Figures of Speech

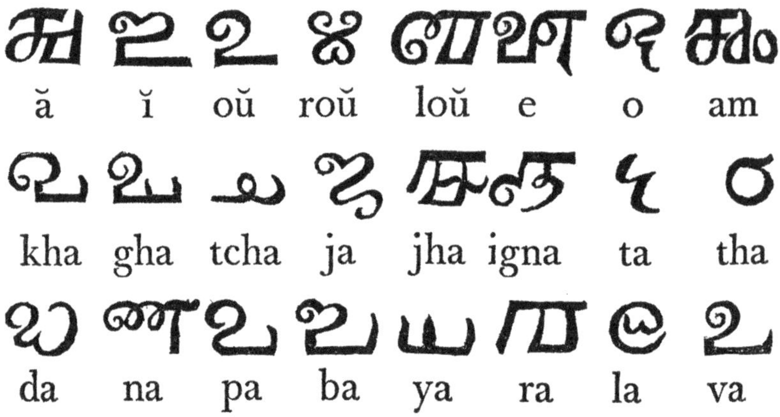

IMPRESSIONS | *Studies in the Art, Culture, & Future of Books*
Matthew P. Brown, series editor

Figures of Speech

Six Histories of Language & Identity in the Age of Revolutions

Tim Cassedy

UNIVERSITY OF IOWA PRESS
IOWA CITY

University of Iowa Press, Iowa City 52242

www.uipress.uiowa.edu
Printed in the United States of America
Design by Sara T. Sauers

The University of Iowa Press is a member of Green Press Initiative and is committed to preserving natural resources.
Printed on acid-free paper

Library of Congress Cataloging-in-Publication Data
Names: Cassedy, Tim, 1981– author.
Title: Figures of speech : six histories of language and identity in the age of revolutions / by Tim Cassedy.
Description: Iowa City : University of Iowa Press, [2018] | Series: Impressions: studies in the art, culture, and future of books | Includes bibliographical references and index. |
Identifiers: LCCN 2018013979 (print) | LCCN 2018033883 (ebook) | ISBN 978-1-60938-613-9 | ISBN 978-1-60938-612-2 (paperback : alk. paper)
Subjects: LCSH: English language—Variation. | English language—Social aspects. | English language—Social aspects—Foreign countries. | Language and culture—History—19th century.
Classification: LCC PE1074.7 (ebook) | LCC PE1074.7 .C37 2018 (print) | DDC 427—dc23
LC record available at https://lccn.loc.gov/2018013979

to Hannah

CONTENTS

LIST OF ILLUSTRATIONS

ACKNOWLEDGMENTS

I COULD NOT HAVE written this book without the generous support I received from the National Endowment for the Humanities, the American Antiquarian Society, the Library Company of Philadelphia, the American Philosophical Society, the Lewis Walpole Library, the Andrew W. Mellon Foundation, and the United Methodist General Board of Higher Education and Ministry. At Southern Methodist University, I also benefited from funding from Dedman College, the University Research Council, and the Department of English. I am grateful for their support.

For assistance gathering the materials that make this book come alive, I thank David Fry, Deirdre Fry, Chelsea Grogan, John Overholt, Kate Petsche, Andrew Wilson, and the Interlibrary Loan staff at SMU. I also wish to thank Matt Brown and the anonymous readers for the University of Iowa Press for their generous and generative readings. I further thank the editors and reviewers at journals where I developed this book's ideas and voice: Chris Castiglia, Lauren Coats, Catriona MacLeod, Sarah Mesle, Dana Nelson, and Eric Slauter. An earlier version of part of chapter 1 was previously published in "'A Dictionary Which We Do Not Want': Defining America Against Noah Webster, 1783–1810," *William and Mary Quarterly* 71 (2014). An earlier version of chapter 5 was published in "Types of Reading, Types of Pleasure: *Pantographia* and the Specimens of Globalization," *Word & Image* 34 (2018).

I am grateful to my colleagues at SMU who have made my work more joyful and creative, including Greg Brownderville, Darryl Dickson-Carr, Irina Dumitrescu, Dennis Foster, Dan Moss, Jayson Sae-Saue, Nina Schwartz, Lisa Siraganian, and Rajani Sudan. I owe a special debt to Ezra Greenspan.

My song forever shall record my gratitude to the curators and librarians at the Library Company of Philadelphia and American Antiquarian

Society who made my hours in their reading rooms so joyful and transformative: Linda August, Vince Golden, Jim Green, Connie King, and Elizabeth Pope.

I also thank the colleagues, collaborators, and friends I met in archives, libraries, and reading groups, whose feedback and intellectual curiosities helped me understand the kind of scholarship I wanted to write: Kelly Bezio, Hester Blum, Michelle Burnham, Ryan Cordell, Lindsay DiCuirci, Paul Erickson, Melissa Gniadek, Glenda Goodman, Molly Hardy, Lucia Hodgson, Toni Jaudon, Jason M. Payton, Joe Rezek, Danielle Skeehan, Jordan Stein, Dan Walden, and Kelly Wisecup. I am also deeply grateful to Laura Fisher and Shirley Wong, comrades; and to Pat Crain, Bryan Waterman, and Tom Augst, mentors.

Most of all and with inexpressible gratitude, I thank Hannah Cassedy.

Figures of Speech

Introduction

Language Makes the Difference between Man and Man

The Character She Represents Herself to Be

A young woman, seemingly in distress, turned up in the spring of 1817 near the resort town of Bath, wearing strange clothes and speaking a foreign language. Concerned citizens trying to communicate with her quickly determined that her language was not French, Spanish, or Greek. When they gave her pen and paper, she wrote a few lines in an elegant but unfamiliar script. Although no one was able to read the text, it was, at least, a graphic clue about her identity. Her well-to-do caretakers sent handmade copies of the note to well-educated and well-travelled people near and far, hoping to find someone who could translate for her. At the London headquarters of the East India Company, a distinguished scholar of Asian languages examined the script but found that it was not Chinese, Sanskrit, Arabic, or Farsi, and could not identify it. Experts at Oxford also drew a blank.[1]

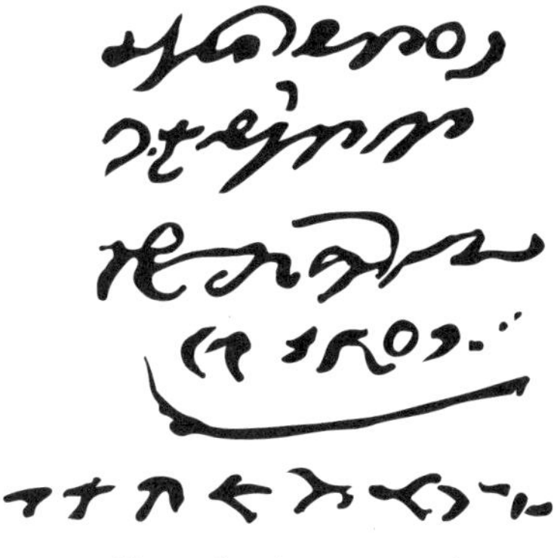

Hey, what language is this? *Bristol Mirror*, June 21, 1817.

The Bath baths being an international tourist attraction, the owner of one of the city's four bathhouses posted a copy of the note in his lively pump room, a see-and-be-seen social

The pump room, Bath, where Caraboo's handwriting was on display. Detail from Robert Cruikshank, *Well Known Characters in the Pump Room* (London, 1826). Courtesy of the Lewis Walpole Library, Yale University.

venue drawing guests from all over the world. Perhaps a visitor would recognize the mysterious writing; in the meantime, it was an exotic display object for the bathhouse's clientele to enjoy. The female stranger was quickly becoming the talk of the town, especially after she used pantomime to explain that her name was Caraboo and she had been kidnapped by human traffickers from her home on a South Pacific island called Javasu, where her father was king.

In a more racialized society, Princess Caraboo's physical body might have figured more prominently in the mystery of her identity. Her complexion was "very triflingly sallow, rather more corresponding to a brunette, with a pleasing colour on the cheeks," according to a physician who made a brief attempt to perceive a yellow ("sallow") tint in Caraboo's skin before acknowledging that she looks "rather more" like a (European) brunette than anything else—complete with that crucial marker of racial whiteness, blushing cheeks. Yet her body was simply not the evidence that drew his attention. For him and many others, Caraboo's physiology was less significant, or less revealing, or less interesting than the unknown Oriental language that she spoke and wrote. "I have seen her write," the physician insisted, "and she writes with grace and facility." He thought that her writing system bore a resemblance to Chinese, or possibly Greek.[2]

Weeks passed, and the Princess continued to inspire considerable detective work and research. Many a visitor came to her temporary residence at the town clerk's mansion to "try his skill at developing the character and nation of the unknown foreigner."[3] From the beginning, her written and spoken language was treated as the most significant evidence about who she was. In Edinburgh, an exiled aristocrat from Ottoman Crimea read several newspaper reports about Caraboo's language and thought he recognized it as Tartar, his mother tongue. He sent down a series of questions for her in that Turkic language, written phonetically in the Latin alphabet in hopes that an English speaker would read them aloud to Caraboo, record her responses phonetically, and return them to Edinburgh without having understood either end of the conversation. Others thought Caraboo might be speaking "an imperfect Javanese," "a mixture of languages used on the coast of Sumatra," or the Circassian language of the North Caucasus. Still others believed that she was not speaking a language at all but babbling gibberish and perpetrating an elaborate hoax.[4]

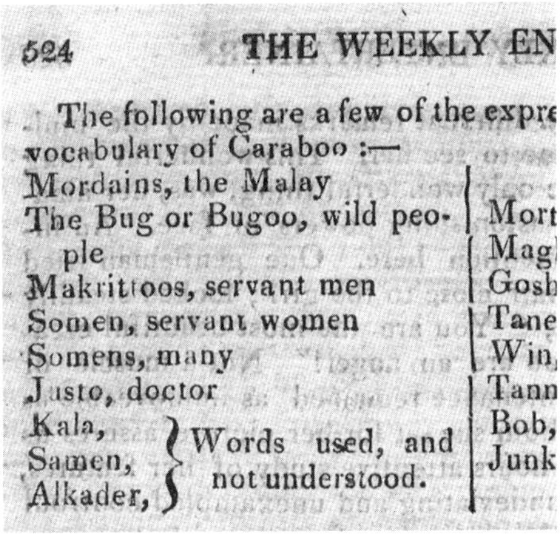

524 THE WEEKLY EN

The following are a few of the expre
vocabulary of Caraboo :—

Mordains, the Malay
The Bug or Bugoo, wild people
Makrittoos, servant men
Somen, servant women
Somens, many
Justo, doctor
Kala, Samen, Alkader, } Words used, and not understood.

Mort
Mag
Gosh
Tane
Win,
Tann
Bob,
Junk

Words from Caraboo's vocabulary, as reported in a country magazine. *Weekly Entertainer*, July 7, 1817. © The British Library Board, General Reference Collection P.P.6046.b.

The plausibility of the hoax theory dwindled as six weeks ticked by and Caraboo continued speaking fluently in her still-unknown tongue, though she was also beginning to pick up a little English. Nevertheless, it remained the firm belief of Hester Lynch Piozzi, the well-connected historian and intellectual who lived nearby, that Caraboo was a con artist, because (as she reported to a friend) the young woman did not write right-to-left "in an Eastern Manner; but beginning from the left Hand—clearly prov[ing] herself to be a novice."[5] Others who doubted

Princess Caraboo's authenticity laid subtle linguistic traps to see whether she would fall into them. A clergyman paid her inappropriately intimate compliments in English to see whether she would blush. (She didn't.) Servants stayed up all night in her room to hear in what language she talked in her sleep. (The foreign one.) Visitors took notes about her language to establish whether she was voicing words with consistent meanings or was just babbling. (They were consistent.)[6] Hundreds of curious, important, and often skeptical people came to converse with the Princess in person, overwhelmingly coming away from those conversations reassured as to her genuine Oriental identity.[7]

The immediate question was not what Caraboo was saying, but what language she was saying it in. In the short term, at least, the intense scrutiny of her language was not an attempt to decipher its meaning but an attempt to identify the language and thereby identify her. The people who were scratching their heads about Caraboo in 1817 were trying to complete a sentence that began with the words "Caraboo is..." The subject was Caraboo; the predicate was uncertain. After many hours in her presence, an enthusiastic visitor declared that "*Caraboo* is the character, she represents herself to be."[8] His tautological grammar highlights what was at stake: Is "she" the same as "herself"? Is her "being" the same as her "representation"? Is Caraboo herself, or someone else? *Who is this person?*

There are ways to approach the question of *Who is this?* other than to study a person's language. One might instead scrutinize her skin color and physiology in an effort to place her within the conceptual landscape of race: *She is a white person*, perhaps, or *She is an Indian*. Yet another strategy would be to look for an answer with reference to her social position: *She is a lady* or *She is a beggar* or *She is a slave*. Caraboo's handlers would attempt those strategies as well. But Caraboo happened to arrive in western England at a time when there seemed to be good reasons to rely on linguistic evidence when evaluating a person's identity. This book is about those reasons. For now, Caraboo remains a linguistic mystery.

Our Languages, Ourselves

This book is a recovery project: it recovers a lost disciplinary moment when language served as a framework for understanding selves and a tool for refashioning selves. When a French refugee in Philadelphia declared in 1806 that "language makes the difference between man and man," he was stating a commonplace. In fact, the "wonderful influence which language exerts over our inmost sentiments and strongest associations" constituted one of the basic assumptions in British and American social thought at the turn of the nineteenth century. Each language was believed to produce its own distinctive constellation of thoughts and feelings in its speakers' minds. "It is an idle mistake to suppose that the study of languages acquires words alone," a Scottish teacher of Urdu testified at the East India Company's headquarters in London; rather, the student of languages "unavoidably acquires, what is vastly more material, the thoughts of the people by whom those languages are spoken."[9] To the extent that English speakers took the "language makes the difference between man and man" idea literally—and that extent varied by time, place, and individual disposition—they believed that different languages facilitated different "ideas," "sentiments," "associations," and "thoughts": different minds and different selves. This was the basis of the *Encyclopaedia Britannica*'s assertion that "the language of any people is a very exact index of the state of their minds."[10] A people's language, therefore, seemed "indexed" to the contents of their minds, the way race was indexed to their bodies and nationality was indexed to their political circumstances.

This hypothesis profoundly affected how English speakers imagined their world, as every aspect of pronunciation, vocabulary, and spelling came to seem like a potential basis for detecting the contours of human diversity—or for shaping them. Like our present moment, the turn of the nineteenth century witnessed the displacement and migration of people in large numbers and worldwide extent. At times, linguistic differences seemed to validate the racial, national, local, and regional identity categories that took shape in the wake of the American, French, and Haitian revolutions; the expanding European presence in Asia and Africa; and the globalization of trade and politics. At other times, however, they strained or resisted those categories—as they did for the many Americans who fought to keep Britain and the United States linguistically united even as they fought to make them nationally separate. This episode in the history of Western identity categories is very little known today. But it is an important episode: a forgotten part of the history of how we have come to understand persons and peoples in a diverse human world.

Figures of Speech is also a recovery project in a more directly archival sense: its chapters revolve around six forgotten individuals, only one of whom even the specialist reader is likely to have encountered before. These six people—a Scottish doctor, an English beggar, a French aristocrat, a Caribbean planter, a London artisan, and Noah Webster—put language at the center of their identities and lived out the possibilities of their era's linguistic ideas. They were all outsiders in ways specific to their newly globalizing world. All of them were geographically mobile, all crossed national borders, and all of them worked for a living. They lived in all four hemispheres and never met each other—but in implicit and occasionally explicit ways, they were all speaking to each other, putting each other's ideas into practice, and building on each other's experiences. Their six histories illustrate how linguistic identity categories were useful to those dispossessed of other identity categories by empire, revolution, and globalization. They undertook linguistic projects that now seem unthinkable and produced texts that now seem bizarre: a talking clock that was never built, an expensive book that wasn't even theoretically possible to read, numerous small fortunes spent on experimental typography, and  than you can shake a stick at. All of them left bold traces in print: if you are in North America or the British Isles, you can likely find all six characters' print legacies in the rare books departments of nearby university libraries. But although these six characters' efforts were preserved widely in libraries and archives, they faded from popular and scholarly memory. Little of their work has ever been seriously researched before, partly because it became difficult to grasp why it was created in the first place.

But this is what you want in a recovery project. Texts that seem illegible, meaningless, wacky, or inexplicable suggest the possibility of new knowledge, different perspectives, unheard voices and ideas—especially when there is evidence that they seemed legible and meaningful to someone in the past. There is an eighteenth-century French proverb that says: "He who is snotty, let him blow his nose." This proverb evidently had a meaning in eighteenth-century France—an obvious, proverbial one!—but that meaning is no longer intuitive. "When we cannot get a proverb, or a joke, or a ritual, or a poem, we know we are on to something," writes the cultural historian Robert Darnton. "By picking at the document where it is most opaque, we may be able to unravel an alien system of meaning."[11] The six unusual characters and their strange linguistic undertakings are this book's incomprehensible French proverbs. One of those six, a Scottish-born planter named Duncan Mackintosh who spent the last decades of the eighteenth century on the Caribbean island of Martinique, invested a considerable portion of his estate in 1797 in publishing a book-length demonstration of his new linguistic invention, a system of diacritics designed to make English pronunciation more predictable. He looked forward to the day "when a soci'ety *of* good' and le*a*rned Gen'tlemen" would publish new, Mackintoshized versions of "*all'* the we*a*lth' and *d* be*a*u'ti*e*s *of* the anc'ients an*d* mo'derns," after which "we ma'*y* ma'k*e* a bon'*ef*i*re* *of* the o'ld books."[12] Mackintosh must have expected the immense cost of replacing all the books in the world to yield correspondingly immense benefits. Such benefits, however, are no longer easy to imagine. People do a lot of crazy things—but *Figures of Speech* is about a world in which Mackintosh's project did not seem altogether crazy.

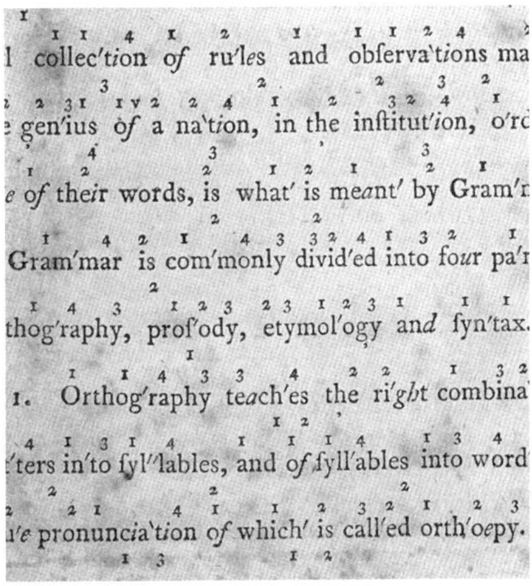
collec'tion of ru'les and obferva'tions ma
gen'ius of a na'tion, in the inftitut'ion, o'rd
of their words, is what' is meant' by Gram'n
Gram'mar is com'monly divid'ed into four pa'r
thog'raphy, prof'ody, etymol'ogy and fyn'tax.
1. Orthog'raphy teach'es the ri'ght combina'
'ters in'to fyl'lables, and of fyll'ables into word
'e pronuncia'tion of which' is call'ed orth'oepy.

Detail from Duncan Mackintosh's phonetic printing system, 1797. Courtesy, American Antiquarian Society.

It is not only the ideas of this book's texts that are difficult to grasp; their materials also resist our understanding and even our representing them. They are hard to describe, hard to catalog, and hard to type. Duncan Mackintosh's phonetic spelling proposal has never been quoted from before now—in part because his proposal never came to pass and no longer seems plausible, but also no doubt because introducing tiny numbers and symbols into the white space between lines of text did not get any easier with the industrialization of printing. The material legacy of that text is as significant as its intellectual legacy. When Mackintosh writes that "Q is al'ways fol'l*owe*d by *u*, and, at l*e*ast', one vow'el besid'*e*s," his words express no very original idea, but the unusual textual materials with which he expresses them bespeak some unfamiliar and deeply felt ideas about language.[13] Excavating those ideas requires addressing the text's materials as well as its words. In the chapters that follow, I draw deeply on media studies and on a cluster of related and overlapping disciplines: book studies, book history, print culture studies, material text studies, and the history of reading. It is an axiom of media studies that *all* textual artifacts communicate through their material form as well as their textual content—but the sources in this book dramatize this with particular urgency, such as when their textual content is mundane, like Mackintosh's "Q is al'ways fol'l*owe*d by *u* . . . ," or inaccessible, like Princess Caraboo's "." The need for material readings is especially vivid in these texts, but they also highlight domains of meaning that material text interpretive methods may illuminate even in less materially conspicuous texts.

Categories of Identity in the English-Speaking Diaspora

The 1780s were the last time in history that most English speakers lived in England: by the 1790s, population growth in Ireland, the United States, Canada, and the British Caribbean meant that the average English speaker was no longer an English national.[14] This inversion had far-reaching consequences. One of the most significant functions of the theory that "language makes the difference between man and man," in fact, was to describe an increasingly diasporic English-speaking world as united by linguistic sameness even though it was divided by geospatial distance. Indeed, the chief goal of Duncan Mackintosh's 1797 phonetic innovation was to ensure that a "unifo'rmity *of* pronunc*ia*'t*io*n . . . ma'*y* be spr*e*ad' thro'*ugh* all' pa'rts *of* the glob'e, where'v'er E'ng-lish shall' be tau'*gh*t."[15] Linguistic concepts of identity helped bridge not only geospatial but also political divisions: the "bold" and "energetic" English language, a Pennsylvania farmer wrote at the outset of the War of 1812, represented a common object of care for both parties to that conflict, "exempt[ ] from the restrictive obligations and ties of nationality."[16] This transatlantic linguistic sameness—partly real, partly imagined—served as a stabilizing counterweight to the era's volatile politics.

But the rising significance of linguistic evidence at the end of the eighteenth century also raised the stakes of time-honored concerns about the glitches and imperfections that English speakers had long perceived in their language. English was "attended with great deficiency and irregularity in its alphabet," for example, and had "such a number of S's . . . as to give a general hiss through the whole tenor of our language, which must be exceedingly disagreeable to every unprejudiced ear."[17] These aesthetic concerns became, at times, existential concerns about the English-speaking self. All manner of linguistic defects seemed likely to generate corresponding mental defects: "What′, ṭhen′, shall′ we sày to ṭho′s*e* who′ prĕtĕ′nd that′ mĭsplă′c′ing the ac′cent ç̣an′ hà′v*e* no′ bad Effec′*t* on ṭhĕ Lĕ*a*′rnĕr?" asked Duncan Mackintosh in 1799. "If so′, ădị*i*êŭ′ tŏ Rĕ*a*′ṣŏn ăn*d* cŏm′mŏn Sĕns′*e*."[18] Correcting such defects promised to make entire generations savvier and more virtuous: put the accents back in their proper places, and bonjour to reason and common sense. In 1814, a clerk at the United States War Department expressed a similar concern that the r-less pronunciations in his native Virginia of "*de hosses*, for the horses, *de gals* or *gaerls*, for the girls" were "unhappy sources of great impuritys, not only of the language, but of morals."[19] This is exactly why Mackintosh thought it would be a good idea to "mằk*e* ă bŏn′*e*fĭr*e*" out of all the books in the world, should phonetically unambiguous replacements become available: if he had indeed created a technology for stabilizing and unifying the English language across vast geographical and social distances, then the principle that "language makes the difference between man and man" suggested that he had also created a technology for stabilizing and unifying the minds of English-speaking people. His plan offered the possibility of reimagining and reconstituting the British Empire not in terms of political power but in terms of linguistic sameness and the shared mentalities that went along with it.

There were, of course, other ways to draw distinctions between people at the end of the eighteenth century. You could take religion as your determining factor and distinguish Protestants from Catholics, Christians from heathens. You could use nationality and distinguish among French, Spanish, American, and British; or English, Scottish, Irish, and Welsh. You could use climate, differentiating the supposedly indolent tropical peoples from the putatively industrious peoples of temperate zones. You could use economic position: rich, poor, middling, propertied, enslaved. You could use skin color: white, black, red, yellow, tawny, swarthy, olive, chestnut. You could use race: Caucasian, Ethiopian, American, Mongolian, Malay. You could use sex: male, female.[20]

Each of these categories called attention to certain differences and glossed over others. They were useful for different purposes in an imperial world. If, like Duncan Mackintosh, you were a Scot occupying an until-recently-French sugar colony in the Caribbean who wanted to claim an elite place in the British Empire, then climatic identity was not the identity category for you, since it posited that the tropics made for a lazy, sluggish self very different from the hardy people living in the rugged north. British nationality might be a more appropriate category for identifying across the transoceanic space of empire—but on the other hand, being Scottish, you would still stand in an awkward and somewhat marginal position vis-à-vis England, the nation at the practical center of British power.

Duncan Mackintosh chose language as his category of identity. He gave himself a way to imagine himself at the intellectual center of an English-speaking community of which he was at the geographic margins. Several twentieth-century fables, including *My Fair Lady* (1956) and *How the García Girls Lost Their Accents* (1991), dramatize the tangible social advantages available to people who speak a prestige dialect: if you lose your Cockney accent, you get to marry a handsome gentleman and join the upper class. But socioeconomic power is not what Duncan Mackintosh was after when he created his system for encoding English phonetics in print—at least, it's not what he claimed to be after. He was not looking for a way to engineer his or anyone else's position in a social hierarchy; rather, he was trying to engineer the mind from the inside. The goal of his project was not to produce colonial subjects who could, like Eliza Doolittle, pass as imperial elites at the embassy ball. The goal was to produce colonial subjects who had the same mental architecture as the imperial elites: colonials who *were* English—morally, intellectually, and sentimentally.[21]

Say Now **Shibboleth***: Linguistic Identity from Antiquity to 1775*

The idea that your language corresponds to your identity is a very old idea, indeed an ancient one. After the Gileadites defeated the Ephraimites in a crucial battle around the twelfth century BCE, the surviving Ephraimites were eager to retreat back across the Jordan River into their own territory. The victors, hoping to neutralize their enemy more fully, set up checkpoints at the river fords and asked everyone who wanted to pass if he was a Gileadite or an Ephraimite. If you said you were a Gileadite, you had to prove it by pronouncing the Hebrew word for an ear of corn. The victorious Gileadites pronounced this word *shibboleth*. The Ephraimites also spoke Hebrew, but their dialect did not have the /sh/ phoneme; they pronounced the same word as *sibboleth*. Those who said *shibboleth* were evidently real Gileadites and could cross. Those who said *sibboleth* were immediately killed.[22]

Language is a communications medium, but it always communicates more than its words literally say: an Israelite says "ear of corn" but at the same time reveals his tribal affiliation. In some sense, languages constitute inevitable dividing lines in a social world: people tend to share a language, as well as a way of life, with those among whom they live. Still, language and its technologies easily become overdetermined, easily used to draw boundaries that have little to do with mutual intelligibility. In ancient Mesopotamia, for instance, peoples who wrote their languages in cuneiform felt a "strong bond" with other cuneiform-writing peoples and sneered at civilizations that used easier, alphabetic scripts.[23] Comprehensibility is not the only dimension of linguistic meaning.

In one sense, these ascriptions of significance to arbitrary aspects of language have been going on forever. Yet European contact with the Americas created dramatic new fields of meaning on which linguistic knowledge and fantasy played out. New World contact was a linguistic endeavor, among other things, not only between Europeans and the American peoples they encountered but between the many European peoples vying for influence in the New World. If you were exploring the contact zones of North America in the seventeenth century, you might well encounter Native Americans speaking Spanish, French, or Dutch. English settlers used pidgin Spanish to communicate with Natives in the Carolinas in the 1670s. As early as the mid-1620s, Natives in New England who spoke disparate languages used English to communicate with each other, but not until centuries later, in the nineteenth century, did it become apparent that English would be the predominant European language in North America.[24] New England was merely a span of "about two hundred miles, betweene the *French* and *Dutch* Plantations," as Roger Williams wrote in his *Key into the Language of America* (1643). Still, from the beginning of their presence in the New World, English speakers were eager to make the English language a force there. British colonists invested significant resources not only in bringing the English language into wide use in North America but also in maintaining linguistic norms that mirrored those in Britain. Throughout the colonial period and even well beyond it, Anglo-Americans were eager to mark themselves as linguistic insiders, fetishizing the same prestige dialect of southeastern England favored by elite English speakers in England.[25]

The linguistic significance of New World contact coincided with developments in the Old World that made language a matter of British public concern. In 1707, the Crown and Parliament of England merged with those of Scotland, creating the new multilingual, multiethnic, and multinational nation of Great Britain. The polyglot nature of the new nation troubled many intellectuals and bureaucrats, to whom such a nation seemed unstable, per John Locke's well-known claim that language is "the great Instrument, and common Tye of Society." The English language became a focal point of efforts to "tye" the British national community together, while ensuring the continuing dominance of the existing English-speaking elite. Perceiving the Gaelic language as a political hazard, the Anglocentric British government began trying to exterminate it, implementing English-only education policies in northern Scotland where Gaelic predominated.[26]

The disintegrative threat of a nation linguistically foreign to itself lay not only in the Scottish Highlands but also in London. Scots flocked to the imperial capital during the eighteenth century, seeking a voice in defining their British nation and empire after centuries of living under

Pantless Scots rain down on London in this detail from Richard Newton, *A Flight of Scotchmen* (London, 1796).

English suzerainty. Scottish accents became increasingly common and, at the same time, increasingly disparaged in London. Books designed to help Scots lose their Scottish accents proliferated. Yet Scots were not the only linguistic aliens in the metropolis. Even the King's English was in some sense a foreign tongue. For forty-six years beginning in 1714, Britain was ruled by kings born and educated in Germany; when George I and George II spoke English at all, it was with a thick German accent. Not until 1760 did Britain again have a monarch whose first language was English. There is a twinge of linguistic relief in William Kenrick's hyperbolic 1773 dedication of his *New Dictionary of the English Language* to King George III, whom he addresses as "the most accomplished Speaker of the English Tongue."[27] He was, at least, the first natively English-speaking British monarch in half a century. The ethnopolitical roots of the British nation ran in divergent Celtic and Germanic directions, but one common link that Britons chose to get behind was the English language: *we are British because we speak English.* Samuel Johnson made the analogy between the language and the polity explicit in 1755 in his famous *Dictionary*: "we have long preserved our constitution, let us make some struggles for our language."[28]

Enlightenment philosophy provided additional reasons to keep a careful eye on the English language as an index of the British self. Scottish and French Enlightenment thinking on language grew out of two ideas presented by John Locke in his *Essay Concerning Humane Understanding* (1689). In Locke's "empiricist" account of human consciousness, the human mind begins as a blank slate, with no ideas innately built into it. The mind and its ideas, Locke argues, are formed entirely through experience—either directly, by witnessing through the five senses, or by combining and examining what has been witnessed. Locke sees this process taking place without language: sequences of ideas pass through consciousness and interact with each other in what one later commentator has called a "wordless discourse of the mind." Later, we assign names to some of those fundamentally wordless ideas and call those names "language." For Locke, therefore, language is a system in which ideas are encoded and decoded, not a system in which ideas are generated. The media theorist Walter Ong once summarized this theory of language in a way that makes it sound patently ridiculous: "My mind is a box. I take a unit of 'information' out of it, encode the unit . . . and put it into one end of the pipe. . . . From the one end of the pipe the 'information' proceeds to the other end, where someone decodes it . . . and puts it in his or her own box-like container called a mind. This model obviously has something to do with human communication," Ong quips, "but, on close inspection, very little." In fact, Locke was aware that human communication did not always work like this, and he found that reality troubling. Words can be imprecise, Locke observed, and in the inexact process of cramming our wordless ideas into the necessarily imperfect words available to us, we can lose track of what we really think. Locke's two key contributions to eighteenth-century linguistic thought were, first, that our minds are formed by sensory experiences apart from words, and, second, that in a perfect world it would be possible to put any idea, any shade of meaning, into words and convey that meaning error-free to another person. But he also observed that we do not live in that perfect world.[29]

As later thinkers realized, Locke's two lines of thinking on language are in conflict with each other: his "admission that words often take an active role in thought" is incompatible with his "faith in word-free mental discourse." Étienne Bonnot de Condillac (1715–80) was the most influential eighteenth-century writer to explore this contradiction. He concluded that Locke was wrong to propose sense perception as the substructure on which language and the other mental faculties rested. Condillac argued that it was the other way around: *language* was the substructure on which sense perception and everything else rested. According to one intellectual historian, this makes Condillac's *Essay on the Origins of Human Knowledge* (1742) "the source of the notion that . . . the language of each nation expresses the character of the people who speak it." At the very least, Condillac was one of that idea's most significant vectors and proponents in eighteenth-century philosophy, especially after his friend Denis Diderot affirmed it in his entry on language in the *Encyclopédie* (1754). An essay competition in 1758–59 at the Prussian Academy in Berlin on the question, "What is the reciprocal influence of the opinions of a people on their language and of their language on their opinions?," also helped draw attention to that "reciprocal influence."[30] Succeeding generations of German Enlightenment and Romantic writers, including Johann Gottfried Herder (1744–1803), Friedrich Schlegel (1772–1829), and Wilhelm von Humboldt (1767–1835), developed this line of thinking and posited a close relationship between peoples, languages, and minds. Their work would be rediscovered by English-speaking linguists and anthropologists toward the end of the nineteenth century, and would come to be seen as a crucial turning point in the protohistory of the modern study of human diversity, thought, and language. "The world in which we live," wrote Humboldt in 1812, "is exactly the one into which the language we speak transplants us." This statement sounds so much like the twentieth-century idea known as the "Sapir-Whorf hypothesis"—more on this later—that numerous linguistic historians have proposed specific lineages of Humboldt's students and their students and their students' students, "to whom we are indebted for having incubated" Humboldt's ideas until they could be properly hatched in the 1920s.[31]

Although Herder, Schlegel, and especially Humboldt would later seem like original founders of the idea that different languages facilitate different thoughts, that is not how they seemed in the English-speaking world in the late eighteenth and early nineteenth centuries. Humboldt may have been an important proponent of this idea in German philology, which later influenced Anglophone linguistics—but Humboldt does not appear in this book, because he did not influence the thinking of this book's characters. To the extent that English speakers' ideas about language and thought in 1800 were based on a formal intellectual tradition, it was not the German one. Rather, the intellectual center of gravity for this subject was in Scotland, where it was explored in major works by Adam Smith (1761), Lord Kames (1762), Lord Monboddo (1773–92), George Campbell (1776), James Beattie (1783), Hugh Blair (1783), Thomas Reid (1785), and Dugald Stewart (1792).[32]

With increasing specificity, eighteenth-century Scottish writers detailed the implications of the thesis that "we really think by signs as well as speak by them." It followed that a person cannot think thoughts for which his language has no words: over time, a people's language and their ideas must always evolve in tandem, new words allowing new thoughts, and new thoughts requiring new words. The theory applied not only to discrete, thinkable "thoughts" but also more broadly to sentiments and character. "Hence the language of a brave and martial people is bold and nervous," the *Encyclopaedia Britannica* stressed in 1797, "while the languages of those nations in which luxury and effeminacy prevail, are flowing and harmonious, but devoid of force and energy of expression." One of the many aspects of this theory that seemed appealing at the time was that it appeared to explain how societies pass down values, temperaments, and attitudes from one generation to the next. "In consequence of the gradual improvements which take place in language as an instrument of thought," Dugald Stewart wrote in 1792, "the classifications both of things and facts with which the infant faculties of each successive race are conversant, are more just and more comprehensive than those of their predecessors."[33] The advancing knowledge of one generation, he suggests, is built into the language learned by the next: depending on which language you acquire, certain "things and facts" may be invisible or plain as day. This reasoning, as developed by Stewart and others, provided a theoretical basis for the widespread notion that each language corresponds to a distinct set of values, assumptions, habits of thought, and patterns of feeling. While the Scottish Enlightenment did not create that linguistic hypothesis, it gave academic and learned communities reasons to endorse and institutionalize it.[34]

By the last quarter of the eighteenth century, therefore, the Western world had already been thinking about individual and group identity in terms of language for hundreds and even thousands of years. The interrelated legacies of Biblical, Classical, and Enlightenment thinking about the relationship between people and language remained present at the turn of the nineteenth century. Late-eighteenth-century English speakers did not invent the idea that language corresponds to the true self, but they found that idea useful in new ways—for several reasons, all of which will be discussed later, including the reconfiguration of national boundaries, increased imperial and commercial contact with the diverse human world, dramatic growth in vernacular literacy rates, and the expanding availability of print. The central idea that each language corresponds to a distinct type of mind and self was not new in the Age of Revolutions; rather, this idea, having long had a place in Western intellectual history, rotated into position at the center of a newly influential account of human identity. That account, I will suggest later, closely anticipates what would come to be called "culture" a hundred years later.

Big Data: How to Tell whether a People Is Barbaric

The president of Yale University proposed this thought experiment in 1816 in a leading scientific journal: Suppose that you wanted to learn about a particular group of people, and your only source of information about them was a bilingual dictionary between their language and yours. Based solely on a review of their language's words, what (if anything) could you tell about them?

It would be difficult to exaggerate just how revealing President Timothy Dwight thought such an analysis would be. "Possessed of vocabularies, containing such words . . . in customary use among them," Dwight wrote, "we should know with indubitable certainty, that the *Romans* were a military; the *Greeks*, a learned, and philosophical; the *Hebrews*, a religious; and the *French*, a polished people." His indubitable certainty rested on patterns that he perceived in the meanings of their words: "The Latin language contains many terms, employed about *war*," the Greek language "pertaining to *art*, and *science*," the Hebrew "to *morality* and *religion*," and the French to "*polite intercourse*." Relying on the theory that language corresponds to thought, Dwight reasons that a concentration of words in a particular domain must be evidence of a corresponding concentration of mental activity in the same domain. "The character of a nation may with absolute certainty be extensively known from this source," he affirms, "with more ease, and more certainty, than in any other manner." In Dwight's view, the most revealing and reliable means of learning about a people through words is not to use their language as a communication technology, but to use it as data: obtain "a dictionary, containing all its words" and analyze those words abstractly, independent of any statements the people in question might actually use them to make.[35]

Duncan Mackintosh, the phonetic-spelling innovator in Martinique, wanted to engineer a linguistic reality; Dwight merely wanted to perceive one. Dwight was less concerned with the effects of a language on a people than he was with the effects of a people on their language. These ideas were complementary and not always fully distinguished. Both men saw a language as a kind of recipe for a particular kind of mind. Dwight wanted to analyze the recipe, Mackintosh to change it. While Mackintosh focused on the phonetic ingredients, Dwight focused on its lexicon, and others looked into syntax, grammar, and prosody. Lord Kames, the Scottish philosopher, noticed that French words are accented on the final syllable more often than English words are. He interpreted the accent on the ultima as a rather bold gesture, linguistically corresponding to "the French [people] being brisk and lively." It was, he thought, "a pregnant instance of a resemblance between the character of a people and that of their language."[36] By the end of the eighteenth century, English speakers had developed elaborate conventions for interpreting the intellectual and moral implications of many different kinds of linguistic evidence, including Kames's ethnology-by-scansion. The languages of less civilized people were said to have fewer words than advanced languages and to be especially deficient in conjunctions. "This we know," wrote the Scottish academic James Beattie: "that barbarous nations have but few [conjunctions]; that cultivated tongues, like the Greek and Latin, have a considerable number."[37] Words ending in vowel sounds indicated "voluptuous indolence."[38] An object-verb-subject syntax signaled that a people was "primitive."[39] (See table 1 for a longer list of linguistic variables about which eighteenth-century writers drew such conclusions.)

Learning how to use these principles to guide conclusions about the world's peoples was a standard element of Anglophone pedagogy. At a school in Calcutta where English and Scottish men were learning Bengali, Sanskrit, Arabic, Farsi, and Hindustani in 1802, students had to demonstrate not only communication proficiency in those languages but also the ability to draw ethnolinguistic conclusions about their speakers. In response to a question about "the manners and customs of the natives of India," one student wrote a prize-winning essay arguing that "from the metaphorical and poetical dress which forms so striking a characteristic in all Eastern languages, we may reasonably conclude, that society among them, is as yet in a state of infancy." Another student noted that from "the openness and boldness of expression in our own [language], we discern evident marks of that nobleness of mind and freedom of spirit, which dignify the Briton."[40]

It is easy to imagine what might have been appealing for these aspiring company men in Calcutta about the idea that English speech exhibited an "openness and boldness" evincing a characteristically British "nobleness of mind and freedom of spirit." Thinking about language this way meant that as long as they remembered their mother tongue, they were fundamentally British, no matter how else India might change them. Furthermore, it provided an opportunity for the students to feel morally superior to Indians by perceiving their linguistic difference as a difference in temperament: "in every sentence of [Oriental languages]," wrote one student, "appear that humility and slavish submission, or that haughtiness and despotic insolence, which have ever been the characteristics of Asiaticks."[41]

In retrospect, it seems clear that the college students in Calcutta, like the college president in New Haven, were not so much discovering new information as having old information confirmed. The students already perceive Asian societies to be primitive and backward, and they

TABLE 1. Linguistic Evidence and Its Implications, c. 1775–1825

ASPECT OF LANGUAGE	IMPLICATION ABOUT PEOPLE
gutturals	primitive[1] "barbarous"[2]
absence of gutturals	"mild . . . agreeable"[3]
frequent use of metaphor	"governed by arbitrary power"[4] primitive (compensating for lexical poverty)[5]
consonant clusters	not "cultivated"[6]
small lexicon	primitive, barbaric[7] "few ideas"[8] "vivacity . . . fire and enthusiasm"[9] island nation[10]
copious lexicon	"a cultivated society"[11] "coolness"[12] "favourable . . . to reason and philosophy"[13] "unprecise"[14]
few conjunctions	"Ignorant people . . . barbarous nations . . . uncultivated"[15]

1. Rev. of Azara, *Voyages dans l'Amérique Méridionale*, in *Analectic Magazine*, Nov. 1818, 390.
2. *System of Geography*, 2:160.
3. M., "On the Origin," [619] (misnumbered 629).
4. Ibid., [619].
5. "Thoughts on the History of Language," *Berwick Museum*, Sept. 1785, 466; Fry, *Pantographia*, xi–xiii.
6. S. Oliver, *A General Critical Grammar*, 13.
7. F., "On Language," *Scots Magazine* (Edinburgh), July 1804, 486; Blair, *Lectures on Rhetoric and Belles Lettres*, 1:283; Fry, *Pantographia*, xiii; Warburton, *The Divine Legation of Moses*, 2:81–82; Pignotti, "Upon the Origin and Progress of the Italian Language," 1:260–61.
8. S. S. Smith, *Essay on the Causes*, 214.
9. Blair, *Lectures*, 1:124.
10. Fry, *Pantographia*, xi–xii.
11. Pignotti, "Upon the Origin," 1:243.
12. Blair, *Lectures*, 1:124.
13. Ibid., 1:125.
14. Pignotti, "Upon the Origin," 1:267.
15. Beattie, *Dissertations*, 482; Blair, *Lectures*, 1:167–68; Murray Cohen, *Sensible Words*, 40–41, 59–60; O. Smith, *Politics of Language*, 113–14.

TABLE 1 (continued)

ASPECT OF LANGUAGE	IMPLICATION ABOUT PEOPLE
homophones	"confused . . . deficient in understanding . . . bedlam"[16]
inflections	valuing "harmony" and "beauty"[17] "superior ratiocination"[18] "more civilized"[19]
absence of inflections	"barbarity and profound ignorance"[20]
contractions	"corrupt[ion] of . . . politeness and morals"[21]
long words	"Barbarous"[22] "harmonious"[23]
short words	"Barbarous"[24]
monosyllables	"taciturnity"[25]
highly vocalic (many vowels per consonant)	"Barbarous"[26] "harmonious softness" in temperament[27]
object-verb-subject word order	primitive[28]
large number of synonyms	"barbarous"[29] "addiction to pleasure and amusement"[30]
words ending in vowel sounds	"voluptuous indolence"[31]
higher pitch	primitive, unmannerly[32]

16. Pinkerton, *Dissertation and Progress of the Scythians or Goths*, 102.
17. Blair, *Lectures*, 1:140.
18. Dwight, "Observations on Language," 383.
19. Monboddo, *Of the Origin and Progress of Language*, 4:19.
20. Pignotti, "Upon the Origin," 1:247.
21. Mackintosh, *Essay* (1797), iv.
22. Monboddo, *Of the Origin*, 4:8.
23. M., "On the Origin," [619].
24. Beattie, *Dissertations*, 270–71.
25. M., "On the Origin," [619].
26. Monboddo, *Of the Origin*, 4:6.
27. Pignotti, "Upon the Origin," 1:265.
28. Blair, *Lectures*, 1:118.
29. Vallancey, *A Grammar of the Iberno-Celtic, or Irish Language*, 3.
30. Dwight, "Observations on Language," [365–66].
31. M., "On the Origin," 620.
32. "Thoughts on the History of Language," 466.

find that language confirms that prejudice.[42] Dwight already believes that the French are "a polished people," and that's why he perceives their language as abounding with words about politeness and taste. In fact, when the lexical data conflict with what Dwight already thinks, he changes the interpretive rules to bring the lexical analysis into line with his preconceptions. At one point, he scratches his head over the fact that "the language of *Arabia* is said to be very copious," which would seem to suggest that its speakers are highly intelligent and possessed of many ideas. Yet, Dwight concedes, "this is morally impossible; because the *Arabians* are, comparatively, an ignorant and uncivilized people." In a breathtakingly circular argument, he concludes that Arabic's surprisingly large vocabulary is probably padded with synonyms rather than composed of words with genuinely distinct meanings. This "multiplication of synonimous words is a proof, not of national improvement, but of addiction to pleasure and amusement," he explains. The revised characterization corresponds to existing knowledge about "the Arabians," and so the problem is resolved.[43]

Dwight's confirmation bias is so obvious to modern eyes that it's tempting to suspect him and his counterparts of arguing in bad faith, knowingly stacking the interpretive deck to confirm what they already believe. Perhaps they knew that what they were really doing was simply bolstering existing stereotypes with the "exact," "absolute," and "indubitable certainty" that Dwight trumpeted. Yet Dwight, at least, was known for neither careless reasoning nor intellectual dishonesty. The much more interesting possibility is that Dwight genuinely believed that a dictionary was a material transcript of a people's collective mind, and therefore an opportunity to do a kind of close reading of the minds and morals of an entire society.[44]

If we grant Dwight et al. the benefit of the doubt and assume that they sincerely believed that they were engaged in objective research, then the linguistic analyses they thought they were conducting were really projective tasks, like inkblot tests. Dwight's conclusions don't provide useful information about the French, the Hebrews, the Arabians, the Asiaticks—just as what I see on the Rorschach cards doesn't provide information about what the inkblots really depict. They provide information not about the object of interpretation but about the person doing the interpreting. By offering an opportunity to leap to conclusions, projective tasks illuminate the interpreter's assumptions and fantasies. They point to what is easiest for him or her to believe.[45] This means that the large body of linguistic "knowledge" generated at the turn of the nineteenth century has little value as evidence about the history of languages, but it has great value as evidence about how the English-speaking world made sense of human diversity in an age of globalization.

Does Language Really Make the Difference between Man and Man?

Figures of Speech is not about whether Dwight, Mackintosh, and their contemporaries were correct when they maintained that "language makes the difference between man and man." This is a work of cultural history, not a work of linguistics or cognitive psychology: it's about how English speakers used this idea to define and navigate identity categories at the turn of the nineteenth century. The characters in this book illustrate how a linguistic account of identity mattered more broadly, to more people, and for more reasons than we have previously understood. The hypothesis was true to them, whether or not it was true in actual fact.

Dwight's once-mainstream methodology for apprehending human difference and Mackintosh's once-plausible strategy for changing it haven't been much reckoned with, partly because they quickly came to be understood as spurious. Under the expanding influence of the New Philology—the comparative-historical method of linguistic analysis developed in nineteenth-century German universities—the intellectual moves epitomized by Dwight and Mackintosh came to seem quaint and unscientific. Professional linguistics turned away from drawing conclusions about the minds of a language's speakers and focused instead on reconstructing how each language had changed over time. The line of inquiry that became the academic discipline of linguistics is traditionally dated from 1786, when Sir William Jones (1746–94) showed that Sanskrit, Latin, and Greek had evolved from a common parent language. Other early figures in this disciplinary tradition include

Jakob Grimm (1785–1863), Rasmus Rask (1787–1832), Jean-François Champollion (1790–1832), and, more distantly, John Wilkins (1614–72), John Locke (1632–1704), and George Berkeley (1685–1753). Dwight and Mackintosh were participating in a different line of inquiry—one that is rarely treated as part of the history of linguistics at all: linguistic historians frequently distinguish "linguistics" proper from the undisciplined, misguided, "eighteenth-century manner" of linguistic scholarship. That "eighteenth-century" tradition is the subject of this book, not because it is valuable to linguistics as we know it but because it mattered a great deal at the moment that this book attempts to understand.[46]

Today, the idea that different languages yield different thoughts is called linguistic determinism. The linguistic determinism hypothesis was one of the most important ideas in twentieth-century academic linguistics—though always a contentious one—after linguist Edward Sapir argued in 1929 that what we think of as "the 'real world' is to a large extent unconsciously built up on the language habits of the group" to which we happen to belong.[47] The implication is that speakers of different languages might have fundamentally different experiences of reality. In the 1930s and 1940s, Sapir's student Benjamin Whorf presented what he believed was empirical evidence for his mentor's claim. The Hopi language, Whorf reported, has no word that means "time," and no words for units of time like seconds, minutes, or days. This linguistic idiosyncrasy, Whorf argued, required Hopi speakers to construe experience otherwise than as a linear flow of moments that lie first in the future, then in the present, and finally in the past. His evidence suggested that time is an aspect of grammar rather than an aspect of reality. Other researchers went on to investigate the possibility that their alternative experience of time might equip the Hopi to understand four-dimensional space-time better than speakers of European languages.[48]

The Sapir-Whorf linguistic determinism hypothesis and its implications overflowed the field of linguistics into other academic disciplines, proving extremely influential and generative in the humanities. "The limits of my language are the limits of my world," wrote Ludwig Wittgenstein, and the interrelated twentieth-century intellectual movements now known as postmodernism, poststructuralism, deconstruction, the "linguistic turn," and cultural studies rest on the premise that our strongest beliefs and clearest perceptions are products of discourse rather than of objective reality. Words that seem to refer to things existing in the real world—such as *nature*, *teenagers*, *privacy*, *Texas*, *white people*—turn out in this perspective to refer to concepts invented since the eighteenth century. They are ways of talking about (and hence experiencing) the world—but we might have had other ways instead, and we should wonder why we have these ones. The central insight of twentieth-century literary studies might indeed be the idea that practically speaking, we live in a system of signification, not in an empirical reality.[49]

Linguists, however, grew increasingly skeptical after World War II about the evidence behind the linguistic determinism theory. Benjamin Whorf's Hopi example collapsed under scrutiny. (Hopi turns out to have an intricate temporal vocabulary that Whorf did not understand.) By the 1970s, linguistic determinism was largely discredited in academic linguistics and the Sapir-Whorf era was regarded as an unfortunate disciplinary folly. In the second half of the twentieth century, linguistic research focused increasingly on the samenesses rather than the differences among human languages. All languages, for example, have pronouns that encode singular/plural and at least three grammatical persons.[50] In the influential view of linguist Noam Chomsky, those common elements imply the presence of a common linguistic architecture or "universal grammar" that is biologically hardwired into the human brain—some innate neurobiology guiding the cognitive development of every physiologically normal infant in certain general directions. This approach suggests that our consciousness (or at least some fundamental portion of it) is constructed not by the arbitrary "language habits" of the social world to which we happen to belong, as Sapir thought, but by our DNA, much as our arms and legs are.[51]

Linguists have overwhelmingly adopted this view since the 1980s. But they have also explored the possibility that some aspects of consciousness really do differ according to language—though in much more limited ways than Whorf and his followers proposed. This "weaker" form of linguistic determinism, sometimes called linguistic relativity, gained momentum in the 1990s as technological breakthroughs in neuroimaging, and attendant developments in cognitive psychology, opened the door to new kinds of data about the mind and brain. As of this writing, neurolinguists seem to be on the verge, or perhaps just over it, of identifying neurophysiological correlates for certain kinds of grammar: paths of neurons that materially exist in the brains of speakers of languages with certain kinds of grammars. This finding would seem to confirm that language makes the difference between brain and brain, at least in some minute ways, although it would not resolve the question of how or whether those neuroanatomical differences generate any differences in cognition or consciousness.[52] Still, some neuro- and psycholinguists are once again willing to advance the "strong" version of the Sapir-Whorf claim. "The structures that exist in our languages profoundly shape how we construct reality," one cognitive psychologist wrote recently. "It turns out that if you change how people talk, that changes how they think." This is, in turn, exactly the line of thinking pursued by Duncan Mackintosh when he claimed that poor pronunciation was "a most dangerous corrupter of . . . politeness and morals."[53]

Figures of Speech is not about whether different languages really do create or reflect different cognitive realities. (My hunch: not really; maybe a little.) It is about what happened when English speakers believed that they did. The world may or may not look different in another language. But it certainly does look different if you *believe* that language has that effect. The empirical question of whether language affects consciousness is a question for a social scientist. *Figures of Speech* is about the historical and representational question of why three generations of English speakers at the turn of the nineteenth century believed that it did, and what that belief allowed them to do.

English Linguistic Identities from France to Javasu

One thing that belief allowed them to do was make a living. The declaration that "LANGUAGE MAKES THE DIFFERENCE BETWEEN MAN AND MAN" first appeared in print in 1806, in newspaper advertisements for a schoolbook composed by one Nicholas Dufief (1775–1834)—a teenaged aristocrat who fled the French Revolution for Haiti, fled the Haitian Revolution for Philadelphia, and went on to a career as probably the most famous teacher of French in the antebellum United States.

Dufief's life and work organize chapter 1, "Linguistic Salves for Political Wounds." He was part of the flood of French-speaking refugees from the Haitian and French revolutions that British and American cities absorbed in the 1790s. The rise of Napoleon (1799–1804) and the later restoration of the Bourbon monarchy (1814–15) would set off additional diasporic waves, as some of the exiles from the 1790s returned to France, and new political refugees fled from it. This Atlantic circulation of refugees created a corresponding circulation of languages and dialects and made for a huge and increasing supply of French teachers in the English-speaking world, as educated and formerly wealthy Francophones arrived in Atlantic port cities and needed to make a living, preferably one that did not involve physical labor. The Age of Revolutions' political refugees suffered great losses—of property, families, homes, homelands, social position, political power, and nationality—but they kept their languages.

The French Revolution was the chief trauma of Dufief's life. After his family, home, wealth, and title were taken from him when he was seventeen, the French language became his locus of purpose and meaning, as well as his profession. As a teacher of French, Dufief invented what he believed was a way to tap into the deep learning processes by which children acquire their mother tongue. He considered his pedagogical technique one of the most significant inventions in the history of the world—"a discovery exceeding in power that of the steam engine"—and he spent his entire adult life promoting it.[54] He had arrived in Philadelphia penniless and speaking no English; it's rich that his greatest achievement (so he believed) was a method for making that kind of linguistic isolation easier to transcend. By thinking about his "difference" as "made" by his French language, Dufief was able to remain, in a way, French, even though he never again lived in France. He bore his francophonicity for the rest of his life in a linguistically English world—forever an outsider, a purveyor of French to non-Francophones, restaging in every classroom the experience of not being understood. It might have been satisfying to watch that incomprehensibility melt away with the advancing proficiency of each new pupil, as language eased the difference between him and them. Or he might have been torturing himself.

Chapter 2, "The United Language of English: Linguistic Separatism and Unionism in the Revolutionary Atlantic," focuses on the alternately reassuring and alarming implications of linguistic identity for English speakers who made their lives far from the historical center of the English language. One of those people is Duncan Mackintosh, the Scottish-Caribbean phonetician who hoped to improve the transmission of English phonetics—and therefore English mentalities—to colonial and otherwise distant populations. Partly because he was promoting his long-distance English pronunciation transmission system while he was himself at a long distance from England, Mackintosh never won the institutional support that he thought his system deserved. But what he was trying to do illustrates a "linguistic unionism" shared by many others in England, Scotland, the British Caribbean, and, perhaps most surprisingly, the new United States. Although Americans did not want to share a government with Britain, they did want to share other things: literature, social rituals, aesthetic fashions, modes of politeness. The English language became a potent symbol of what they wanted to share, an index of how well they were sharing it, and (they believed) a unique mental architecture that supported those particular values, rituals, tastes, and modes. Numerous Americans proposed new alphabets and new spelling systems around 1800, not in the spirit of rebellion against the language of England, but for the same reason as Duncan Mackintosh: they wanted to prevent the emergence of a distinctively "American" strain of English, just as Mackintosh wanted to prevent or reverse the emergence of a Caribbean English. Americans imagined the English language as a reassuring foundation for their daunting political independence.

When, therefore, Noah Webster (1758–1843) called his fellow Americans in the 1780s to join him in driving a wedge between British and American forms of English, many Americans were horrified. Webster tried harder than anyone else to get Americans to disavow their "English" linguistic identities. But far from the eminent lexicographer and American patriot who would be beatified after the publication of his *American Dictionary* in 1828, the Noah Webster of the turn of the nineteenth century was widely known as a radical lunatic trying to foment an unwanted linguistic schism. Although Webster's linguistic nationalism has earned him a reputation as the founding father of American English and a beacon of early American cultural independence, Webster's eagerness to declare linguistic independence was in fact very unusual in his day. The second half of chapter 2 depicts Webster, the linguistic separatist, as an outlier within an American linguistic ideology that was often more closely aligned with the linguistic unionism epitomized by Duncan Mackintosh.

English was one of many languages that English speakers wanted to exchange across imperial distances. From the edges of empire trickled raw linguistic data that promised to sustain conclusions about the newly visible diversity of the human world. But transmitting that data was a task poorly suited to English speakers' most efficient text transmission technology: the movable-type printing press and its corresponding cabinet full of alphabetic type. While texts in the Latin or Greek alphabet could be distributed very widely at small expense, other scripts were logistically and financially prohibitive to print.[55] This presented a constant problem for missionary societies, scholars, bureaucrats, and magazine reviewers. The alternative to commissioning custom-manufactured type was to transliterate the foreign text—Turkish, Russian, Tamil, or whatever it might be—into Latin characters and print it that way. But this was a very imperfect solution. There are about forty meaningfully distinct sounds, or phonemes, in English, which we represent (rather ambiguously, as Mackintosh noticed) by means of twenty-six letters. All told, however, the world's various languages use at least a hundred sounds other than the English ones. Very few of these are easy to describe in English, but one of them is the back-of-the-mouth consonant in *loch* or *chutzpah*, and another is the click that you make with your tongue when you want a horse to go faster. The vast majority of non-English phonemes, however, have no loanword from Scottish or Yiddish or horsemanship to refer to. Absent such a point of phonetic reference, unfamiliar phonemes are practically impossible to describe qualitatively. (Try using words to describe the horse-acceleration sound: *it's like a cluck, but frothier . . . ?*)

Indeed, before the advent of recorded sound in the 1870s, the only really reliable means of transmitting unfamiliar language sounds from one place to another was to send a living person to vocalize them.[56]

One effect of this was that few people in Britain had a clear idea of what non-Western languages sounded like because few people had occasion to talk face-to-face with a speaker of a non-Western language. (Things were different in North America.) Yet the expanding linguistic diversity of the British Empire created practical and ideological needs to circulate the sounds of non-European languages. Chapter 3, "The Abecedarian Clock: Recording Speech before Recorded Sound," is organized around John Gilchrist (1759–1841), a teacher and translator who spent more than twenty years in India compiling the world's first English-Urdu bilingual dictionary—and then, frustrated with the alphabetic difficulties of transmitting the knowledge he had gained, spent a quarter century inventing a universal alphabet of one hundred letters "***komprehendeŋ evure leteral swnd utturabl artekyoletle bie te hyoman vœs.***" Intent on redressing the "notorious cacography" of the world's many mutually illegible writing systems, Gilchrist joined the ranks of the small cadre of English speakers who had dreamed up universal alphabets over the preceding three centuries. He was one of the very first who went so far as to cast such an alphabet into a physical fount of working type. Gilchrist's "***yoneversul***" alphabet is an utterly forgotten forerunner of the much later International Phonetic Alphabet (1888) that would underpin the modern discipline of linguistics. Gilchrist's alphabet appears in print in these pages for the first time since 1826.

"comprehending every literal sound utterable articulately by the human voice"

Typefounder Edmund Fry (1757–1835) also confronted the linguistic diversity of the world and the difficulty of representing it in movable type. But instead of trying like Gilchrist to reduce that difference into a single universal alphabet, he did the opposite: he created type for every known alphabet and writing system in the world. His *Pantographia*, published in 1799, featured "specimens" of 164 languages and 208 alphabets—a purportedly complete compendium of human writing made possible by Fry's own sixteen years of artisanal labor manufacturing the book's custom type. *Pantographia* was widely purchased, appreciated, and celebrated as a work of "national importance." This highly unusual textual object anchors chapter 4, "How to Read the World: *Pantographia*, Print Specimens, and Linguistic Identity." Since even the most learned polyglot can know only a small fraction of the languages in the book, *Pantographia* is impossible to "read," if reading means comprehending visual symbols as words. *Pantographia* evidently invites a different kind of textual engagement, and I argue that it was a kind practiced by eighteenth-century print consumers when they heeded a publisher's invitation to visit a print shop to evaluate a "specimen" of the paper and type on which some large-scale work was to be printed. *Pantographia* recognizes an analogy between suspending the textual content of a specimen to evaluate its material form and suspending the semantic content of a language to evaluate its formal properties. The book links the consumer pleasure of evaluating a "specimen" of print to the imperial pleasure of evaluating a specimen of language.

Pantographia made worldwide linguistic diversity available in parlors everywhere. Twenty years after its publication, the hosts of the distressed young woman known as Caraboo sat her down with a copy of *Pantographia* and turned its pages, hoping that she would recognize one of its languages as her own. But she didn't. Chapter 5, "Mary Willcocks's Caraboo Tongue," is about that young woman. Her real name, or at least her legal name, was Mary Willcocks. Born to working-class parents in southwestern England, Willcocks (1791–1864) had little formal education and had never traveled farther than London. The exotic language that she spoke and wrote was of her own invention. A brilliant and troubled twenty-five-year-old, Willcocks became Caraboo when forced into a legal and economic corner: she was begging her way through the English countryside, trying to earn £5 to pay for a ticket to America, when, threatened with arrest for vagrancy, she adopted an *I-don't-speak-English* defense that worked far too well. Willcocks's Caraboo was exactly the British gentry's Orientalist fantasy of how a South Pacific lady of quality would speak and behave. She tried twice to slip away from the mansion at which she, as Princess Caraboo, was being fêted as an exotic guest, but her well-to-do hosts mobilized search parties and tracked her down before she got far enough away. The Caraboo persona, which she had originally deployed defensively, thus became a prison—a linguistic and behavioral mask that she could not take off without risking criminal prosecution.

So she made the best of it. Trapped in the Caraboo identity, Mary Willcocks took advantage of its liberating potentials. Willcocks's demographics (poor, rural, female) made her unlikely to be listened to—but elite audiences and newspaper readers hung on Caraboo's every word. Mary Willcocks had been physically abused by her father—Caraboo was also a trauma victim, but one far more likely than Mary Willcocks to be heard and compassionated. Willcocks had been institutionalized twice for a mental illness that today might be diagnosed as bipolar disorder—but in the person of Caraboo, her manic creativity, her eccentric leaps of thought, and her extraordinary linguistic ability were relished, not pathologized. As Mary Willcocks, she was obligated to follow gender norms against which she clearly chafed: during her adolescence, she had been punished for cross-dressing and beaten by her father for an unspecified intimacy with a young woman. As Caraboo, however, she was allowed outside the confines of European heterosexuality: she fenced, shot arrows, rowed a boat, climbed trees, carried a knife, swam naked, refused to be alone with men and recoiled at their touch, and placed herself at the homosocial center of elite female society. Caraboo's queerness was viable in a way that Mary Willcocks's was not. Her extraordinary linguistic skill gave her access to a subject position from which she could be wild, eccentric, imaginative, athletic, queer. At the same time, that skill condemned her to near-total linguistic incommunicability: she found a way for her language to be heard, but not understood.

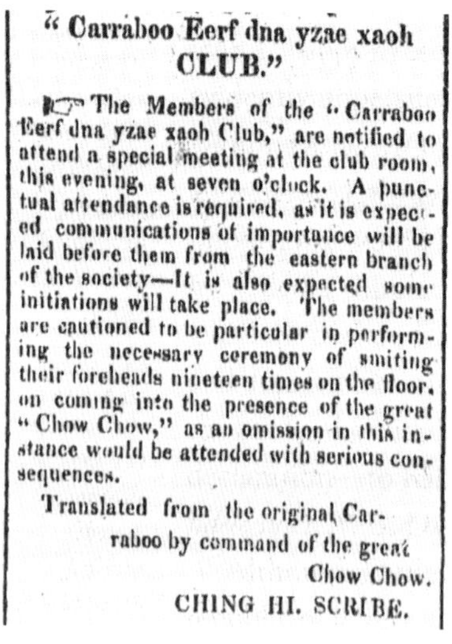

"Carraboo Eerf dna yzae xaoh CLUB."

☞ The Members of the "Carraboo Eerf dna yzae xaoh Club," are notified to attend a special meeting at the club room, this evening, at seven o'clock. A punctual attendance is required, as it is expected communications of importance will be laid before them from the eastern branch of the society—It is also expected some initiations will take place. The members are cautioned to be particular in performing the necessary ceremony of smiting their foreheads nineteen times on the floor, on coming into the presence of the great "Chow Chow," as an omission in this instance would be attended with serious consequences.

Translated from the original Carraboo by command of the great Chow Chow.

CHING HI. SCRIBE.

An American newspaper editor takes Caraboo as an occasion to play with fake Asian language in this joke: an announcement in the voice of "the great Chow Chow" regarding a meeting of the "Carraboo Eerf dna yzae xaoh CLUB" (Caraboo free-and-easy hoax Club). *National Messenger* (Georgetown, D.C.), Nov. 3, 1817. Courtesy of Readex.

After Caraboo was identified as Mary Willcocks, she became an instant transatlantic celebrity. A sympathetic admirer bought her a ticket to America, and crowds were waiting for her at the dock when she arrived in Philadelphia. Hundreds of articles appeared about her in American newspapers over the next few months. To Americans, Willcocks was the clever autodidact from humble beginnings who had hoaxed the English intelligentsia. A constant stream of visitors came to her lodgings seeking autographs—in Caraboo's script, of course—and

Willcocks performed her Caraboo act on stage at a six thousand–seat theater in Philadelphia to cheers and applause. In spirited newspaper drollery, Americans joined Caraboo-Willcocks in playing with language and playing with their identities: playing Chinese, playing princess, playing not-American, playing not-British. Willcocks had proved that an ingenious linguistic performance could dramatically alter one's perceived racial, national, and socioeconomic position. Americans took Willcocks's identity-bending linguistic play as an invitation to engage in the same kind of subversive experimentation.

From Language to Culture

One story that has been told about the history of identity is that the eighteenth century saw a shift in Western thought from more fluid, changeable categories of identity to more fixed and rigid ones. During the early part of the century, for example, changing environmental factors, such as climate, dominated European thinking about why people were the way they were. In one 1720 novel, an Englishman whose wife cheated on him in Jamaica reflects that the liaison "was not so much the Fault of the Woman as of the Climate, believing 'twas not her natural Inclination, but that cursed malevolent Planet [Venus] which predominates in that Island, and so changes the Constitution of its Inhabitants, that if a Woman land there as chaste as a Vestal, she becomes in forty-eight Hours a perfect *Messalina*." On the other hand, the husband worries, perhaps "her now having liv'd five Years in *Jamaica* was time long enough, not only to tincture, but to change her whole Mass of Blood, and totally alter her Nature." Either way, environmental circumstances could apparently "alter her Nature," and her national and ethnic Englishness provide no guarantee against the sensual influence of the tropical clime. At that early period in the eighteenth century, typical Europeans knew which nation-state(s) they belonged to, but identified less with "the abstract concept of their 'nation'" than with "their monarch, their religion, or their native region." By 1800, however, nationality had become a core component of a person's sense of who she was—a component over which she could exercise little control unless she had an unusual degree of influence on state politics. And while the word "race" had a loose meaning and was generally interchangeable with "nation" before about 1780, it subsequently developed a stricter sense "as a term for the biological subdivision of humanity" into four or five distinct groups with recognizable physiological differences. The emerging significance of racial and national identity categories has been seen as illustrating the end of a period in which identity was tied to a person's always-changing experience, and the beginning of a period in which identity became something permanent and fixed.[57]

The linguistic approaches to identity that appealed to English speakers around the turn of the nineteenth century don't quite fit into this paradigm because language is neither entirely fixed nor entirely fluid. While language can be changed more easily than skin color, my power to change my language is seriously constrained, especially after childhood. In some ways, then, my mother tongue is something I'm stuck with, like my complexion. But in other ways, I can intentionally control it—like *My Fair Lady*'s Eliza Doolittle, or like Mary Willcocks's Caraboo. Language straddles the inside/outside, essential/inessential, nature/nurture, hereditary/environmental line. This is precisely what made language such an appealing element of identity discourses at the turn of the nineteenth century: it is sticky, but not inalterable. Thinking about identity in terms of language meant conceiving of identity as something that is difficult but not impossible to change; for the geopolitical, ideological, and media-technological reasons discussed in this book, that kind of identity needed to be conceivable.

Today, the category that we use to describe identity as socially (not biologically) determined, and difficult (but not impossible) to change, is "culture." Although that word did not exist in this sense until 1860 at the earliest, the early-nineteenth-century use of language to mark identity may represent an early version of the concept of "cultural identity" that would emerge explicitly a century later. The idea that each community has a "culture"—a distinctive body of shared strategies for experiencing and making sense of the world, socially transmitted from generation to generation—is not an inevitable conclusion to be drawn from reality. It's a hypothesis and interpretive strategy that had to be invented. During the twentieth century, culture became the primary category of human identity in the West: it came to seem worthwhile to look for people who shared those deep assumptions, habits, and instincts; understand that set of people as a group with meaningful ties to each other; and give a name ("culture") to designate the thing that those people had in common.

Like what would later be understood as "culture," language seemed at the turn of the nineteenth century to shape all members of a given community, conditioning their expectations and assumptions in ways that were almost impossible to resist. Like the later concept of culture, language was understood as a social phenomenon, but one that was only obliquely accessible to human will—difficult to change through deliberate intervention but nevertheless susceptible to neglect and corruption. As with a culture, to the extent that people shared a language, they ostensibly shared fundamental strategies for understanding their experiences, no matter what other differences they might have. The literary scholar Michael Elliott has argued that "before the early twentieth century, the vocabulary of social identity provided no reliable lexicon for dividing those characteristics that people inherited from their ancestors from those they did not." Elliott and others have seen "culture" as the concept that popularized the notion that "group-based differences" may be "socially determined."[58] I am suggesting that "language" began to serve as a vocabulary for nonbiological group-based differences a century earlier.

This matters because it calls into question the assumption that cultural identity is unlike racial and national identity. Those categories, for all of their explanatory and community-making power, are fraught with perils that the English-speaking world spent the nineteenth century learning about. We like to think that cultural identity provides a more evolved account of human diversity: culture is about values and morals and practices—about consciousness, not about the body or power. Indeed, nineteenth- and early-twentieth-century anthropologists made sure that "culture" was understood in contrast to racism.[59]

I am far from the first person to wonder whether cultural identity isn't a disguise for something much uglier.[60] But I am suggesting a new historical lineage, from the linguistic protoethnography practiced at the turn of the nineteenth century to the modern "cultural" thinking of the twentieth. To the extent that this lineage obtains, we should be troubled by how effortlessly it reinforces the observer's existing assumptions. We watch as Timothy Dwight's prejudices about Arabs sail through his linguistic analysis unaltered; he ends up with exactly the same Orientalist fantasy about Arabs that he had before, but now certified as racism-free. One of the many functions served by linguistic thinking at the turn of the nineteenth century was to provide evidence for things that you already want to believe; or, to put it another way, it was a way of making prejudices seem justified. Culture might be the same thing.

CHAPTER ONE

Linguistic Salves for Political Wounds

Well, Perhaps You Are a Frenchman

If this were a nineteenth-century French class, I might begin by asking you to open your copy of Monsieur Dufief's book to page 255 and repeat each phrase and keyword after me:

> European. *Européen.* I took him for an European. *Je l'ai pris pour un Européen.*
> Asiatic. *Asiatique.* You were mistaken; he is an Asiatic. *Vous vous êtes trompé, c'est un Asiatique.*
> African. *Africain.* His father was an African. *Son père était Africain.*
> American. *Américain.* I thought he was an American. *Je croyais qu'il était Américain.*
> Creole. *Créol.* Are you not a Creole? *N'êtes-vous pas Créol?*
> German. *Allemand.* A colony of Germans was sent thither. *On y envoya une colonie d'Allemands.*
> Englishman. *Anglais.* You look like an Englishman. *Vous avez l'air d'un Anglais.*
> Bohemian. *Bohémien.* Is he not a Bohemian? *N'est-il pas Bohémien?*

Dane. *Danois.* No, he is a Dane, I am sure of it. *Non, il est Danois j'en suis sûr.*

Frenchman. *Français.* Well, perhaps you are a Frenchman. *Peut-être bien êtes-vous Français.*

Spaniard. *Espagnol.* I was told he was a Spaniard. *On m'a dit qu'il était Espagnol.*

Fleming. *Flamand.* For my part, I think he is a Fleming. *Quant à moi, je crois qu'il est Flamand.*[1]

Dufief's was one of the nineteenth century's most popular schoolbooks for teaching French to English speakers, used widely on both sides of the Atlantic from the 1810s to the 1850s, so over the years, countless British and American learners recited this twelve-sentence introduction to the vocabulary of racial, ethnic, and national identities. It didn't have to turn out this way, of course. Dufief was just one of many writers of his day who composed new French-for-English-speakers books and launched them into the British and American print markets to compete with standard texts that were now being published in their fifteenth and twentieth editions. These upstart imprints, with titles like *The First Step to the French Tongue* (1795), *A Guide from the English Language to the French* (1799), and *A New Grammar of the French Tongue* (1804), rarely gained any traction against the established standbys. But Dufief's did. His first edition, published in Philadelphia in 1804, quickly sold out, and he continued selling out edition after Philadelphia edition for the rest of his life: 1806, 1810, 1817, 1823, 1827, 1834. In 1817, he moved to London and launched the book there with equal success, turning out London editions in 1818, 1819, 1828, 1831, and 1834. He arranged a verbatim adaptation of the book for teaching Spanish (I took him for a European, *Creí que fuese Europeo*—His father was an African, *Su padre era Africano*, and so on) and published editions of that on both sides of the Atlantic too (1811, 1817, 1825, 1826).[2] His book commanded the print marketplace, and its reprints, new editions, and translations illustrate how material commerce and material design help shed light on this unusual moment in the history of linguistic thinking.

That Dufief's book, as opposed to someone else's, should have achieved such dramatic transatlantic and translingual commercial success involved a bit of luck. But it was not only luck. In several significant ways, Dufief had his finger on his audience's pulse: his book connected a cultural moment in which language seemed a plausible basis for a stable identity category to a political moment in which national, racial, and class identities were disrupted by the three Atlantic revolutions. The vocabulary lesson from the book is a case in point—its national and racial sample phrases dominated by uncertainty about the very nouns they are exemplifying. *A European*, *an American*, and the other identity nouns turn out to be rather unreliable descriptors of what "he is" or "you are," and the prevailing grammar is a grammar of ambiguity: *I took him for . . .* , *Are you not . . . ?*, *Perhaps you are . . .* , *I was told he is . . .* The "Asiatic" is mistaken for a European and an American. "His father was an African," but what was his mother, and what is he? "You look like an Englishman," but are you really? By the time the page issues a definitive statement ("No, he is a Dane, I am sure of it"), that kind of certainty seems out of place, and it's no surprise that the rest of the phrases undermine it. In a literal sense, this is a lesson about how to express confusion about whether these national, ethnic, and racial nouns apply to someone. They seem to name categories that (at least in this lesson) cannot be reliably detected or known for sure.

Of course, the content of these sentences is not exactly the point. The students reciting them were studying French, not sociology, and the lesson's stated goal is to teach not the ideas that these sentences say but the words and syntax used to say them. The learner would stash away these linguistic materials so that he could later use them to express ideas of his own, "drawing supplies for the formation of phrases from his continually increasing stock of words."[3] Hence the many other colorful counterfactuals appearing in the book's eight thousand practice sentences—some of which embellish this chapter's margins—such as "my fosterbrother has attempted to murder me"—a sentence that students were no doubt unlikely to have occasion to utter, but which they learned so that someday they might say something else about a foster brother, an attempt, or a murder.[4] Still, the uncertainties attending *an American*, *an African*, and the other identity nouns that don't quite accomplish their nominative work might be said to reflect the chaotic state of identity in the Atlantic world during the

FOSTER-BROTHER. My foster-brother has attempted to murder me.

FRÈRE DE LAIT. Mon frère de lait a voulu m'assassiner.

extremely tumultuous decades following the American, French, and Haitian revolutions. Between 1775 and 1825, political revolutions obliged many people to rethink their identity vocabularies. In North America, English-speaking whites grew up in the 1750s defining themselves as "English," in contradistinction to the ostensibly brutal and violent "Americans" (i.e., Natives). In the 1760s and 1770s, however, those same people began to define themselves as "Americans" in contradistinction to the brutal and violent "English" (i.e., British). Similarly head-spinning changes took place around the Atlantic. A person born in 1792 on the Caribbean island of Martinique could have reached her early twenties having changed nationalities eleven times without ever leaving the island, which was governed successively by France, Britain, free blacks, Britain, France, Britain, France, Britain, France, Britain, and France by 1815. Over the same period of time, a person living in Paris would have been the subject of a kingdom, a republic, an empire, a kingdom, an empire, and a kingdom.[5]

If you were a cartographer in those years, these developments were extremely disruptive, but they had a straightforward (if time-consuming) solution: draw new maps with the political boundaries in different places.[6] The solutions available to noncartographers were less obvious. This is the situation dramatized by Washington Irving in 1819 in the character of Rip van Winkle, who gets drunk and passes out before the American Revolution, awakening in the 1790s to find himself accosted by townspeople asking bewildering questions about "on which side he voted?" and "whether he was Federal or Democrat." Disoriented, Rip "doubted his own identity, and whether he was himself or another man." This is one of the earliest known uses of the word "identity" in its modern sense: an awareness of an individualized self, continuously present through time and space, and of that self's position within socially defined categories such as race, nationality, and (in Rip's case) partisan affiliation. Rip neatly illustrates how political revolutions can strain this self-perception—a strain without a release mechanism as simple as the mapmaker's. "Every thing's changed," Rip exclaims, "and I'm changed, and I can't tell what's my name, or who I am!"[7] Things turn out okay for Rip van Winkle, though: he happens to have an adult daughter willing to pay his living expenses, so he never needs to adapt to his new sociopolitical reality. He resumes his prerevolutionary activities of lazing around and shooting the breeze.

The author of the "I took him for an European" schoolbook was not so lucky as Rip in resolving the challenges presented by Atlantic revolutions to "his own identity, and whether he was himself." Nicolas Gouin du Fief spent his childhood in western France on an estate to which his father, grandfather, great-grandfather, and great-great-grandfather had all been *seigneur*, or lord. Young Nicolas was in line to become the fifth Lord Gouin du Fief and enjoy a nobleman's privileged life until a crowd of antimonarchy protesters stormed the Bastille, and the National Assembly voted to "completely eradicate the feudal system" just before his fourteenth birthday.[8] Three years later, the young man's father was in exile, his mother was a counterrevolutionary insurgent personally leading battles against the French army, and Nicolas, the ex-future Lord Gouin du Fief, was a political refugee on the other side of the ocean—first in Saint-Domingue and then in Philadelphia.

When he wrote his French-for-English-speakers schoolbook a decade later, "Nicholas Gouin Dufief" had a new Anglicized name, a new American citizenship, a new proficiency in the English language, and a carefully cultivated relationship with President Thomas Jefferson.[9] "Well, perhaps you are a Frenchman": the sample sentence that he wrote to drill the word *Français* might have been about as nationally concrete as Dufief could be about himself, and he made sure that his readers knew it. He prefaced his schoolbook with a detailed account of the revolutionary circumstances that had led to its composition. When his customers bought his book, they were also buying the biography of a refugee who had lost his national identity when the French nation-state to which he was loyal gave way in 1792 to a French nation-state that he despised. He kept that loss on full display in every edition of his schoolbook; it was part of the product. He never developed a meaningful connection to any particular national identity after he lost his French one. Instead, Dufief embraced a linguistic account of identity. In 1806, now thirty years old, he placed advertisements in Philadelphia, New York, and Boston newspapers announcing a second edition of

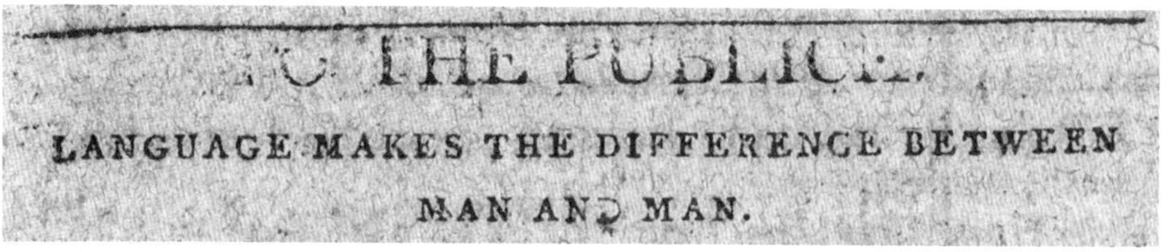
TO THE PUBLIC.

LANGUAGE MAKES THE DIFFERENCE BETWEEN MAN AND MAN.

Dufief makes his thesis statement easy to find. *United States' Gazette* (Philadelphia), July 11, 1806. The Library Company of Philadelphia.

his French-for-English-speakers schoolbook. The advertisements ran under the heading "LANGUAGE MAKES THE DIFFERENCE BETWEEN MAN AND MAN."[10]

He meant it quite literally. Dufief saw language the way eighteenth-century climate theorists saw climate, the way Freud saw childhood, the way a psychopharmacologist sees neurochemistry, the way a racist sees biology: the cause of observable differences among different peoples, and the thing that makes you the way you are—smart or dull, strong or weak, cautious or impulsive, tenacious or capricious. "Language," Dufief wrote, "is the very creator of the thinking faculty itself." Like Duncan Mackintosh, Timothy Dwight, and the Scottish Enlightenment philosophers discussed in the introduction, Dufief believed that a language bequeaths to its speakers a kind of mental inheritance.[11] He believed, for example, that languages abounding with prepositions, adverbs, and conjunctions had "a decided superiority over other languages" because their speakers' "faculty of reasoning receives a greater degree of accuracy" (cf. table 1).[12] For John Locke, such "accuracy" had been the chief dimension along which languages differed from each other, but Dufief and his ilk envisioned a much more complex picture. Dufief wrote that each language "gives wings to the imagination, by opening new views for meditation and reflection," with different languages apparently offering different "views" of the world.[13]

This way of thinking about language emphasizes how a language differs from a secret code. Learn a code, and you can send and receive messages; learn a language, Dufief indicates, and new dimensions develop in your "thinking faculty"—your cognition, your consciousness, ultimately your self. To make language a defining attribute of the self is to root the self in an institution that cannot be changed by fiat (like nationality) but can be bent, changed, or shaped through the exquisite and intentional effort of the speaking subject.

Such an identity suited Dufief himself, in that it allowed him to belong to both the Francophone and Anglophone worlds. The French language was almost the only thing he was able to bring with him from his childhood in the Old World to his adulthood in the New, and no one could rob him of it the way the French Revolution had robbed him of his national and aristocratic identities. As an English speaker, Dufief was self-made, the product of his own bootstrapped effort. As a French speaker, Dufief remained connected to a life that, although he was now geographically and sociopolitically distant from it, he could keep alive within himself as long as he spoke French. He abhorred the French Revolution, but he came to see himself as the flag-bearer of a pedagogical revolution that was (he believed) far more historically significant: he believed that he had discovered the linguistic basis of consciousness, a truth "DISCOVERED, after SIXTY CENTURIES of almost IMPENETRABLE DARKNESS."[14] He built a linguistic identity out of the ruins of his national identity and started his own linguistic revolution to eclipse the political revolution that displaced him.

Dufief was far from the only Atlantic subject who found a linguistic salve for political wounds in that revolutionary era, but in his life the relationship between political revolution and linguistic identity is visible in especially high relief. National exile was the central trauma of his life, and his identity became that of a Franco-Anglophone and Anglo-Francophone—a person who bridged the French-speaking and English-speaking worlds. He devoted his life to the idea that language could replace what he had nationally lost, and he sold that idea, along with his French pedagogy, to British and American readers.

The Refugee's Language

Revolutions need metaphors, and one of the chief metaphors of the American, French, and Haitian revolutions was that the revolutionaries were rebellious adolescents. A famous 1776 print, for example, stages the

American Revolution as family drama: "I'll force you to obedience you rebellious slut," says Britain, as a tattooed and scantily clad America hollers for "Liberty liberty mother for ever." Detail from *The Female Combatants* (1776). Courtesy of the John Carter Brown Library at Brown University.

imperial crisis as mother-daughter domestic drama: mother Britain commanding obedience as her adolescent daughter punches her in the face and demands liberty.[15] For Dufief, however, the revolution-as-adolescence trope was not a metaphor. The French and Haitian revolutions coincided with his actual adolescence, and defined it. He had the bad historical luck to come of age exactly at the moment that two revolutions destroyed the institutions around which he might otherwise have organized his adult self: the Bourbon monarchy, the colony of Saint-Domingue, and his own family, wealth, and nobility. The evaporation of those institutions undermined everything from his nationality to his name. His language was what he had left.

Nicolas Gouin du Fief's father was the *seigneur du fief*, or lord of the manor, of an estate in the far west of France with the unfortunate name of le Fief (the Manor): he was seigneur du fief du Fief, lord of the manor of The Manor. Like others in the region, Dufief's family was ethnically Celtic—descended from the people known as Bretons who, a thousand years earlier, had fled the Anglo-Saxon settlement of their native Britain and established themselves just across the English Channel in the extreme northwest corner of continental Europe. Their duchy of Brittany was absorbed into the French state in 1532, but the region retained its Celtic language and distinct political and legal institutions.[16] Dufief's surname, Gouin, is Celtic; English speakers know it as Gwen. (It means "white" and makes up part of the word "penguin"—the white part.) By the time Dufief was growing up in the late eighteenth century, aristocratic families like his shunned the Breton language and spoke French instead. By surname and ethnicity, however, he was transnational from birth.[17]

IN THE BEGINNING. In the beginning things were very different.

AU COMMENCEMENT. Au commencement les choses étaient bien differentes.

Stripped of le Fief during the French Revolution, members of the Gouin du Fief family took divergent approaches to renaming themselves. Dufief's brother Jean-Baptiste-Désiré dropped his manorial title and became Désiré Gouin for a time. The parents steadfastly remained Nicolas-Henri and Victoire-Aimée du Fief.[18] Dufief altered *du Fief* to *Dufief* after he arrived in the English-speaking world in his late teens and experimented with several different given names in the 1790s: Nicholas G. Dufief, Chevalier Nicholas Gouin Dufief, Gawain Dufief, Gouin Dufief Junr., and Mr. Gouin Dufief.[19] He stabilized his onomastic identity in his midtwenties by eliding both his given name and his ethnically Celtic surname, becoming simply "Dufief." He was N. G. Dufief on paper, Monsieur Dufief in public. The name was easy for English speakers to pronounce even though it was conspicuously French, which suited his purposes as he built a public identity as a teacher and general purveyor of the French language to the English-speaking world.

Born in 1775, the oldest of five children, Dufief grew up in a mansion near the port city of Nantes, thirty miles up the Loire River from where it empties into the Atlantic Ocean.[20] These were flush and cosmopolitan times in Nantes thanks to the city's long-established dominance of the French slave trade. Known as the *ville des Négriers* (the city of "Negro-mongers"—that is, slavers), Nantes ran three times as many slaving voyages as any other port in eighteenth-century France, transporting to the French Caribbean perhaps 450,000 enslaved persons all told. The economy of Nantes was vertically integrated for transatlantic slave commerce, boasting powerful banks to finance voyages, manufacturers of textiles and trinkets to trade for slaves in West Africa, a shipbuilding industry producing the necessary vessels, and metalworkers forging the numerous chains, handcuffs, and torture instruments that such ships required. After moving their human cargo from Africa to France's West Indian colonies—especially Saint-Domingue, but also Martinique and Saint Lucia—the ships returned to Nantes carrying brown sugar that had been grown and processed by last year's slaves. Nantes's twelve sugar refineries further processed the muscovado (brown) sugar into refined (white) sugar, as well as rum and brandy. "Nantz brandy" was a staple of British and American liquor cabinets until well into the nineteenth century.[21]

CHILDHOOD. Childhood is the happiest time of life.

ENFANCE. *L'enfance est le temps le plus heureux de la vie.*

BRANDY. We import a great deal of brandy from France.

EAU DE VIE. *Nous tirons beaucoup d'eau de vie de France.*

Aristocrats like Dufief's parents were as eager as Nantes's bourgeois to share in the lavish fortunes being made by investors, ship captains,

Prerevolutionary Nantes. Drawing attributed to Nicolas Ozanne, ca. 1776. Musée Dobrée, Grand Patrimoine de Loire-Atlantique.

and plantation owners in the slave-and-sugar trade that was centered on Saint-Domingue, a colony the size of Maryland that at its peak produced half of the world's sugar. It was the most lucrative territory in the world, constituting at least 10 percent of the entire economy of France and organizing virtually all of the economy of Nantes. Although four thousand miles of ocean and a two months' journey separated Nantes from the colony on which its prosperity depended, Saint-Domingue was socially and imaginatively close by; one historian has written that eighteenth-century Nantes was an "Atlantic and American" city at least as much as it was a French city.[22]

YEAR. In six years he will enjoy the full possession of his estate.

AN. *Dans six ans il jouira de tout son bien.*

Saint-Domingue's ruling class contained many expatriate *nantais*, including siblings of both of Dufief's parents, and if things had gone differently, Dufief might well have ended up owning a Caribbean sugar plantation. Some of the sample phrases in the learn-to-speak-French schoolbook that he would write in his twenties might have been imaginary snatches of that lost future. His students would learn the French word for "sugarcane" by reciting "*Cette habitation roule beaucoup de cannes à sucre.* At this plantation they grind a great number of sugar-canes." The book's agricultural vocabulary features a number of phrases idealizing landowner-fieldhand relations, such as "this lord is much beloved by his peasants" and "he ordered that a glass of brandy should be given to his reapers."[23] As things turned out, though, Dufief had no opportunity to be beloved by his peasants, reapers, or slaves. Instead, when he was thirteen years old, a revolutionary legislature in Paris declared France's feudal system and all its privileges to be null and void.[24] That was the end of the *seigneurie du Fief* that Nicolas Gouin "du Fief" would have otherwise inherited.

Dufief and his parents went to war against the French Revolution. In 1791–92, the sixteen-year-old made his way up the English Channel, around revolutionary France, and into central Europe, where exiled aristocrats had turned the German city of Coblenz into "a small extra-national Versailles." From there, a coalition of armies led by these "Emigrants" was planning to invade France with the support of Prussian military forces, overthrow the revolutionary government, and restore the crippled monarchy to its formerly absolute sovereignty. Dufief joined a military outfit that called itself, rather ambitiously, the Marine Royale (royal navy) of France, and, with other Emigrant forces, embarked on a brief, ill-fated counterrevolutionary invasion of France.[25]

Not long after crossing from German territory into France, the Emigrants found their path to Paris blocked by the rocky Argonne Forest, the passable areas of which were strategically occupied by French troops sent by the republican government. Skirmishes ensued. After three rainy weeks of military deadlock, the French army won a critical victory, effectively ending the royalist invasion. Word of the Emigrants' defeat reached Paris the next day, where the revolutionary legislature, stirred by the news, voted unanimously to abolish the monarchy and proclaim the French Republic.[26] It was Dufief's seventeenth birthday.

GROAN.
The groans of the wounded filled me with horror for war.

GÉMISSEMENT.
Les gémissements des blessés m'inspiraient de l'horreur pour la guerre.

The Emigrant armies now beat an urgent and chaotic retreat out of France through what the novelist Johann Wolfgang von Goethe, who happened to be traveling with a Prussian regiment supporting the Emigrant invasion, described as "the worst weather in the world." Aristocrats who had weeks earlier toasted the imminent restoration of the monarchy now found themselves in conditions of extreme privation. Most units ran completely out of food, and the October rain provided the only source of drinking water. Carriages that overturned were left in

An eighteenth-century satirist depicts the Emigrants and their Prussian allies in retreat, terrified to the point of incontinence. Detail from Isaac Cruikshank, *The New Prussian Exercise* (London, 1792). Courtesy of the Lewis Walpole Library, Yale University.

the thick, clayey mud beside the road, next to dying horses and naked human corpses plundered of their clothing. The aristocratic abjection was surreal. Goethe saw "the elegant carriages of the Emigrants . . . painted in all colours, and covered with gold and silver" lying abandoned, their expensive luggage spilling out of them. Dufief's unit, the Marine Royale, made it out of French territory after a grueling fifty-mile march in two days of cold rain. Tears in his eyes, the commanding "admiral" disbanded the Marine Royale, and the seigneurs and barons who comprised it dispersed to their respective exiles.[27] A few weeks later, in Paris, the National Convention voted to sentence the king to death. He was beheaded on January 21, 1793.

HEAD. He was condemned to lose his head.

TÊTE. *Il fut condamné à perdre la tête.*

That winter marked the beginning of the worst year of Dufief's life, the year that he would highlight in the introductions to his many schoolbooks. Draft riots broke out near his home in Nantes and quickly evolved into a general antigovernment revolt that drove the French Republic's administrative and military presence out of the region. Seizing an opportunity, the regional nobility threw their financial and logistical support behind the peasant uprising, which became a devastating conflict that would turn the lower Loire valley into a war zone for the next three years. Around this time, Dufief boarded a ship bound for the New World.[28]

AGAINST ONE'S WILL. He is gone to the West-Indies against his will.

A CONTRE-CŒUR. *Il est parti pour les Indes-Occidentales à contre-cœur.*

The rest of his family would regroup on the island of Jersey, a British possession in the English Channel just fifteen miles from the coast of Normandy, where his father would spend the next decade conspiring to undermine France's revolutionary governments. But for reasons unknown, Dufief embarked on a different, New World exile. His schoolbook, written years later, offers this sample sentence for the French idiom that means "against his will": *he is gone to the West-Indies against his will.* Whether willingly or not, Dufief left his mother, his five- and seven-year-old brothers, and his three-year-old sister, and boarded a ship bound for Saint-Domingue.[29]

If you were trying to escape a popular revolution in 1793, Saint-Domingue was an unfortunate destination, as the conflict that would come to be called the Haitian Revolution was already well underway there. But refugees often have only bad options to choose from. When Dufief arrived in Saint-Domingue that spring, the slave revolt that had begun two years earlier had coalesced into an army of tens of thousands of ex-slaves and free people of color, at war with the French government and with the white planter class. The planters, who opposed the French Revolution, were also at war with the French government. Seeing political chaos descend on the so-called Pearl of the Antilles, both Spain and Britain invaded the colony. By the time of Dufief's arrival, thousands of people had died in the conflict; one of the colony's two largest cities had burned to the ground; and many whites had fled to other parts of the Caribbean, to France, and to the North American mainland.[30]

COLONY.
The negroes rebelled in the French colonies.

COLONIE.
Les nègres se sont révoltés dans les colonies françaises.

Yet in early 1793 it was still possible to believe that the slave revolt could be contained and peace negotiated between the colony's 31,000 white inhabitants, 28,000 free people of color, and 465,000 slaves. If on his arrival Dufief cherished any optimistic prospects, however, they would have been short-lived. On June 20, Le Cap, the city that had not already burned down, erupted into what one historian has called "the most murderous instance of urban conflict in the entire history of the Americas," and it was rapidly becoming clear that the days of white rule in Saint-Domingue were numbered. In Dufief's spelling book, the specimen sentence for the word *colony* is "The negroes rebelled in the French colonies."[31] Most of Saint-Domingue's remaining white population began rapid preparations to leave the island. For the second time that year, Dufief became a political refugee, fleeing like thousands of others to Philadelphia. It's not clear what happened to his Saint-Domingue relatives, but by the time Dufief arrived in Philadelphia in July, he was on his own.[32]

TO CLIMB UP.
The mountains of Saint-Domingo are not easy to be climbed up by Europeans.

GRAVIR.
Il n'est pas facile à un Européen de gravir les montagnes de Saint-Domingue.

Dufief did not speak English, but Philadelphia boasted a huge population of French-speaking refugees, and the city and federal governments were remarkably accommodating to them. Perhaps with the help of one of the municipal grants available to French refugees, Dufief signed up

TO RECOVER ONE'S SELF. You have nothing to fear; recover yourself.

SE RASSURER, SE REMETTRE. Vous n'avez rien à craindre; remettez-vous, rassurez-vous.

for English lessons and purchased nine books: two French-language introductions to English grammar, a French-English dictionary, an English pronunciation dictionary, book-length poems by John Milton and James Thomson, and English-language histories of England, Rome, and the Holy Roman Empire. Evidently, the seventeen-year-old hoped to give himself a crash course in European political history.[33]

Instead, he received an unplanned lesson in epidemiology. Less than a month after his arrival, the worst urban epidemic that had ever struck North America broke out in Philadelphia. Ten percent of the city's population would be dead from yellow fever within three months. After treasury secretary Alexander Hamilton contracted the virus in September, the federal government suspended operations and pulled out of the capital city. Half of Philadelphia's population followed suit: 25,000 medical refugees fled the city, including Dufief, who was now making his third emergency migration of 1793.[34] A family in Princeton took him in, and Dufief, making the best of the situation, was determined to begin an immediate and rigorous study of the English language. Unpacking his new books in New Jersey, however, Dufief discovered that he had left the grammars in Philadelphia. Traffic in and out of the city had been suspended, and no replacements were to be found nearby. Dufief's unhappy grammarlessness threatened a considerable delay to his intended acculturation, for he found that "it was deemed impossible to learn English without the help of" a French-language introduction to English. Dufief was devastated. He collapsed into a deep depression, "more sensibly affected by this omission," he later wrote, "than by all the misfortunes that had befallen me in the French revolution."[35] Perhaps he was mourning more than just the grammars. Dufief lost his home, his family, his title, his wealth, and his nation that year, but he had retained the capacity to communicate. Perhaps those grammars seemed like precious fragments of France that would have told him what he needed to know to make his way in America. Perhaps with their loss he felt himself, finally, alone. This transnational trauma and identity crisis became an origin story that Dufief would tell for the rest of his life.

TO DIE. He died of the yellow fever at Philadelphia.

MOURIR. Il est mort de la fièvre jaune à Philadelphie.

Our hopes, alas! are all come to nothing.

Toutes nos espérances, hélas! s'en sont allées en fumée.

If he had had one of the grammars he had left in Philadelphia—perhaps Thomas Berry's popular *Vraie méthode pour apprendre facilement à parler, à lire, et à l'écrire l'anglois* (True method for easily learning to speak, read, and write English)—he would have begun his English education by learning the names of the parts of speech, along with rules given in French about how to use them, such as (in French) "when nouns end in *ch*, *sh*, *ss*, *s*, or *x*, you must add *es* to form the plural." It was a deductive process: learn principles, then apply them. Using Berry's book, Dufief would not have seen a complete English sentence until page 90.[36] The crucial first eighty-nine pages—the pages explaining principles on which English proficiency would depend—were back in Philadelphia. Here in Princeton, Dufief had only books designed for people who already know how English sentences work.

Dufief resolved to find his linguistic way without a guide. He isolated himself in his room with his large bilingual French-English dictionary, which happily contained not only definitions but also sample phrases for each word. On blank paper with a line drawn down the center, Dufief began copying hundreds of sample phrases out of the dictionary into two corresponding columns, French and English, hoping "to imprint on my mind the acceptation or sense of words," and soaking up what he called "the genius and analogy of the English language"—what we might call English syntax and morphology, the patterns governing the formation of words and phrases. He was learning inductively: starting with examples and generalizing principles from them. He used his English pronunciation dictionary to work out the sounds of the English phrases he was learning. After six weeks of this, Dufief made his first shy attempts to speak to the other members of the household. "To my great surprise," he later wrote, "I found myself able to enjoy and support a social conversation with them."[37]

TO SHUT UP IN. He shut himself up in his closet, and would speak to no one.

ENFERMER. *Il s'enferma dans son cabinet, et ne voulut parler à personne.*

RECLUSE, SOLITARY. This young man is too recluse for his age.

SOLITAIRE. *Ce jeune homme est trop solitaire pour son âge.*

This is how Dufief made the discovery that became the basis of his career: it was possible to learn a second language by jumping straight into complete sentences without yet understanding them. The idea is counterintuitive, a bit like studying algebra without first learning to add and subtract, and although Dufief had an inflated sense of the earth-shattering originality of his insight, it is true that the learning process he outlined was unusual for his day. His strategy anticipates what is now called the "direct method" of second-language pedagogy, an approach that only came into widespread use at the end of the nineteenth century.[38]

Dufief's origin story—perhaps exaggerated here and there, but verifiably true in its general outlines—has the shape of a conversion narrative. Wandering in the Atlantic wilderness, suffering ordeals and tribulations, a despairing Dufief turns to a large, authoritative book: a dictionary. In that book's light, he is reborn. In Princeton, his phrase-by-phrase study "became more easy and agreeable," and he began to tackle extended English prose. Like Saint Augustine obeying the angelic directive in the garden to "pick up and read, pick up and read," Dufief "read with unspeakable delight" Gibbon and the other histories. He found himself "even capable of relishing, in a high degree, many of the beauties of Thomson's Seasons." (No word on Milton.) This was accomplished—as he shouted from the rooftops for the rest of his life—"*without the assistance of a teacher*, in the short period of four months," and, even more remarkably, "without *grammatical rules.*" As far as he could tell, he had stumbled onto "nature's method" of teaching language: the process by which we learn our mother tongues.[39]

Speechlessness Is next to Helplessness

The yellow fever subsided in November, when temperatures dropped enough to kill the mosquitoes that spread the virus. Evacuees returned to the metropolis.[40] Armed with his new linguistic competency, Dufief did what young men alienated from their families have been doing since Benjamin Franklin: he went to Philadelphia to make his fortune.

Dufief was unskilled in any craft, nor had he received a proper gentleman's education; as he later admitted, he "had never paid much attention to literary pursuits." He might have supported himself through manual labor, such as by driving carriages or making shoes, as other French aristocrats in exile did, though it shocked the conscience. He had arrived in Philadelphia without financial or social or artisanal capital, but language is a resource that you cannot easily take away from refugees, even if you take away everything else. "Seeking subsistence, in the character of Teacher of the French Language," as he wrote, represented perhaps his only chance to earn his living without losing his dignity. And although Philadelphia was teeming with French exiles offering language lessons, it was also teeming with paying students. "Perhaps no language was

AIR.
We recognized him by his noble air.

AIR.
A son air noble nous le reconnûmes.

ever studied at once by so many persons at a time, in proportion, as the French is now studied in America," John Adams had written a few years earlier. The Age of Revolutions was an age of language classes.[41]

Dufief in Philadelphia, age twenty-five or twenty-six, in a coat with fashionably high collar and fashionably broad lapels. His eyes were blue. Engraved portrait by Charles Févret de Saint-Memin, 1801. Library of Congress.

Guided by his own recent experience, Dufief began offering private lessons in which he began inductively with complete phrases instead of starting with a deductive overview of the parts of speech or the conjugation of a regular verb. Word got around that Dufief was teaching French without teaching French grammar. "The principal French teachers" in town scoffed ("jealous," as Dufief believed) and prospective students began to insist that he "teach them the language *grammatically*." Since he needed the money, he gave in and "pursued the old, *stale*, *threadbare*, *grammatical system* . . . [t]o obtain *bread* in *peace*," as he wrote later in contemptuous italics. The grammatical method may have been "stale," but it paid for fresh bread. At the end of his second year in Philadelphia, Dufief rented a shop on Market Street in an area that was becoming known as "French-Town," and began offering two-and-a-half-hour group classes three times a day.[42]

TEACHER OF THE FRENCH LANGUAGE. He follows the profession of teacher of the French language.

MAÎTRE DE FRANÇAIS. Il exerce la profession de maître de français.

Keeping his unpopular pedagogical innovations to himself for the time being, Dufief began putting down roots, working to build a social presence and a capital reserve so that he could afford to rock the pedagogical boat. He befriended the U.S. attorney for the district of Pennsylvania. He mingled with émigrés at the American Philosophical Society and read up on the philosophy of language. He wrote away to his commanding officer from the failed invasion of France and obtained from him an affidavit attesting to his honorable service in the Marine Royale. He started a side business dealing in rare books and scored Thomas Jefferson as a regular client.[43] And he worked to put his ideas about language pedagogy on paper. A decade after arriving in the United States, he sent the manuscript for his schoolbook to press.

The French pedagogical niche of the American print market was already crowded in 1804. The two most popular introductions to French in the United States at the time were both titled *A Grammar of the French*

Tongue—one by John Perrin (1768), the other by Louis Chambaud (1750). Unlike his competition, however, Dufief regarded his book not just as an English-to-French pedagogical text but as a radical breakthrough in language pedagogy. His title, therefore, defines a much more ambitious project than just a grammar of French: *Nature Displayed, in Her Mode of Teaching Language to Man*—and halfway down the page, in smaller type, . . . *Adapted to the French.*

Almost all of the English-language introductions to French published in the century before Dufief began with some sort of definition, usually of "grammar," and always stated in English. The first words of the first lesson in Perrin's book, for example, are: "Grammar is a collection of Observations to which the manner of speaking or writing, used in a language, may be reduced." It is hard to overstate how formulaic these opening definitions were: "Grammar is the art of . . . ," "An Art is a rational method . . . ," "Grammar is the science of . . . ," "Grammar, in general, is . . . "[44] Dufief makes a point of starting very differently. The first lesson in *Nature Displayed* opens like this:

Loaf.	BUY me a three pound loaf.
Pain. m.	Achetez-moi un *pain* de trois livres.
Bread.	Which bread do you wish to have?
Pain. m.	De quel *pain* voulez-vous?

No orienting definitions. No basic rules. Just sample sentence after sample sentence, all the way through the entire volume—eight thousand sentences, each in English and French, organized thematically, with virtually no exposition or instruction. In volume 2, the student will find material more reminiscent of a conventional introduction to French grammar—such as the useful principle that some nouns are considered masculine and preceded by *le* and others considered feminine and preceded by *la*—but Dufief's idea was to keep the emphasis on the absorption of complete sentences, picking up only a bare minimum of abstract principles and rules along the way.[45]

Perhaps Dufief was thinking of his own experiences of bodily privation as a teenage soldier in the Argonne when he made bread the subject of the learner's very first French utterance. It is not an unreasonable place to begin, especially at a time when bread accounted for most of the calories consumed in Philadelphia. (The city's urban poor averaged more than a pound of bread each, per day.[46]) But Dufief's opening line also echoes one of American literature's most iconic scenes of beginning a new life, the seventeen-year-old Benjamin Franklin's arrival into Philadelphia eighty years earlier. In 1723, Franklin had disembarked in Philadelphia and walked up Market Street in search of breakfast. Finding a bakery, he had asked for "a three-penny loaf," which, because he did not understand the exchange rate, was far too expensive for any loaf of bread. Being "told that they had none such," Franklin asks for "three-penny worth of any sort" of bread, and receives "three great Puffy Rolls," which, too embarrassed to disclose his mistake and take just the one, he accepts, "and walk'd off with a roll under each arm, and eating the other," passing the very spot where Dufief would first open his language school seventy years later.[47] Dufief puts his novice reader-learner in much the same place: like Franklin, the student asks for a threeish loaf; and, like Franklin, he receives words instead of bread—a request for clarification ("*Which* bread . . . ?"). In the same way that Franklin's narrative strips its protagonist down to his most basic biological need for food in order to launch a new life as an economic subject, Dufief puts his speaker in the same condition as a starting point for a new life as a new linguistic subject. He organizes the sentences of *Nature Displayed* into themes that radiate from an increasingly extensive self: the first thousand sentences are about food, clothing, shelter, and the body; the next thousand are about civics and social relations; then "the Country"; then "the Universe."

SCHOOLBOY.
He is only a schoolboy, and already pretends to decide on every thing.

ECOLIER.
Ce n'est qu'un écolier, & déjà il décide de tout.

The centerpiece of the Dufief system is a bilingual call-and-response aimed at forming mental associations between the meanings in each language. It is a kind of incantation—operating, according to Dufief, on the deep reaches of the student's mind, "a miracle which analogy and analysis, without his knowledge, will do for him."[48] Dufief gives this example of an ideal classroom workflow:

TEACHER	STUDENTS (IN UNISON)
Bonjour, Charles.	*Bonjour, Charles.*
Good day, Charles.	Good day, Charles.
Bonjour, Charles.	Good day, Charles, *Bonjour, Charles.*

Venez vous asseoir.	*Venez vous asseoir.*
Come and sit.	Come and sit.
Venez vous asseoir.	Come and sit, *venez vous asseoir.*[49]

The strategy differs greatly from using abstract reason to learn grammatical rules. Because Dufief sees language as a substructure of thought, not a product of it, he regards the conscious learning of grammatical rules as a fundamentally superficial exercise. Tellingly, the sample sentence in *Nature Displayed* for the word "grammar" is: "He forgot the rules of grammar."[50] Dufief's "natural" oral-aural method is designed to penetrate more deeply into the mind. Dufief even imagined a nefarious mind-control scheme based on his pedagogy: "A conqueror," he suggested, "might even, by this means, extinguish the language of the conquered, and substitute any other suited to his political views." If each language is a different blueprint for thought and behavior, then each is "suited" to a distinct politics. "God forbid that such a measure should ever be resorted to, with the help of the means afforded by this work!" Dufief exclaimed in print, but the point of his system was its power to effect less malevolent but equally sweeping transformations of the self.[51] "No one can read these volumes with the attention and zeal they deserve," a London reviewer agreed decades later, "without becoming a Frenchman."[52]

GRAMMAR. He forgot the rules of grammar.

GRAMMAIRE. *Il a oublié les règles de la grammaire.*

The French (Pedagogy) Revolution

Dufief's schoolbook found an immediate and unusually transregional American audience. Using a subscription model to fund publication of the 1804 first edition, Dufief sold advance copies to customers in fifteen of the seventeen United States, and beyond. Less than two years later, he put up his own capital to finance a second edition in 1806, and a third in 1810. He expanded to the British market in 1818, and the book's commercial success went on for decades, with Dufief overseeing at least seven American and five British editions during his lifetime. Thomas Jefferson sent copies to his grandchildren and included it on a list of "the best books I am acquainted with." Edgar Allan Poe, Washington Irving, Lidian Jackson Emerson, and John Jacob Astor all studied from

Nature Displayed. Even forty years after his 1834 death, the name "Dufief" was still being used to market French pedagogy.[53]

Dufief, now in his mid-thirties and looking considerably more relaxed. Stipple engraving by David Edwin from a miniature by Pierre-Julien Méance, ca. 1809; frontispiece to *ND* (1810).

By all accounts, Dufief was a gifted teacher whose book was practical and helpful—but he wanted to be something more. While he had advertised his services in the 1790s as "Gouin Dufief, teacher of the French and English Languages," the later years of his career found him styling himself "N. G. DUFIEF, the Discoverer of the New System of Education."[54] His claims about the power of his pedagogy grew more extravagant over the years: he initially claimed that he could teach a person French in six months; later, he said "three or four" months; still later, he said he could do it in one.[55] Numerous book reviewers were repelled by the "quackish *tone* in which he speaks of the merits of his own system."[56] So while *Nature Displayed* (as a book for learning French) was widely appreciated, it was also (as a purported scientific breakthrough disclosing a fundamental law of nature) ridiculed, parodied, and dismissed. Boston's *Monthly Anthology* magazine published an appreciative review of *Nature Displayed* "as a *practical* work" and "a valuable acquisition to the student of the French language . . . which reflects credit on the literature of our country." But the magazine's reviewer also noted gently that "the author, with that pardonable degree of vanity and ardour so natural to a young man, lays greater claim to originality, than we think he would be able to support."[57] Eventually, Dufief was claiming that his pedagogical system was "a discovery exceeding in power that of the steam engine, and more important in its application, inasmuch as mental is superior to merely physical power."[58] He wanted his discovery to have been a radical turning point in intellectual history.

METHOD, MODE. He is author of a new mode of teaching languages.

MÉTHODE. *Il est auteur d'une nouvelle méthode pour enseigner les langues.*

SCHOLAR. One of my scholars learned French in less than three months.

ECOLIER. *Un de mes écoliers a appris le français en moins de trois mois.*

For someone whose life had been ruined by revolution, Dufief was remarkably eager to describe what he was doing as "revolutionary." *Nature Displayed* brought upon him "a most virulent persecution" from "the enemies of *truth*," he said, but his new ideas had won the day: "so complete was the revolution, that in Philadelphia, the center of opposition, the natural method completely prevails," he wrote in 1806. "The old system of teaching living languages by grammatical rules," he predicted, "will ere long be driven from this country."[59] Dufief, who in 1793 had been part of "the old system" and been driven from his own country by revolution, was now staging his own pedagogical "revolution" in which he would inflict on pedants the alienation and exile that he had suffered.

WHOLE. The whole nation rebelled.

EN MASSE. *La nation s'est soulevée en masse.*

Both times that Dufief had a chance to introduce his pedagogical innovation to a print public—in Philadelphia in 1804–6 and in London in 1818—he took out combative advertisements announcing an almost apocalyptic conflict between the pedagogical status quo and his new "system, which must ere long annihilate every other."[60] He certainly was advocating a shift in pedagogical strategy, but he spoke as if he was manning a barricade: he intended "the overthrow of a method which, by its baneful influence, has, for centuries past, paralyzed the most precious faculties of the human mind." Though ostensibly censuring conventional pedagogy, he was closely echoing the language of tyranny in which French revolutionaries denounced the monarchy.[61] Dufief conceived of himself with the moral seriousness of a Kant or Marx: he was "informing genius of its own existence . . . and unbinding the fetters by which it is too often restrained."[62] His students had nothing to lose but their chains, and a world to win: thanks to his discovery, "THE GREAT DESIDERATUM OF ENABLING NATIONS TO ARRIVE AT THE HIGHEST DEGREE OF MENTAL PERFECTION" was now at hand.[63]

CENTURY, AGE. The last century has been famous for great events.

SIÈCLE. *Le siècle passé a été fertile en grands événements.*

These grandiloquent pronouncements did Dufief no favors in the mainstream press, unless his goal was to offend the intellectual communities that he otherwise seemed eager to impress. The *Edinburgh Magazine* ran a scathing parody announcing the imminent publication of a book called *Nature Perfected*, by means of which anyone could learn a language in a week, compose better poetry than Homer, sculpt the Venus de Milo, and travel to the sun.[64] Yet even the *Edinburgh Magazine* conceded that Dufief's "method has its advantages," the main problem being that "he has thrown an air of quackery round the whole."[65] This typified the general response to *Nature Displayed* throughout Dufief's three decades marketing it. In the 1820s, the Philadelphia press explicitly set aside "the philosophical merits of this work, upon which so much stress has been laid in Europe," since "in our opinion it is fitted to facilitate, more than any other extant, the communication and acquisition

WHIMSICAL. I hate whimsical people.

CAPRICIEUX. *Je hais les gens capricieux.*

of the French language."[66] In other words: the book works, whatever the merits of the philosophical chip on Dufief's shoulder.

Perhaps this was the way Dufief wanted it, or needed it. He had a strong persecution complex and felt himself "surrounded by savage and barbarous assailants" who attacked him with "a rage bordering on madness."[67] Perhaps Dufief also discovered that revolutionary conflict sold books. If his sense of being under attack came from his early experiences of violence and dispossession during the French Revolution, he never said so, though he would hardly have been the first person to respond to a traumatic experience by becoming hypervigilant. But he never wrote about the French Revolution. Nor did he write in detail about any other aspect of his childhood, his adolescence, his transatlantic passage, his experiences in Saint-Domingue, or anything else of the life he lived before learning English—with one important exception: he wrote about his mother.

HAUGHTY. He is so haughty that every body hates him.

HAUTAIN. *Il est si hautain que tout le monde le hait.*

In fact, Dufief's lifelong devotion to his mother tongue was also quite explicitly a devotion to his mother. Every edition of *Nature Displayed* opens with a conspicuous and elaborate three-page dedication "TO MY MOTHER." "How numerous and how just are the claims You possess!" Dufief writes in that dedication, capitalizing "You" as if he is addressing royalty, or God. "You, who considered it of less moment to have given me existence than to have cultivated my mind; You, who, to the care of an anxious father for my education, added Your persevering attention." Dufief's father's role in the dedication (and perhaps the household) seems to be to provide a contrast with Dufief's much more engaging and impressive mother: while "an anxious father . . . endeavored to improve my mind, and form my taste for knowledge, by frequently describing the glory of *Montesquieu*, *Buffon* and *Pascal*, You strove to exalt my sentiments, by fixing generous principles in the glowing breast." He calls his mother "my Affectionate Parent," in noticeable emotional contrast with his other parent, "an anxious father," who does not even receive the possessive "my."[68]

TO SUCKLE. It is a crime in mothers not to suckle their own children.

ALLAITER. *C'est un crime dans les mères de ne pas allaiter leurs enfans.*

The dedication pages to Dufief's book develop a pedagogical contrast between his parents that maps exactly onto the pedagogical contrast that Dufief would draw between himself and the "old school." His mother seeks to inspire him in the deepest way, providing a moral and even spiritual pedagogy, "exalt[ing]" his very feelings and kindling virtue in his "glowing breast." She addresses her pedagogy to his heart and soul: "You . . . evinced that those principles ennobled Your own soul, which it was Your ambition to implant in mine." In comparison, the father's pedagogy looks trivial and inept, "describing" the work of dead intellectuals instead of bringing them to life, "endeavor[ing]" to interest his son in academic knowledge but evidently without success, per Dufief's confession elsewhere that he "had never paid much attention to literary pursuits."[69] Meanwhile, the values that his mother "implant[ed]" in his soul and "cultivated" in his mind apparently took root.

FOSTERFATHER. How many fathers are there in this world who are nothing more than fosterfathers!

PÈRE NOURRICIER. *Que de pères dans ce monde qui ne sont que des pères nourriciers!*

The difference between his father's routine rehearsal of the canon and his mother's inspiring, fertile pedagogy is the same difference that Dufief asserts between learning "the grammar" and learning "the genius" of a language: one boring, rote, and abstract; the other vivid, soul-changing, and relevant to the present world. He pervasively describes his own pedagogy in gendered, maternal terms; his book, after all, titularly displays nature in "*her* mode of teaching languages." Typical schoolroom pedagogy was "dark, tedious and fruitless," he wrote, in ways that "tender mothers will much better comprehend than cold grammarians!" While the cold grammarians' students were studying grammatical principles and memorizing decontextualized lists of words, Dufief's students would undergo the same process "by which we have been taught to speak our vernacular tongue, and by which we taste, in the mutual effusions of the heart, the first delights of human life."[70] The "cold," "fruitless," masculine pedagogy of the grammarians contrasts sharply with the maternal process that Dufief extolls: embodied and generative, making language something "we taste," "effusions" flowing like milk from the mother's breast. In Dufief's telling, mother-child language acquisition is inherently intimate and intersubjective—a scene of "mutual" affection, a scene of the "heart," a scene of "delights." This is the scene that he dedicates his career to re-creating. What Dufief calls "nature's mode of teaching languages" has more than a little in common with the blissful mother-child intimacy of what Freud called the oral stage.[71]

He does not resemble his father in principles. *Il ne tient pas de son père, du côté des sentiments.*

This boy resembles his mother very much; does he not? *Ce garçon tient beaucoup de sa mère; n'est-ce pas?*

If Dufief had been looking for a way to practice the kind of intimate shaping of mind and sentiments that he wrote about so ardently in his dedication, he could hardly have chosen a better vocation than a professional purveyor of language, at this moment in the history of ideas. The best science and the prevailing social thought of his day held that languages did much of the same kind of work as he valued in his mother: nurturing, empowering, cultivating, making you who you are. His book is all about language; its dedication is all about making you who you are and doesn't mention language at all. But Dufief lived at a moment when *language* and *making you who you are* already seemed like the same endeavor: "language makes the difference between man and man." Dufief's cultural and intellectual milieu encouraged him to link *making you who you are* to language; his reasons for drawing an additional link to mothering were perhaps less historical than personal. In numerous books and advertisements, he explicitly related language acquisition to fetal gestation: "language . . . is the very creator of the thinking faculty itself, which would exist merely in embryo without such a vehicle," he wrote. The metaphor makes language a kind of womb in which the learner's embryonic mind is nourished before it is ready to exist independently. Dufief had been torn out of his mother's protective enclave by revolution. One implication of the linguistic account of the self that he promoted was that language was a protective enclave that you couldn't be torn from.

French for the Masses

The forty-one-year-old Dufief planned a short visit to Britain in 1817 to find a London publisher for *Nature Displayed.* He told Thomas Jefferson he would be gone for "several months," but in fact he stayed six years.[72] He built a new teaching practice, publishing business, and social reputation in London. In Philadelphia, Dufief had highlighted the speed and ease of learning à la Dufief; in London, he emphasized scale. Dufief believed that his system entailed students creating mental associations by speaking the same meaning aloud in two languages. The key operation was the act of speaking—the response part of his classroom's call-and-response rhythm. Because the teacher engaged the students in unison rather than individually, there was no need to keep class sizes small. A single teacher, Dufief suggested, "may, entirely unassisted, instruct several thousand pupils at the same time, and thus

EUROPE. Europe is the most enlightened of the four parts of the world.

EUROPE. *L'Europe est la plus éclairée des quatre parties du monde.*

completely monopolize the business of a whole town."[73] But the truly attention-grabbing aspect of this suggestion was not the possibility of lucrative pedagogical monopolies—it was mass public education.

FREEHOLDER. None but freeholders ought to have a right to vote.

FRANC-TENANCIER. *Il n'y a que les francs-tenanciers qui dussent avoir droit de suffrage.*

Britain was beginning a long and difficult national conversation about public education when Dufief arrived in the late 1810s, spurred by explosive population growth, urbanization, the rise of industrial manufacturing, and a corresponding decline in the apprenticeship system. The question of "whether it was proper that education should be diffused amongst the lower classes" was debated in Parliament for the first time in 1807, and no consensus was reached.[74] For decades, elites expressed grave concerns about the destabilizing effects that universal education might have on the social order: "now, when every man fancies he can think and act for himself, his first desire is to question the authority by which others presume to do it for him," the *Royal Lady's Magazine* editorialized in a review of the twelfth edition of *Nature Displayed*. "It remains to be seen, however, how a nation . . . of would-be philosophers, will manage their affairs."[75]

For those who thought national public education was even theoretically desirable, the staggering costs presented an enormous practical hurdle. There were not enough teachers to effectively teach every child in the nation, and nowhere near enough money to pay them even if they had existed. Experimental schools on the so-called Lancasterian and Madras models tried having students spend part of their time learning and the rest teaching the students in the classes behind them, and other strategies for doing effective education with a high student-to-teacher ratio were keenly sought and discussed.[76] With his characteristic confidence, Dufief now announced that he had "completely solved the great problem of national education—so long a desideratum" because his method was conducive to large class sizes. Thanks to his system, it was now "readily in our power to meliorate the morals of the lower classes, and to enable minds to rise to distinction, which are now lost to themselves and to the world, for want of the means of culture."[77]

Dufief's vision of a single instructor and a theater full of students addressed not only the problem of cost but also some of the concerns of those who worried about the chaotic potential of an educated proletariat.

A Dufiefian classroom was highly structured and did not entail critical thinking. A journalist described standing "beneath the open windows of the large saloon in which the undaunted Dufief vociferated a word at a time to a long column of pupils, all of whom bawled the sound back to him at once. The process was very entertaining to passengers along the street."[78] The system entailed disciplined repetition, in some ways like industrial labor. It also corresponded nicely to the sort of "panoptic" arrangement envisioned in the 1780s by Jeremy Bentham and famously taken by Michel Foucault as emblematic of modern institutions. In Bentham's model prison, prisoners' knowledge that they might be under surveillance at any given time causes them to behave as if they are under surveillance at all times. They act, as it were, as their own guards. In the halls where Dufief gave classes to large crowds, even a student in the back of the room was surrounded by neighbors who could hear when he or she made a mistake. "The advantage," noted a writer in the London *Literary Chronicle*, "is, that by an ingenious contrivance of Mr. Dufief, all the scholars, however numerous, are a check upon each other, and all under the immediate eye of the teacher."[79] As for Dufief, he was eager to describe his system as institutionally efficient in the same ways as other nineteenth-century innovations: he advertised "the powerful Principle of the Economy of Labour by Scientific Means applied to the Improvement of Education and of the Human Mind."[80] This industrial vocabulary reassured some people, and bothered others. The *London Magazine*, a literary journal to which Keats, Hazlitt, the Shelleys, and other Romantics were frequent contributors, called it "a mode of discipline (we would almost say mechanical) to which few *English people* will submit."[81]

But submit they did. In 1827, Dufief persuaded the London Mechanics' Institution—a charity providing inexpensive adult education—to let him offer an introductory French course to its members, tuition-free, on Thursday evenings.[82] The course began in mid-June. By the end of July, the course was so overenrolled that it had to be moved into the institution's theater "so that those Members who wished to join, and were prevented on account of the want of accommodation, will now be admitted."[83] Independent reports place the number of students who took the course at between 200 and 300—even though the class required students to purchase *Nature Displayed* at a price equivalent to nine months' membership in the institution.[84]

By the 1820s, Dufief seems to have given up on the idea of being a national of any particular state. He deployed British, French, and American nationalities according to his strategic needs: he advertised *Nature Displayed* in Britain as "the True British System of Education,"[85] but he ran exactly the same advertisement in the United States, deleting only the word "British" from the header and tacking on a nationalistic exclamation at the end: "What a triumph for the American method."[86] In the London editions of *Nature Displayed*, Dufief emphasized a brief layover he had made in British territory thirty years earlier, on his way to join other displaced aristocrats in invading eastern France: he invoked "the enlightened hospitality of England, when I first landed in 1792 . . . happy to escape from the revolutionary frenzy."[87] Yet even he was evidently unpersuaded by his own anglicism: he decided not to adapt *Nature Displayed* for English students learning English, since, "Being a foreigner, I always thought that a production of such great national importance would be better received . . . if written by a native."[88] Still, he added a supplementary dedication page to his British editions in which he declared himself King George IV's "Most obedient, Humble, and devoted Servant, Nicolas Gouin Dufief." But he also sent a copy of the book—bound in silk and gold and still containing that very British declaration—to King Charles X of France, an "*Humble Offrande de son fidèle sujet, N. G. Dufief*," a humble offering from his loyal subject.[89]

GOD SAVE. God save the king and all the royal family.

DIEU SAUVE. Dieu sauve le roi et toute la famille royale.

TO DRINK SOME ONE'S HEALTH. Let us drink the health of Thomas Jefferson, President of the United States.

BOIRE À LA SANTÉ DE QUELQU'UN. Buvons à la santé de Thomas Jefferson, Président des Etats-Unis.

Although Dufief always wanted to participate in the international republic of letters, that was never the transnational sphere in which he was taken seriously. He addressed his advertisements to "the friends and lovers of Education, the Learned, the Curious, and all who are desirous of observing by what simple means Nature produces great and permanent effects," but he never managed to persuade the intellectual elite that he had indeed discovered the basis of consciousness.[90] A different community did, however, take shape around him in Britain: a community of elite bilingual expatriates offering language lessons, a significant number of whom found it expedient to ally themselves with Dufief. One expediency was that his system did not require much

English-language proficiency of its teachers: the teacher had only to read aloud the English sentences from *Nature Displayed*.[91]

In this respect Dufief was lending a hand to the continental elites who followed in his footsteps—financially depleted by political upheaval; unskilled in a trade and not eager to endure the humiliation of practicing one; marketing their language instead of their manual labor. The Napoleonic Wars sent a wave of political refugees across the English Channel in the 1810s, some of whom became instructors offering tutoring à la Dufief. A student at an elite military academy in Napoleonic France, for example, had to flee the country when the Bourbon monarchy was restored to the throne in 1814. Two years later found him in London, advertising in the *Times* that he taught French "according to the new and ingenious plan of Mr. Dufief."[92] Another political refugee, formerly a staff secretary to Napoleon's naval minister, set up a teaching practice in Bristol and billed himself as the region's "first Introducer of the Dufief System."[93] Nor was this an exclusively French phenomenon: one Italian aristocrat, forced to relinquish his property during the Risorgimento, advertised in an Ipswich newspaper in 1825 that since being "a Teacher of Languages [was] the only means now left him for supporting his unhappy family," he was now offering French and Italian lessons according to Dufief's method.[94]

In the end, therefore, Dufief found himself at the center of a community of political refugees teaching their native languages to English-speaking students. His community—his people—were bilinguals in exile in the English-speaking world. He was always between nationalities; he found other people who were between them, too, and let them share his linguistic home. On some level, it might have been important to him not to assimilate into the American or British nations. He spent a career deliberately and carefully articulating oral language, but he doesn't seem to have made much of an attempt to pronounce English like a native. According to one of his protégés, he always spoke English with "a horrible French accent."[95] That, at least, was a French identity that he could control.

Dufief is an extreme example of forces that in less acute ways affected much of the English-speaking world. Most people's coming-of-age, separation from their families, and assertion of an adult self were not literally provoked by political revolution as Dufief's were. There were many English speakers who were forced by the era's revolutions and wars to imagine new ingroups and outgroups. Few people had occasion to pledge allegiance to the king of Britain, the king of France, and the president of the United States, as Dufief did. But there were many who rethought their identities in the wake of political revolutions, and many for whom the other available categories of identity—national, ethnic, racial, religious, climatological—did not make adequate sense of the circumstances they faced.[96] There were many who processed the Age of Revolutions' political upheavals by doing what Dufief did: thinking and talking about languages and their relationship to the self. As I discuss in the next chapter, Americans—like other British colonials and postcolonials in the eighteenth and nineteenth centuries—used linguistic evidence to think of themselves as linguistically (and hence mentally) English, even when they were no longer nationally English.

Of Mothers and Mother Tongues

When Dufief left home at seventeen, his father was already in exile fifteen miles off the coast of France, on the Manhattan-sized island of Jersey, where he would spend the remaining decade of his life conspiring with other displaced aristocrats about how to restore the monarchy. Dufief's mother, however, fought the revolutionary regime more directly, embarking on an extraordinary military career as a counterrevolutionary soldier. Around the time that Dufief left for Saint-Domingue in the spring of 1793, draft riots near his childhood home started a chain reaction of protests and crackdowns that evolved rapidly into an antigovernment insurgency known as the War of the Vendée, named for the region where the fighting intensified. Dufief's mother personally distributed weapons and ammunition to the peasants of le Fief and hosted strategy sessions for the regional nobility considering how to support (or, in another view, co-opt) the peasant uprising.[97]

Supposedly at the peasants' request, aristocrats with military experience assumed command of the "Vendéan" antigovernment forces. In late summer—around the time that 3,500 miles away Dufief was discovering that he had left his grammar books in yellow-fevered Philadelphia—state troops sent from Paris to quell the Vendéan uprising clashed with the insurgents about twenty-five miles from the Gouin du Fiefs' house. Vendéan fighters panicked and began to retreat, until a crowd of pitchfork-wielding women at the army's rear is said to have blocked the way and shamed the men into turning around and fighting anew. The day ended in a key victory for the insurgency.[98]

Mother Britain and daughter America kiss and make up. Detail from Thomas Colley, *The reconciliation between Britania and her daughter America* (London, 1782). Courtesy of the John Carter Brown Library at Brown University.

Victoire-Aimée Libault Gouin du Fief—Dufief's mother—was not at the rear, armed with a pitchfork: she was in the battle, armed with a rifle.[99] She sustained a minor wound. It was a turning point for Madame Gouin du Fief, then thirty-nine years old. After that battle, she became a full-time soldier. She was a good shot with a pistol, managed a horse expertly in battle, and had a natural flair for leadership. In memoirs written years later, soldiers from both sides of the conflict remembered her, "always at the heaviest part of the fighting, inspir[ing] the royalist cavaliers with her voice and her example," "wheeling about on a horse at the head of a squadron," "shooting upon the Republicans and cursing any and all Vendéan cowards" who moved to retreat.[100]

WOUNDED. This courageous woman was severely wounded.

BLESSÉE. *Cette femme courageuse fut blessée grièvement.*

In the dedication of *Nature Displayed*, Dufief would write about his mother's military career. "When the French Revolution burst forth," he wrote, she had displayed "those principles . . . which it was [her] ambition to implant in" him. These were the "generous principles" and "exalt[ed] . . . sentiments" that she had kindled within Dufief—that profounder education than his father's "descri[ptions]" of "the glory of *Montesquieu*."[101] Notwithstanding Montesquieu's philosophical relevance to the toppling of the monarchy, it was evidently his mother's pedagogy of principles and sentiments that the French Revolution called for. Her kind of pedagogy—the kind that Dufief thought his teaching embodied—was what you drew on to make it through a revolution.

BREAST. They say the Amazons used to burn their right breast.

MAMELLE. *On dit que les Amazones se brûlaient la mamelle droite.*

With three small children in tow, Victoire-Aimée Gouin du Fief

Céleste Bulkeley, one of several other upper-class women who saw combat in the Vendée insurgency, fires a pistol in the battle of La Roche-sur-Yon, August 26, 1793. Illustrated postcard (Sables-d'Olonne: Victor Marsault, 1907).

spent two years traveling with the Vendéan insurgency as it wrestled with the French army for control of northwestern France. It was a devastating conflict that has been controversially described as the first modern genocide.[102] A staggering third of the population in the Vendée region would die between 1793 and 1796, either in battle, from starvation and disease, or by execution—including in unspeakably violent ways, such as the mass executions of royalist sympathizers by drowning in Nantes in the winter of 1793–94.[103] After a failed invasion of the Vendée region by British-backed royalist émigrés in 1795, and thousands of additional deaths, Madame du Fief and her children climbed into an open boat and pushed off from the French coast for Jersey, just as Dufief's school on Philadelphia's Market Street was beginning to prosper.

Dufief closed the dedication of *Nature Displayed* with a promise to his mother "to emulate Your virtues" and a wish that this promise might "efface, my dear Mother, from Your mind, the remembrance of the horrors of an unexampled revolution!" Perhaps Dufief was also addressing himself and, in another way, his readers. He devoted his life to emulating his mother's pedagogy—teaching the French language and hence (he believed) French principles and sentiments. Perhaps he was modeling for his audience how holding onto language could be a way of letting go of revolutionary horrors. Dufief proposed in *Nature Displayed* a theory of what "makes the difference between man and man" in which a language could cultivate a virtuous mind, generous principles, and exalted sentiments, as his mother had cultivated in him. In his linguistic account of identity, he found a theory of the self in which revolution had not torn him away from what made him who he was after all.

CHAPTER TWO

The United Language of English

Linguistic Separatism and Unionism in the Revolutionary Atlantic

AS WAR WITH BRITAIN loomed in 1812, a Princeton-educated farmer in western Pennsylvania was tinkering with two inventions. One was a new kind of gun: a very early machine gun, the design for which he eventually sold to the United States Navy. The other was a new alphabet and spelling system designed to eliminate phonetic ambiguity and thus halt the diversification of English pronunciation. He had noticed a "vEry predominant corruption ov the constituent sounds" of English words, a corruption that threatened "to debàse, & extinguiſh the harmòni'us propòrtions" of the language, both in Britain and in what he called "United America." The cause of this phonetic deterioration was English spelling: "the Engliſh written language, as now extant, is confounded & disgràced with such an àwkward clumsy system ov orthography" that it was nearly impossible to be certain of the true sounds that a sequence of written letters was supposed to represent. As a result, pronunciation drifted randomly, phonetic diversity multiplied, and with each passing year English deteriorated and fragmented—and would continue to do so, unless an alphabet like his could be implemented before it was too late. With these two projects underway, the Revolutionary War veteran divided his time between building guns to keep Britain and America nationally separate and building alphabets to keep them linguistically united.[1]

Although he acknowledged that "great and weighty political interests" had pushed the two English-speaking nations to the brink of war, the Pennsylvania gunsmith/alphabetician/farmer, whose name was Joseph Chambers, believed that the protection of the English language transcended those interests, warranting an "exemption from the restrictive obligations and ties of nationality." English was of equal importance to "patriotic citizens of both nations," he wrote. When he prepared a pamphlet explaining his new phonetic alphabet, therefore, he prefaced it with dual dedication pages: one to President Madison, and the other to His Royal Highness the Prince Regent, soon to be known as King George IV.[2]

Similar expressions of linguistic unionism echoed from both sides of the Atlantic during the half century between 1775 and 1825, even as political conflict within that world intensified. One London publisher, for example, gushed in 1791 that "the western world will have possessed no language so uniform and so universal as our own is likely to be; when the British Americans shall once have peopled their new continent."[3] Such writers expected not only that English would spread across North America but that it would be a "uniform" English—uniform in lexis,

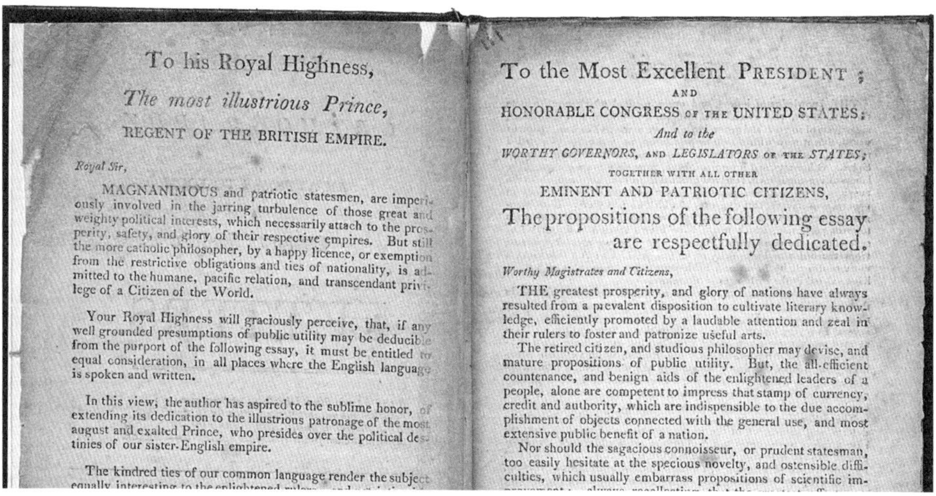

To his Royal Highness,

The most illustrious Prince,

REGENT OF THE BRITISH EMPIRE.

Royal Sir,

MAGNANIMOUS and patriotic statesmen, are imperiously involved in the jarring turbulence of those great and weighty political interests, which necessarily attach to the prosperity, safety, and glory of their respective empires. But still the more catholic philosopher, by a happy licence, or exemption from the restrictive obligations and ties of nationality, is admitted to the humane, pacific relation, and transcendant privilege of a Citizen of the World.

Your Royal Highness will graciously perceive, that, if any well grounded presumptions of public utility may be deducible from the purport of the following essay, it must be entitled to equal consideration, in all places where the English language is spoken and written.

In this view, the author has aspired to the sublime honor, of extending its dedication to the illustrious patronage of the most august and exalted Prince, who presides over the political destinies of our sister-English empire.

The kindred ties of our common language render the subject

To the Most Excellent PRESIDENT;

AND

HONORABLE CONGRESS OF THE UNITED STATES;

And to the

WORTHY GOVERNORS, AND *LEGISLATORS* OF THE *STATES;*

TOGETHER WITH ALL OTHER

EMINENT AND PATRIOTIC CITIZENS,

The propositions of the following essay are respectfully dedicated.

Worthy Magistrates and Citizens,

THE greatest prosperity, and glory of nations have always resulted from a prevalent disposition to cultivate literary knowledge, efficiently promoted by a laudable attention and zeal in their rulers to foster and patronize useful arts.

The retired citizen, and studious philosopher may devise, and mature propositions of public utility. But, the all-efficient countenance, and benign aids of the enlightened leaders of a people, alone are competent to impress that stamp of currency, credit and authority, which are indispensible to the due accomplishment of objects connected with the general use, and most extensive public benefit of a nation.

Nor should the sagacious connoisseur, or prudent statesman, too easily hesitate at the specious novelty, and ostensible difficulties, which usually embarrass propositions of scientific im-

Facing dedication pages to the British (left) and American (right) heads of state, in Joseph Chambers's *Elements of Orthography* (Zanesville, Ohio, 1812).

grammar, phonology, and orthography. Many linguistic projects undertaken during this period were designed—like Joseph Chambers's phonetic alphabet—to ensure or defend this transnational English uniformity.

From the perspective of political history, this bidirectional linguistic unionism is counterintuitive, since these are also the years in which a sharp division was established between the British and American nation-states.[4] Because British and American historiography has traditionally been organized around national boundaries, we know much more about the linguistic separatism that also existed in the English-speaking world in the Age of Revolutions than we do about its linguistic unionism. The goal of this chapter is to reestablish the significance of the "exemption from . . . nationality" that Joseph Chambers and others believed the English language deserved. Despite American national independence—or possibly because of it—linguistic transnationalism inspired a flurry of intellectual creativity and ingenuity on both sides of the Atlantic. This chapter is about that flurry, with special attention to Duncan Mackintosh, the Scottish-Caribbean typographic innovator mentioned in the introduction, who hoped to transmit English phonetics to colonial and otherwise distant populations. It is not a coincidence that his story takes place in a geographical space outside Britain and the United States: he wrote from the French and British Caribbean for British and American audiences. With Mackintosh as a case study, I outline who worked to preserve the British-American linguistic union, why they wanted to preserve it, and how they tried to do so. Mackintosh's experiences illustrate the liminal status, transnational audiences, and primarily phonetic concerns of this cohort of linguistic innovators.

These alphabetic experiments are challenging to write about—partly because it can be hard to empathize with their authors' sense of urgency about their linguistic ambitions and nightmares, but also because their texts are literally difficult to type. We lack the letters they require. They put us—at least temporarily—in a kind of pre-Gutenberg condition in which reading is easy and publication is hard. The letters for these texts don't already exist in type metal or its virtual equivalent, ready and waiting for us to use them. Instead, they have to be formed by the hands of a skilled artist—a scribe, or in this case a graphic designer. Nor are the material shortcuts taken by eighteenth-century alphabetic experimentalists generally applicable to our text technologies: in 1775, it was a trivial matter for Thomas Spence's printer in Newcastle to file off half of an A so that Spence could use ƛ to represent the vowel in "fat" and A to represent the vowel in "fate," but getting that character onto the page you are reading now was considerably more complicated. Texts that resist representation remind us how an eye toward materiality can reveal what after-the-fact history conceals. They strain to express meaning beyond the ordinary limits of their linguistic technologies and ours. They are unfamiliar voices. They have something to say that hasn't been much heard.

The unionist fantasy of a transatlantic English undivided by new nationalisms also helps refute two myths about Noah Webster, the American writer and lexicographer who for generations of intellectual and literary historians has exemplified the linguistic dimensions of early American nationalism. Webster, who called on Americans to "seize the present moment, and establish a *national language*, as well as a national government," was the most conspicuous linguistic nationalist in the early republic.[5] A recent history of the early United States cites Webster as evidence that "Americans expected the development of an American English that would be different from the English of the former mother country, a language that would reflect the peculiar character of the American people."[6] It is clear that Webster expected that, and looked forward to it. But if we are interested in whether Americans other than Webster expected to forge a distinctively American linguistic path, it seems important to note that in the early United States, Noah Webster was widely regarded by Americans as a crackpot and buffoon. By 1800, according to one writer at the time, Webster had "by his vanity and presumption, rendered himself successively, an object of indignation, contempt, ridicule, and pity."[7] In the early republic, his name was proverbial for linguistic wrongness. Abigail Adams corrected herself after misspelling a word by joking parenthetically, in a 1790 letter to her son, that "if you should perceive that the spelling of this Letter is different from what you have been accustomed to, you must Set it down for Websters New plan."[8] While Webster's texts tell a story about their author's American linguistic nationalism, therefore, it's not at all clear that they tell the same story about their audience.

To rescue the significance of Noah Webster's linguistic nationalism for early American thinking, writers have usually either ignored the early American hostility toward him or explained it away with reference to Webster's many nonlinguistic activities. For example, Webster's strident interventions in Federalist politics made him plenty of partisan enemies. His conspicuous self-promotion and evident economic ambition also seemed distasteful according to existing (if decaying) norms about anonymity and deference in print. Furthermore, he seems to have been a difficult person to get along with: aggressively confident, easily offended, prone to absolutist thinking, obsessed with his reputation, and known to hold a grudge.[9]

But while Americans no doubt had sufficient extralinguistic reasons to dislike Noah Webster, the bad reception of his linguistic nationalism should also be understood on its own terms. From the perspective of the significant and ongoing tradition of transatlantic linguistic unionism—the subject of this chapter—the public thud of Webster's linguistic separatism in the early republic is hardly surprising. Americans were thoroughgoing participants in well-developed efforts to prevent exactly the transatlantic linguistic schism that Webster was trying to encourage. When Webster announced, therefore, that "America should have her *own* [language] distinct from all the world," he was stating a position that was counterintuitive to his audience.[10] The first myth that I intend this chapter to debunk, therefore, is that Noah Webster's writings are representative of early American thinking about American national identity. The overlooked public rejection of Websterian linguistic nationalism adds to the growing evidence that Americans were deeply ambivalent about the implications of their postrevolutionary independence. Webster's audiences demanded to stay connected to a British literary and linguistic past, as departing from it seemed like an abandonment of knowledge and virtue. At the same time, they demanded to feel connected across state lines and to believe in the coherent reality of an American national community. Imagining their own linguistic unity with Britain permitted Americans to claim for themselves the parts of "Englishness" that they wanted to preserve, even as they rejected English nationality—and Webster made himself the linguistic enemy of this ambivalence. He denounced his contemporaries' linguistic efforts to have their Englishness and reject it too. He insisted that Americans pick a side, as much in language as in nationality. And since the early twentieth century, it has often been said that he succeeded, at least a little, in splitting British and American English: he is credited for British-American spelling differences such as *honor/honour* and *center/centre*. This is the second Webster myth that I intend to undermine: at the end of the chapter, I present evidence that these national spelling differences are not attributable to Webster.

Noah Webster and Duncan Mackintosh were both native English speakers who were not natives of England. Both were upwardly mobile middle-class subjects whose financial well-being was never quite secure, and both of them risked their own capital to publish their experimental linguistic texts. From their homes in the New World, both of them tried to alter written English so that it would be more representative of spoken English. They produced texts designed to make English more accessible to geographically dispersed audiences in a newly globalized world. Both believed in the affiliative power of linguistic sameness: they saw language as the boundary of a meaningful community that might or might not coincide with a nation. Their chief difference was that Webster wanted a nationally distinct language that would reinforce national distinctness, while Mackintosh wanted a transnational English-language community transcending nationality and geography. Not every person in the English-speaking world was an ocean away from England, using a language that had been transplanted from across the sea—but around 1800, for the first time, most were.[11] The trend at the turn of the nineteenth century was that English speakers were in less physical proximity with each other and in more physical proximity with non–English speakers. In this respect, these Anglo-Caribbean and Anglo-American language experimentalists are representative figures. And while Webster and his linguistic nationalism have been better remembered, the linguistic unionism of Mackintosh and of Webster's opponents illustrates the global, Caribbean, and profoundly transnational imaginative horizons shared by English speakers in both of the English-speaking nation-states in the Age of Revolutions.

The Silence of Print

Fifty years before Joseph Chambers tried in western Pennsylvania to form a more perfect alphabetic union between British and American speakers, and thirty years before Duncan Mackintosh tried it in Martinique, Benjamin Franklin explored the same concept in London. Living in London in 1768, Franklin remarked that "from the want of public examples of pronunciation in his own country, it was often difficult to learn the proper sound of certain words . . . which of course every American very well understood as to their meaning." Dreaming of a world in which Americans could learn "the proper sound" of words as easily as they could learn "their meaning," Franklin experimented with a phonetic spelling system that he hoped would convey "correct" pronunciation more accurately to the provinces.[12]

Indeed, many non-English English speakers felt that they lacked access to reliable information about English pronunciation despite having excellent access to English-language print culture. Print is always silent. Americans imported "pronouncing dictionaries" from Britain in large

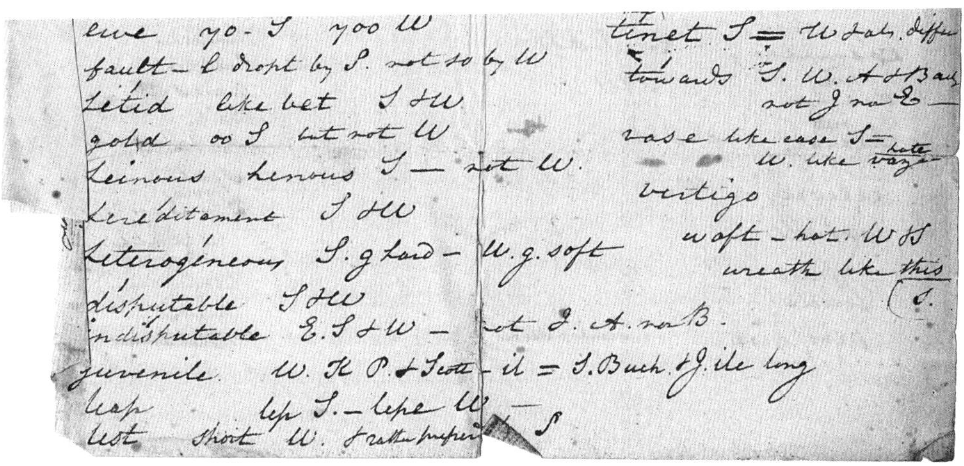
ewe 70 - S 700 W
fault — l dropt by S. not so by W
fetid like bet S & W
gold oo S but not W
heinous henous S — not W.
hereditament S & W
heterogeneous S. g hard — W. g. soft
disputable S & W
indisputable E. S & W — not J. A. nor B.
juvenile W. K P. & Scott — il = S. Buch. & J. ile long
leap lep S. — lepe W —
lest short W. & rather proper S
tenet S = W & als. differ
towards S. W. A & Bai
not J nor E —
vase like case S — late W. like vaze
vertigo
woft — hot. W & S
wreath like this (S.

Part of a comparison of the pronunciations recommended in fifteen English dictionaries, probably compiled in Philadelphia in the late 1790s. At bottom left, for example, the last syllable of "juvenile" rhymes with *bill* in the dictionaries of Walker, Kenrick, Perry, and Scott, but with *bile* in those of Sheridan, Buchanan, and Johnson. Courtesy of the American Philosophical Society.

numbers—but even when those dictionaries succeeded in penetrating the phonetic opacity of English spelling, the pronunciations that they recommended did not always agree.[13] Phonetically minded Americans could consult additional pronunciation manuals in hopes of identifying a consensus, although one did not always emerge, as one Philadelphia dictionary owner vividly discovered after embarking on an amateur project of comparative phonetic research. Starting with a list of fifteen dictionaries and eighty-four uncertain words, he tabulated the pronunciations recommended by the respective dictionaries. Was "diamond" two syllables or three? Sheridan said two, Walker three. Where was the accent in "indisputable"? It was in dispute: Entick, Sheridan, and Walker put it on the second syllable; Johnson, Ash, and Bailey on the third. Was the *l* in "fault" silent? Sheridan said yes, Walker no. The *g* in "springy": hard or soft? Consensus: soft. The *g* in "heterogeneous"? Sheridan hard, Walker soft. The dictionary owner discontinued the tabulation after 180 lookups, nowhere near to completing the list.[14]

The alternative to consulting the not-indisputable phonetic texts was to track down a well-bred native of southeastern England. This was not always feasible. A Massachusetts lawyer compiling a list of "Americanisms" in the 1810s consulted with two English gentlemen to make sure that the words, usages, and pronunciations on his list really were specific to the United States; but their assessments were uncertain, because "they have often observed to me, that although they were educated in England, yet having resided in America a long time, (about twenty years) their ear had lost much of that sensibility to deviations from the pure English idiom."[15] Similar uncertainties about "pure English" phonetics existed in Scotland, Ireland, and Wales, in many counties in England, and on the imperial frontiers—including on the Caribbean island of Dominica, where, while Franklin was conceiving his phonetic alphabet in the 1760s, Duncan Mackintosh arrived just as the British army seized the island from a small population of French colonists, native Caribs, and free and enslaved Africans.

The phonetic spelling system that Franklin drew up in 1768 replaced six letters of the Latin alphabet with new characters and restricted the meaning of the remaining twenty, so that "*all* the Letters, Vowels, and Consonants . . . wherever they are met with, or in whatever Company,

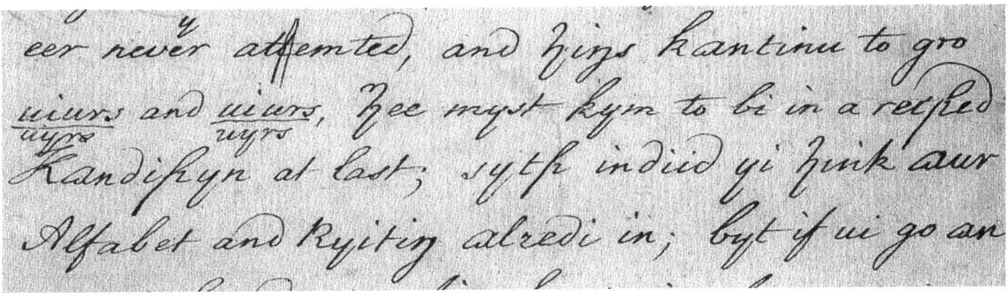
eer never attemted, and ɧiŋs kantinu to gro
uiurs and uiurs, ɧee myst kym to bi in a respekted
kandiſhyn at last; syth indiid yi ɧink aur
Alfabet and Ryitiŋ alredi in; byt if ui go an

Franklin's system removes the Latin letters *c*, *j*, *q*, *w*, *x*, and *y*. He adds two vowels, *a* and *y*, and consonants representing /th/, /dh/, /sh/, and /ng/: *ɦ*, *ɧ*, *ſh*, *ŋ*. At the beginning of the second line, Franklin can't decide whether to write "*uiurs*" or "*uyrs*" for *worse*. The first option would appear to rhyme with "fierce"; the second, with "verse." (Cf. "*ui*" for *we* and "*myst*" for *must*.) From Benjamin Franklin to Polly Stevenson, July 20, 1768. Courtesy of the American Philosophical Society.

their Sound is always the same." He used his experimental alphabet to send a flirtatious letter to his friend Mary Stevenson, suggesting that she collaborate with him on developing the system. Using the same experimental alphabet, Stevenson politely declined. While acknowledging that it could be helpful to people "*hu uiſh ta akuyir an akiuret pronynsieſhyn*,"* she thought that the costs of Franklin's orthographic reformation greatly outweighed its benefits, and concluded: "*yi biliiv ui myst let piipil spel an in ɧeer old ue*."† Franklin countered that a reform would become necessary "*sym tyim ar yɧyr . . . ar aur ryitiŋ uil bikym ɧi sêm uiɧ ɧi Tſhyiniiz*."‡ But his correspondent, who already spoke the metropolitan prestige dialect as her native tongue, perhaps did not share Franklin's sense of urgency about the phonetic opacity of English writing.[16]

* "who wish to acquire an accurate pronunciation"

† "I believe we must let people spell on in their old way"

‡ "some time or other . . . or our writing will become the same with the Chinese"

It did not get easier during the next half century to know how faraway speakers pronounced their English. When Duncan Mackintosh was working on a second edition of his phonetic spelling proposal in Barbados in 1805, he apologized that "my′ present *vast′* dis′tance from the metrop′olis has ren′dered it impos′sible for me to procu′re any oth′er o′ral assist′ance than that′ of va`gue opin′ions." Expecting that British readers would find phonetic errors throughout his book, he emphasized that his main contribution was not the pronunciation he had encoded, but the code in which he had transcribed it. He hoped that some "frie′ndly, gen′erous, good′ Proso′dians" in England would correct any Scottish, Caribbean, French, or otherwise nonstandard pronunciation quirks that his "va`*gue*" information about London pronunciation had allowed into the volume.[17] In the future, he explained, books could be prepared "pla`*i*nly point′ing out′ to all′ na`t*i*ons the quan′tity an*d* qual′ity *of* ev′ery letter, syl′lable, an*d* word′ in ou′r tong′*ue*," and the phonetic information vacuum in the English-speaking Caribbean would be a vacuum no longer.[18] A magazine critic back in England agreed that what Mackintosh was proposing could be of particular benefit to "foreigners or other persons who are not in the way of hearing the English language correctly pronounced"—a class of persons in which Mackintosh, like Franklin, explicitly placed himself.[19]

Franklin in 1768 and Mackintosh in 1797 were British colonials, and there is a well-understood history of eighteenth-century colonial hypervigilance about "correct English." It is less well known, however, that Americans remained strongly committed to those same standards long after London ceased to be their capital—and not just as a form of lingering colonial mimicry.[20] Even though the American Revolution fundamentally changed the power dynamics between American and British English speakers, Americans remained extremely interested in knowing how British English speakers spoke and bothered by the obstacles to finding out. "It has been very difficult," complained a New Englander in 1805, "for the Natives of North-America, to attain the true and most approved Pronunciation of the words and names in English Books which are in use in England, and America."[21] His concern closely echoes Franklin's problem forty years earlier, and it was still on Americans' minds a quarter century later, when a New York schoolteacher wondered whether it would be possible to create "a pitchpipe of simple vowel sounds" that could be sent "from one country to an other, and handed down to future times": a mechanical device that would faithfully reproduce the twelve or so English vowels, much as a musical pitch pipe could faithfully reproduce the twelve notes of the chromatic scale. Like the phonetic alphabets of Franklin and Mackintosh, this phonetic pitch pipe was envisioned specifically as a transnational object, circulating "from one country to an other" much as Mackintosh's system would send correct English pronunciation "to all′ n`at*i*ons."[22] This would finally make English phonetic accuracy available worldwide—for vowels, anyway.

An imaginary "pitchpipe of simple vowel sounds" could be set to different vowels, the way this actual pitch pipe could be set to different notes by sliding the end in or out. From *Illustrated Vocabulary for the Deaf and Dumb* (London, 1857). Washington University Libraries, Department of Special Collections.

Although a few other pipe dreamers contemplated mechanical devices for circulating human phonemes (see chapter 3), most of the era's efforts to record and transmit English phonetics were, like Mackintosh's, alphabetic and typographical, not mechanical. Rendering English spelling more representative of English pronunciation became something of a hot topic, to the point that in 1805 a magazine essayist gushed that "there are few subjects in which schemes of reformation have been more frequently recommended, than in the arrangement and the sounds of the English alphabet."[23] A steady stream of proposals for English spelling reform came off British and American presses. The national orientation of modern scholarly disciplines, however, has hindered historians' and literary scholars' recognition that these British and American alphabetic experiments constitute a single genre. Those published in America have usually been taken as evidence of American nationalism, while the British ones are most often linked to British social reform and education movements.[24] They are better understood, however, in relation to each other. (I have summarized seventeen alphabet reform projects, from both sides of the Atlantic, in table 2.)

Innovators who wanted to make printed English spelling more phonetically reliable had two material alternatives, neither of which was ideal: creating new characters, or repurposing old ones. New characters required new type—a severe impediment, since type was an eighteenth-century printer's single largest capital investment, much more expensive than the printing press it was used on. (In 1796, Boston printer Isaiah Thomas owned twelve printing presses, worth $732, and eight tons of type, worth $12,200.) The wholesale replacement of all the type owned by all printers everywhere was almost unthinkable. Moreover,

TABLE 2. Alphabetic and Orthographic Reforms Published in English, 1775–1825

DATE AND PLACE	CREATOR	SPECIMEN	TITLE OF PROPOSAL
1775 Newcastle	Thomas Spence	Ɨt ma hile pĭrplĕks a karlĭs Redĭr ŏv nu Kărĭktĭrz, tꝏ dĭsifĭr thĭ trꝏ Sĕns tharŏv; ħo ĭt ſhŭd be eze ĭnŭf tꝏ no ĭt bi a lĭtĭl Ⱥplĭkaſhĭn ănd Prăktĭs.	*The Grand Repository of the English Language*
1779 London	Benjamin Franklin	*ɥi si meni inkanviiniensis, az uel az difikɥltis, ђat uuld atend ђi briŋiŋ iur letɥrs and arђagrafi intu kamɥn ius*	*Political, Miscellaneous, and Philosophical Pieces*
1786 London	James Elphinston	Dainger must attend dhe repprezentacion ov won sound by various symbols.	*Propriety Ascertained in Her Picture*
1789 Boston	Noah Webster	hed, giv, brest, frend, speek, beleev, laf, dawter, plow, tuf, proov, blud, draft, karacter, masheen	*Dissertations on the English Language*
1791 Philadelphia	Joseph Chambers	The Englıſh lɑnguage, ɪɴ ɑddítıoɴ tω ᴛhe ᴇxŭberaɴᴛ varɨety, ɑɴd mɑsculɨɴe dıstínctɴess ov ıts vꝏwelƨ, abꝏuɴdƨ ɪɴ ᴛhe mȯre sȯɴor'us vȯcular cɵɴsoɴaɴᴛs.	"Elements of Orthography"
1793 London	James Alderson	By lis'ning to wize admonishuns, and tempuring the vivasety of yuth with a proppur mikstshure of sereus thawt, you may inshure tsheerfulnes.	*Orthographical Exercises: In a Series of Moral Letters*
1793 Philadelphia	William Thornton	ᴆi Amɜrikɜn laŋguidȷ uil ᴆɜs bi az distiŋt az ᴆɜ gɜvɜrmɜnt.	*Cadmus: Or, a Treatise on the Elements of Written Language*
1797 Boston	Duncan Mackintosh	màny àdvàn′tàgès ṭhàt wò*ul*d′ nèç′èssàrıly̆ àccrù′*e* fròm à stà′ndàrd òf prònùnçia`ṭion	*A Plain, Rational Essay on English Grammar*

TABLE 2 (continued)

DATE AND PLACE	CREATOR	SPECIMEN	TITLE OF PROPOSAL
1798 Trenton, NJ	James Ewing	ʎe furst âttêmts ât rytiq wêr prʌbabli vêre rw̄d ând impêrfêkt	*The Columbian Alphabet*
1800 London	Charles Allen	Too bee, or not too bee? that iz the kwestshun;— Hwether tiz nobler in the mind too suffer The stingz [sic] and arro'z of outrajeus fortshune	*New Orthographical Exercises, for the Use of English Seminaries*
1805 New York	Enos Weed	ʊr Faɱer vɘi♀ art in hevven; Halloed be ♂i n××m. ♂i ki↥dum kum. ♂i wil b doon as in hevven, so in er∠.	*The American Orthographer*
1807 Walpole, NH	Abner Kneeland	Orashun, pronʊnst befor th' Skꝏlmɛstur Ɛssoseashun bi ƐBNUR NELƐND	*A Brief Sketch of a New System of Orthography*
1807 London	Thomas Young	HŪcN LuVLɩ ŪuŪMEN STŪPS TE FΩ̆Lɩ, END FEɩNDZ TU Lēt ΔET McN BɩTrēɩ	"A Description of Articulate Sounds, with Appropriate Characters"
1808 Boston	William Pelham	their hèàrtș wéře cȧn̊kĕred with diṡcôntént	*A System of Notation*
1813 Philadelphia	Thomas Embree	ɐ pϱrsn kɐn lərn tσ red ɐnd riit ɪŋglɪſh prɵpϱrlɪ ɵn ɿhɪs plɐn	*Orthography Corrected*
1816 Richmond, VA	Samuel Boyle	~t3em 3nd ~t3ed 4el 4aat f22r no m3n	*Orthography Corrected*
1825 London	John Gilchrist	*ɯ am nɯ goeŋ on e pelgremeȷ and haveŋ performd mɯ devoɹɯnz wel en e fyɵ dez retɯrn*	Gilchrist's Universal Character

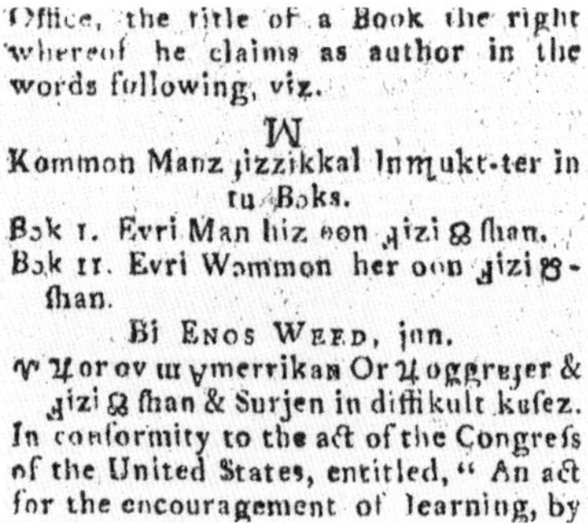
Office, the title of a Book the right whereof he claims as author in the words following, viz.

W

Kommon Manz ʒizzikkal Inʒtrukt-ter in tu Boks.

Bok I. Evri Man hiz oon ʒizi ʃhan.

Bok II. Evri Wommon her oon ʒizi ʃhan.

Bi Enos Weed, jun.

Orʮoggrɐjer ov ʎmerrikan Orʮoggrɐjer & ʒizi ʃhan & Surjen in diffikult kasez.

In conformity to the act of the Congress of the United States, entitled, "An act for the encouragement of learning, by

Copyright registration for a home medical reference, "The Common Man's Physical Instructor," issued by a Connecticut doctor named Enos Weed in 1798 in a reformed spelling system of his own design. *Connecticut Journal*, June 20, 1798. Courtesy of Readex.

the expense of designing and casting enough custom type to print even a small demonstration pamphlet—let alone implementing it at scale—was prohibitive for all but the very rich and very optimistic.[25] "It would have been easy to form a new set of characters to compose my alphabet," sighed the sitting mayor of Trenton, New Jersey, who proposed a new alphabetic scheme in 1798, "but . . . before it could be brought into use, every printer must have a new set of types to represent those characters. . . . These would have been insurmountable obstacles to the adoption of the system; I therefore determined in favor of the old characters."[26] His system called for more than twenty-six letters, but with a little creativity he found additional glyphs in the type that was already in the print shop, such as by turning existing Latin characters upside-down. His alphabet of thirty-three characters includes *k*, *y*, *v*, as well as *ʞ*, *ʆ*, *ɑ*, and it repurposes the long *ſ*, which most printers were phasing out anyway, to mean /sh/. A hypothetical printer wishing to use the Trenton mayor's alphabet would have had to obtain extra *k*'s to turn upside down as *ʞ*'s—but that was easily done. Some of the era's other phonetic spelling proposals took advantage of typefounders' existing infrastructure for manufacturing astrological and mathematical symbols in the same sizes as Latin letters.[27]

The kulumbeân âlfabêt of Mayor James Ewing, the ʎmerrikan Orʮoggrɐjer of Dr. Enos Weed, and the *nu letɥrs and ɑrɦɑgrafi* of Benjamin Franklin had the upside of requiring little or no new manufacturing, but the downside of looking illiterate. At a glance, they all resembled texts produced by imperfect spellers, such as Franklin's sister, Jane Mecom, who in her correspondence with her brother frequently apologized for "the Incorectnes of my Leter."[28] Franklin reassured her: "You need not be concern'd in writing to me, about your bad Spelling, for in my Opinion, as our Alphabet now stands, the bad Spelling, or what is call'd so, is generally the best." Part of the idea of Franklin's system, therefore, was to collapse the difference between phonetic spelling and bad spelling: "*ȝoz hu du ncat spel uel . . . natyrali fcal into ȝi nu meħyd alredi*," he wrote; "*ȝêr prezent bad speliŋ iz onli bad, bikcaz kcantreri to ȝi prezent bad ruls: yndyr ȝi nu ruls it uuld bi gud*." Under his system, the "*prezent bad speliŋ*" of writers like his sister would become *gud speliŋ* by fiat.[29] This orthographically egalitarian promise of Franklin's system has tended to dominate later understandings of it—somewhat to the exclusion of his top-down anxiety to replace all regional dialects with the London metropolitan standard.[30]

"those who do not spell well . . . naturally fall into the new method already; their present bad spelling is only bad, because contrary to the present bad rules: under the new rules it would be good"

But it has often been difficult to convince elites and would-be elites to give up distinctions between elite and nonelite language. The sociologist Pierre Bourdieu suggests thinking about acts of linguistic expression as "symbolic goods," each act having a quasi-economic value within the particular "linguistic market" in which it is offered. Speakers accrue more symbolic capital by using linguistic forms with higher values—the highest values usually being found in linguistic forms associated with sociopolitical elites. For Bourdieu, this explains basically all linguistic preferences: when people prefer one pronunciation, spelling, or syntax over another, they "often talk as if the language they favour could have some value outside the market, by intrinsic virtues such as its 'logical' qualities; but, in practice, they are defending the market"—that is, the social hierarchy that rewards people who speak that way.[31] Conformity to linguistic norms has socioeconomic benefits, and signing on to any reform of linguistic standards is socioeconomically riskier than pursuing what one critic has called "the trusted path of linguistic improvement to augmented social respectability."[32] In this view, the social expediencies of upward mobility motivated English speakers outside of England to double down on their commitment to existing notions of English linguistic correctness. Franklin's system and others like it may have been doomed, therefore, by their being close enough to standard English orthography to register visually as bad English. The inventor of a different system of "inglish orthoggraphy" in the late 1780s tried to head off this problem by arguing that, alarmingly illiterate as his system might appear, it was not as bad as Franklin's, "an exemplificacion ov [hwich] wood but terrify dhe reader." But as long as the words were mostly in Latin characters, they looked wrong unless they were spelled right.

"Many schemes have been devised by speculative writers for improving the orthography, and assimilating it to the oral tongue," wrote the poet Robert Southey in 1808, "but they have all so disfigured the appearance of the language . . . that they have only excited ridicule."[33]

Writing from the Caribbean in the 1790s, Duncan Mackintosh took a different approach, one evidently designed to avoid that ridicule, and one under which Jane Franklin Mecom's "*bad speliŋ*" would have remained bad. Mackintosh prioritized the preservation of the existing Latin alphabet and the existing English spellings, so that his text still looks like literate English. The trade-off is in efficiency: adding phonetic information to the presently ambiguous Latin characters requires more marks on the page—more ink—in the form of an interlinear gloss, which occupies a lot of space. His system relies mostly on superscript and subscript numbers to clarify the phonetic values of ambiguous letters, italics to mark silent ones, and accent marks to indicate stress and quantity. He concludes that English speech uses forty-nine discrete sounds, most of which can be signified in more than one way: the sound represented by *z* in "daze," for example, is also represented by the *s* in "days." Meanwhile, there are also three other things that *s* can mean. Mackintosh assigns numbers and other marks to all of these: the *s* of "days" is $\underset{2}{\mathrm{s}}$, as distinguished from $\underset{1}{\mathrm{s}}$ ("cots"), $\underset{3}{\mathrm{s}}$ ("sure"), and $\underset{4}{\mathrm{s}}$ ("vision"). The quadruplicate ambiguity of the old *s* yields to four distinct certainties: $\underset{1}{\mathrm{s}}$, $\underset{2}{\mathrm{s}}$, $\underset{3}{\mathrm{s}}$, and $\underset{4}{\mathrm{s}}$. Counting each variant as a separate letter, this enlarges the alphabet from twenty-six ambiguous letters to 105 reliable ones: $\overset{1}{\mathrm{a}}$ $\overset{2}{\mathrm{a}}$ $\overset{3}{\mathrm{a}}$ $\overset{4}{\mathrm{a}}$ b $\underset{,}{\mathrm{b}}$ $\underset{1}{\mathrm{c}}$ $\underset{2}{\mathrm{c}}$ $\underset{3}{\mathrm{c}}$ $\underset{,}{\mathrm{c}}$, and so on. Unlike the English letter *e*, which can correspond to many different sounds, Mackintosh's letter $\overset{4}{\mathrm{e}}$ always indicates a schwa. Since a schwa may also be represented as $\overset{4}{\mathrm{i}}$, $\overset{4}{\mathrm{o}}$, or $\overset{1}{\mathrm{u}}$, Mackintosh's system does not make English any easier to write: one must still memorize arbitrary spellings. But while it does not make English speech easier to write, it makes English writing easier to speak and does so without "disfiguring the appearance of the language."[34]

Mackintosh finished his system in 1797 while living in Martinique. His entry into print illustrates the vast flow of people, texts, capital, goods, and ideas within and between the West Indies and other parts of the Atlantic world: as scholars have recognized in recent years, the Caribbean was enormously significant around the Atlantic, profoundly shaping the experiences, literature, and culture of Britons and Americans, even those who never crossed an ocean.[35] For archival and other reasons, however, taking stock of the circumatlantic importance of the Caribbean frequently means investigating writers writing *about* the West Indies rather than writers writing *from* the West Indies. There were four printers in Martinique in 1797, none of whom had the infrastructure necessary to print Mackintosh's two-hundred-page proposal, or two hundred pages of anything else: they produced newspapers, broadsides, government proclamations, legal forms, and pamphlets, but all of the codex books on the island were imported.[36] Yet texts did not only circulate transnationally in the Atlantic world after they were printed; they also circulated transnationally in order to be printed. In this case, the Scottish-British-Dominican-Martinican Mackintosh hired a respected printing firm in Boston to undertake the unusual and time-consuming task of setting 237 pages of alternately roman and italic text, interlined with around eighty thousand 4.5-point numbers. Mackintosh's *Plain, Rational Essay* highlights the cultural production actually taking place in the Caribbean—and how that production is easily obscured: printed in Boston and addressed to "British and American ladies and gentlemen" by a writer with a conspicuously Scottish name, the *Essay* would be easy to take as a transatlantic (rather than circumatlantic) object. In fact, though, it is Caribbean, imperial, and colonial—not only in its compositional origin but also in its intended purpose of synchronizing pronunciation across imperial distances and in the political circumstances that prompted its publication.

The Vast′ Dis′tance from the Metrop′olis

Mackintosh's efforts to reach phonetically across his "present *vast′* dis′tance from the metrop′olis" came near the end of a life lived at the linguistic and geospatial margins of empire.[37] He was born in Inverness, in the extreme north of Scotland—about as far as you can get from London and still be in the British Isles.[38] He spent his adult life in places of multiple and conflicting languages, nationalities, loyalties, and ways of life, moving among several Caribbean islands that were themselves changing hands among several empires. When he composed his phonetic spelling proposal in Martinique in the mid-1790s, Mackintosh was situated in a British occupation of a French enslavement of a majority African population on a formerly Amerindian island. His "lit'tle patriot'ic book'" was, among other things, a technology of imperial assimilation aimed at resolving such multiply identified complexities in favor of a coherent Englishness.[39]

Mackintosh had come to Martinique as a refugee two decades earlier, when the island was French territory and Mackintosh was in legal trouble on the British-occupied island of Dominica. With his pregnant wife and his one-year-old daughter, he sailed from Dominica out of the British Empire and crossed twenty miles of ocean to seek asylum in Martinique, a French sugar colony the size of New York City. By that time, Mackintosh was accustomed to life as an English speaker in the Caribbean *francophonie*; a decade earlier, he had arrived in Dominica just as the British Navy seized the island from the French during the Seven Years' War. He had spent from 1761 to 1774 in Dominica as part of the English-speaking population to whom the British government sold lands seized from the island's colonial French, free African, and native Carib communities. Mackintosh owned two hundred acres and was a partner in hundreds of acres more. But a financial dispute with his creditors in 1774 led to the seizure of Mackintosh's estate by "a designing Cabale," sending the family to Martinique.[40]

Mackintosh's experience as a refugee in Martinique went a lot better than it might have. He gained the favor of Martinique's French aristocracy, securing legal protection against his Dominican creditors and talking his way into a grant of two hundred acres of land in Martinique to replace his lost Dominica estate. Still, he resented having to start over: "like another Adam driven from his Paradise, I endeavour to earn my Bread by the Sweat of my Brow," he complained five years later.[41] Cognizant of their precarious legal and social circumstances as British citizens in French territory, Duncan and Elizabeth Mackintosh walked a careful political tightrope. They formalized their relationships with the local French elites: their children's godparents included the governor's wife, the commander in chief of the militia, and the island's naval commander.[42] They confirmed their English marriage under French law, and Elizabeth converted to Catholicism.[43] Later, when Mackintosh wrote to Saint Lucia to solicit a British military commander's assistance in recovering some money that he was owed in Dominica, he appealed to his and the officer's shared Scottish Highland origins (referencing their "native Country" and prefacing the name of the person who owed him money with the Gaelic honorific *Maishter* rather than the English *Mister*), but he also emphasized that he was not in a position to advance the interests of their other native country, Britain, against his French hosts. "By extraordinary Indulgence I enjoy all the Privileges of a french Subject yet I have hitherto preserv'd the Title of a British One," he explained; "Honor enjoins me to observe the strictest Neutrality during my present position . . . among Foreigners."[44] Certainly, he was enjoined not only by honor but also by prudence to keep his national identification somewhat indeterminate.

Twenty years passed, until in the 1790s the French Revolution threw Martinique and the rest of the French Caribbean into chaos. The Martinique planter class, deeply concerned about the consequences for their slave economy of *liberté*, *égalité*, and the rest, pursued increasingly hostile relations with the French government, eventually dispatching an envoy to London to negotiate British protection from revolutionary France, as well as from their own slaves, who comprised 89 percent of the island's population. The British obliged, seizing control of Martinique in 1794, guaranteeing the continuation of slavery and helping to put down the incipient slave rebellions that followed the 1791 onset of the Haitian Revolution a thousand miles to the northwest.[45] Under the British occupation, Mackintosh found himself in circumstances similar to those he had enjoyed thirty years earlier in Dominica: he belonged to a minority occupying force of English speakers, on an island where most of the people spoke non-European languages and most of the Europeans spoke French.[46] It was in the aftermath of that British invasion in 1794 that Mackintosh put together his phonetic proposal under the deceptively ordinary title of *A Plain, Rational Essay on English Grammar.*

Mackintosh was evidently impatient to rejoin the English-speaking world—or to have the English-speaking world rejoin him. He expressed frustration about the linguistic lag that followed British political conquest: "$\overset{3}{\text{a}}$lm$\overset{1}{\text{o}}$st $\overset{3}{\text{a}}$ll′ $\overset{2}{\text{o}}$ûr $\overset{4}{\text{a}}$d$\overset{1}{\text{o}}$pt′$\overset{4}{\text{e}}$d s$\overset{1}{\text{u}}$b′j$\overset{1}{\text{e}}$c*t*s," he complained, remain "*w*h$\overset{1}{\text{o}}$l′l$\overset{3}{\text{y}}$

ig′norant *of* ôur tong*ue* [and] retâ*i*n′ a ver′y par′tîal a′nd fa`tal attach′ment to their na`tive coun′try, la′ng-ûage, la*ws*, cus′toms and prej′udices; all′ which′ they fo′ndly transmit′ to th*ei*r chi′ldren a′nd domes′tics bo′rn in ôur col′oni*es*—wit′ness Grena′da, St. Vin′cent, Domini′ca, &c.," all of which Britain had seized from France thirty years earlier. He blamed the slow pace of anglicization on the unpredictable relationship between written and spoken English, which confused and discouraged foreign learners: "the pronunc*i*a`t*i*on . . . s*e*em′s to them′ a′s a me′*re* wa′ndering va`por or phan′tom." His goal was to make the British Empire easier to join, not just in a formal political sense ("la*w*′s") but also in terms of shared subjective experiences ("cus′toms an*d* prej′udices"). One of the "man`y advan′tages that wo*ul*d′ nec′essarily accru′*e* from a sta′ndard *of* pronunc*i*a`t*i*on," he predicted, would be "a ver′y consid′erable incre*as*′*e* to the nu′mber *of* ôur fâi`thful sub′jec*t*s," encompassing Grenadians, Martinicans, Dominicans, and generally people who were nationally, but perhaps not yet experientially, British. Writing from an island in the West Indies that was only barely (and temporarily) part of the Anglophone world, Mackintosh nevertheless adopted the perspective of the imperial center, including himself within the superior part of the us/them grammatical division separating the British rulers from "ôur fâi`thful sub′jec*t*s."[47]

Yet even though Mackintosh writes in the first-person plural of the British imperial center, he goes out of his way to define an English-speaking "us" that is American and colonial as well as English and British. His title page is "respectfully inscribed to British and American Ladies and Gentlemen," and he interweaves references to English, Scottish, and American people and places within its text. A sample sentence that name-checks a British military hero is paired with a sample sentence that name-checks an American one: "*W*ho′ can be′ a Pitt′?" as well as "*W*ho can be a Washington?" He registers an American as well as a British copyright and goes out of his way to say so. The book seems to be working to integrate the same transnational currents as those of Mackintosh's own life, integrating the diversity of the English-speaking world into one single "pla`*i*n, rat*i*onal and pe′rmanent *standard of pronuncia`tion*."[48]

In 1797, of course, there was no longer a common government linking Britain to its former American colonies. In the absence of a political state encompassing all English speakers, Mackintosh returns again and again to a rhetorical strategy in which the English language does the same work. He repeatedly replaces the actual nation-state of Great Britain with a metaphor in which the English language is itself a state: "ĕtỳmŏl′ŏgỳ, ănăl′ŏgỳ ăn*d* eŭphŏnỳ mā`*y* bĕ căll′ĕd thĕ *pā′rlĭamĕnt*, ăc′cĕnt thĕ *mŏn′ărch*, ănd ŏûr stā′ndărd ăc′cĕnt rŭ′l*e*s, thĕ *măg′nā chărt′ă* ŏ*f* E′nglĭsh prŏnŭnc*ĭā*`t*ĭ*ŏn," he writes. He notes that English pronunciation sounds best when "sŭbmĭt′tĕd tŏ ĭts nā′tĭv*e* lĕgĭslā`tŭr*e*" and remarks that accentual stress is the "Gŏ′vĕrnŏr in chĭ*ef*′ ŏ*f* ŏûr prŏnŭnc*ĭā*`t*ĭ*ŏn." Elsewhere, he reimagines the English language not as a function of the British Empire but as itself an empire, "hā`vĭng ĕnrĭch′ĕd ĭtsĕlf′ bỳ thĕ wĕ*a*lth′ ŏ*f* ăll′ pŏl′ĭshĕd lā′ng-ûāgĕs" through "glō′r*ĭ*ŏ*u*s ăcqûĭsĭt′*ĭ*ŏns ŏr cŏnq′ûĕsts."[49] In this linguistic empire, as in a political empire, "wealth" flows inward from "acquisitions" and "conquests" from other languages.

Mackintosh thus sought to reconcile a national vocabulary with the transnational reality of his book's audiences: "E′nglishmen," "Scotch′men," "American Ladies and Gentlemen," "ŏûr ădŏpt′ĕd sŭb′-jĕc*t*s [in] Grĕnā′dă, St. Vĭn′cĕnt, Dŏmĭnĭ′că, &c.," "nŏt ŏ′nlỳ nā`tĭv*e*s, bŭt Fŏ′rĕĭgnĕrs lĭk′*e*wĭs*e*."[50] He goes out of his way to detach the English language from English geography: "pe*o*p′le in gen′eral a′r*e* apt′ to imagine that′ the ver′y best′ E′nglish is spoken in the cap′ital," he writes, when in fact many Londoners "he*e*d′lessly prac′tis*e* som′*e* *of* the cock′ney vu′lgar-isms." Invoking the well-known and much-maligned provincial dialects of England's Yorkshire and Lancashire counties, he scoffs at fools who believe "that′ *all*′ E′nglishmen ha`ve *one uniform pronuncia`tion*," confronts "tho′se pu′erile vu′lgar prej′udices which′ affirm′ that′... a Scotch′man can′ *nev′er* spe*a*k′ good′ E′nglish," and insists that "a good′ E′nglish schol′ar, wheth′er bo′rn on this′ or that′ side *of* the [River] Twĕed′, ma`*y* *write* an*d* spe*a*k′ good E′nglish." In an indication of the declining prestige of climatic accounts of human difference, he needs only a rhetorical question to dismiss the notion that different geographical realities could produce essentially different peoples to the north and south of the river dividing Scotland from England: "Hàve the op′posite sid′es *of* the Tweed′ the mirac′ul*o*us pow′er *of* fo′rming heterogen′e*o*us or′gans *of* speech′?"[51] The implied answer: certainly not. The categories of belonging that matter in Mackintosh's project depend not on geopolitical reality but on linguistic reality: the “adopt′ed sub′je*c*ts” who have not learned English are outside, even though they are geopolitically inside; while a colonial with excellent English like himself is inside, even though he is geographically outside. His phonetic spelling proposal was an effort to collapse linguistically the geopolitical distance between the imperial center and the marginal spaces in which he made his home. The goal of Mackintosh's project is to provide a linguistic means for Americans, Scots, and West Indian colonials to assert membership in a British elite from which they were otherwise excluded by distance, ethnicity, or nationality.

Although Mackintosh is only one person who undertook one linguistic experiment, his is part of a larger story about the significances of language in his era. Mackintosh was pushed by revolutionary and imperial forces across borders: class, national, geographic, political, imperial, and religious. His book works to obviate or soothe or reframe at least some of these borders, and maybe all of them. His multinational status, geopolitical marginality, and extensive contact with French speakers are characteristic of his era. Like Nicholas Dufief, Duncan Mackintosh was an ethnically Celtic European in the Western Hemisphere, dislocated in the 1790s by empire and revolution, surrounded by foreigners national and linguistic, purveying in the New World phonemes that he remembered from the Old. Both of them worked to make the voices in their present New World realities sound like the voices of their Old World pasts—Dufief shaping his students' voices through his distinctive classroom call-and-response, Mackintosh hoping to shape his Caribbean neighbors' voices by providing them with an unprecedented degree of phonetic specificity. In their own necessarily singular ways, their efforts to preserve a phonetic continuity despite the political and geographic discontinuities they endured outline the conceptual possibilities of language for people living through their era's imperial and revolutionary changes. For them, the categories of “foreigner” and “native” turn out to be overlapping and not fully distinguishable, such as when Mackintosh writes that “forei*g*ners an*d* na`tives just′ly complain′ that′ *ou′r* pronunc*i*a`t*i*on is an impen′etrable mys′tery.” If English was to be “the univers′al tong′*ue* o*f* Eu′rop*e* and Amer′ica,” what would it mean to be “forei*g*n” or “na`tive”?[52] Foreign or native to what?

Transnational Linguistic Patriotism in the Age of Ex Uno Duo

Among the many questions raised by the Age of Revolutions was this one: what is the relationship between a language and a nation-state? Before the eighteenth century, as Benedict Anderson has influentially argued, governments tended to rule communities that were not imagined as having a single nationality or language. In the second half of the eighteenth century, however, these "polyvernacular" and multinational states began to give way to (notionally) mononational and monolingual states. Anderson links this development to the emergence of new "print-languages" that evolved because producing separate texts for each regional linguistic niche market was, for printers, financially impracticable. As a result, readers in Paris and Provence, or Boston and Charleston, found themselves reading the same books and newspapers as their distant countrymen and came to think of themselves as belonging to the same community. Anderson identifies a veritable "philological-lexicographic revolution" in the form of dictionaries and linguistic initiatives to promulgate these standardized print-languages—projects often backed by nation-states, which invested in them because standardized languages "naturalized" the state entities that already existed, drawing far-flung readers into expansive (national) reading communities. This account highlights how attention to language facilitated "the origin and spread of nationalism."[53]

Yet we should also recognize the parallel value of linguistic sameness in the English-speaking world circa 1800 as a way to imagine communities *other than* nations, such as the supranational community that Duncan Mackintosh had in mind. There was no precedent for two distinct nation-states sharing a vernacular language in common: there was no nation-state speaking "French" other than the Kingdom of France, none speaking "Spanish" other than the Kingdom of Spain, none speaking "Dutch" other than the Dutch Republic.[54] Nobody knew quite what to expect from this new transnational linguistic reality. Nor was it entirely possible to know just how similar the two nations' versions of English actually were, thanks to the technological and alphabetic opacities already mentioned. Postrevolutionary Americans knew that they were foreigners relative to the English and British nations, but they were unsure of how foreign they were to the "English" language. Uncertainties about the likeness of American and British English presented nagging and sometimes pressing problems when English speakers thought about their individual and community identities. Most people were not entirely sure of whether Americans were linguistic insiders, nor had they entirely made up their minds about whether they ought to be.[55]

To what pa′triotism, therefore, did Mackintosh's "lit′tle patriot′ic book′" appeal? It might be the same one invoked by the gunsmith-alphabetician in Pennsylvania who dedicated his alphabetic proposal to the British and American heads of state and addressed "patriotic citizens of both nations." Nor would these have been the only linguistic innovators to articulate a transnational "patriotism" for which the underlying *patrie* is the English language, not England or Britain or the United States of America. Writing from Germany in the same year that Mackintosh was writing from Martinique, the British novelist Herbert Croft thought that the time had come "for making some grand attempt, with regard to fixing the *standard* of our language" and halting the chaotic evolution of its sounds and senses: "Deservedly immortal would be that *patriot, on either side of the Atlantick*, who should succeed in such an attempt" at "the national task" of compiling an "English and American dictionary."[56] This transnational linguistic patriotism was imaginatively useful to postrevolutionary Americans struggling to reconcile their ambivalent desires for self-differentiation from Europe, their uncomfortable sense of diversities within and among the United States, and their enduring commitments to transnational norms and identities.

This postrevolutionary transnational linguistic patriotism, however, was written out of American history later in the nineteenth century, and it continues to be obscure today in academic as well as popular historiography. A different postrevolutionary linguistic ideology survived in American historiography: the linguistic nationalism, and even separatism, promoted by figures such as Noah Webster. Like most histories, this one is embellished with tall tales. According to a story that has been going around since the 1780s, for example, revolutionary America was so hostile to everything "English" that the United

States Congress once seriously considered the possibility "that Hebrew should take the place of English." In another well-worn anecdote, the Pennsylvania legislature came very close to adopting German as the state's official language, the measure being defeated by a single vote.[57] Both of these stories are apocryphal. But anti-British language hostility certainly did exist in the early national United States. A South Carolina plantation owner said so flatly in a letter to Thomas Jefferson in 1791: "As a Nation, it is a misfortune that we speak the English Language."[58] A French soldier reported encountering some linguistic isolationists during the Revolutionary War who were uncomfortable with "the language of their country being that of their oppressors"; they insisted on complimenting his English by telling him "you speak American well."[59] John Adams tried to get "American" to catch on as the name of the language spoken in the United States, while others hoped to change more than just the name.[60] The young man who won the 1793 design competition for the U.S. Capitol building had, just weeks earlier, won another prize for a different nation-building effort: the American Philosophical Society had awarded him a gold medal for his plan of an "AMERICAN LANGUAGE... as distinct as the government."[61] These and other very real early national expressions of distaste for the English language illustrate an important dimension of early U.S. thinking about the English language and the construction of American national identity.

This linguistic nationalism, however, coexisted with powerful fantasies of transatlantic linguistic union that have frequently been ignored or treated as quaint vestiges of colonial mentalities. Early American linguistic transnationalism deserves more attention than it has received, however, because it illustrates a different and less familiar side of the early U.S. relationship to language, corresponding to a different side of early U.S. identity—one that registers overlapping commitments to local, national, and transnational communities. English linguistic unionism certainly did not seem un-American to the young man who gave the oration at Boston's July Fourth ceremonies in 1825 and marked that anniversary of a declaration of national independence by recognizing the language that had *not* been declared independent of Britain. "In spite of all that has passed, we owe England much," said the speaker, a young poet named Charles Sprague, citing various British affronts and outrages to elaborate "all that has passed." The debt he acknowledged was linguistic: "for the living treasures of her mind," he asked rhetorically, "who that has drawn from the deep fountains of her wisdom, who that speaks, and reads, and *thinks* her language, will be slow to own his obligation?" Even as he demeaned England, Sprague celebrated England's essential linguistic contribution to the American self: those "treasures of her mind" still "living" in anyone who "speaks, and reads, and *thinks* her language." He presents the "English" language as a vector delivering desirable values, temperaments, and wisdom into American minds.[62]

In reemphasizing transnationalist linguistic fantasies such as this one, I join with the many cultural and literary historians who in recent decades have brought a welcome scrutiny to the subject of early American nationalism, emphasizing eighteenth- and nineteenth-century Americans' deeply ambivalent feelings about being American—and about not being English and British. These critics have shown that late-eighteenth- and early-nineteenth-century Americans frequently wanted not to break with English values but rather to live up to those values and outdo the English on their terms. This area of research has contextualized the well-known challenges of *e pluribus unum* alongside the parallel but lesser-known challenges of what might be called *ex uno duo*: the transformation of Britain and British North America from one imagined community into two. The phonetic alphabets of Benjamin Franklin and Joseph Chambers exemplify the unionist impulse to halt the transatlantic linguistic drift and nudge American English speakers back toward British correctness. Of course, other early American linguistic innovators were linguistic separatists who wanted a language "as distinct as the government." And still others were somewhere in between: they wanted British and American speakers to share a common standard, but they thought Americans should take the lead in setting it. One American advocate of "ɐ kǫrə*k*t *ɵ*rt*hɵg*rɐfị" (a correct orthography) predicted in 1813 that "If the United States should adopt a correct orthography, the English will find it in their interest to do the same," even though the two nations were fighting a war at that time. His system, therefore, was "not limited to our own nation" but would allow "such . . . inhabitants of each country as have not good English . . . to speak, read and write English properly." We misunderstand such projects, and the attitudes they represent, if we conflate them with the linguistic-separatist efforts to widen the gap between British and American language. They envision reinforcing, not dismantling, a British-American linguistic community.[63]

The alphabetic reforms proposed by Americans after the revolution are best understood as part of a transoceanic project to record and transmit English pronunciation, the same project in which Duncan Mackintosh was engaged in Martinique. Both before and after the revolution, American attitudes toward the English language largely mirrored British attitudes. During the colonial period, English speakers in British North America behaved toward the English language much as nonmetropolitan English speakers did in England: they tried not to sound provincial. The founders of the Philadelphia Academy (later the University of Pennsylvania) fretted in the 1750s, for example, that the colonies' distance from the metropolis put them at risk of losing "the true pronounciation and writing of our own language."[64] Like English speakers elsewhere, American colonists generally believed that there was a correct English dialect, that its speakers were concentrated in and around London, and that their own speech should be measured against its standard—which is why Franklin fantasized in the 1760s about transmitting the "*akiuret pronynsiefiyn*" of London to North America. When colonial Americans visited London, their speech sometimes stood out as provincial, but it usually did not stand out as American: a patchwork of dialects covered British territory on both sides of the Atlantic, and none of those dialects was consistently recognizable as North American during the colonial period.[65]

For most English speakers in British North America, the revolution did little to change their thinking about "the true pronounciation" or the "*akiuret pronynsiefiyn*" of their language: the same *pronynsiefiynz* that had seemed correct in 1775 still seemed correct. Consumer trends bear this out: given the opportunity to exercise some lexicographical nationalism, American consumers repeatedly chose not to do so. During the first fifty years of the United States, the standard dictionaries used in English-speaking North America were the same as those used in

Britain: John Entick's *New Spelling Dictionary* (London, 1765), William Perry's *Royal Standard English Dictionary* (Edinburgh, 1775), Thomas Sheridan's *General Dictionary of the English Language* (London, 1780), John Walker's *Critical Pronouncing Dictionary* (London, 1791), and, of course, Samuel Johnson's *Dictionary of the English Language* (London, 1755). These five works comprised thirty-six of the thirty-eight non-abridged English dictionaries printed in the United States before 1820. The other two were critical as well as commercial failures.[66]

Massachusetts printer Isaiah Thomas, for example, printed Perry's *Royal Standard English Dictionary* in 1788, 1793, 1794, 1796, 1800, 1801, 1802, 1809, and 1812. Although Thomas was an enthusiastic supporter of U.S. national independence, he made no effort to Americanize Perry's *Royal Standard* or to downplay its *Royal* allegiance. He advertised the royal title in large type and altered the volume only by adding a dedication page affirming that the publication was "intended to fix a standard for the pronunciation of the English language, conformably to the present practice of polite speakers in Great-Britain and the United States." The first four editions alone sold 54,000 copies.[67] Like Duncan Mackintosh, Thomas affirms the norm that "polite speakers in Great-Britain and the United States" would all pronounce English the same way: a single linguistic ideal, or prestige dialect, to be sought by English speakers the world over. British writers continued to hope that Americans would retain "the language of our common forefathers . . . the only badge that is still worn of our consanguinity," and many American writers shared the same hope. A strong stigma against "Americanisms" existed in the American press. John Pickering, who published a glossary of Americanisms in Boston in 1816, spoke for this position when he wrote that "*our English* . . . has in so many instances departed from the English standard, that our scholars should lose no time in endeavouring to restore it to its purity."[68]

Noah Webster happened to be friends with Pickering's father, so he was uncharacteristically restrained when he wrote a fifty-page rebuttal to Pickering's work, although he still accused Pickering of "arrogat[ing] to himself a dictatorial authority" "to decide what is or is not correct in language." By this time Webster had been trying for thirty years to persuade Americans that they should embrace linguistic Americanisms, not reject them. He wanted to accelerate the divergence of American English from British English. But as Webster conceded in his 1816 response to Pickering, he had not been very effective in winning over the public to his form of linguistic nationalism: he still found himself "attempting to counteract a current of opinion."[69]

Webster played many roles in the early national United States—schoolbook author, itinerant lecturer, newspaper editor, Federalist pamphleteer, epidemiologist, copyright advocate, and "probably the most prolific writer in America" during his lifetime—but one of his most significant, if unintended, achievements was to become the occasion for an enormous public outpouring of linguistic hostility.[70] Although Webster's name is familiar to historians of early America, not to mention anyone who has owned a dictionary, his unpopularity in the early national period has frequently been overlooked. When Webster wrote "wharves" instead of "wharfs" in 1787 and defended his spelling as "the *American* plural," one of his many newspaper opponents called this recourse "the most ridiculous refuge that could be conceived," and asked: "Pray, sir, do not the Americans speak the English language? Why, then, should we suffer such a barbarism as *wharves*, when we are sure that the proper English word to be used instead of it is *wharfs*?"[71] A different writer demanded to know "who are the *Columbian* authors who do not write in the *English* language and spell in the *English* manner, except Noah Webster, junior Esq.?" These writers insisted that Webster was a bizarre "except[ion]" and outlier.[72] To many Americans, Webster seemed like a linguistic extremist. He became an occasion for considerable numbers of Americans who disagreed with him to articulate other visions of the English language and the United States. The language controversies that Webster elicited and stoked underline the significant interest among the postrevolutionary generations in preserving the value of existing cultural resources and authorities, even as they also sought to define a coherent American identity.

Defining America against Noah Webster

Like Franklin, Chambers, Mackintosh, and the other linguistic experimentalists of his day, Noah Webster was aware of the logistical challenges of synchronizing speech practices across the Atlantic Ocean. "It is very difficult to convey sounds on paper," he confessed to Benjamin Franklin. "In many parts of America, people at present attempt to copy the English phrases and pronunciation," Webster noted, but in his view they were always fighting an uphill battle to catch up with the inevitable shifts and changes in British English: communication between the continents was simply too slow for Americans to keep up. "How shall we know when we are writing or speaking, whether Englishmen are acquainted with this or that particular word, which we wish to use?" he asked rhetorically in 1817. "Shall we send across the Atlantic to ascertain? And to whom shall we send?" Unlike Mackintosh et al., however, Webster did not conceive a new kind of alphabet or pitch pipe to improve the transatlantic transmission of linguistic norms. Instead, he abandoned the very idea of transnational linguistic norms: Britain, he argued, was "at too great a distance to be our model, and to instruct us in the principles of our own tongue."[73]

In fact, Webster was glad for the distance, since he believed that sharing a language with Britain was not only impractical but also detrimental to the United States. "Customs, habits, and *language*, as well as government should be national," he wrote in 1789. "America should have her *own* distinct from all the world. Such is the policy of other nations, and such must be *our* policy." He touted numerous benefits of linguistic separatism, such as that it would inspire nationalist sentiment at home and project independence abroad. But Webster does not seem to have arrived at his linguistic separatism by weighing costs and benefits. Linguistic independence was part of what he believed a nation *is*. "As a nation," he wrote, "we have a very great interest in opposing the introduction of any plan of uniformity with the British language." He wanted American linguistic identity to correspond strictly to American national identity: be American, speak American. Casting himself as a linguistic republican who would strip away imperial restraints on language the way the (other) Founders were stripping away imperial restraints on civil liberties, Webster anticipated a major theme in the twentieth-century historiography of early American nationalism. He believed, with Christopher Looby, that "nations are not born, but made" and "made, ineluctably, in language." In Webster's view, American obedience to British linguistic authorities was "abridging the nation of its rights." Declaring linguistic independence, he urged, was essential to allowing Americans to be American.[74]

Although he anticipated a twentieth-century consensus, Webster was aware that in his own historical moment his position was atypical. Early in his career, for example, he proposed "the omission of all superfluous or silent letters" such as the "*a* in *bread*," noting that "a capital advantage of this reform . . . would be, that it would make a difference between the English orthography and the American." But he freely admitted that an English/American orthographic schism would not seem like an "advantage" to the general public. "This will startle those who have not attended to the subject," Webster wrote in 1789.[75] If he really believed that Americans only opposed linguistic independence because they had not "attended to the subject" enough, however, then he had seriously misjudged the spirit of the times.

The young Webster could be forgiven for overestimating the appeal of linguistic independence, given that he was in the process of discovering a massive American print market for linguistic Americanness. The conspicuously American spelling book that he published in his midtwenties in 1783 was a staggering success: at a time when almost no books sold more than a few thousand copies, Webster's *American Spelling Book* sold a million copies by 1804, when the total population of the United States was only six million.[76] The "blue-backed speller," as it was sometimes called, virtually defined the possibilities of mass culture and national commercial integration in its era. It went on to sell seventy million copies over the course of the nineteenth century. Thanks to his speller and its crude woodcut frontispiece of its twenty-four-year-old author, Webster's name and person were known to hundreds of thousands of Americans, making him certainly the best-circulated and probably the most famous American author of his day. In an era of limited interregional communication, Webster achieved a truly national reputation.[77]

Noah Webster, the linguistic radical in 1798. Pastel drawing by James Sharples or Ellen Wallace Sharples. The Metropolitan Museum of Art, New York. Bequest of Charles Allen Munn, 1924.

Noah Webster, the lexicographical eminence in 1833. Engraving by E. Parker of a painting by James Herring.

But Webster found few Americans who were as eager as he was to throw out the linguistic baby with the colonial bathwater. He was largely unable to stir up public hostility to British English. But he was extremely successful in stirring up public hostility to himself. Contemporary observers of "that *pestilential* writer, Noah Webster"[78] called his linguistic vision "absurd"[79] and "insane"[80] and said it "ought to be scouted from the land."[81] For twenty-five years, attacking "the eccentric Noah Webster" in print became one of the most reliable ways for Americans to talk about the Englishness that they wished to preserve and the Englishness that they wished to abandon.[82] Webster was a maddeningly ubiquitous "typographical incendiary," as one contemporary put it, busily foisting upon American print culture his own too-stark solutions to the thorny problems of defining American identity.[83]

Although generations of Americans continued to buy Webster's "American" speller in droves after its initial publication in 1783, he spent the next forty-five years trying unsuccessfully to sell them on his other ideas about American linguistic independence—until, at the age of seventy, he broke his long losing streak with the book that won his name a place at the center of English-language lexicography: *An American Dictionary of the English Language* (1828). After that, and especially after his death in 1843, Webster would be recuperated in popular memory into the linguistic founding father he had always believed he was. By the end of the nineteenth century, there was a historiographical consensus that Noah Webster had been to American English roughly what George Washington had been to American government. By and large, this consensus still remains in place: a 1936 biography dubs Webster *Schoolmaster to America*; a 2010 biography frames him as *The Forgotten Founding Father*. A well-known historian praised the more recent biography by agreeing that "Noah Webster forged American nationalism by creating an American language."[84] Because Webster was a strong and articulate cultural nationalist, it can be tempting to use him as a representative voice or exemplar in the story of how "European Americans firmly established their separateness from Britain" or "cast off all things British." In another recent history of the early national period, Webster is presented as evidence that "Americans expected the development of an American English that would be different from the English of the former mother country, a language that would reflect the peculiar character of the American people."[85]

I see Webster differently. While it is clear that *Webster* "expected" (and desired) "the development of a distinct American English" reflecting a distinct American character, the generalizability of his attitude is less certain.[86] However much early national linguistic separatists such as Webster later seemed to personify the Americanizing of America, they did not always seem like nation-builders in their own time. For the novelist Charles Brockden Brown, Webster's "Scheme of an American Language" evoked the linguistic apocalypse that God had once before visited on mankind. ("Behold, the people is one, and they have all one language," God says to himself in Genesis, frowning at the Tower of Babel rising from the desert. "Now nothing will be restrained from them, which they have imagined to do. Go to, let us go down, and there confound their language, that they may not understand one another's speech." And so he does.) "Diversity of language was introduced to weaken, disperse, and annihilate the power, by retarding the knowledge, and by disuniting the efforts of the species," Brown wrote in a Philadelphia magazine in 1800. Yet "this evil . . . we are permitted to repair and diminish in some degree, and surely it is every good man's duty to exert himself for this end."[87] Although elite scholars repeatedly and publicly endorsed Webster—who invested significant resources in developing and publicizing his relationships with numerous college presidents—the anti-Webster discourse raged on in the local newspapers and regional magazines that dominated the early American periodical press. His public fate underscores how deeply ambivalent Americans felt about American language. When Webster's opponents rejected him, they saw themselves as affirming their commitment to sharing a form of personhood with Britain, with each other, and with the past. A Boston magazine contributor wrote bluntly that Webster was trying to "furnish us with a dictionary which we do not want."[88]

Why didn't they want it? The anti-Webster backlash reflected a range of sometimes overlapping concerns rather than a singular problem. At different times and for different antagonists, opposing Webster's linguistic nationalism represented a principled stand for knowledge and correctness, a mask for partisan or socioeconomic conflict, an aesthetic response unconsciously determined by politics, or some combination of these and other factors. Webster was a slippery and inconsistent writer given to definitive statements that he would later contradict just as definitively, so the hostile responses to him were not straightforward responses to a coherent linguistic program outlined by Webster as much as they were a somewhat inconsistent collection of responses to a somewhat inconsistent set of linguistic pronouncements uttered and publicized over many years.[89] Three themes, however, predominated.

One was the threat of a broader literary and cultural isolation. Many Americans took Webster as an opportunity to imagine the nightmarish consequences of a full-fledged linguistic schism in which the American and English languages might become mutually unintelligible. Charles Brockden Brown, for example, joined a chorus of other newspaper and magazine contributors in mocking Webster's claim that "as we are politically independent and distinct from other nations, we should likewise be so in literature and language": those efforts to create "not only a government that shall be American, but likewise an American *language*," Brown wrote, were "absurd and pernicious." "We already possess the admirable lexicon of [Samuel] Johnson," wrote one of the many other pseudonymous critics who blasted Webster's proposal for an "American" dictionary in 1800–1801, so Webster's as-yet-unwritten dictionary would either be "superfluous . . . or else must contain vulgar, provincial words, unauthorized by good writers, and in this case, must surely be the just object of ridicule and censure." John Pickering cited Webster forty-one times in his 1816 takedown of "thirsty reformers and presumptuous sciolists, who would unsettle the whole of our admirable language." Pickering's compendium of Americanisms quickly became a standard reference list of words and usages to avoid, while the dictionary that Webster had proposed in 1800—his *Compendious Dictionary of the English Language* (1806)—languished on booksellers' shelves.[90]

Americans affirming their commitment to English linguistic unity also cited the value of the British literary patrimony, and their anxiety about some future illegibility of canonical British texts for American readers underscores the conceptual weight that the British literary canon carried for postrevolutionary American identity. "If Webster's absurd project were adopted," wrote one anonymous commentator, "we should in a few years be obliged to have recourse to Glossaries to explain the *Spectator*, the exquisite Poetry of [Alexander] Pope and [Erasmus] Darwin, and the elegant Junius." Boston's *Monthly Anthology* wondered what would happen to "the purest writers in our language" if Webster's linguistic separatism were to prevail: "must they all be published with a glossary? and who shall make it for them? The printer would be thought insane, who should print Addison, Swift, or Pope, with such an appendix."[91]

In reality, Webster's isolationist reputation far outstripped the actual radicalism of his dictionaries and speller. His *American Spelling Book* differed little from older British spellers except in the "American" in its title, its aggressively patriotic preface, and the American place-names in its geographic appendix.[92] He advertised on the title page of his *Compendious Dictionary* of 1806 that the volume contained "Five Thousand Words" not found in previous (British) English dictionaries, but few of those words were genuinely novel or uniquely American: most were scientific terms ("Molybdenous"), adjectival forms of names and places ("Pennsylvanian," "Newtonian"), or inflectional derivatives of existing words ("jurisprudential"). Still, Webster's lexicography always seemed more iconoclastic and separatist than it was, for the simple reason that he promoted it that way. Advertising his *Compendious Dictionary* in 1806, he insisted that "*New* ideas require *new* terms" and that "there *is not a page of any English Dictionary which does not require emendation*."[93] The actual blandness of Webster's lexicography mattered less to his reception than the sweeping, separatist terms in which he framed it.

A second perceived danger of Webster's lexicography was its regionalism. For the same reasons that Webster's American linguistic permissiveness seemed to threaten the Anglo-American linguistic union, his regional permissiveness seemed to threaten the united language of the United States. Early in his career, Webster had rhapsodized about instituting a common "*federal language*."[94] But he largely abandoned those dreams of a federal American English by the end of the 1790s and wrote instead about bridging the gaps among linguistically distinct American communities. By the first decade of the nineteenth century, Webster was unapologetically including regional forms and meanings in his *Compendious Dictionary*. "How are we to carry on mutual intercourse without understanding each other's terms?" Webster asked rhetorically, in a newspaper essay defending his principles of inclusion. Yet his protestations about the innocent practicalities of making oneself understood in distant regions elided his contemporaries' fears that he was fueling the centrifugal forces that threatened the United States' coherence. He made visible linguistic fault lines within the diverse and fragmentary new nation.[95]

In this way, Webster was caught between competing cultural fantasies—at once too American and not American enough. His affirmation of distinctively American words and meanings symbolized an excessive and dogmatic American patriotism, portending unwanted differences between Americans and Britons. Yet his recognition of regionalisms such as "slump" (New England), "deputize" (Connecticut), and "salts" (South Carolina) evoked a countervailing dystopian fantasy about the de-Anglicized people of the United States becoming a plurality of separate peoples. "Is it not madness to endeavour to establish, not only an *American* or *United States' dialect*, the eldest and proudest daughter of old mother *English*, but a Connecticut, a Massachusetts, a Vermont, and a Pennsylvania dialect?" asked a contributor to an Albany newspaper in 1806, disturbed to find regionalisms in Webster's recently published *Compendious Dictionary*. Invoking an existing assumption that pre-Columbian America was a place of extreme linguistic diversity, the writer warned that "if all the corruptions, perversions, barbarisms, provincial words and phrases which exist in the United States, are to be recognized by lexicographers, and treated as legitimate words of the language of the nation, we shall soon have dialects equal in number to those of that long catalogue which the names of Mohawk, Seneca, Chipeway and Choctaw, contribute to compose."[96] At least for that writer, Webster presaged a tribalized North America in which the (white) inhabitants of Buffalo and Boston would be as unable to understand each other as the Iroquoian and Algonquian peoples who once lived in those respective places. "Instead of defending local usages," editorialized the *New-York Evening Post*, Webster should be working to "establish a standard which should be free from the provincialisms of New England, N. York or Virginia."[97]

Many of his opponents associated him with the threat of interregional linguistic ridicule: "*Crock* is indeed common enough in this section of the country," wrote a Boston critic of Webster's 1806 dictionary, "but it is not an English word, and our Southern brethren ridicule us for using it."[98] Webster's opponents might have valued British linguistic authorities not so much because they were British as because they were recognized authorities who could adjudicate the mutual ridicule and alienation that accompanied regional linguistic variation in a diverse postcolonial America. Writing in a Washington, D.C., newspaper in the wake of the 1820 Missouri Compromise that narrowly averted a civil war, "A Citizen of Ohio" noted a "breach between the pronunciation of the North and the South" and worried about its "political" consequences: a northerner in the south, he wrote, "never speaks a sentence without exciting a smile among the better informed, and a rude and boisterous laugh among the less refined." Why did they laugh at the northerner? The Ohioan gave a straightforward reason: "because Noah

Webster has spoiled his pronunciation."[99] Perhaps pinning the blame for North-South conflict on Noah Webster was more appealing than confronting the conflict's social and political dimensions. It was also an issue that political adversaries could agree on. To some extent, therefore, rejecting Webster was a way of replacing one set of "ugly feelings" with another: instead of an interregional linguistic disgust that might undermine the delicate process of creating a shared national imaginary, a joint anti-Webster linguistic antipathy became a transregional common cause.[100]

Finally, concerns about Webster also dramatized a sociopolitical conflict about the admission of nonelites into the spaces of cultural authority. Arbitrary linguistic differences, such as Webster's devoicing of "wharves" to "wharfs," have real socioeconomic implications.[101] Webster typified the noninstitutional middle-class subject without a social pedigree who now had access to mass print. At times, therefore, the hostility to him foregrounds the contrast between the idealized egalitarianism of democratic culture and the scarier prospect of actually extending social authority to hitherto disenfranchised populations. "If every one has a right to accent as he pleases," wrote George Washington's former aide-de-camp, David Humphreys, in 1804, "and use whatever words are current among his associates, unknown to good authors, as Noah Webster and other conceited innovators assert, then language will soon degenerate into a Babylonish dialect, and be fit only for the lowest of the populace." The critique associates the extension of a "right" to "every one" with social breakdown and points to the anarchical dark side of democracy. Meanwhile, an essay appearing in newspapers in three states in 1800 sarcastically offered to put Webster in touch with "my footman (a true born American)" to "sanction the word *walkable*." To the extent that Webster wanted an American linguistic divergence, therefore, critics feared that he was encouraging a situation in which authority would devolve to the servant class.[102]

Still, it would be reductive to understand the response to Webster mainly as a sociopolitical program driven by elites jealously guarding their cultural capital, or by aspirational nonelites who hoped to rise within the existing sociolinguistic hierarchy and feared its modification or collapse.[103] Whatever coded socioeconomic battles may have been being fought out in these complaints about "wharves" and "slump," social status was not the only issue (or even the primary issue) that his antagonists understood themselves to be fighting about. Very often, they rested their opposition to Webster on the conviction that his language was wrong in a way transcending logical explanation: wrong because it was *wrong*. His name became proverbial in expressions of linguistic wrongness very early in his career. A magazine contributor jeered that under Webster's guidance the English words "her's, and your's" would "be changed into *hern*, and *yourn*, fetch, and catch, into *fotch* and *cotch*; and roof and hoof into *ruff* and *huff*," and a New Hampshire newspaper recalled "a similar attempt at innovation many years since, in which the word '*usage*' was spelt '*yowzitch*.'!"[104] Two other newspapers printed a fake letter to the editor from "a stranger in this city" who was disturbed when he heard a man calling in the middle of the night something about its being "Ba-ash'd won a cloak un Gloady more nan." The traveler's landlord reassured him the next morning that it was just "a teacher of *Webster's American Language*" rehearsing his lessons—but the joke is that it was actually a German-speaking night watchman calling "Past one o'clock, and a cloudy morning" with a thick foreign accent.[105] These objections relied on sarcasm, exclamation points, italics, and exaggeratedly nonstandard language much more than they relied on propositional claims about what makes these so-called errors erroneous. When Webster announced his plans in 1807 for what would become the *American Dictionary* two decades later, several newspapers parodied his polite circular by rewriting it in a phonetic orthography unlike anything Webster was proposing. No accompanying commentary was needed to make the point that Webster's dictionary was a dictionary of an alien tongue:

> i hav devoted the gratest part of mi life to the study of langwij so that now tho i sa it miself, fu if anny kan kompare with me in filolojekal nollij. az the rezult ov ol mi talents & labors i intend to publish a nu dikshunerry of the kolumbian langwij. "i hav evver thort that as sitizens ov an independant naishun we ort not to reli surville on the inglish naishun for books to explane the langwij spokn in our kuntry."

For the implied readers of these essays and parodies, "fotch," "yowzitch," "Gloady," and "dikshunerry" were wrong for reasons that seemed too obvious to explain. "The English have a right to their language," wrote an anonymous Philadelphia newspaper contributor, "and we have no right to *murder* it, any more than they have a right to dictate laws or a form of government for us, or to murder our citizens."[106] The analogy between the Americanization of language and the death of American people reflects the perceived threat that Webster's language would destroy a form of personhood. It construes the English language not as a form of social or political capital but as a repository of the Anglo-American self.

"Honoring" America

Webster largely disappeared from public view for fifteen years after 1810, living off the royalties of his spelling book, and composing the *American Dictionary* in a room that he had soundproofed by pouring sand into the walls.[107] When he emerged in 1826 to announce that his dictionary was nearing completion, his place in the American imagination had shifted dramatically. The *New-York Evening Post* published a note recanting several anti-Webster articles that it had published twenty years earlier. The new *American Dictionary* belonged not to the revolutionary and early national world that Webster had irritated but to a different one. By the 1830s and 1840s, "Americanisms" no longer represented a source of widespread concern. Even John Pickering, who had tried to rid the world of them in 1816, changed his mind by 1830.[108]

Although Webster had often seemed bizarre and distasteful in the early national period, now in the second quarter of the nineteenth century he seemed like a learned patriot—partly because he himself had changed but mostly because the linguistic commitments that he had violated declined in significance with the ascendancy of racial and national accounts of identity. Meanwhile, Webster's own antitransatlanticism mellowed. He sent a copy of the *American Dictionary* to Queen Victoria with a respectful note in 1841.[109] Within a few decades, Webster's name was the watchword of American lexicography, and by the twentieth century historians were celebrating Webster as a "founding father": father of the American language, American culture, American nationalism, or simply America.[110] With the specific cultural politics of linguistic identity that had marginalized him long superseded, Webster came to be embraced for ostensibly having helped early national Americans feel American—even though early national Americans had never embraced the kind of linguistic nationalism that he had advocated. Viewing Webster's linguistic nationalism as representative of his era became a way of erasing the deep ambivalence that the revolutionary and postrevolutionary generations felt about American independence. In truth, revolutionary Americans were enthusiastic about overturning their political environment, but far less enthusiastic about the prospect of overturning their cultural or mental environment. The English language seemed to them like one of the most promising ways to preserve a connection to values, thoughts, and feelings that they did not want to lose.

Two centuries later, most of the dialects of English spoken in the United States do indeed register as distinctively American to both British and American speakers, so Webster was in a sense correct when he predicted in 1789 "a future separation of the American tongue from the English." The present-day differences between British and American English dialects are readily noticeable in oral speech, but much more subtle in written English; differences between British and American spelling affect only a few hundred words in all.[111] Still, since the early twentieth century, it has been conventional to attribute those few hundred spelling differences to Webster. "American spelling," wrote language historian John W. Clark in 1965, "is the result almost entirely of the deliberate, systematic, and . . . sensible efforts of a learned and devoted philologist and lexicographer, Noah Webster." That assessment has come down to the present day as a truism: "we owe to him most of the spellings labeled 'chiefly American' in modern dictionaries," writes one recent historian of American English: "he kicked the *u* out of *colour*, reversed the *r* and *e* in *theatre*, and traded the baffling *-ugh-* for an *f* in *draught*." Writes another: "Webster wanted to emancipate the United States from English cultural models. Hence his new dictionary, with its attempt to create a new spelling system for the United States; to spell 'plough' as plow, or to omit the 'u' from colour, was to make a cultural declaration of independence from Old World obscurantism."[112]

Yet the evidence that Webster is responsible for these spelling differences ranges from the doubtful to the preposterous.[113] While it is true that Noah Webster endorsed a number of spelling changes that now read as "chiefly American," historical trends in those spellings are very difficult to square with the dates of Webster's speller (1783), dictionary (1828), and death (1843). A temporal correlation between Webster's "deliberate, systematic, and . . . sensible efforts" and these national orthographic differences would not, of course, establish that Webster actually *caused* those differences. But as the following examples demonstrate, it is not clear that such correlations exist in the first place:[114]

musick/music, publick/public "It is thanks to Webster that users of English no longer write *public* with a *k* at the end," one historian wrote recently, but in fact this transition began in the 1740s. English dictionaries were already recommending the *k*-less *music* by the 1770s, when Webster was still in college.[115]

colour/color, honour/honor, labour/labor "He can also be credited with the well-known American preference for *color, odor, humor* and *labor*." But this divergence began before Webster was born and widened at a constant rate from 1750 to 1850. The Declaration of Independence, for example, reads *honor*, and Webster actually opposed the *color/honor/labor* spellings at first, calling them "absurdities" in 1783.[116] He later supported them, but the trend toward *honor*, etc., proceeded at a constant rate before, during, and after Webster's lifetime.

organise/organize, recognise/recognize, civilise/civilize "Webster for etymological reasons taught us to write *civilize* and the like, rather than *civilise*."[117] But in reality, it was the British spelling that changed, from *civilize* to *civilise*. The standard spellings on both sides of the Atlantic were *organize* and *recognize* until the 1790s. Over the next fifty years, British writers switched to the *-ise* forms; Americans did not follow suit. Webster does not appear to have played a role in Americans' preservation of the old spellings.

draught/draft Both spellings were common on both sides of the Atlantic until the American Civil War, with *draft* being used about half the time in both nations. In 1863, the U.S. Congress created a national conscription system and spelled the word *draft* in the text of the bill, permanently tipping the scales in the United States. Both spellings remained common in Britain.

centre / center During the eighteenth century, *center* was the dominant spelling on both sides of the Atlantic. Both communities adopted *centre* as the standard form by the early nineteenth century. In the second half of the nineteenth century, *center* made a comeback in the United States.

plough / plow This is the most plausible candidate for having been meaningfully influenced by Webster. Both spellings were widely used in both locations in the eighteenth century, but the spelling standardized as *plough* on both sides of the Atlantic by the 1810s. Usage diverged shortly after the publication of Webster's *Dictionary*, and *plow* was the standard form in the United States by the 1860s.

A generous reading of Webster's role in these shifts would be to say that his dictionaries were increasingly influential after his death. But if something happened to American attitudes about distinctively American spellings in the 1850s, it is awkward to attribute it to Webster, since his dictionary was two decades old by then, and he himself was dead. It is probably more accurate to say that Webster got out ahead of, or anticipated, changes that were happening anyway: as early as 1806, he was recommending the forms that would eventually be known as "chiefly American": *honor*, *center*, *defense*, *recognize*, *plow*, and *draft*. On the other hand, Webster also recommended a host of other spelling reforms in his 1806 and 1828 dictionaries that did not catch on at all: *envelop* (envelope), *wimmen* (women), *thum* (thumb), *fantom* (phantom), *ieland* (island). One of several problems with crediting *honor*, *center*, etc., to the "deliberate, systematic, and . . . sensible efforts of a learned and devoted philologist and lexicographer, Noah Webster," therefore, is that it requires ignoring the spellings that never caught on—a form of selective attention, or the logical fallacy known as cherry-picking.

The two Webster myths are interrelated: the myth that Webster represented the spirit of his age and the myth that Webster introduced the handful of spelling differences that most clearly differentiate

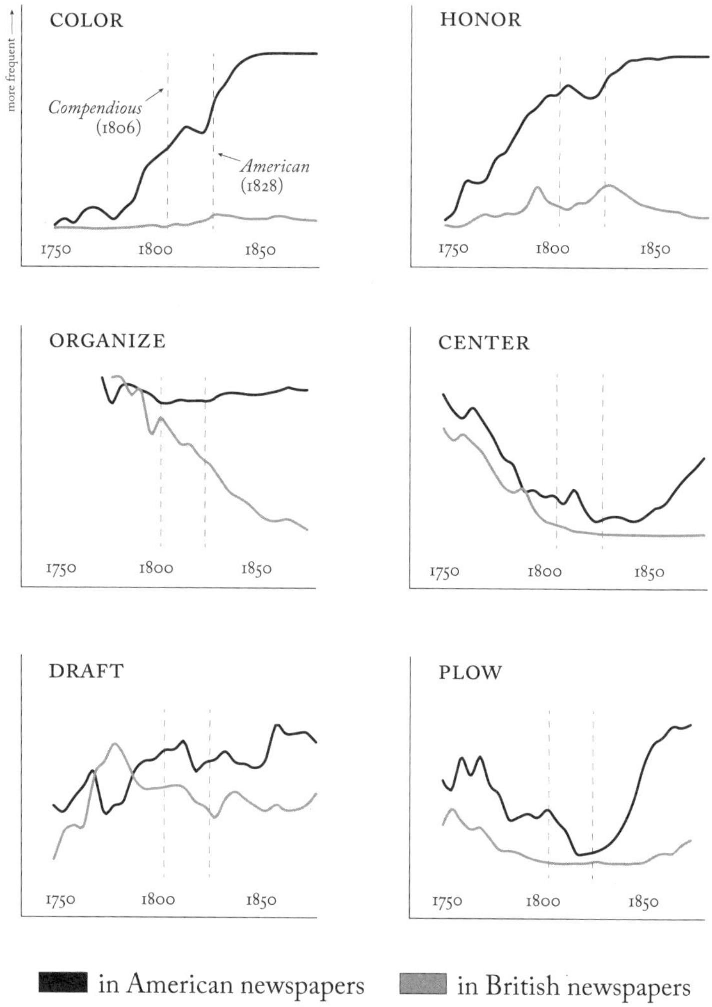

Relative frequencies of "American spellings" of six words in British and American newspapers, 1750–1885. Dashed lines indicate the publication of Noah Webster's *Compendious Dictionary* (1806) and *American Dictionary* (1828).

American from British written English. It is not uncommon to set up semilegendary figures as founders and lawgivers to languages as well as nations. There is a transcultural fantasy of long standing that words are created through the deliberate intervention of authorial figures, like so many poems or novels. Shakespeare is often said to have "invented" or "coined" now-common words including *amazing*, *enchanted*, *downstairs*, and *bump*. This is a much more exciting story than the truth, which is that Shakespeare is merely the author of the oldest known written texts using those words. The list of possible Shakespeare coinages is always shrinking, as older usages turn up in obscure documents.[118] Whatever this need reflects, it is in the case of Webster a need that existed in the later nineteenth century, after Webster's death, and was projected back onto him retrospectively. Our Noah Webster—the founding father of American English who unleashed American identity by emancipating *honor* from its oppressive *u*—has more to tell us about the search for national identity in the postbellum United States than he does about the ambivalent and transnational identities of the United States in which Noah Webster actually lived.

CHAPTER THREE

The Abecedarian Clock

Recording Speech before Recorded Sound

The Sound Like a Long-Necked Juglet

From 1799 to 1804, John Gilchrist was in charge of teaching Urdu to new employees of the East India Company when they arrived from Britain in Calcutta.[1] Happily, many of his students arrived in India having already studied the Urdu dictionary and grammar that Gilchrist had spent the previous decades compiling. Unhappily, their pronunciation was terrible—indeed, incomprehensible. This was partly a matter of students not doing the reading: many of them had skipped the preface in which Gilchrist explains how he has transliterated Urdu sounds into Latin letters. He figured that the students were pretty annoyed when they arrived in Calcutta and found that they had to learn Urdu pronunciation all over again: "Why, the authour must have been mad," he imagined a student muttering to himself, "when he expected that I would read *qŏran* قرآن otherwise than *kworan*." Still, Gilchrist scolded, the learner who neglected the phonetic key "must blame himself entirely, if he be not immediately understood by the natives of India, so well as he could wish."[2]

In fact, however, Gilchrist was aware that his British students' garbled interpretation of the Urdu phonemes in his printed works was not "entirely" their fault. Like Duncan Mackintosh, Noah Webster, and the other alphabetic innovators discussed in chapter 2, Gilchrist encountered difficulties in representing the necessary phonetic information in the Latin alphabet that his audience understood. His task was considerably more daunting than Mackintosh's, however, as he was trying to introduce his readers to phonemes they had never heard before. English has twenty-four consonant sounds; Urdu has eighteen of those consonants, plus fifteen other ones. Even the students who diligently studied his pronunciation key, therefore, might well have scratched their heads as Gilchrist struggled to explain the non-English consonants. To produce the sounds transcribed as *kh* and *gh*, for example, Gilchrist told the student to make "an effort to hawk up tough phlegm from the throat" for *kh*, and "an effort to gargle the throat" for *gh*. If he made the sound of "the rattle in the throat of a dying man," he was doing it wrong. "The true articulation of kh, and gh," Gilchrist concludes helplessly, "depends on ruffling the throat in a particular manner."[3] As for the *q* of *qŏran*, it was to be "produced by clinking the root of the tongue against the throat, so as to cause a sort of nausea. The same sound will be recognised when pouring water in a particular manner from a long necked guglet."[4]

A long-necked guglet. Pour water out of this in a particular manner to hear the correct sound of *qŏran*. Illustration from *The Art Journal Illustrated Catalogue* (London, 1851).

Go ahead and try it if you like, and then try attaching that glug-glug *q*- to the rest of the word that we know as *Qu'ran*. Confident that you've got it? In the end, Gilchrist backs himself up against the opacity of advising "a particular manner" of throat-ruffling and "a particular manner" of water-pouring. Tacitly acknowledging the futility of his nauseous instructions, Gilchrist assured his reader that "the letters which belong to the oriental alphabets, and that we have not in our's, may of course be readily acquired *viva voce* in this country." He recommended nagging your Indian domestic servants to talk to you constantly and to repeat your every Urdu utterance back to you in a native speaker's accent.[5] The Urdu-English phrase books that would make Gilchrist rich included commands that the learner could use to this end, such as:

Show me how you pronounce this letter.	Mŏŏj,he buta,o tŏŏm is *h*urf ko kyoonkur tuluffŏŏż kurte ho.
Tell me a short history, the news of the day, do any thing but sit silent.	Ek mŏŏkhtu*s*ur qi*ſſ*u, ya aj kul kee khubur kuho, ya uor kŏŏch,h pur chŏŏp mut buet̆,ho.
Unless we speak much together, how can I learn to speak?	Ugur hum bahum khoob gŏŏf-togoo nu kureň, to mueň bol chal kyoonkur ſeek,hoonga.
Your business is to teach me the real pronunciation and practice of the language.	Tŏŏm,hara yuhee kam hue ki *ſ*u*h*ee*h* tuluffŏŏż uor zuban ka isti,*a*mal mŏŏj,he ſik,ha,o.

Grammar can be explained in declarative sentences; a lexicon can be recorded in a dictionary; idioms can be listed in a phrase book; but pronunciation can't be written down without prior agreement about the sounds to which a set of visible marks refer. "Pronunciation being the soul of a living or colloquial language, too great attention cannot be paid to acquire this, as accurately as possible," Gilchrist advised.[6] But the only satisfactory way he could think of to learn Urdu pronunciation was to go to India and pay Urdu speakers to converse to you.

This is how Gilchrist came up with the idea for a machine that he called an abecedareloge or "abecedarian clock": a sort of souped-up cuckoo clock capable of mechanically producing any phoneme. "Our coarsest clocks now distinctly articulate *kookoo*," he pointed out; "why not construct similar machines to indicate an alphabet in all its changes, for ever, with as much certainty as they at present tell each passing hour[?]" Rather than present a bird figurine and call *cuckoo* on the hour, the abecedareloge would "simultaneously discover [i.e., reveal] the figure and sound of any letter yet known in the world, more accurately than a common wooden clock already strikes two of them, viz.

oo and k, in *kukoo*." This imagined machine would be a much more reliable point of phonetic reference than the Latin alphabet; it would be a phonetic standard in the form of an enduring physical object that could be consulted as needed, like the platinum bar deposited in the National Archives of France in 1799 as the permanent and irreducible definition of the length of a meter.[7]

I imagine an abecedareloge, perhaps tuned by Gilchrist himself, installed in a lecture hall in the East India Company's London headquarters, faithfully gargling aloud the Urdu sound that Gilchrist called *gh*, or the nauseating one that he called *q*, as rows of aspiring company men listen attentively. Gilchrist worked on his abecedarian clock idea, off and on, for more than forty years, and the scope of the project grew over time. Since he was envisioning a multimedia device that would "simultaneously discover the figure and sound of any letter," Gilchrist had to decide what "figure" to display with each "sound." Finding all existing alphabets, including the English one, "replete with absurdity, intricacy, and contradiction," Gilchrist resolved in the 1810s to subject the Latin alphabet to "a radical reform in its first elements."[8]

By this time, almost a half century had passed since Benjamin Franklin had experimented with modifying the Latin alphabet to improve the phonetic reliability of English orthography, hoping to address the problem that "from the want of public examples of pronunciation in his own country, it was often difficult to learn the proper sound of certain words." In one sense, Gilchrist's abecedareloge tackled the same problem as Franklin's alphabet and the other alphabetic schemes discussed in chapter 2: "I . . . can well conceive the use which might be made of it," Gilchrist wrote of the abecedareloge in 1798, "to perpetuate among any nation with certainty, the precise power of every letter in this or that alphabet, that they might choose to adopt," such as in "America in respect to the English [language]." But Gilchrist's project was fundamentally different from those of Franklin, Mackintosh, Chambers, Webster, and the other alphabetic innovators discussed in the previous chapter, because Gilchrist was not just trying to capture the sounds of English: he had in mind the sounds of "any letter yet known in the world." From an initial slate of thirty-nine characters representing what he believed to be the thirty-nine phonemes of English, therefore,

Gilchrist's phonetic alphabet grew over the course of a decade to one hundred characters "***komprehendeŋ evure leteral sond utturabl artekyoletle bue te hyoman vœs.***" By 1825, Gilchrist had become sufficiently wealthy (or sufficiently unhinged, or both) to commission several hundred pounds of custom-manufactured type and begin issuing experimental publications in his new "***yoneversul karektur.***"[9] By this time, he had come to believe that a worldwide fleet of abecedarian clocks could revolutionize education and facilitate universal literacy, "to the great annoyance of terrestrial Despots" who depended on keeping their subjects in a state of ignorance.[10]

"comprehending every literal sound utterable articulately by the human voice"

The challenge of conveying Urdu pronunciation at a distance thus sent Gilchrist down two interrelated technological paths: one mechanical-acoustic path toward the audible reproduction of all linguistic sounds, and one alphabetic-typographic path toward the graphic representation of all linguistic sounds. For Gilchrist, these were two branches of a single project—the transmission of linguistic sounds over distance—that intersected in the material form of the abecedarian clock. But neither his ***karektur*** nor his ***klok*** ever received the attention Gilchrist thought they deserved—partly because Gilchrist suffered a nervous breakdown shortly after taking delivery of his ***yoneversul*** type and had to set aside his four-decade-long quest to invent a speech machine and a universal phonetic alphabet to go with it. His project was quickly forgotten: I have been unable to locate any mention of Gilchrist's abecedarian clock since his death in 1841, nor have I found more than a single reference to ***gulkrusts yoneversul karektur*** in the many historiographies that it intersects, including literature, typography, print, linguistics, phonetics, Indology, and empire.

Gilchrist did not live to witness the international adoption of a universal alphabet, or the creation of a machine that could reproduce all possible linguistic sounds. But those events did happen, within a few years of each other, roughly four decades after Gilchrist's death, in the form of Thomas Edison's phonograph (1877) and the International Phonetic Alphabet (1888). The phonograph and the IPA no longer seem to have much to do with each other, partly because the phonograph came to be used more for musical than for phonetic purposes. But as media historians Lisa Gitelman and Matthew Rubery have shown, phonographs' earliest audiences in the 1870s and 1880s did not expect the machine to create a revolution in music, so much as they expected it to create a revolution in speech and in texts.[11] The first decade of plans for monetizing the phonograph overwhelmingly involved selling phonographs to businesses to take dictation, and nineteenth-century audiences wondered whether reading literature would become obsolete once you could listen in your parlor to your favorite author reading the book aloud. The conceptual history of sound technology as a means of reproducing speech, rather than of reproducing sound per se, is reflected in our calling electroacoustic transducers "loudspeakers," not "loudsounders," even now.[12] The origins of sound recording turn out to be more verbal, textual, and literary than we have chosen to remember.[13]

If we look back still further, it becomes clear that the conceptual prehistory of sound recording is also more phonetic than we have remembered. "Phonography" was the name of several phonetic alphabets before it was the name of a technology for engraving sound waves on a rotating surface. The "phonography" that consists of a machine and the "phonography" that consists of an alphabet share the same name because of the significant extent to which they were two efforts to solve the same problems. In the mid and later nineteenth century, the chief value of both kinds of phonography seemed to be their capacity to record utterances word for word, such as in the contexts of legislative debates, courtroom testimony, and public speeches. But Gilchrist represents an earlier, lesser-known, and different set of phonographic fantasies: his generation fantasized less about capturing words than about capturing pronunciations. Numerous others who envisioned mechanical sound-reproducing devices assumed that their purpose would be to regularize pronunciation. A young scientist who was working on a speech machine in the later years of Gilchrist's life doubted that such machines could ever be built "with voices so loud and sonorous as to command an army or instruct a crowd"; rather, he predicted in 1837, "the most important uses to which they will perhaps in future times be applied, will be to fix and perpetuate the pronunciation of different languages."[14] This expectation deserves more attention than it has received, especially as it was not entirely wrong: the present-day concepts of "BBC English" and American "Network Standard" English illustrate

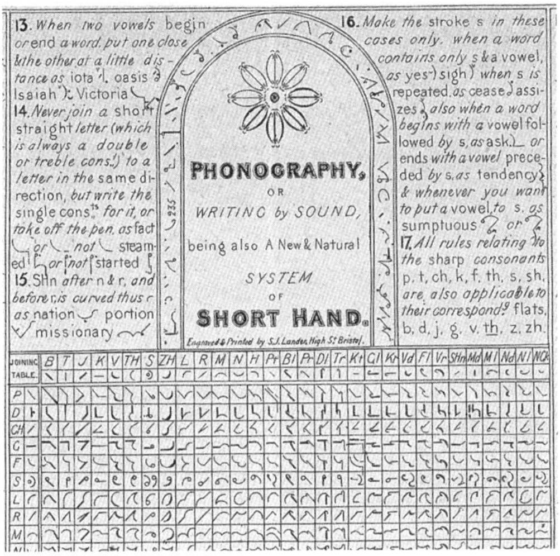

Phonography in 1840. Detail from a broadside by Isaac Pitman, *Phonography, or Writing by Sound* (Bath, 1840). Beinecke Rare Book and Manuscript Library, Yale University.

Phonography in 1889. From *The Century Dictionary* (New York, 1889).

how one function of long-distance sound reproduction technologies (though perhaps not "the most important" one) has been to "fix and perpetuate" certain pronunciation norms, with corresponding social consequences within and across national contexts.[15]

Both the ***karektur*** and the ***klok***, therefore, overlap the history of identity in a globalized world and illustrate how linguistic thinking provided alternatives to national and racial paradigms of belonging for people whose lives took them beyond those paradigms—not just within the English-speaking world, as discussed in chapter 2, but across vaster and more diverse geographies and peoples. Gilchrist was a true citizen of the British imperial world; he lived in the Northern, Southern, Eastern, and Western hemispheres—tamed a hummingbird in Grenada—grew a beard in India—owned land in Australia. Like Nicholas Dufief and Duncan Mackintosh, Gilchrist lived an in-between life. He mastered and manipulated his national, geographic, and socioeconomic in-betweenness by mastering and manipulating language. Gilchrist's abecedarian clock—like Dufief's "natural" pedagogy, Mackintosh's "lit′tle patriot′ic book′," and Webster's "American English"—was a carefully pronounced phonetic response to imperial dislocation. It is a reminder that linguistic failures are records of experiences that lie outside of what is ordinarily representable—and it is equally a reminder that treating the materiality of texts can help us recover the alien and unrepresentable. John Gilchrist's life did not fit within national or racial boundaries. It is not a coincidence, I think, that he left a body of text that does not fit within the letters of the alphabet, and plans for a talking machine that wasn't designed to speak a single word.

John Gilchrist, Eurpasian

John Gilchrist arrived in British India in 1782 in his early twenties and landed a job as an assistant surgeon to the East India Company's private army of 200,000 Indian soldiers. The conventional British wisdom about language in India at this time was that there were four main languages in the region: Arabic, introduced by conquest, and of religious significance to Muslims; Persian (Farsi), introduced by conquest and the region's chief administrative language; Bengali, used in the east; and Sanskrit, the dead language of sacred texts. Gilchrist began learning Persian, the language in which the EIC did business, as well as Sanskrit. But as he traveled with the army in northern India, he found that neither his patients nor the locals spoke those languages. They spoke something else. Asking around, he was told by company officials and European scholars that the vernacular he was referring to was called Moors, that it was "a jargon, without rules or grammar of any kind, and that many much more clever fellows than [he], had vainly attempted to make any progress in such studies." Nevertheless, Gilchrist applied for and received a paid leave in 1785 to study this "Moors." He went full immersion: shunning the European presence in Bombay, Gilchrist moved a thousand miles inland to the city of Fyzabad, near Nepal and the foothills of the Himalayas.[16] He "changed his European appearance as much as he possibly could," grew a long beard, dressed in native clothes, engaged in "unrestricted intercourse with all classes of the inhabitants," and paid to have himself "surrounded by several learned *Hindoostanees*" who would teach him their vernacular language. After satisfying himself that no dictionary of this vernacular existed,

Gilchrist decided that he would have to make one and set about compiling a wordlist by systematically uttering every possible combination of linguistic sounds he could think of, and asking his native assistants whether he was saying words: *abab*—is that a word? *abach*—is that a word? *abad? abaf?* The dictionary took more than a decade to finish—"a lexicographical slavery of fifteen long years," as he later said, rather melodramatically—and by the time it was done he had become a much better student of languages than he had ever been a student of medicine.[17] He never worked as a surgeon again.

Gilchrist had come to believe that the disregarded patois called Moors was neither a patois nor "Moorish" at all but was actually "the grand living popular speech of all Hindoostan"—a robust vernacular language indigenous to the subcontinent and understood more widely than any of the other Oriental languages that Europeans were learning. Gilchrist called the language Hindoostanee and spent the next forty years promoting its relevance to British audiences, trying to "charm the hobgoblin jargonick notions we have imbibed [about it], out of our heads for ever." He set in motion the East India Company's eventual divestment from Persian and its reprioritization in the 1810s of "Hindustani" (as everyone but Gilchrist spelled it) as the chief language of Indian colonial administration, before it switched to English in 1837. Later in the nineteenth century, the British Raj would encourage Muslims to write Hindustani in an Arabic script and Hindus to write it in a Devanagari script. (Gilchrist learned and taught both scripts.) The former was called Urdu; the latter, Hindi. This is how there came to be two "languages" in the Indian subcontinent that are mutually intelligible when spoken but mutually illegible when written.[18]

The long career of John Gilchrist comprises many strange and fascinating episodes that deserve more attention than I can give them in these pages. His significant role in defining and shaping Hindustani language and literature has been widely recognized by historians of British colonialism, Indian nationalism, and Muslim-Hindu relations in South Asia. To a lesser extent, Gilchrist is also known to historians of South Asian and colonial linguistics for the romanization scheme that he invented and promoted—a method for transcribing Hindustani into Latin letters that was widely adopted in the nineteenth century. But the second act of his linguistic career, the part involving the abecedarian clock and its hundred-character universal alphabet, is unexplored and unknown.[19]

The Hindustani dictionary and grammar occupied Gilchrist's attention through most of the 1780s and 1790s, although he also found time to father a number of biracial children. In 1798, with the dictionary and its related materials complete, Gilchrist had the good fortune to impress the incoming Crown-appointed governor-general of India with his linguistic zeal. When that administrator, Richard Wellesley, presently decided to open a language academy in Calcutta—aiming to improve the Indian-language skills of the young British men who arrived from Europe eager to get rich in the East India Company's employ—he hired Gilchrist as its first professor. This institution, the College of Fort William, became the focus of a decades-long power struggle between the Crown, which had wide-ranging strategic interests in superior communication with native peoples, and the company, which did not at all appreciate a new requirement imposed by Governor-General Wellesley that all new EIC employees demonstrate proficiency in Persian and one other vernacular language before commencing work.[20]

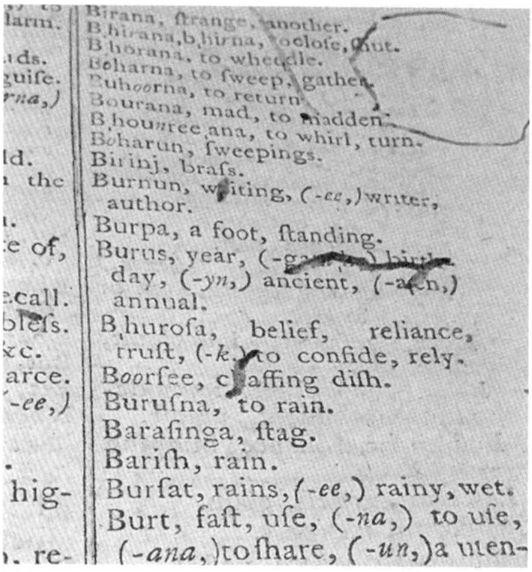
Birana, ſtrange, another.
B,hirana, b,hirna, to cloſe, ſhut.
B,horana, to wheedle.
Boharna, to ſweep, gather.
Buhoorna, to return.
Bourana, mad, to madden.
B,hounree ana, to whirl, turn.
Boharun, ſweepings.
Birinj, braſs.
Burnun, writing, (-ee,) writer, author.
Burpa, a foot, ſtanding.
Burus, year, (-g[illegible]) birth-day, (-yn,) ancient, (-a[illegible]n,) annual.
B,hurofa, belief, reliance, truſt, (-k.) to confide, rely.
Boorſee, chaffing diſh.
Buruſna, to rain.
Baraſinga, ſtag.
Bariſh, rain.
Burſat, rains, (-ee,) rainy, wet.
Burt, faſt, uſe, (-na,) to uſe, (-ana,) to ſhare, (-un,) a uten-

From a copy of the Hindustani-to-English volume of Gilchrist's *Dictionary, English and Hindoostanee* (1786–98) at the Library of Congress. This copy belonged to the library at the College of Fort William and suffered extensive worm damage.

The college's politicized conflicts suited Gilchrist just fine. A paranoid streak ran deeply through his personality, and like Nicholas Dufief and Noah Webster, he thrived on the perception that his enemies were conspiring against him. It was a prolific time for him. He was a highly effective and well-liked teacher. In addition, Gilchrist took charge of the college's press, partly because he needed Hindustani texts to assign to the students in his Hindustani classes. He recruited a cohort of Indian writers and poets to collect, transcribe, and edit Hindustani literary manuscripts, and began publishing at a furious rate. Between 1801 and

1804, the "learned natives in the Hindoostanee Department, in the College of Fort William, under the direction and superintendence of John Gilchrist," published at least fifty books in Hindustani. During the same period of time, Gilchrist himself also authored fifteen book-length pedagogical texts for English-speaking learners of Asian languages.[21] These are the years in which Gilchrist undertook the editorial and authorial work for which he is known to history, institutionalizing and shaping Hindustani literature and language. In 1804, however, he requested a leave of absence to return to Britain—and when his request was denied, he promptly caused a diplomatic incident, then resigned his professorship, packed up his Calcutta household, gathered his seven biracial children—what became of their mother(s) is unclear—and left the subcontinent where he had spent half his life, never to return.[22]

Months later, he arrived in Britain for the second transoceanic homecoming of his life. A quarter century earlier, twenty-year-old "Jockey" Gilchrist had returned from three years' naval service in Grenada (1776–79) to a vibrant social life in Edinburgh. He had embarked for India two years later with great reluctance. "Oft with a friend Ive trod the dewy lawn / Or bathd in Fortha's cooling silver stream," he had written in 1781, referring to Scotland's River Forth in one of several mournful poems composed on the long voyage out—"now all vanisht like a faithless dream."[23] But if Scotland had ever been to him the pastoral idyll that he figured in his youthful poetry, that is not what it was to him when he returned with seven young children a quarter century later in his middle age. After fighting with the East India Company in London about his pension for a year and a half, he established himself in Edinburgh in 1806 and passed a volatile decade there. He started a bank, married a woman half his age, acquired an aristocratic title, and made a lot of enemies. He became outraged at the structural oppression of Britain's working poor and got involved in radical politics. By 1816, however, Edinburgh had become "a place which my soul abhors with the completest detestation."[24] Protesting that he was being run out of Scotland because of his political activism, Gilchrist moved to London—compelled, he wrote, "to disown and deny my country, as a tyrannical stepmother."[25] Leaving that metaphorical stepmother, he also left his actual mother and at least three of his teenaged children.

He would return only for one or two brief visits in the remaining twenty-five years of his life.[26]

In the long run, Gilchrist was never quite at home anywhere. In India, he went out of his way to live among strangers whose language he did not know. He wanted to leave Grenada in 1779, wanted to leave India in 1804, wanted to leave London in 1806, and wanted to leave Edinburgh in 1816. Yet he spent most of his post-India life teaching and thinking about Indian languages, spent much of his post-London life back in London, and spent part of his post-Edinburgh life trying to get Edinburgh to name a city square after him.[27] He lived between and outside communities, and he thought a lot about being between and outside. He had a strong opinion, for example, about what to call the growing biracial population (such as his own children) with European fathers and Indian mothers: "I would recommend the adoption of the epithet *Eurpasian*," he wrote, "instead of Indo-Briton, Anglo-Indian, Eurasian, &c. as the most melodious, *comprehensive*, and inoffensive appellation which could be conferred on an encreasing community."[28] He might have been writing, too, about himself: his was a profoundly "Eurpasian" life. His abecedarian clock and universal alphabet were his two most ambitious attempts to make a Eurpasian life more melodious, comprehensive, and inoffensive.

te abesedιereun klok

By the time he moved down to London in 1816, Gilchrist had drawn up actual plans for the abecedarian clock that he had first referenced in print some twenty years earlier. The machine would be an actual working clock, its face encircled by the thirty-nine letters of his new alphabet instead of the twelve numbers usually found there. The clock's "literal index," or minute hand, would make an ordinary hourly circuit around the face. Every ninety seconds, as the hand reached a new character on the dial, the clock would loudly pronounce that character's corresponding sound. At nineteen and a half minutes past the hour, for example, the hand would reach Gilchrist's new letter *ɷ*, and the clock would utter that vowel, three times, and then fall silent until the next letter. In this manner, he wrote, the clock "carries the pupil, in

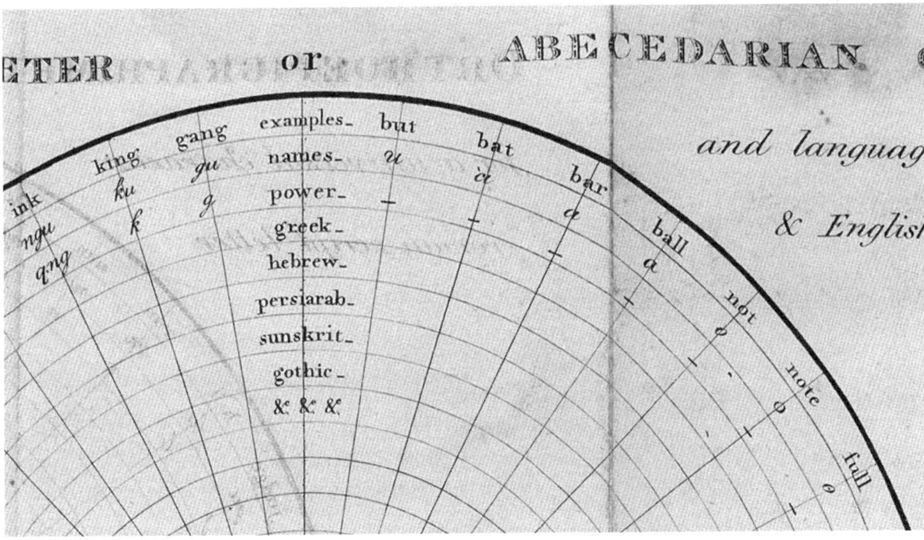

Detail from one of Gilchrist's abecedarian clock designs, as printed in the *Asiatic Journal*, November 1816. Photo courtesy of the Newberry Library, Chicago, call no. A51.097, v.2.

the course of one hour, slowly over the whole alphabet" (with "a sort of symphony" at the top of the hour).[29] To serve more pupils at a time, Gilchrist suggested that a single abecedareloge mechanism could drive eight clock faces arranged in an octagonal configuration, "and thereby convey the sounds required to a numerous audience, looking to the literal figures under such rehearsal in regular rotation." By the fall of 1816, Gilchrist claimed to have spoken to "a gentleman of the very first mechanical genius of this age," who assured him that "there can be little doubt of the invention being practicable, though the expense may be considerable."[30] Gilchrist mocked up an illustration of the clock face and persuaded the *Asiatic Journal* to include it as an engraved plate with their November 1816 issue.

In retrospect, it is less than intuitive that Gilchrist should have imagined his device as an abecedarian *clock* rather than, say, an abecedarian piano, an abecedarian doll, or an abecedarian steam engine. But clocks frequently provided the conceptual undergirding of Enlightenment mechanical automata. Cuckoo clocks were cutting-edge acoustic technology at the time that Gilchrist was conceptualizing the abecedareloge, having been perfected in southern Germany in the 1750s and become ubiquitous around Europe by the 1770s. Gilchrist was not the first person to imagine a noisemaking clock with a wider vocabulary. Benjamin Franklin once mentioned hearing about an Irish clock from which a night watchman popped out and called "*Past twelve a Clock*," at twelve o'clock, and Gilchrist appears to refer to a garbled version of the same anecdote when he mentions a rumor that "an automaton was once exhibited in Ireland, which could distinctly repeat and pronounce the whole of the Lord's Prayer."[31] Gilchrist's clock is different from other real and imagined speaking automata, however, because it was designed not to speak words with meanings, but to pronounce phonemes out of context: it abstracts phonetics from semantics, the way a typewriter keyboard or a case of metal type abstracts graphemes from semantics. It is also unusual in affect: cuckoo clocks and exhibited automata were usually whimsical, but the abecedareloge was deadly serious. Perhaps seeking to emphasize the abecedarian clock's value as a scientific instrument rather than an entertainment object, Gilchrist suggested that the device could alternatively be called an orthoepigraphemeter (ortho-, epi-, graphe-, -meter: correct-speech-writing-measurer)—a neologism that apparently invokes the "chronometer," an extremely precise clock that could remain synchronized with London during a marine voyage of many months. The development of chronometers in the eighteenth century had made transoceanic sea voyages vastly safer and easier than before by providing the first reliable means of calculating longitude. (The difference between the "noon" shown on your chronometer and solar noon at your location indicates your degrees of longitude from home.) In the way that a chronometer was a portable mechanical object that could provide a fixed reference point for the otherwise intangible passage of time, Gilchrist's envisioned orthoepigraphemeter was a portable mechanical object providing a fixed reference point for the otherwise intangible human voice.[32]

The chronometer had enabled global commerce and the British Empire to exist at a new scale in the eighteenth century. The orthoepigraphemeter, Gilchrist believed in 1816, could do the same thing for the English language. During his ten relatively nonlinguistic years in Edinburgh, Gilchrist's enthusiasm about non-English phonemes seems to have dwindled: the abecedarian clock that he outlined in 1816 did not include the *q*, *kh*, *gh*, and other sounds that had vexed his students in India. Rather than use the machine to transmit these phonemes orthoepigraphemetrically, Gilchrist now wanted to use the machine to eliminate them: the ten aspirated Hindustani consonants were merely "ten more difficulties in a learner's way, than our own, with no one commensurate advantage." Why have fifty phonemes when thirty-nine will do? "Let other nations boast . . . about the great variety and number of their alphabetical signs," Gilchrist suggests, "while we, in English, rest satisfied with the thirty-nine, at present extant." For the same reason, he wanted to replace the "multiformal a, A, *a*, *A*, *A*, **A**, a, A" with one singular form used in both writing and printing: *a*. The world's extant alphabets, and those alphabets' extant scripts, added up to "a complicated mass of inconsistency and disorder." If English speakers could get their alphabetic house in order, he argued, then English would become dramatically clearer and easier to learn than any other language—and "every nation on the face of the earth," Gilchrist predicted, would eventually conclude that "they may all gain much, while they can lose very little, by its substitution for their vernacular tongue." Build a better language, and the world will beat a path to your abecedareloge. Gilchrist began now to describe a future in which "British Monologigraphy" would reach "the remotest people on every continent" by means of his "Orthoepigraphiloge," "abecedarian clock," or "Polyglossal British Atlas."[33]

Like Nicholas Dufief and many others, Gilchrist was a firm believer that each language sets up its own distinct horizon of possibilities for what its speakers can think and feel. Reversing a common idiom, he liked to ask a student not whether he had mastered a language but whether "*it be master* of his cogitations or not."[34] To learn a language, he believed, was to submit oneself to that language's particular cognitive system. "It is an idle mistake to suppose that the study of languages acquires words alone," he would later tell an audience at an East India Company shareholders' meeting: the student of languages "unavoidably acquires, what is vastly more material, the thoughts of the people by whom those languages are spoken." For this reason, Gilchrist's vision of an orderly alphabet, a reliable phonetic standard, and a universalized English language seemed to him to promise incalculably vast benefits. The "chaos" of the world's present alphabets stood in the way of learning and knowledge; beyond them lay "an immediate diffusion of rational liberty, commerce, morality, and religion, from the river to the ends of the Earth," and "the unlimited amelioration of mankind."[35]

Gilchrist's linguistic imagination widened still further, however, after his alphabet failed to win the 1823 *Prix Volney*—a prize competition held by the Institut Royal de France for the creation of an alphabet "suitable for transcribing Ethiopic, Persian, Turkish, Armenian, Sanskrit, and Chinese" into Latin letters.[36] Gilchrist blamed his loss on the prize committee's favoritism toward an inside candidate. But while "a similar disappointment might have terrified most men from a second attempt," he bragged, "it rather stimulates my ambition to throw the gauntlet on this theme."[37] The better to throw the gauntlet, Gilchrist raised the stakes: his next attempt would be applicable "to all the languages of the universe," not just the six languages specified by the institute's committee, and it would greatly exceed the Latin alphabet. He stopped using terms like "Polyglossal British Atlas" and "British Monologigraphy" and started using totalizing words and prefixes in his descriptions of what he was proposing: "an omnilingual . . . universal or catholic litraeclature," a "universal grammaclature," "the Panglossal Diorama," or simply "gilchrist's universal character." He added sixty-one letters representing non-English phonemes to the thirty-nine characters that he had defined on the clock face in 1816. This alphabet, he now advertised, would "communicat[e] pure Hindoostanee rapidly to Englishmen, and good English equally so to the natives of British India." This marks a key difference between his alphabet and those of Mackintosh, Franklin, Chambers, and his other predecessors: "the venerable american's views," Gilchrist noted, referring to Franklin, "were limited to english . . . ; while my project is generally extended to human speech, under all the variable or varying aspects it can well assume."[38]

Still, as Franklin had done a half century earlier, Gilchrist kept most of the Latin alphabet's existing characters, restricted their meanings, and supplemented them with new letters in the graphic spirit of the old ones. The throat-ruffling, juglet-pouring Hindustani consonants that

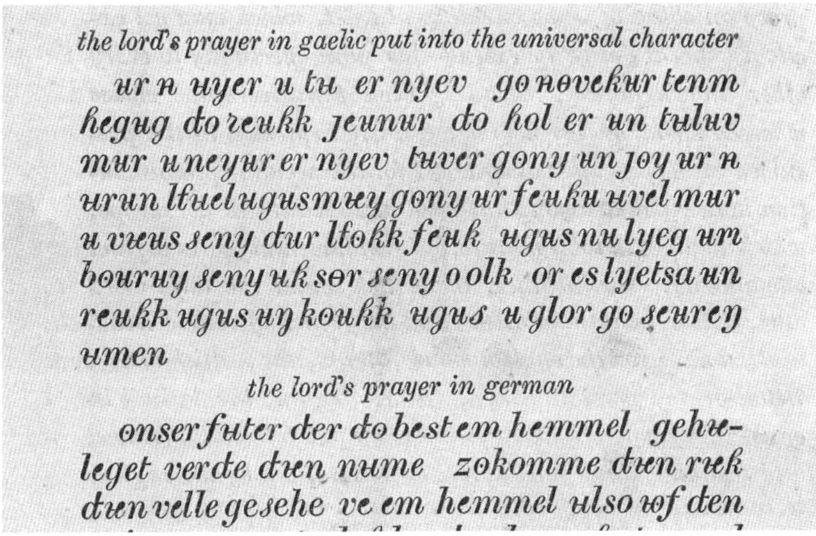
the lord's prayer in gaelic put into the universal character

ur n uyer u tu er nyev go nevekur tenm hegug do reukk jeunur do hol er un tuluv mur u neyur er nyev tuver gony un joy ur n urun lfuel ugusmuy gony ur feuku uvel mur u vueus seny dur lfokk feuk ugus nu lyeg urn bouruy seny uk sor seny o olk or es lyetsa un reukk ugus uŋ koukk ugus u glor go seureŋ umen

the lord's prayer in german

onser futer der do best em hemmel gehu-leget verde dun nume zokomme dun ruk dun velle gesehe ve em hemmel ulso uf den

Gilchrist's universal character, representing the Lord's Prayer in Gaelic (top) and German (bottom). From Gilchrist's *Dialogues, English and Hindoostanee*, 4th ed. (London, 1826). The Thomas Fisher Rare Book Library, University of Toronto.

Gilchrist had represented as *kh* and *gh* thirty years earlier are back, now represented as *k* and *g*—not to be confused with *k* and *g*, which have their usual English values. A lucrative contract teaching Hindustani and Persian in London to India-bound EIC physicians gave Gilchrist the financial resources in 1825 to take the financially and symbolically significant step of hiring typefounder Vincent Figgins to cut and cast a fount of 14-point type in **gulkrusts yoneversul karektur**.[39] The commercially preposterous decision to take this typographic plunge made a loud material statement: Gilchrist had now gone far beyond the point where phonetic alphabet proposals had usually sputtered in the past. Casting type asserted that his system was no one-off specimen sheet or mere curiosity; it was a global alphabetic revolution ready to go at a moment's notice.

gulkrusts yoneversul karektur was one of the very first universal phonetic alphabets ever cast—one of the first physical founts of type said to contain characters representing every sound in every language in the world. I know of only two predecessors, both of which were much more limited in scale: an unattributed pamphlet titled *The Methodist* [. . .] *a New and Universal Alphabet* (1741) and Francisco Mirambell y Giol's *Anocújeni, ó alphabéto* [. . .] *universal, para todas las lenguas* (1813). Given their primacy, Gilchrist's 1825 universal character and these earlier universalist typographies are surprisingly obscure; they have almost never been discussed by historians of language, linguistics, and print. Much better known are various universal alphabets that were proposed but never cast into type, including those of John Wilkins (1668), Francis Lodwick (1686), and Charles de Brosses (1765). Several nonuniversal phonetic alphabets are also relatively well known, including Franklin's phonetic alphabet for English (1768), John Pickering's transcription system for American Indian languages (1820), William Jones's romanization scheme for "Asiatick words" (1788), and Constantine Volney's sixty-character alphabet for six Asian languages (1819). Gilchrist's own contribution to that nonuniversal phonetic tradition has been recognized: his "Hindee-Roman Orthoepigraphical Ultimatum" (1804) became a widely used romanization system for Hindustani, Persian, and Arabic.[40] But his much more ambitious ***yɵneversʉl*** alphabet (1825), the one representing every sound "***tat kan nacyɵrale egzest en ene dɨealekt amʉŋ mankɨend***," has not been remembered.

"that can naturally exist in any dialect among mankind"

To demonstrate the new alphabet and type, Gilchrist arranged for fold-out extravaganzas with titles like "The Panglossal Diorama" to appear in a few magazines, along with a few sample pages of type—a feat that likely involved hauling a few hundred pounds of loose type, or perhaps already composed into formes, from one London printer to another one three-quarters of a mile away. He also evidently talked the editor of a London weekly into running an advertisement that included 250 characters in Gilchrist's type (along with a few thousand pieces of ordinary Latin type).[41] But by far the most impressive showcase for ***gʉlkrʉsts yɵneversʉl karektʉr*** was a typographic spectacle that he issued in 1826, about a year after he first had the type cast. Although he had tried to distribute earlier specimens of his universal alphabet by selling them, he did not do so now. Nor did he give them away; instead, he made sure that this spectacle would circulate widely by appending it to a book that he knew would sell well anyway, a fourth edition of his *Dialogues, English and Hindoostanee* (first published in Calcutta in

1804). The new 1826 edition of this steady seller was almost 50 percent larger than the previous version—not because it includes more dialogues but because after the last page of the *Dialogues*, Gilchrist resets the page numbering to zero and launches into more than a hundred pages of new, nondialogue material on his new custom-made *yoneversul* type. He apologizes—sort of—for increasing the book's bulk: "when a man feels a deep-rooted conviction, during a period of forty years," he writes, "that some notions, well concocted by him, upon any particular theme, are consistent with truth, reason, and eventual practicability . . . he should not, to please even a respectable majority of opponents, rashly be guilty of treason against his own matured judgment." He acknowledges this "respectable majority" who would have preferred the volume without the appended "scheme of practical grammagraphic perfection"—but includes that grammagraphically perfect scheme anyway.[42]

The showcase that nobody had asked for includes text in fifteen languages: Aesop's fable of "The Fox and the Stork" in *hendostune* (Hindustani), *furse* (Farsi), *bhukhu* (Brij Bhasha), *boŋlu* (Bengali), *sunskret* (Sanskrit), and *yurube* (Arabic); the Lord's Prayer in Gaelic, German, Chinese, and English; and scattered words and phrases in Greek, Latin, French, Italian, and Spanish. Instead of the seven or eight different alphabets in which those languages were usually printed, Gilchrist needed just one. "The Bible Society alone," he pointed out, "may yet save thousands of pounds on an endless variety of uncouth, untractable types, which are at present required."[43] There were very few specialty printers in Britain who could have printed a book in those fifteen languages in 1825, since very few printers ever had a reason to invest in having Devanagari or Persian or Arabic type on hand. Gilchrist was proposing a new alphabetic world order under which any printer could print any language.

our	wo	吾
daily	ze	日
bread	yoŋ	用
	leuŋ	糧。
forgive	men	免
our	wo	吾
trespasses	tsœ	罪、
for	kue	蓋
we	wo	吾
also	ye	亦
forgive	men	免
debtors	fo	負
our	wo	我
those	ce	者。
not	wu	勿

The Lord's Prayer in English in Latin characters, in Chinese in Gilchrist's universal character, and in Chinese in Chinese characters. From Gilchrist's *Dialogues, English and Hindoostanee*, 4th ed. (London, 1826). The Thomas Fisher Rare Book Library, University of Toronto.

In fact, Gilchrist wanted nothing less than the linguistic reintegration of a world that had been condemned since Babel to labor under the "needless incumbrances" of a "whole tribe of superfluous symbols." He envisioned the end of history as a world community speaking a single language and conceiving of itself as a single people.[44] Evoking the consolidation of many peoples into one, he referred to Cervantes's knight-errant, Don Quixote, who has "apparently three or four different names, though only one in reality": ***kweksot*** in England, ***keɹot*** in France and Italy, and ***kekote*** in Spain and Germany. Even Latin, the common linguistic medium of the (printed) republic of letters, was often incomprehensible in face-to-face contexts because its pronunciation varied so radically across Europe: "the british sound the latin word mus, ***mus***, the italians ***mos***, and the french of course ***mos***." Gilchrist longed for a world in which everyone, faced with the same letters, would utter the same sounds. In this manner, "every national discrepance might speedily be reconciled through the panglossal diorama, with one grand cosmopolitan scheme." He believed that his universal alphabet was "the appropriate precursor of a universal tongue" and dreamed of that "grand beneficial feast, of which all nations might freely partake, were a single mode of human speech, such as it originally existed, with one vehicle for it, rendered universal."[45] Gilchrist's life spanned nations, languages, religions, ethnicities, and governments. It is apt, therefore, that at his most ambitious he was envisioning a world united in a single language, "all nations" sitting down to a common banquet of meaning. For a mobile life like Gilchrist's, the prospect of belonging to a "grand cosmopolitan scheme" in the form of a language might well have seemed more relevant than the prospect of belonging to Scotland or England or Britain.

Gilchrist's "Panglossal Diorama" of 1825 and fifteen-language sampler of 1826 got around, in both the short and the long term, as interest in phonetic typography greatly increased in the 1830s. A *Gentleman's Magazine* contributor in 1829 referenced "those outrageous overturnings of the whole fabric [of spelling] proposed by Franklin and Gilchrist"; twenty years later, the *Edinburgh Review* indicated that Gilchrist's was still "perhaps the best known" of the universal phonetic alphabet proposals. It was at that time, in the 1840s, that social reformers Isaac Pitman and Alexander John Ellis declared a "crusade . . . to exterminate heterotypy from the face of the earth" and proposed their own universal phonetic alphabet—or "phonographic alphabet," as they called it. Although Pitman and Ellis did not mention Gilchrist's system explicitly in their *Plea for Phonotypy and Phonography* (1845), they knew about his proposal and included his name in a list of luminaries who had supported alphabetic universalism. Forty years later, the Pitman-Ellis "phonographic" alphabet, tweaked over the years, would form the basis of the International Phonetic Alphabet (IPA) that was adopted at a scholarly conference in 1888, providing the new science of linguistics with the medium for recording and reporting data that it has used ever since.[46]

Yet, curiously, Gilchrist has never been considered as part of the intellectual genealogy of the IPA. One possible reason for this is the rising stature of Sir William Jones (1746–94) in nineteenth-century linguistics. Gilchrist and Jones had developed competing romanization schemes for Indian languages in the late eighteenth century, and for most of the next century, scholars and institutions had to decide which system to use and endorse. The Gilchrist-or-Jones question became, at times, quite contentious; even in 1890, a Jones partisan assailed "the hostile camp formed by Dr. Gilchrist's treatment of vowel-transliteration" in a scientific paper.[47] Meanwhile, during the course of this conflict, scholars were discovering the profound implications of a paper that Jones had given in 1786 in which he had shown that Indian and European languages derived from a common source. This hypothesis became the founding insight of the modern discipline of linguistics—the discipline that would formally adopt the IPA in 1888.[48] Although Jones's and Gilchrist's romanization schemes had no bearing on the Indo-European hypothesis, Gilchrist's structural position in the nineteenth century as the anti-Jones probably worked against his being memorialized in a discipline founded on Jones's work.

Then, too, Gilchrist was not an academic; his interests lay in what he called "*practical* Orientalism." Rita Raley has suggested that the contrast between Jones and Gilchrist was "not quite that of an amateur-professional divide, but Jones emblematizes a model of scholarship that values surplus knowledge," while Gilchrist "adheres to notions of functionality and practicality," disadvantaging his reputation during the nineteenth-century professionalization of knowledge. Finally, it is worth noting that Gilchrist embraced the idea that a person's language is the "*master* of his cogitations" and that different languages facilitate different kinds of thinking—aligning himself with an intellectual tradition that academic linguists would firmly reject during the nineteenth century.[49] Whatever the reason for his remaining out of historical sight, Gilchrist is an unacknowledged founder of "universal" phonetic typography in the English-speaking world and an unacknowledged contributor to the alphabetic kind of "phonography" that eventually became the International Phonetic Alphabet.

The other kind of phonography—the acoustic kind—came to be associated more with music than with speech in the 1890s. Yet phonographs retained the name of "talking machines" long after they were primarily used as music machines.[50] That term, "talking machine," registers the phonetic heritage of recorded sound, and it has its own intellectual history that goes back to exactly what Gilchrist had in mind when he envisioned a phonetic cuckoo clock called an abecedareloge. The earliest "talking machine," so called, was built in Vienna in the second half of the eighteenth century by a Hungarian engineer named Wolfgang von Kempelen—better known to history as the creator of a celebrated fake chess-playing automaton—at the same time that Gilchrist was dreaming up the abecedareloge in India. Gilchrist and von Kempelen had essentially the same idea about building out the acoustic technology of a cuckoo clock to make human speech. Inside a cuckoo clock, a bellows blows air through a wooden chamber, the interior of which has been carved, like a whistle, into a shape that causes the air to resonate at a particular frequency. (There are two bellows and two resonant chambers: one that says *cuc-* and one that says *-koo*.) When von Kempelen began trying to build his *Sprechmaschine* in 1769, he started with the design principles of the cuckooing automatons that already worked so well. Like a cuckoo clock's cuckoo mechanism, von Kempelen's artificial vocal tract was a bellows (corresponding to lungs) connected to a wooden resonating chamber (corresponding to a mouth). Instead of being carved by the clockmaker, however, von Kempelen's wooden chamber could be shaped by the machine's user in real time—including by raising and lowering a wooden flap inside the box (functioning as a tongue), opening a valve to a small auxiliary chamber above (nose), and manipulating a rubber gasket at the end of the device (lips).[51]

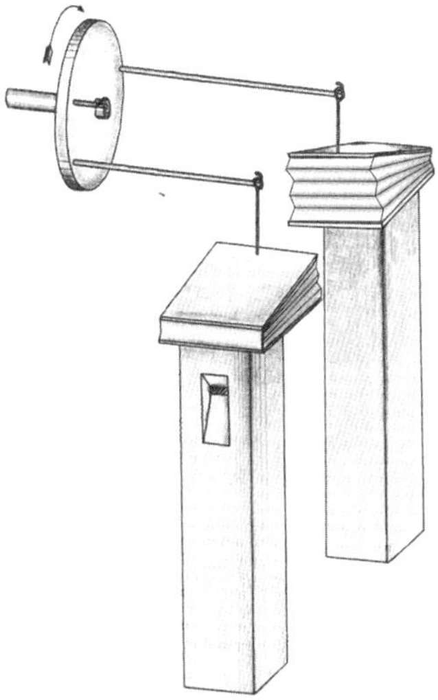

Inside the cuckoo clock. Two resonating chambers—one for *cuc-* and one for *-koo*—each topped with a leather-hinged bellows.

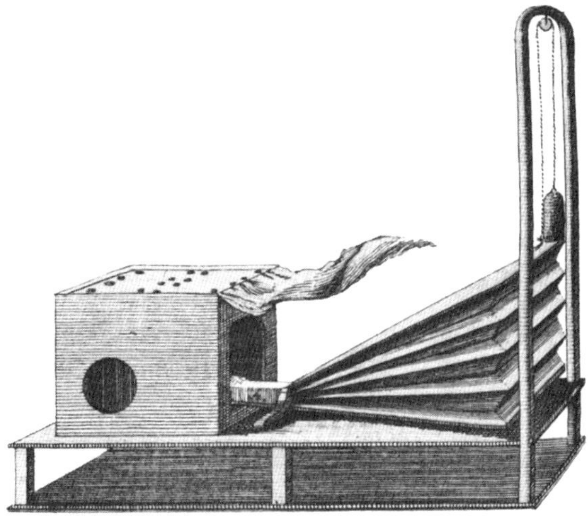

Inside the talking machine. Von Kempelen's talking machine relies on a mechanism similar to that of the cuckoo clock. From C. F. Hindenburg, *Ueber den Schachspieler des Herrn von Kempelen* (Leipzig, 1784).

Von Kempelen spent twenty years tinkering with his "talking machine" and never perfected it. Yet his cuckoo-clockish mechanical mouth played a pivotal role in the history of sound technology anyway. Although von Kempelen couldn't really get the talking machine to work, he did publish a 400-page monograph about what he had learned, with copious illustrations, in 1791. Some decades later, a British inventor named Charles Wheatstone tracked down von Kempelen's talking machine design and made some breakthrough improvements to it, so that it worked well enough that people would pay to witness it. A phonetic enthusiast named Alexander Melville Bell, while working on one of the most ambitious phonetic alphabets ever conceived, took his teenage son to see a demonstration of Wheatstone's talking machine in 1863. The son was fascinated. He bought von Kempelen's book and began his own experiments with speech reproduction machines. A decade later, he got the telephone working—and that device, not his father's phonetic alphabet of "self-interpreting physiological letters," is the phoneme-transmission system for which the Bells are mostly known to history. This is a more or less direct lineage from cuckoo-clock-like mechanical voicebox devices like what Gilchrist was envisioning to modern telephony.[52] Even as late as 1897, cuckoo clocks and phonographs still seemed similar enough that you might buy them from the same specialty store: there was in Troy, New York, "a dealer in the talking machine, graphophones, and cuckoo clocks."[53]

Gilchrist played no role in the future development of the acoustic phonograph and only a distant role in the creation of the IPA. His significance is perhaps not as an ancestor of either technology but as an eccentric spokesperson from a moment when those two technologies were the same thing. But although he was eccentric, he was also, like Nicholas Dufief and Duncan Mackintosh, oddly representative of the broadest possibilities of empire at the time, and the diverse ways in which language wove through those possibilities as an orienting strand of identity that could be grasped and traced back to a place of belonging. Dufief, Mackintosh, and Gilchrist all tried to extend the reach of that strand; all of them were trying to make language more possible to exchange. Dufief wanted to make it possible to learn a new language in a month. Mackintosh wanted to make it possible to pronounce à la London in Barbados or Boston. Gilchrist wanted to make it possible to hear the sounds of any language, anywhere. All of them came to their linguistic innovations as responses to being displaced by the forces of revolution and empire. And all of them believed that language makes the difference between man and man, which meant that all of their projects had very high stakes.

It is probably not a coincidence, therefore, that Gilchrist's, Mackintosh's, and Dufief's very different innovations would have gone a long way toward solving the others' problems. The abecedareloge would have been an excellent countermeasure against the regional linguistic diversification that Mackintosh was trying to prevent and that Noah Webster's antagonists feared. In Martinique, Mackintosh was trying to simplify English pronunciation so that French speakers could learn the language more easily when they were thrust suddenly into the Anglophone world because of the French Revolution. Those are exactly the circumstances that set the seventeen-year-old Dufief on his life's linguistic path. And both Dufief and Gilchrist envisioned transforming the linguistic realities of mass audiences, with potentially vast mental benefits.

Actually, Gilchrist happened to be on the board of the London Mechanics' Institution in 1826 when Nicholas Gouin Dufief offered to teach a French class there, free of charge.* That was the class that at times contained as many as three hundred students, who gathered on Thursday nights in the institution's theater (built under Gilchrist's supervision) for Dufief's call-and-response lessons, repeating en masse Dufief's proffered phrases—English, French, English, French (see chapter 1). Gilchrist had already decided years earlier that he hated Dufief, however, and had written contemptuously that those who "prefer a regal turnpike to a common passage" were welcome to choose the "celebrated French nobleman's *royal road*." To Gilchrist, Dufief seemed less interested in "stimulating the minds" of his students than in "surfeiting their memories"—stuffing them with insubstantial obedience instead of developing their capacity for autonomous thought. Still, one wonders whether Dufief's packed classrooms aren't part of what Gilchrist was thinking about when he suggested later the same year that an abecedareloge, the speech machine that he had been dreaming about for decades, could be useful "for teaching hundreds of children simultaneously."[54]

*Required textbook sold separately.

The Lingual Cure

Shortly after launching ***gulkrusts yoneversul karektur***, the sixty-six-year-old Gilchrist collapsed into a crippling illness of both body and mind. He spent the next six years traveling around Europe, consulting with doctors, and submitting to painful treatments that left him sicker than before. He endured two months of experimental subcutaneous electrotherapy, an injection of nitric acid into his urethra, and a chemical-induced blister covering his entire abdomen. He suffered "constipations, cholics, flatulencies . . . the most disgusting tastes in the mouth, secretions of clammy saliva . . . gusts of discontent, ill-humour, and misanthropic feelings against man and beast, strange internal whiffing sounds between the brain and the top of the head"—(this sentence goes on for

Gilchrist in his sixties, in 1825, seated before a pedestal that reads "oriental philology, universal language." Frontispiece to Gilchrist's *Hindoostanee Philology* (London, 1825).

more than a page)—"a sense of acidity as if the teeth had been steeped in vinegar . . . anticipation of a thousand evils, apathy and indifference to every body and thing, unamiable and invidious thoughts." He was cured (so he believed) in the winter of 1833, by eating several pounds of grapes per day and taking small doses of sulfuric acid, prescribed by mail by a homeopathic physician he never met.[55]

In an ecstatic and rambling hundred-page pamphlet dashed off in the early months of his recovery, Gilchrist sang the praises of homeopathy, which was at the time a new and promising medical discipline. Homeopaths rejected the diverse panoply of conventional medical interventions in favor of extremely small doses of medicines dissolved on the tongue. After forty years of teaching other people what to do with their tongues, Gilchrist now returned his lingual attention to himself. Speculating about why the lingually administered medication was so effective, he suggested that the tongue was one of the nervous system's central nodes, "the lingual papillae having nerves as slender as the finest filaments in a little spider's web," extending out to every part of the body. Medication applied to the tongue, he proposed, was absorbed directly into the nervous system, bypassing the digestive tract and reaching the nerves in a purer and more potent form than was possible through the stomach. Whether or not he was primed by a linguistic life to believe in the power of the tongue, there is a poignancy to the peaceful, intimate scene of lingual treatment that he describes. A "dexterous assistant" dispenses the tiny pills directly into your mouth, and, "carefully placed on the tongue, they dissolve there by the moisture of that member, when raised gently to the roof of the mouth previously rinsed with a little tepid water only."[56] Very unlike the lingual activities of yesteryear, when he taught students to pronounce *kh* "in the very act of hawking up phlegm from the throat, which becomes tremulous and ruffled," this eucharist demands no tremulous hawking.[57] All that Gilchrist required of his tongue anymore was to lift it gently to the roof of the mouth, almost as if he were about to say *l . . . anguage.*

Duncan Mackintosh, who died in the West Indies just as Gilchrist was returning to Britain from the other Indies, was a Scot who made his life in the Caribbean *francophonie*; Gilchrist was a Scot, a political radical, and a father of mixed-race children born in India. They were both national, political, and racial outsiders. But they were linguistic insiders. Perhaps part of what drew their attention to language was that language offered them a better chance of belonging within their British social worlds than the other identity categories available to them. Gilchrist was at home in the teaching of radically foreign languages for many more years than he was at home in Scotland, England, or India—or in France, where he spent most of his last decade. It is ironic, therefore, and a little sad, that a dispute over Gilchrist's estate would cause British judicial institutions to spend fifteen years evaluating whether he had been legally English or Scottish at the time of his death. Gilchrist had made out his will in Paris, leaving almost all of his £25,000 estate to found a charitable organization "for the benefit, and advancement, and propagation of education and learning in every part of the world." A nephew, however, challenged the will's validity on the grounds that Gilchrist was Scottish and therefore should have executed his will according to Scottish legal protocols, not the English protocols he had followed. The case thus hinged on whether Gilchrist was "domiciled" in Scotland, England, or France at the time of his death in Paris in 1841. Had he *emigrated* from England to France in 1834, or was he merely living there as an expatriate? If an expatriate, was he an expatriate from Scotland or from England? After leaving Scotland in 1816, had he remained "a Scotchman" living in England, or had he become "a non-Scotchman—an Englishman, in truth"? The law required that Gilchrist be assigned a singular, nonoverlapping political nationality: he had to be one or the other, not both or in-between.[58]

The case eventually reached the House of Lords, where members pored over Gilchrist's publications and private papers, weighing textual evidence about his subjective relationship to England at the time of his death. They considered the fact that he had furniture in storage in

London, that his will referred to him as "J. B. Gilchrist, of the city of Edinburgh," and that he had declared in a "strange wild incomprehensible rhapsody" of an 1820 pamphlet that he had been forced "to disown and deny my country, as a tyrannical stepmother."[59] The Lords concluded that Gilchrist had considered himself to be an Englishman when he died, thus upholding the will. That decision, *Whicker v. Hume* (1858), is still occasionally referenced in common law countries when a person's domicile or residence is in dispute. So Gilchrist, who spent his life crossing borders and dreamed of a world in which a common language made national borders irrelevant, in the end became part of the legal mechanism by which the state makes exclusive determinations of national identity.

While the estate was tied up in litigation, 550 acres of Australian land that Gilchrist had acquired in 1801 became the thriving Sydney suburb of Balmain—named for its previous owner, a colleague of Gilchrist's in India who had signed it over to him to settle a debt of £17. By the time Gilchrist's charity took control of his estate in 1865, the Australian property was worth £70,000, an enormous sum. This endowment allowed the Gilchrist Educational Trust to become a major sponsor of working-class adult education programs, fellowships for women at Oxford and Cambridge, and scholarships to British universities for students from British colonial possessions well into the twentieth century.[60] Among Gilchrist's papers was found a note in which he expressed a wish that the charitable organization operate "on the most benevolent principle, connected, nevertheless, with my system of a universal language."[61] The note, however, was not legally binding, and his trustees (probably wisely) chose to ignore the part about the universal language. So Gilchrist got a legacy. But it was not the abecedarian legacy he wanted.

CHAPTER FOUR

How to Read the World

Pantographia, Print Specimens, and Linguistic Identity

Of Form and Content

John Gilchrist, who was very fond of Greco-English neologisms, once described his ***yoneversul*** alphabet as "pantagraphical."[1] In describing his alphabet this way, he was nodding to the title of a book he greatly admired: *Pantographia*, a putatively comprehensive catalog of languages, containing hundreds of linguistic "specimens" in 208 different alphabets: "ALL THE KNOWN ALPHABETS IN THE WORLD; TOGETHER WITH . . . ALL WELL-AUTHENTICATED ORAL LANGUAGES; FORMING A COMPREHENSIVE DIGEST OF PHONOLOGY." Conceived and executed during the 1780s and 1790s by a London type manufacturer named Edmund Fry, *Pantographia* was the most multialphabetic book in the history of the world when it was published in 1799: no previous book contained text in more alphabets and writing systems. Its specimens include three Carolingian scripts, a poem by Alexander Pope translated into Javanese, the Lord's Prayer in Algonquian, a thirty-word Eskimo vocabulary, three varieties of French, twenty-one specimens of English, and on and on in alphabetical order—page after page of exotic type and foreign words in Abyssinian, Amharic, Angolan, Arabic; Cadeaux, Carnish, Catalonian, Celtic; Mendaean, Mexican, Mercian, Mohawk; and all the way through the alphabet to New Zealand. It's like a salesman's sample case, containing one or two or three of each item in the catalog—not for using, but for examining. In this instance, the catalog is the world, the goods are its languages, and the case is *Pantographia*.

Gathering specimens of 164 languages was no easy task in eighteenth-century London, but *Pantographia*'s most impressive feat is a technical achievement, not a research one. Only half of the book's specimens appear in the Latin alphabet or in one of the other alphabets for which movable type was ordinarily manufactured in Europe: Greek, Hebrew, Arabic, and a few others. The other half of *Pantographia*'s specimens required custom type made from scratch—about two hundred different typographic alphabets, hand-cut in metal type, letter by letter, used in *Pantographia* and then never used again. The fact that it exists at all is astonishing. The "simple representing of the existing alphabets," a magazine essayist wrote in 1808, a decade after *Pantographia* was published, "is physically possible to execute," but "so tedious, laborious, and difficult, that in reality we have nothing of this kind"—except for a single work, "the copies of which, however, are excessively scarce. This is called 'Pantographia.'"[2] All told, cutting the type for this cabinet of

Details from four of *Pantographia*'s 405 linguistic "specimens," three of them printed from Fry's handmade custom type. Courtesy, American Antiquarian Society.

typographic curiosities would have required upwards of ten thousand hours of skilled labor.[3] Between 1782 and 1798—the years during which Gilchrist was compiling his Hindustani dictionary, Duncan Mackintosh was confronting the opacity of English pronunciation, Noah Webster was insisting that "there iz no alternativ" to radical American spelling reform, and Nicholas Dufief was discovering nature's method of teaching languages—typefounder Edmund Fry (1757–1835) personally undertook the artisanal labor of cutting *Pantographia*'s type. If he had billed himself at his usual rate, *Pantographia*'s type would have cost more than £8,000, a sum that could have paid for the building of three or four churches.[4]

Gilchrist called his alphabet "pantagraphical" because it was a system for "writing all" languages; Fry called his work *Pantographia* because it contained "all writing" systems (or tried to). These two ambitious experimental type-manufacturing projects were both responses to the world's increasingly evident linguistic diversity and the challenge of representing that diversity in ink. Both projects aimed to surpass the representational horizons of the Latin alphabet and thereby make the world's languages available in British print. But they approached that goal in opposite ways: Gilchrist by reducing typographic diversity, Fry by proliferating it. Gilchrist was frustrated with the ever-increasing multiplicity of the world's known scripts—they were "needless incumbrances among all the languages of the earth," he thought, since a single alphabet would do just as well.[5] By contrast, what a reviewer called Fry's "curious production in diversified typography" sought to extend alphabetic multiplicity.[6] Fry's stated goal was to "put it into the power of philologists to extend the sphere of our knowledge; and to furnish them with a centre of communication, to which their researches and discoveries may be directed."[7] So whereas Gilchrist proposed to eliminate alphabetic diversity, Fry instead tried to render every conceivable linguistic diversity in physical, metallic form.

Like Dufief, Webster, Mackintosh, and Gilchrist, Fry was trying to do something with language other than communicate. When Dufief says, "My fosterbrother has attempted to murder me," he is not reporting an actual attempt on his life. When Mackintosh writes that "Q $\overset{2}{\text{i}}\underset{2}{\text{s}}$ $\overset{3}{\text{a}}\text{l}'\text{w}\overset{2}{\text{a}}\text{y}\underset{2}{\text{s}}$ $\text{f}\overset{1}{\text{o}}\text{l}'\text{l}\overset{3}{\text{o}}$*w*ed $\text{b}\overset{2}{\text{y}}$ *u*," he is less interested in conveying a piece of orthographic

"Divers that shrink from monsters of the main / through rocks or shoals may search for pearls in vain."

information than in conveying a pronunciation. When Gilchrist places a newspaper advertisement in which he writes that "***dıevurz fat ʂreŋk from monsturz ov ŧe men / ŧro roks or ʂolz me serc for perlz en ven***," his communicative agenda has very little to do with pearls, or with ***perlz***, or with the moral of his didactic couplet, which appears to be something like "fortune favors the bold." These utterances are not chiefly efforts to use the semantic dimensions of language; they are efforts to discover and make "the difference between man and man." Likewise, although *Pantographia* is irreducibly linguistic, it is by design mostly illegible to any given reader. Even the most learned polyglot could read only a fraction of its 405 linguistic specimens, at least to the extent that "reading" means comprehending graphic symbols as semantically meaningful words:

COURLANDIC: Tews mûs kut tu esch in debbes. Sweérti to tau waêrtsch . . .

ETHIOPIC I: አቡነ፡ ዘበሰማያት፡ ይትቀደስ፡ ስሙብ . . .

FINLAND: Isa meiden joca olet taivvaisa, pyhittetty stolcon sinum nymes . . .

FORMOSAN: Diameta ka tu vullum lulugniang ta nanang oho, maba tongal ta tao tu goumoho . . .

HEBREW 8: אבינו שבשמים: יקדש שמך: תבוא מלכותך . . .

IRISH 6: Ar naṫ ata ar neam, Naomṫar hainm . . .

LETTICE: Musso tæwss kass eeksch dæbbæsim. Swættizlay toop tauwss wardz . . .

MANDARINE I: Caí tien ngò tem fú chè ngò tem yuén. Ul mîm c'hîm xîm . . .

MOHAWK: Songwaniha ne karongiage tigsideron. Wesagsanadogegtine . . .

NAGARI 2: वा पितर गोमितर ञो पक इक मनितमड . . .

PERSIAN 2: اِي پَدَرْ مَا كِه دَرْ أَسمَانْ پَكْ بَشَ نَمَّ تُوْ . . .

PHILOSOPHIC 2: Hαι coba ȣȣ ιa ril dad, ha bαbι ιo sȣymtα . . .

POCONCHI: Catat taxah vilcat; nimta incaharçihi avi . . .

RUSSIAN 2: Оптче нашъ, иже еси на небесѣхъ . . .

SAMARITAN 7: ࠀࠁࠉࠍࠅ ࠔࠁࠔࠌࠉࠌ: ࠉࠒࠃࠔ ࠔࠌࠊ ࠕࠁࠅࠀ ࠌࠋࠊࠅࠕࠊ . . .

SERVIAN 4: Otse nash ishe jeszi v nabeszih, poszueti sze ime tvoje . . .

Yet *Pantographia*'s original audiences evidently found the book meaningful. Despite its high price—at £2.2s, *Pantographia* cost as much as seven pairs of shoes or sixty pounds of beef—the book enjoyed a warm reception on its publication in 1799, counting among its subscribers a roster of influential British intellectuals and politicians.[8] Reviewers hailed it as a work of "national importance" that "must long have been reckoned one of the *desiderata* of Literature."[9]

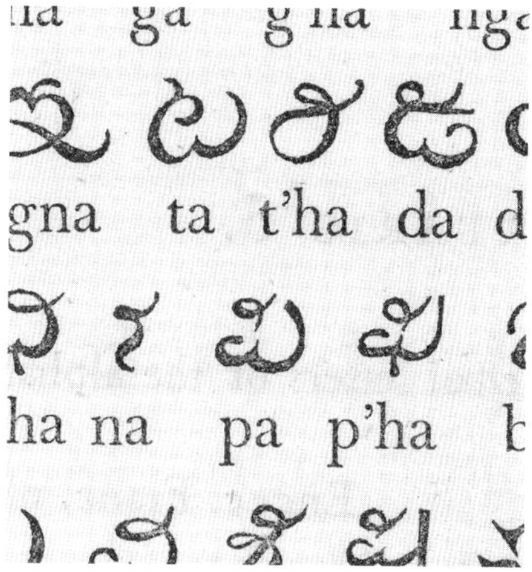

Detail of "Talenga" (Telugu) specimen in *Pantographia.*

The basis of *Pantographia*'s perceived importance was the hypothesis that linguistic difference corresponds to human mental difference. This principle had recently been affirmed by the *Encyclopaedia Britannica*: the entry on "Language" had been updated for the 1797 edition to state that "the language of any people is a very exact state of their minds."[10] *Pantographia* brought together the data one would need to investigate the minds of "any people." It was an unprecedentedly wide-ranging collection of linguistic "specimens" taken from around the globe, organized and digested and ready to be interpreted. The book's linguistic content is not to be read for meaning but to be examined as evidence: how long are the words? how many vowels are there? which guttural consonants does it use? The book presents an opportunity to classify and organize the human world according to language and to see the linguistic differences between man and man. One of *Pantographia*'s early reviewers suggested that "those who compare the idioms of different nations" could use *Pantographia* to "distinguish sister dialects and radical diversity."[11] Apprehending the "radical diversity" of the human race in linguistic terms is fundamentally the same endeavor that Dufief, Webster, Mackintosh, and Gilchrist were engaged in. Unlike them, Fry was not trying to alter any linguistic identities, only to catalog them—but he was cataloging them for some of the same reasons that Gilchrist was inventing universal type, Webster was revising American English, Mackintosh was creating a phonetic notation, and Dufief was discovering the linguistic basis of consciousness: *Pantographia* promises to contain the vast human diversity that was increasingly visible to English speakers at the end of the eighteenth century.

Fry's innovation is to connect the idea that "language makes the difference between man and man" to eighteenth-century media theory. Eighteenth-century readers were highly attuned to the material and ideological formations through which communications take place—in other words, to mediation—in part, scholars have recently argued, because the newly universal availability of print heightened readers' awareness of the differences between printed and written communication. Even if a handwritten document and a printed document contain the same text, they do not have the same meaning in terms of their trustworthiness, affect, official status, and so forth. This eighteenth-century awareness that print-mediated communication differs from manuscript-mediated communication set off a chain reaction of other kinds of media consciousness. Readers became extremely interested in orally transmitted texts such as ballads and ancient poetry—convinced that even though voices, manuscripts, and print can all transmit verbal texts, those texts that had been transmitted mainly by voice were of a different order of meaning because of their different medium of transmission. They also became aware of the mediating effects of new genres (the novel, the newspaper) and new institutions (postal systems, coffeehouses).[12]

Pantographia recognizes the hypothesis that "language makes the difference between man and man" as a kind of media consciousness. It represents each language as a medium for communication and thought, and it posits that one linguistic medium conveys different kinds of meaning from another—much as the print medium conveys different kinds of meaning from the scribal. *Pantographia* connects the "language makes the difference" hypothesis to eighteenth-century media theory by presenting its 405 linguistic specimens in a familiar material format that was explicitly designed to highlight media differences: a type specimen book. It leverages a mode of reading that print professionals and consumers alike already knew how to apply to specimens of typography. In so doing, it shows how the linguistic identity hypothesis was a response not only to globalization but also to media shift.

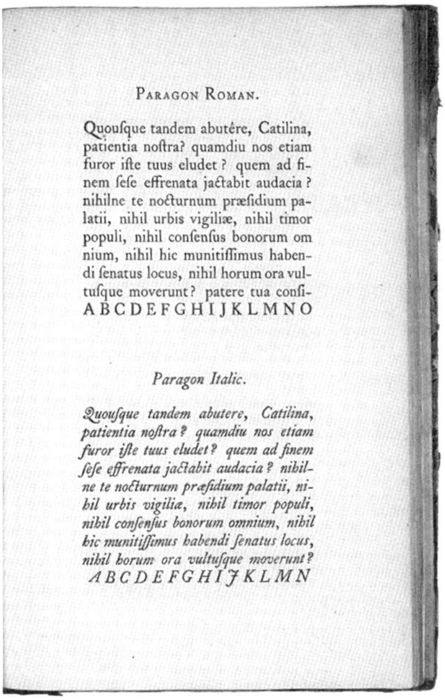

Paragon Roman.

Quoufque tandem abutêre, Catilina, patientia noftra? quamdiu nos etiam furor ifte tuus eludet? quem ad finem fefe effrenata jactabit audacia? nihilne te nocturnum præfidium palatii, nihil urbis vigiliæ, nihil timor populi, nihil confenfus bonorum omnium, nihil hic munitiffimus habendi fenatus locus, nihil horum ora vultufque moverunt? patere tua confi-
ABCDEFGHIJKLMNO

Paragon Italic.

Quoufque tandem abutere, Catilina, patientia noftra? quamdiu nos etiam furor ifte tuus eludet? quem ad finem fefe effrenata jactabit audacia? nihilne te nocturnum præfidium palatii, nihil urbis vigiliæ, nihil timor populi, nihil confenfus bonorum omnium, nihil hic munitiffimus habendi fenatus locus, nihil horum ora vultufque moverunt?
ABCDEFGHIJKLMN

Page from a 1785 specimen book by typefounder William Caslon. Courtesy, American Antiquarian Society.

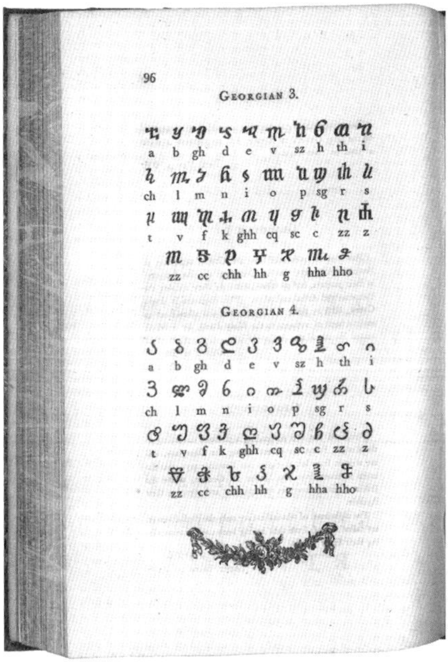

"Georgian" specimens in *Pantographia.* Courtesy, American Antiquarian Society.

Types of Reading

By being unreadable—at least in the usual semantic sense of reading—*Pantographia* forces its audience into contact with the shapes and sounds of language rather than letting readers look *through* those shapes and sounds to their semantic meanings. *Pantographia* insists on the significance of those shapes and sounds, over and above and next to whatever they are used to say. For example, *Pantographia* indicates that these three phrases have identical semantic meanings:

1. Amproy antsica izau hanautangh andanghitsi angharanau hofissahots, vahoüachanau hoaui aminay . . .
2. Abâtâyn bassamaj jalach. Jynzalyn mangystcha . . .
3. Our Father who art in heaven, hallowed be thy name . . .

The similarities of linguistic content yield to differences of linguistic form, especially since the content is not really perceptible to readers who do not happen to read Malagasy (1) and Amharic (2) as well as English. What the monolingual English speaker can perceive is that Amharic takes only five words to say what English and Malagasy say in ten. Or that Malagasy appears to take more than thirty syllables to say what English and Amharic say in half that number. Or that Malagasy makes extensive use of nasal consonants. Or that almost all Malagasy words terminate in vowels. Today, these observations no longer seem like meaningful evidence about these languages' speakers or the "state of their minds." But *Pantographia* is founded on the idea that these differences are significant.

In the book's long preface, Fry endorses a standard argument about the correspondence between a language and its users' social, moral, and intellectual horizons: "the improvement and copiousness of [a people's] language would keep pace with their own progress in knowledge, and in the arts of civil life" over historical time, he states, using language taken verbatim from the *Encyclopaedia Britannica*. Imagining the spread of various peoples over the habitable world, Fry offers *Pantographia*'s readers a conjectural history of how different groups of people developed different ideas and invented new words to represent those ideas: "they would every where meet with new objects, which would occasion the invention of new names," so that eventually "a vast number of words would in one country be fabricated, to denote complex conceptions, which must of course be unintelligible to the body of the people inhabiting countries where those conceptions could never be formed."[13] Different peoples apparently had different "complex conceptions," and each language was fitted to a particular set of conceptions that were allegedly "unintelligible" to other peoples. In this account, each language was a unique system of meaning and signification that constituted a unique way of conceiving the world—much as Dufief conceived of a language as "the very creator of the thinking faculty itself."[14] Accordingly, *Pantographia*'s linguistic specimens ask to be read as comparative glimpses into other ways of being and other modes of personhood.

Those who put *Pantographia* to ethnographic use might not have reached many shocking conclusions about the world's peoples. The book's specimens reinforce familiar imperial and Orientalist fantasies. For example, by providing different kinds of specimens for peoples

SUMATRAN.

One	*Chit*	Two	*Nung*
Three	*Sa*	Four	*See*
Five	*Ingo*	Six	*La*
Seven	*Chee*	Eight	*Poë*
Nine	*Ca*	Ten	*Tsap*
The sun	*Jet*	A man	*Tapò*
The moon	*Geuex*	A woman	*Tsawà*
The stars	*Tchee*	The head	*Taow*
The sky	*Thee*	The hair	*Tamung*
Rain	*Hò*	The face	*Beeïn*
The sea	*Haï*	The eyes	*Bwaclieu*
Wind	*Whang*	The nose	*Pee*

TARTARIC 1.

يا بابامز كه يوكسك ݣوݣده سن
آدݣ آري اولسون
پادشاهلغݣ ݣلسون

NEW ZEALAND.

One	*Katahè*	Father	*Papa*
Two	*Karooa*	Son	*Hetamàeh*
Three	*Katarroo*	The eyes	*He matta*
Four	*Kawha*	The nose	*He eih*
Five	*Kareema*	A dog	*Egoorree*
Six	*Kàònoo*	Fish	*Teyka*
Seven	*Kawhetoo*	Ear-shells	*Hepaooa*
Eight	*Kawarroo*	A stone	*Powhattoo*
Nine	*Kàeeva*	Water	*Hewai*
Ten	*Kacahaoro*	A house	*Hèàwhài*
A hedge	*Pateéà*	A nail	*Ewhàò*
A hatchet	*Kochee*	Victuals	*Eëi*
A garment	*Hecacahoo*	Tataow	*Emaho*
A canoe	*Hewaca*	To paddle	*Hoggee*
To speak	*Orero*	Good	*Apoorotoo*
Yes	*A a*	Bad	*Ekeeno*
No	*Kaowra*	Look you	*Eta eta*

The elementary concerns of South Pacific islanders, against the complex Oriental mystery of the "Tartaric." Fry's preface rehearses the standard argument that these limited vocabularies correspond to the limited conceptual range of their people's minds. Courtesy, American Antiquarian Society.

thought to be at different stages of human progress, *Pantographia* steers the reader toward seeing Africans and Polynesians as uncivilized, and Amerindians as incipiently civilized thanks to European contact. The specimens for the Hottentots and Tahitians are brief transliterated vocabularies of concrete nouns, inviting the standard conclusion that these speakers don't need many or complicated words because they don't have many or complicated ideas. By contrast, the specimens of Amerindian languages are typically the Lord's Prayer transliterated into Latin characters, which verifies that their languages have words for abstract concepts such as "hallowed," "kingdom," "thy will," and "trespasses." Given the prevailing assumptions about the superior mentalities that correspond to abstract language, the book's data appear to validate the hierarchy of civilizations that Europeans already believed in.

In this respect, *Pantographia* is like other totalizing literary and scholarly projects in the eighteenth century, such as the *Encyclopaedia*

Britannica, that facilitate imperial judgments about the many peoples of the world—often while also making specific and timely interventions in the politics of British identity vis-à-vis its English, Scottish, Welsh, and Irish constituents. *Pantographia* works to imagine a British linguistic identity that is centered on the English language but that also incorporates the authenticity that elite Britons projected onto Gaelic during the eighteenth century's "Celtic Revival."[15] It achieves this by distinguishing an abstract Celtic linguistic essence from the Celtic languages themselves: the volume includes more or less ambivalent entries on SCOTS, IRISH, and WELCH, but it glowingly evaluates CELTIC under a separate heading. The CELTIC specimen is atypical for *Pantographia* in that it is a secular poetic text: twenty lines from the epic poem ostensibly composed by the third-century Scottish bard named Ossian and transmitted orally through the centuries until it was "discovered," translated, and published in the 1750s and 1760s by James Macpherson:

> 'S e guth anaim mo ruin a tha 'nn,
> O! 's ainmach gu aislin Mhalmhin' thu

and so on, with a prose translation on the facing page. The contrast could not be starker between the CELTIC specimen and the other language that happens to be on the same page, "CERAM," a Polynesian language for which *Pantographia*'s specimen is a vocabulary of the numbers one to ten: "Oeenta, Olooa, Otoloo, Opatoo, Oleema, Oloma, Opeeto, Oaloo, Oteeo, Opooloo." Fry is merely following alphabetical order in placing CERAM after CELTIC, but the difference between the visually and phonetically intricate Ossianic poetry and this most basic of vocabularies built of just five consonants and four vowels is fortuitous for the argument Fry wants to make about the comparative mental richness available within the CELTIC language. "This language," Fry writes on the facing page, "under all it's disadvantages from the subjecting powers of Greece and Rome; and afterwards from Saxon innovations in this country, is still spoken with much purity upon a great part of the continent, and in the islands of Scotland; and it exists at this day one of the greatest living monuments of antiquity." Linking the CELTIC to "this country," *Pantographia* invites its Anglo-British reader to take pride in the CELTIC language, imaginatively rejecting the "subjection" of ancient empires and the "innovations" of the Germanic Saxons. The maneuver suggests a way for non-Celtic English speakers to feel the autochthonous connection to British personhood they had projected onto Celts, without allowing actual Celts into social acceptability.[16]

The linguistic identity that develops around Fry's twenty-one specimens of "ENGLISH" responds to the same revolutionary disruptions that prompted Mackintosh's, Webster's, and Dufief's linguistic endeavors. *Pantographia* explicitly describes English as a language that survives revolutions. "There is not, perhaps, any language in the world, which has experienced so many revolutions as this," Fry writes, "and, like the political constitution of the country, it seems to have gained both strength and energy by every change." In Fry's telling, the history of the English language is the history of successive waves of political upheaval. After the Norman conquest, William the Conqueror, "in imitation of other conquerors, endeavored to make the language of his own country [i.e., Norman French] as generally received as his commands," Fry writes, and the serial imposition of new language regimes by new political regimes meant that "the ancient English became an entire medley of Celtic, Latin, Saxon, Danish, and Norman-French." More recently, Enlightenment science had introduced "innumerable terms . . . from that inexhaustible source, the GREEK," and "Italy, Spain, Holland, and Germany, have also contributed something, so that the present English may be considered as a selection from all the languages of Europe."[17] This upbeat narrative about the history of English translingualism advertises not only the language's reassuring capacity to survive political change but also a basic imperial value: the capacity to be enriched by other people's productions, linguistic or otherwise, which Fry locates at the core of the English language. Four thousand miles away, on the English linguistic frontier in Martinique, Duncan Mackintosh was writing the same narrative into his own linguistic extravaganza at almost exactly the same time, boasting of English's "hȁ`vĭng ȅnrịch′ȅd ĭtsȅlf′ bȳ ṭhȅ wȅ*a*lth′ ȍ*f* ȁḷl′pŏl′ĭshȅd lȁ′ng-ûȁgȅṣ." Mackintosh's interest in mythologizing English as inherently global and absorptive is straightforward: he is in a distant multilingual environment on the front lines of empire, in territory that could change national hands at any time, but his imperial mythology of the English language places him at the heart of linguistic Englishness, not at its margins. *Pantographia*, a decidedly metropolitan production, illustrates how the mythology of an imperial, revolution-proof English language had purchase as a locus of "English" identity not only in the colonies but also at the empire's metropolitan center.

Types of Difference

Yet *Pantographia* may be less significant for its particular ideas about speakers of English and other languages than for the sort of engagement that it asks its readers to undertake: it asks them to evaluate the languages of the world in the same way that they would evaluate a specimen of typography. In most contexts, typography works hard to be unnoticeable. Reading founts are designed to "prevent[ ] us from noticing anything about the letters over and above the words they make." But eighteenth-century readers directed a certain amount of attention to typography, precisely because bad type becomes conspicuous and distracting. The post-1700 migration of typographical vocabulary out of the print shop and into general English is one index of how typography has never really been invisible: uppercase and lowercase, stereotype, typecast, cliché, mind your p's and q's.[18]

High-quality printing involves a great deal of careful labor, but none of that labor is quite as immediately apparent in the printed product as the condition of the type used in the printing. Sloppy proofreading causes imperfections, but they are rarely as conspicuous as the imperfections caused by worn-down or low-quality type. Type quality, therefore, became a potential competitive advantage for printers who had the capital and the supplier relationships needed to maintain crisp type. This required considerable resources, as type was expensive and had to be regularly replaced: it wore down over time, becoming smudgy or broken, at which point it would be sold on the secondhand market to an undercapitalized or provincial printer, and eventually sold back to a foundry to be melted down and recast.[19] One of the many hints that Benjamin Franklin drops in his autobiography as to his printerly superiority over his older brother James is that James's type was in terrible shape when he died in 1735. Franklin set James's son up with "an Assortment of new

Types" and congratulated himself for having "thus . . . made my Brother ample Amends" for the three years of apprentice labor of which he had deprived him by skipping out early on his indenture in 1723. When printers had new type, they were eager to say so. One Scottish printer, for example, advertised in 1800 that he had "disposed of his old materials" and "purchased, from the first founderies in the kingdom, a complete and elegant assortment of Types"—reiterating again, later in the advertisement, that he had "the advantage of his materials being *new*, and from the most approved makers."[20]

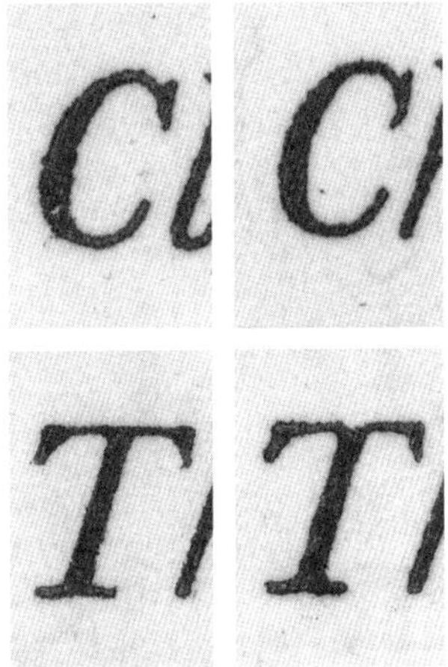

Detail from *Pantographia*, reflecting type in excellent condition (left) and type showing wear (right); note the buckling of *C*'s serif and erosion at the joint of the *T*.

Similar assurances of the material superiority of print objects are almost ubiquitous in eighteenth-century printers' and booksellers' advertisements for large projects, and these advertisements also kept typography in public view. A "New and Elegant Quarto Edition of The celebrated WORKS of VIRGIL," for example, was advertised in 1788 as being "Beautifully and correctly printed on superfine Paper, with new Types, cast on Purpose by the inimitable FRY and Co."[21]—that is, brand-new type cast by Edmund Fry's firm, specifically for this publication. The *Monthly Mirror*, a lively entertainment magazine focused on British theater, referenced the same material superlatives when it boasted in 1800 that it was not raising its price even though it had "procured an entirely new Type . . . and we trust its superior excellence will be no less conspicuous than the acknowledged taste and accuracy of our printer." That the *Mirror* cost just a shilling illustrates how far type quality was relevant to middle-class audiences, not just to the luxury market (although it certainly was relevant there as well).[22]

While eighteenth-century printers competed with each other with respect to the condition of their type, they generally did not compete with respect to its design. For most of the eighteenth century, almost all printers in the English-speaking world used a single type design, created in the 1730s by the typefounder William Caslon. When their type wore out, they bought more from Caslon's foundry (operated by the patriarch's heirs after his death in 1766), or from another foundry: the standard product at virtually every foundry was an in-house replication of Caslon's design, as close to the original as the foundry's punchcutter had the skill to make it. As a result, almost all eighteenth-century printing is set in Caslon or a Caslon knockoff. Mackintosh's *Essay*, printed in Boston: Caslon. Gilchrist's Urdu-English dictionary, printed in Calcutta: Caslon. This type design remains iconic today as the body text of *The New Yorker*.

This paragraph, like the rest of the book, is set in Caslon.

Edmund Fry was nine years old when his father opened London's third typefoundry in 1766 with the unusual and ill-fated business plan of breaking the Caslons' aesthetic monopoly on British typography. Instead of casting type in the Caslon tradition, Edmund Fry's father drew inspiration from John Baskerville, the Birmingham businessman who had recently attracted considerable attention by publishing an impressive edition of Virgil on type of his own design and manufacture. Baskerville's type was lighter and more slender than Caslon's, with starker contrasts between the thick and thin parts of letters. Fry's father thought Baskerville's design was the type of the future, so the type that he began manufacturing actually exaggerated Baskerville's most distinctive qualities: the Fry foundry's version of Baskerville's design is even thinner, sparer, and lighter than the original.[23]

This paragraph is set in Baskerville.

The elder Fry was correct when he predicted that Baskerville's tall and thin design was the design of the future, but he got ahead of the demand curve by more than a century. Baskerville's type, as refined by Fry Sr., was among the most widely used and influential designs in twentieth-century typography. During the eighteenth and most of the nineteenth centuries, however, it was considered too avant-garde for general use. Eighteenth-century readers found it difficult to look "through" the medium of Baskerville typography to the words of the text; the medium was distractingly strange. One of Baskerville's contemporaries warned the designer that "the exceeding sharpness of his letter . . . beyond anything we had been used to, would certainly offend."[24] And offend it did. The difference between Caslon and Baskerville may be extremely subtle to the modern reader; but type, like other aesthetic objects, is a matter of taste, which is to say that

This paragraph is set in Fry's Baskerville.

Quouſque tandem abutere

Quouſque tandem abutere

Quouſque tandem abutere

From top to bottom, Caslon (c. 1730), Baskerville (1757), Fry's Baskerville (1766), as digitized by Carol Twombly for Adobe Systems (1990), by Monotype Design Studio (1995), and by an open-source collective led by Simon Pascal Klein (2011–12), respectively. From top to bottom, the thinnest parts of the letters become much thinner, the serifs terminate more sharply, and short (*x*-height) letters such as *m* stretch vertically to rise higher relative to tall letters such as *d*.

its beauty is in the eye of the beholder, for reasons that are beyond the beholder's conscious awareness and intertwined with class, ideology, and power. Benjamin Franklin tells a story about getting into an argument with a gentleman in London in 1760 who predicted that Baskerville's type "would be a means of blinding all the readers in the nation, for the strokes of [the] letters, being too thin and narrow, hurt the eye."[25]

Even if Baskerville-style type did not literally blind the reading public, it evidently represented some shift in "national" meaning or culture that Franklin's interlocutor was detecting and anxious about. That attunement to the nonsemantic dimensions of linguistic communication exemplifies the media consciousness that Fry would call on in *Pantographia*—although Fry would encourage readers to direct that attunement toward ethnographic purposes rather than toward predictions of optic catastrophe. Fry demonstrates how to draw conclusions from letterform design, for example, when he asserts that the alphabetic specimen labeled Irish 5 "bears strong marks of a barbarous age."[26] The age that produced that alphabet was evidently a barbarous one, and to Fry that barbarity was detectable in its alphabet, even without arranging that alphabet into the form of barbarous words. The evidence of barbarity was in the letterforms, not the words.

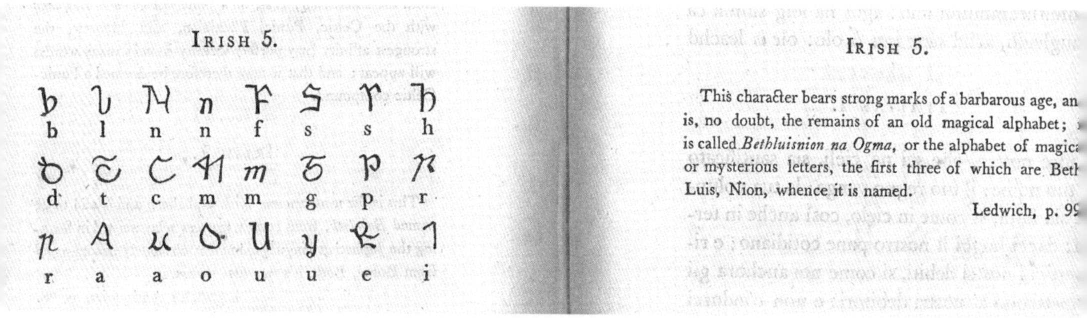

No doubt the remains of an old magical alphabet.

By the time the twenty-five-year-old Edmund Fry became a partner in his father's foundry in 1782, the firm's experiment in avant-garde typography had pretty well failed. The Frys adopted a new strategy: instead of producing distinctive type, they would produce type utterly indistinguishable from Caslon's—the best, most precise, most meticulous Caslon clone available. Unlike his father, whose professional background was in medicine, Fry was an expert cutter of type. He spent the first few years of his partnership in the firm cutting punches for exceptionally precise copies of the dominant Caslon type.[27] This aspect of type manufacturing was a highly skilled and laborious process. The first step was to stamp, cut, and shave the end of a chunk of steel into the shape of each letter that needed to be cast. This steel "punch" was then tempered (hardened) and driven into a bar of soft copper to make an impression or "matrix" into which molten type metal would later be poured. Making a punch and its corresponding matrix took at least four hours, but the result was an extremely durable and valuable object. In the hands of a skilled foundry worker, a matrix could yield hundreds of pieces of type per hour: ladle a spoonful of molten type metal (an alloy of lead, tin, and antimony) into the matrix, and it hardens almost instantly into a piece of type. Matrices last essentially indefinitely: Britain's last operating typefoundry was still casting type from some

A steel punch (not one of Fry's) for the numeral 1. Fry evidently made more than 4,000 punches for *Pantographia*. Norwick Center for Digital Solutions, Southern Methodist University.

of Fry's Baskerville matrices as recently as 1986.[28] The characters for *Pantographia* would have required the same meticulous punch-cutting process, but without the future payoff; as Fry was no doubt aware, there was no commercial market in eighteenth-century London for Bulgarian type, Burmese type, or the vast majority of *Pantographia*'s other alphabets.[29]

Casting type. The worker in the middle is preparing to ladle a spoonful of molten typemetal into the wooden mold in his left hand. The matrix for a single character is mounted inside the mold. After pouring in the typemetal he will open the mold to let the piece of type fall into the tray. The operation takes about fifteen seconds per piece of type. From *Illustrated Vocabulary for the Deaf and Dumb* (London, 1857). Washington University Libraries, Department of Special Collections.

Fry had an artistic and scholarly mind, and the business of executing someone else's designs might have bored him. He started working on *Pantographia* as soon as he joined the firm. If a part of him longed for an outlet for more original, creative, or aesthetic typefounding, *Pantographia* was that outlet. When his father retired in 1787 and Fry became lead partner, he was advertising eight sizes of his new Caslon-compatible type—8-, 9-, 10-, 11-, 12-, 14-, 18-, and 20-point type, each in roman and italic—designed to "mix with, and be totally unknown from" a printer's existing stock of Caslon, as well as eighteen sizes of the more avant-garde Baskervillesque type, ranging from 4.5 to 72 points.[30] In the end, the Fry operation ended up as the more aesthetically conservative foundry, as the Caslons, perhaps seeking to outmaneuver Fry's perfect clone, developed a new design in the 1780s and 1790s. In any case, Fry's Caslon imitation succeeded at turning the business around. The Caslon firm held the title of "letter-founder to the king," but in 1786 the Frys scored the coup of being named letter-founders to the king's son, the prince regent and future George IV.[31] Fry's commercial retreat from his father's failed typographical experiment, therefore, provided the relative financial stability from which he went about accumulating the linguistic materials for a typographical experiment of his own. He acquired an eclectic library of polyglot Bibles, travelogues, treatises, dictionaries, encyclopedias, histories, and a great deal else; and developed epistolary relationships with scientists and intellectuals such as John Nichols, editor of the important *Gentleman's Magazine*.[32]

How to Read a Type Specimen

Caslon's and Fry's foundries, which were situated around the corner from each other in central London, kept up a vigorous commercial rivalry, taking passive-aggressive shots at each other in their promotional materials.[33] Neither firm advertised regularly in newspapers, although they benefited from the hundreds of newspaper advertisements taken out by publishers who bragged about using type cast by "the ingenious Mr. Caslon" or "the celebrated Edmund Fry and Co."[34] The chief promotional materials of both firms were the specimen books that they produced every few years and distributed at no charge to printers, who in turn used them in discussions with clients. Fry, for example, threw in six free specimen books and a stack of two-page specimen sheets with a 1786 shipment of type to the Massachusetts printer Isaiah Thomas, asking Thomas to "distribute [them] according to thy own Discretion" to other printers.[35] But although specimen books have a practical commercial purpose, they also (like most forms of advertising) exceed the formal business purpose that they explicitly serve. A type specimen book exercises its audience's familiarity with a mode of textual engagement or "reading" that depends on ignoring the semantic meaning of its words. Type specimens depict printed language, but they seek to do so without presenting linguistic content: they call for their "readers" to suspend the process of interpreting ink shapes as letters composing meaningful words and instead apprehend them as graphic shapes per se. This is exactly the opposite of how reading usually works. "Reading," writes one design historian, "begins when letters vanish" into the page and we become "conscious of words, not letters."[36] By contrast, reading a type specimen depends on making the words vanish and becoming conscious of the letters. This is why type specimens maintain identical semantic content from page to page, book to book, and foundry to foundry: what varies is the size, design, execution, and other aspects of the material form. In the Fry and Caslon specimen books, per conven-

The learned Dr. Edmund Fry, M.D., about seventy years old, a quarter-century after *Pantographia*. His right hand rests on a copy of his magnum opus. Oil on canvas, by Frederique Boileau, c. 1830. Courtesy of Deirdre Fry.

tion, each roman and each italic face is composed into the opening lines of Cicero's first Catilinarian oration—the same text on every page so that the semantic meaning drains away by repetition.[37] The specimen book wants the reader to ignore Cicero's dispute with Catiline and look instead at the shapes of the ink. In this way, type specimens are "meta-mediating" texts; they ask their audiences to focus on an aspect of print communication that is usually looked through. They foreground the graphic medium rather than allowing it to recede. A typefounder needs his audience to cultivate this mode of reading, because a typefounder is in the business of selling letterforms, not texts.[38]

In its conspicuous display of technical excellence and typefounding chutzpah, *Pantographia* could be understood as a type specimen book taken to the genre's logical extreme. Its pages visually echo the type specimen genre and depend on the same subordination of textual content to the form or medium in which it is represented: like a type specimen book, *Pantographia* exists not to communicate any particular linguistic content but to illustrate a diversity of linguistic forms. The book certainly had an advertising function and helped make Fry's reputation as a specialty typefounder. Impressed by the "ingenuity and industry exhibited in this publication," one of *Pantographia*'s early reviewers announced his view that "if the typographic art be still capable of improvement, few persons are better qualified than Mr. Fry to bring it to perfection." Fry rebranded his operation as "The Polyglot Foundry," and during the first decades of the nineteenth century he was a leading manufacturer of non-Latin type. After he earned a medical degree from the University of Aberdeen in his early forties, he went by "Dr. Fry"—and although he never practiced medicine, the credential enhanced his reputation as the typefounder for the learned. John Gilchrist, who praised *Pantographia* as a "guide through the very elements of literature," associated Fry with exotic, exceptional type and expected that his readers would too. When he had his own experimental type cast by one of Fry's competitors in 1825, he was careful to assure the public that the foundry he used was "at least on a footing with fry."[39] Comprehensive, reiterative, and typographically conspicuous, *Pantographia* calls for the same mode of reading as the specimen book—a mode of reading in which language is a visual object to look at rather than a semantic object to understand. It turns this mode of reading, however, not just to the commercial purpose of selling type but to imaginative, aesthetic, and ideological purposes of classifying human diversity.

The elite readers who bought *Pantographia*, however, were mostly not the authors, publishers, and printers who ordinarily encountered type specimen books, so it would be fair to wonder how much of its audience saw the same analogy between ignoring words to focus on letterforms in a type specimen and ignoring words to focus on linguistic form in *Pantographia*. In fact, though, while type specimen books were not part of a typical eighteenth-century reader's print landscape, other "specimens" of material print did come routinely to a typical print consumer's attention, especially via a widespread but little-remarked protocol of eighteenth-century subscription publishing

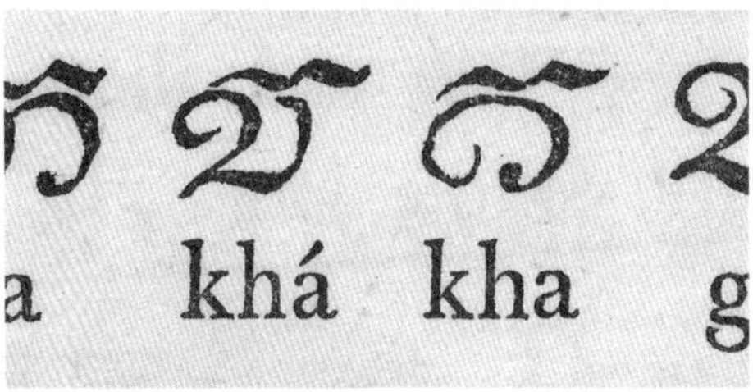

Detail of "Bali" (Balinese) specimen in *Pantographia*.

that made evaluating printed "specimens" part of the normative consumer experience of late-eighteenth-century print culture. Publishers contemplating capital-intensive projects standardly issued short "specimens" illustrating the material form of the larger whole and encouraged retail customers to inspect them.[40] In newspaper advertisements, publishers referred customers to booksellers or print shops where such specimens could be examined: "Specimens of the type, &c. may be seen at the different booksellers," for example, or "Specimens of the Types on which the above Works are printed, may be seen by applying to the Printers of this Paper."[41]

These small printed "specimens" illustrating the paper, ink, type, and design of larger consumer print objects existed in far greater numbers and circulated much more widely than the type specimen books used within the printing trade. For example, the London publisher of a *New, Complete, and Universal System of Geography* to be delivered in eighty weekly installments in 1792 announced in newspaper advertisements that the first week's installment was "intended as a public specimen of this performance, and may be returned if not approved." The publisher urges "country booksellers . . . to order a quantity of the first numbers . . . for the perusal and inspection of their customers."[42] Among the publisher's goals in this advertisement are to enlist country booksellers to teach their customers the norm that responsible book-buying entails first inspecting the type and other materials. When Noah Webster's publisher sent around a specimen sheet of the lexicographer's forthcoming *American Dictionary* (1828), he was very careful to note that this sheet was *not* representative of the type: "The following is a Specimen of the lexicography of Webster's Dictionary; but not of the type, paper and printing—the type and paper not being yet procured. The type will be new, and the oriental words printed in their proper characters."[43] Such advertisements promoted not only a specific print product (Webster's *American Dictionary*) but a way of thinking about print products that maintained a rigorous conceptual distinction between a printed object's semantic content (in Webster's case, "the lexicography") and its material form ("the type, paper and printing").

It was in publishers' interests to promote that media theory, especially in Britain after the 1774 legal decisions that radically changed British intellectual property law by ending perpetual copyright protection.[44] These decisions released thousands of valuable texts into the public domain and sent printers scrambling for competitive advantage. With copyright limited to fourteen years (renewable once), printers could no longer rely on the exclusivity of their steady sellers' textual content but had to compete on the material form in which they presented that content: the ink, the paper, and the movable type used to transfer the one to the other. (They also competed on price, of course.) By issuing specimens of consumer print products, publishers were arguing implicitly for the material specificity of their textual products. They were claiming that their products' value rested to a meaningful extent on an irreducibly specific set of typographic and other materials on which they would be printed, which could not be described in words or replicated on anyone else's equipment. This was certainly true of *Pantographia*, which depended on a singular assemblage of one-of-a-kind material types. *Pantographia* makes the experience of evaluating typography as a medium into a luxury consumer good. In this way, Fry—like Dufief, Mackintosh, Webster, and Gilchrist—was trying to sell a product that rested on the "language makes the difference between man and man" idea. Evidently anticipating some demand for *Pantographia* in an even more luxe form than it already took, Fry had a few copies printed on vellum and extravagantly priced at ten guineas. One of those vellum copies wound up in Calcutta, in the library of the multilingual college where John Gilchrist had been hired as the first professor in 1799, just as *Pantographia* was going to press half a world away.

Types of Pleasure

Pantographia cannot be reduced to the ethnographic conclusions toward which it often gestures. The sheer visual exuberance of *Pantographia*'s typographic diversity seems to be at the heart of its meaning, at least as much as any of its ideas or claims. It is not a treatise, and exposition is not its main strategy: it relies on the rhetorics of repetition, variation, glossing, and accumulation—performing and materializing (rather than explicating) its meaning. Its basic move is to repeat itself over and over with slight differences. In this respect, *Pantographia* has much in common with Nicholas Dufief, who also sought the depths of linguistic knowledge by repetition rather than by rational explication. There are 201 alphabetic tables in the book—the letters of an alphabet lined up in order rather than arranged into words—so if you wanted to, you could come away from the book with 201 different symbols with which to graphically represent a single sound, such as the voiced bilabial stop: ب, β, ב, ࠁ, Б, 𝔅, B, ब, etc. While *Pantographia* contains a preface and some glosses and headnotes, it seems unlikely that many of the people who have ever looked at the book have spent as much time reading its expository sections (the preface, the headnotes) as they have spent thumbing through its pages, savoring and scrutinizing the visual and sonic exotics of foreign languages that they cannot understand. This is one implication of its being in the form of a type specimen rather than in the form of a treatise. A treatise declares its own authority; a specimen declares its examiner's authority.

Pantographia can be engaged as a text, but it also exceeds its own textuality: it is about the line where words become sounds, and letters become shapes. It makes the arbitrariness of the reader's linguistic reality visible: we make these sounds and draw these shapes, but other people make other sounds and draw other shapes. The book may require letting go of the conceit that the main point of books (or any material texts) is to yield knowledge. What if the point of *Pantographia* was to yield pleasure? One 1799 book review of *Pantographia*, in fact, closes with the prediction that readers "will find much pleasure, and some information in the perusal of it."[45] *Much* pleasure; *some* information: in *Pantographia*, the visual pleasure of type makes contact with the imperial pleasure of otherness. Perhaps type was already a locus of aesthetic pleasure, and what Fry did was to provide a way for that pleasure to feel useful or relevant by linking it to the scholar-approved mode of ethnographic knowledge that languages supposedly yielded. Or perhaps *Pantographia* was less for "using" than for "perusing"—for aspects of the human encounter with material texts that we still don't have much of a vocabulary for and that are often frowned on, such as judging a book by its cover, or flipping through it and looking at the pictures. The Amharic, Malagasy, and English Lord's Prayers quoted earlier take their place in the volume along with 153 other versions of the Lord's Prayer—some of them in non-Latin alphabets, but most of them transliterated into Latin letters with roughly English phonological values so that an English-speaking reader could ostensibly vocalize and perceive these other sonic representations of the meaning that in English sounds like "Our Father who art in heaven, hallowed be thy name . . . ," without understanding anything else about how those sounds correspond to that meaning. The semantic meaning remains stable while the sonic form varies:

Abyssinian: Abbahn shirfifu. Selenskgi zebonsha . . .
Bengallee: Bappa kita, jang adda de surga, Namma-mou jadi bersakti . . .
Ancient British 2: Ein tad yr hwn wytl yn y nesoedd. Sanctedidier dy enw . . .
Ethiopic 2: Abuna xabashamajath. Yithkadash shimacha Thymtsa mangystcha . . .
Gothic 4: Atta unsar thu in himinam; veihnai namo thein . . .
Icelandic 1: Fader vor thu som ert a himnum, helgest thitt nafn . . .
Irish 7: Ar nathair atá ar neamb, naomhthar hainm . . .
Madagascar 2: Amproy antsica izau hanautangh andanghitsi angharanau hofissahots, vahoüachanau hoaui aminay . . .
Mexican: Ore rure u bacpe Ereico: Toicoap pavemga tu a va . . .
Molqueeren: Oes Veer der iin de hiim'len binne. Jimme nemme word heil'ge . . .
New England: Nooshun kesukquot, quittiana tamunach koo wesuonk . . .
Persian 3: Ei padere ma kih der osmon. Pak basched nâm tou . . .
Savanna: Keelah nossé kitshah awé heyring. Yah zong seway ononteeo . . .
Siamic 2: Po raou you savang, scheu pra hai prakot touk heng kon tang tai . . .
Virginian: Nooshun kesukquot. Quittiana tamunach koowesuonk . . .
Walloon: Pærinthele nostru cela ce esti en cheri. Svintzas cæse numele teu . . .

Is this a cacophony? a symphony? The final words of *Pantographia*'s long title suggest thinking of it as "A COMPREHENSIVE DIGEST OF PHONOLOGY." But whatever the word "phonology" means to us is not what Fry had in mind: *phonology* is his own coinage, and the title page of his *Pantographia* prospectus is its first known usage in English.

The two coinages that bookend the title page—"PANTOGRAPHIA . . . PHONOLOGY"—declare the book's aspiration to be a complete record of two media by which language emerges from the mind into physical phenomena: a "graph"-ic medium addressed to the eyes, and a "phon"-ic medium addressed to the ears. Writing and speaking are the most common mechanisms for rendering language empirically perceptible, but they are not the only possible ones. Several of Edmund Fry's extrapantographic activities suggest that he had a broader interest in the mediation of language per se, not just its mediation in the "graphic" and "phonic" forms covered by *Pantographia*. He was very interested in lip-reading and became involved with the first institution in Britain at which that skill was systematically taught, the London Asylum for the Deaf and Dumb Children of the Poor, which opened in 1792. He name-checked the Asylum in *Pantographia*'s preface, mentioning that "several children have already been discharged capable of understanding what they read or see, and of expressing all their wants by articulate language."[46] (His involvement with this organization seems to have led a nineteenth-century biographer to conclude that Fry himself was deaf, which he was not. The error has been repeated in subsequent accounts of him.[47])

In addition to those graphic, aural, and labial mediations of language, a tactile medium became one of Fry's significant interests toward the end of his life, some decades before Louis Braille's system gained worldwide momentum. Twenty years after the publication of *Pantographia*, Fry was once again cutting type for an alphabet that no one had ever printed before—not a design by John Baskerville or William Caslon, but Fry's own design for an alphabet of twenty-six letters to be read through the fingertips. It had already become clear by the 1810s that embossed printing for tactile reading would be a workable system for blind literacy. The printing technology necessary to appropriately deform the paper already existed. But reading materials for blind people were not produced in large quantities until decades later, not because of a technological hurdle but because of the institutional hurdle of agreeing on a standard alphabet.[48] Much as John Gilchrist intervened in the long process of standardizing a set of graphic symbols for phonetic transcription by designing and manufacturing ***gulkrusts yoneversul karektur***, Edmund Fry intervened in the long process of standardizing a set of tactile symbols for alphabetic transcription by designing and manufacturing a fount of type to be read through the fingertips. He tinkered with this project in the 1810s and got *Blackwood's Edinburgh Magazine* to mention in 1820 "that Dr Edmund Fry has printed a sheet, on which the letters are raised on the paper, and capable of being felt and read by the fingers' ends"—but of course, as had been the case with magazine reviews of *Pantographia*, magazine notices about his tactile typographic undertaking could not illustrate that undertaking because they lacked the type necessary to do so.[49]

Another decade passed before Fry found an appropriate forum in which to present his tactile alphabet: in 1832, the Royal Scottish Society of Arts announced a prize competition for the "Best Alphabet and Method of Printing for the Use of the Blind." The Society received twenty entries, including Fry's. When these designs for tactile alphabets were eventually all printed together, they amounted to their own little *Pantographia*—no longer bespeaking an epic investment of type-manufacturing labor, however, because in the three decades since *Pantographia*'s publication, the new technology of lithography had made specimens of unusual typography trivially easy to print.

As in all type specimens, the twenty proposals all strive to represent the same content, depicting a new diversity of solutions to the one representational task of making the letters of the Latin alphabet haptically perceptible. The contest had in fact been poorly designed: in the four years that intervened between the prize deadline and the selection of a winner, the prize committee changed its mind about what it was looking for, deciding that "the best alphabet for the blind" would be one that preserved the forms of the Latin alphabet and thus remained legible to sighted readers. Fry's was the only entry of this type, so he won the prize by default, on May 31, 1837. He wasn't able to accept the honor, however. He had died a year and a half earlier, just before Christmas 1835.

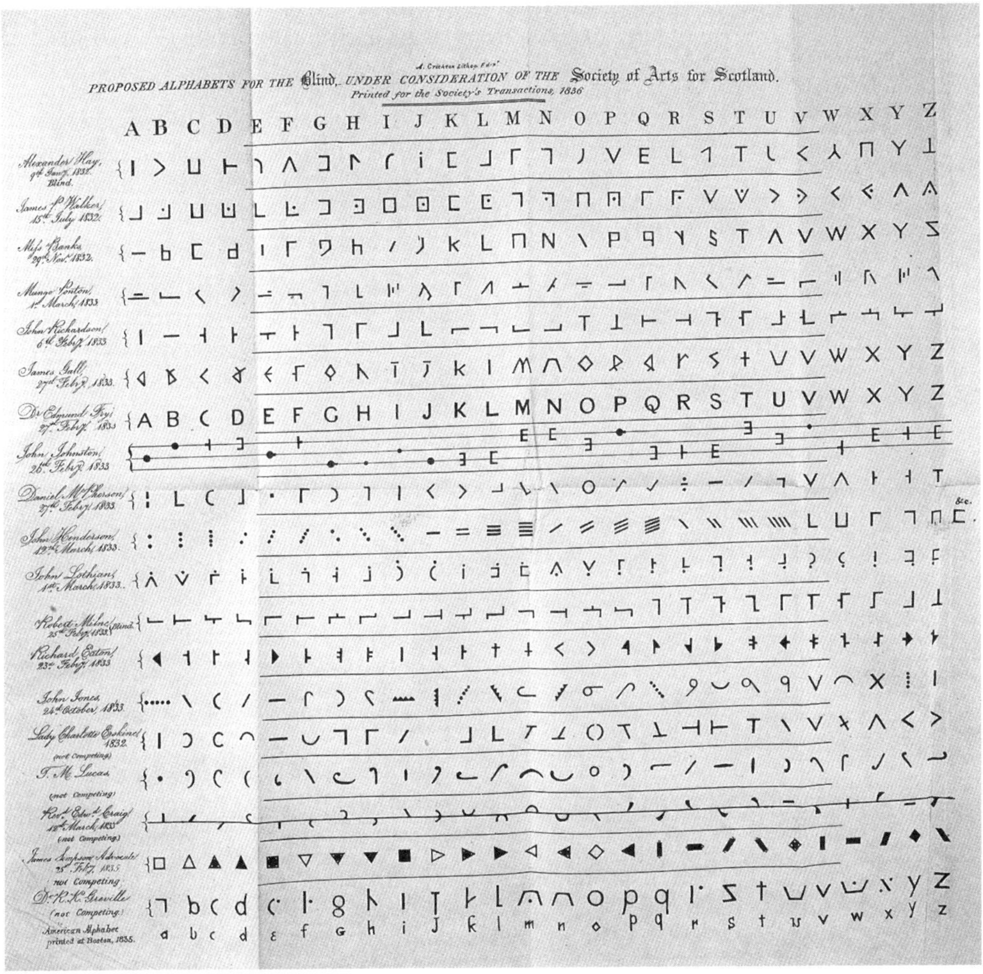

Tactile alphabets evaluated by the Scottish Society of Arts for its 1833 prize contest "on the best alphabet and method of printing for the use of the blind." Edmund Fry's proposal is seventh from the top. Lithograph in *Transactions of the Royal Scottish Society of Arts*, vol. 1 (Edinburgh, 1841). © The British Library Board, RB.23.a.34000.

From beyond the grave, therefore, Fry was still issuing specimens of alphabetic type. Tactile printing did not go in the direction he envisioned—Braille characters have no relationship to the shape of their corresponding Latin letters. But Fry's tactile alphabet was anticipatory in other ways. It was a very different design from the eighteenth-century Caslon, the slimmed-down Baskerville that had caused such a ruckus, the even-slimmer Fry take on Baskerville, or the so-called modern faces that rapidly replaced Caslon at the beginning of the nineteenth century. No one knew quite how to describe the letters that Fry had entered into the Scottish prize competition. One of the competition's judges wrote that Fry's letters were "what, I believe, are called by printers the Egyptian letters." But later he corrected himself: "I find I am not correct in calling these letters *Egyptian*; but what I mean is a plain letter without *feet*, and having all lines the same thickness."[50] The term he was looking for, of course, is *sans serif*, but the terms *serif* and *sans serif* were scarcely known at the time. (Despite appearances, *sans serif* is not a borrowing from French but an English coinage with

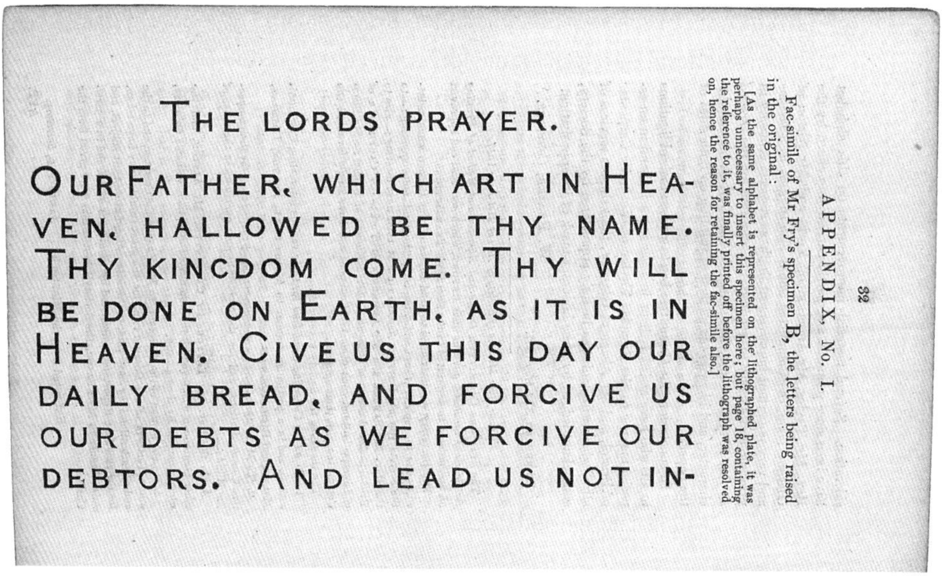

32

APPENDIX, No. I.

Fac-simile of Mr Fry's specimen B, the letters being raised in the original:

[As the same alphabet is represented on the lithographed plate, it was perhaps unnecessary to insert this specimen here; but page 18, containing the reference to it, was finally printed off before the lithograph was resolved on, hence the reason for retaining the fac-simile also.]

THE LORDS PRAYER.

OUR FATHER, WHICH ART IN HEAVEN, HALLOWED BE THY NAME. THY KINGDOM COME. THY WILL BE DONE ON EARTH, AS IT IS IN HEAVEN. GIVE US THIS DAY OUR DAILY BREAD, AND FORGIVE US OUR DEBTS AS WE FORGIVE OUR DEBTORS. AND LEAD US NOT IN-

Fry's winning entry in the 1833 tactile alphabet contest. © The British Library Board, RB.23.a.34000.

murky origins.) Fry's tactile type specimen is one of the very earliest appearances of sans serif type, though it is not the absolute first.[51] The specimen that he submitted to the Scottish Society was, like 156 of his *Pantographia* specimens, the Lord's Prayer.

If *Pantographia* was about making language physical, so was Edmund Fry. As a typefounder, he lived his life surrounded by tiny particles of language that flowed in alphabetical order (or, just as often, not in alphabetical order) out of his foundry in London, silent and uncommunicative linguistic potentialities waiting to be realized as text. In *Pantographia*, those particles—indeed, every conceivable linguistic particle—are ordered and contained; the owner of *Pantographia* will (allegedly) never confront a script he cannot pronounce, and he will never think of a people without being able to imagine how their language sounds. The book holds out the possibility of the linguistic reintegration of a human world that seemed increasingly fragmented. For those who believed that language makes the difference between man and man, the fantasy of *Pantographia* was that it marks the difference between man and man.

CHAPTER FIVE

Mary Willcocks's Caraboo Tongue

The Invention of 

On a Tuesday night in September 1817, concertgoers gathered at Philadelphia's largest theater to watch a twenty-five-year-old woman write and speak in a language that they knew did not exist. After the crowd had been warmed up for a half-hour with stirring orchestral music and several popular songs, the woman of the hour was escorted to the stage by two male attendants as "the room shook with applause."[1] She was dressed from head to toe in satin and lace, with elaborate silver embroidery, and a silver lace turban on her head.[2] "Paper was handed to her," a newspaper reported, and the audience watched as she wrote a letter in the imaginary language that she had famously invented, "that language which had puzzled the Universities of Oxford and Cambridge, and the most learned professors of the Oriental languages in Great-Britain." The crowd ate it up, "particularly the ladies." Finally, the young woman spoke briefly to the audience in her invented language, a performance that was "highly applauded." She gave her audience what they had come for: a disorienting encounter with what seems like language but isn't, a disorientation familiar to anyone who has ever 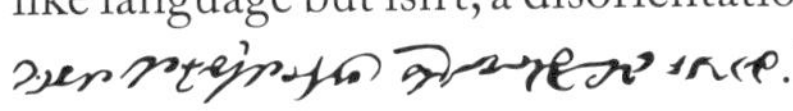. Newspapers declared that she had verified "the purity of her character and views" and proven herself to be "an innocent and unoffending female" who was "highly accomplished

The star of the show. Detail from an engraving by Nathan Cooper Branwhite, 1817.

in her manners." She canceled a planned second Philadelphia concert and headed to New York, where she found it difficult to leave the house without being hounded by crowds of curious onlookers.[3]

Six months earlier, the same twenty-five-year-old woman was a beggar on the streets of Bristol, England. Six months before Bristol, she was let go from a servant job outside London after intentionally setting two beds on fire, though her mistress swore that except for the fire she was "the best servant she ever had." Two years before that, she dressed as a man and held a job as a male farmhand near Bath. A year before that, she was kicked out of London's Magdalen Home for Penitent Prostitutes after indignantly denying having ever been a prostitute. (Six months before that, she applied for admission to the Magdalen Home for Penitent Prostitutes.) Two years before that, she learned to write. A year before that, she was hospitalized for "a brain fever" (acute insanity). A year before that, she almost committed suicide. A year before that, she was a domestic servant on a country estate in western England. Eight years before that, she was put to work spinning wool. Eight years before that, she was born.[4] Her name was Mary Willcocks.[5]

But Mary Willcocks was not the name under which she took the stage in Philadelphia. In notices about the event in local newspapers, she gave her name and this postscript: "P.S. As you may probably not know me by my subscribed name, you will by that of Carraboo."[6] Nor was she being overly presumptuous when she asserted confidently that "you will" know her. Her arrival in Philadelphia a few weeks earlier had touched off a nationwide media event. By the time she appeared on stage, articles had appeared about her in seventy American newspapers. In Vermont, a satirist reported that Caraboo had been spotted "more than 20,000,000 times in the U.S." and that fashionable American babies were forgoing "the old expression '*ah goo!*'" and saying "CARRABOO" instead.[7] Her brief celebrity became an occasion for Americans to play with identity by playing with language. Among the characters in this book, Willcocks illustrates the fullest and strangest possibilities of linguistic identity in the Age of Revolutions.[8] The era's linguistic thinking intersected with her unique linguistic talents and gave her an opportunity to exercise a stunning amount of control over the racial, national, socioeconomic, and gender dimensions of her social identity. Language made the difference between Willcocks and Caraboo, and in this chapter I set up Willcocks's life in considerable detail in order to illuminate the aspects of her identity that were accessible to her linguistic intervention. In a broad sense, she was doing what all the characters in this book did: manipulating, transforming, and experimenting with language in the service of creating a new kind of self.

Mary Willcocks's transformation from beggar to celebrity is not a classically American bootstrap narrative in which the protagonist achieves economic self-sufficiency through diligent labor and honest dealing. Instead, she achieved her brief economic self-sufficiency through linguistic skill and cunning. That spring, in England, she had persuaded hundreds of scholars and socialites that she was an Asian princess by speaking a pseudo-Oriental language of her own invention. For two solid months, the gentry of Bristol and Bath knew her as Princess Caraboo. When it emerged in June that she was not Asian or a princess after all, she seized a lucky opportunity to get very far away on a Philadelphia-bound ship. And even before she landed, American newspapers were reporting the story, celebrating her as a trickster-hustler who had cleverly hoaxed the British intelligentsia—an early practitioner of the showmanship and hucksterism that would later be celebrated as quintessentially American in P. T. Barnum's American Museum (1841–65), Herman Melville's *The Confidence-Man* (1857), and Mark Twain's *Huckleberry Finn* (1884).[9] The fact that Willcocks-Caraboo never tried to rob her wealthy hosts despite ample opportunities to do so led her contemporaries to conclude that she had "no apparent object, but an ambition to excel in deceit."[10] She parlayed a lie into a livelihood—for a time, anyway—and she went down in history as "the most amusing, and perhaps the least noxious, of modern cheats," the purveyor of a deception so clever and harmless that you want to overlook its mendacity and just admire its execution.[11]

Mary Willcocks's real story, though, is less jolly, and not really a hoax. She didn't intend to become Princess Caraboo, nor was the Caraboo persona part of any larger "ambition to excel in deceit." Unlike Duncan Mackintosh, Noah Webster, John Gilchrist, and Edmund Fry, who created linguistic innovations because they wanted to, Mary Willcocks invented her language for self-preservation: she was trying to avoid being arrested. Detained in a Bristol suburb for illegal begging, she deployed a desperate *I-don't-speak-English* defense that worked better than she could have possibly imagined. It was only "with reluctance, nay, almost with force," that she was conducted by well-intentioned locals to the suburban mansion where she became known as Princess Caraboo.[12] She had a natural talent for glossolalia, the practice otherwise known as speaking in tongues, and could effortlessly produce a steady stream of speech sounds that sounded convincingly like language. Interviewed by the Bristol town clerk, the town clerk's wife, their Greek-speaking manservant, and the local Overseer of the Poor, Willcocks responded to questions unhesitatingly in her incomprehensible glossolalia and allowed her auditors to draw their own conclusions about what she was trying to say. The episode could be thought of less as a hoax than as a brilliant linguistic defense against institutionalization—a defense that nightmarishly becomes its own prison. She couldn't take off the linguistic mask without exposing herself to criminal prosecution.[13]

The town clerk's wife, Elizabeth Worrall, took a special interest in the apparently unfortunate young foreigner. When she indicated that she wished to know the female stranger's name, Willcocks pointed to herself and cried "Caraboo, Caraboo."[14] After a few days' uncertainty, and a great deal of pantomime, and some intriguing suggestions from a Portuguese sailor on a brief layover in Bristol who claimed to have picked up a little of "Caraboo's" language in the East Indies, it was settled: instead of being removed to the Bristol poorhouse as an English vagrant charged with begging, the young woman would be removed to the Worralls' mansion as a Malaysian princess shipwrecked in a foreign land. For the next two months, Mary Willcocks lived with the Worralls as Caraboo, speaking only her increasingly elaborate invented language. Prompted by her eager hosts to flesh out her backstory, and using the details hazarded by the Portuguese sailor as a starting point, and drawing on several different literary genres, Willcocks explained through pantomime that she was a princess from a Pacific island called Javasu, had been kidnapped by human traffickers, and, after a five months' captivity at sea, had leapt overboard and swam to shore in what turned out to be England.[15]

Week after week, a stream of tantalizingly opaque linguistic evidence poured out of Caraboo's mouth. Visitors flooded the Worralls' house, "eager and solicitous to examine and listen to the unknown foreigner."[16] But the many scholars and travelers and curiosity seekers who tried to identify Caraboo's language (and, thereby, identify her) were stymied. The excitement about her in general, but about her language in particular, illustrates how thirsty Britain was for linguistic knowledge about its imperial world—the same knowledge that Gilchrist and Fry were also trying to make available through their typographic innovations. In fact, the Worralls procured a copy of Edmund Fry's *Pantographia* and paged through it with their guest, hoping that Caraboo would point to her language and thereby locate herself within the known diversity of humankind.

No linguistic identification was forthcoming from the volume. But without quite realizing what they had done, the Worralls had just given Willcocks a detailed account of her audience's linguistic expectations. She began incorporating details from *Pantographia*'s diverse vocabularies into Caraboo's language, such as the word "Alla-talla" (God) from a specimen labeled "LAMPOON . . . one of the principal languages spoken in the island of Sumatra." With *Pantographia* as a reference guide to her patrons' linguistic ideology, Willcocks was able to reverse-engineer a faux language that exactly matched elite British expectations about Oriental languages in the early nineteenth century. She also quickly developed a written counterpart to her spoken glossolalia, ingeniously synthesizing the graphic qualities of known Oriental languages without quite being identifiable as any one of them. Caraboo's language thus seemed very much like it belonged to a missing page from *Pantographia*—partly because of Willcocks's own knowledge and intuition and partly because she was literally working from *Pantographia*.[17]

Word began to circulate that the Worralls had an Oriental princess staying at their house—"Indian," "Chinese," "Japanese," "Javanese," or "Malay," depending on the report—initially by mouth, then by mail, then in the local newspapers in Bristol and nearby Bath, then in the London and Edinburgh press, and then in newspapers in every part of the British Isles. A Bristol newspaper joked that her presence had "excited uncommon bustle amongst the *Greeks*, *Malayans*, *Chinese*, *Shanscritians*, *Arabians*, *Persians*, *Sumatrans*,—and ALLAH TALLAH only knows how many Ans besides."[18] It is as if Caraboo opened a door to limitless numbers of identities—the God-only-knows-how-many "-ans" superadded to an already long list of exotics. She was every possible Oriental identity in one, a canvas on which Britain briefly projected its global imagination.

Caraboo turned out to be a delightful guest, exhibiting a fascinating panoply of seemingly Oriental practices. She climbed onto the roof to worship the sun. She cooked curry and ate a vegetarian diet. With cloth that was offered her, she sewed clothes in her native fashion. She swam expertly in the Worralls' pond, practiced scrupulous hygiene, shot a bow and arrow, danced in "an infinite variety of attitudes . . . bend[ing] her body in numberless shapes," banged a gong, climbed trees, and beat Mr. Worrall at fencing.[19] In other words, she performed a nineteenth-century British fantasy of southeast Asian ways of life, in addition to a nineteenth-century British fantasy of southeast Asian written and spoken language.

The backstory that Willcocks invented for Caraboo—or, really, the Caraboo narrative that she co-created with the curious visitors whom she coaxed into leaping to conclusions—drew on the standard

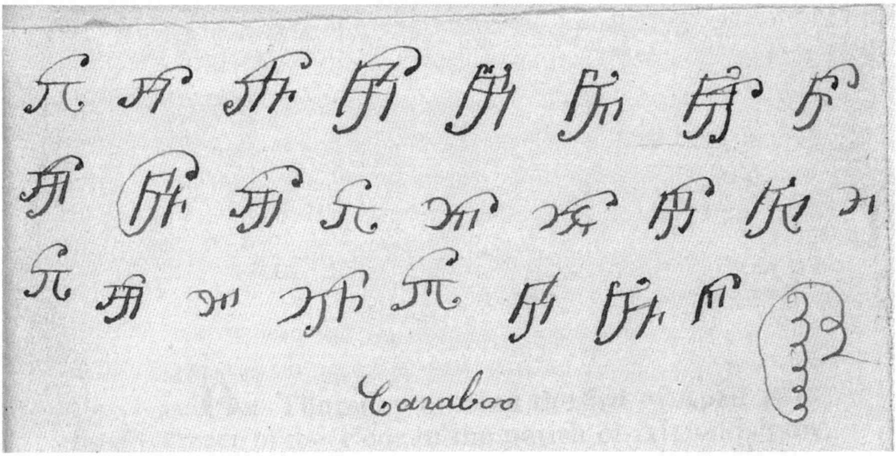

The only surviving document in Mary Willcocks's hand: a souvenir that she gave to one of the many curiosity seekers who visited her after her Caraboo persona was debunked. Tipped into a copy of the Gutch–Worrall Caraboo pamphlet. *EC8.B1752.817C. Houghton Library, Harvard University.

adventure-romance trope of the highborn woman threatened with rape by pirate kidnappers. Six months before her appearance at the Worralls', it seemed, Caraboo and her female attendants were strolling through her garden in Javasu when they were set upon by pirates. Armed with a dagger, Caraboo fought back, killing one pirate and wounding another, but was nevertheless seized, bound, and taken on board a ship. The pirate chief then sold her to what appeared to be a sex slavery operation trafficking Asian women among Dutch and British spheres of influence. The ship picked up four more women in Batavia (Jakarta) and delivered them to Cape Town, Africa. Months later, the ship reached the North Atlantic. Sighting land, Caraboo made a daring escape by jumping overboard into the Bristol Channel and swimming to shore through the frigid February waters. She wandered helplessly around Gloucestershire for six weeks until fortune found her at the Worralls'.[20]

While the Caraboo persona helped Mary Willcocks avoid one kind of imprisonment, it imposed a different kind on her: the prison of being a character in someone else's fantasy. During her two months as Caraboo, she twice attempted to escape from the Worralls' mansion, hoping to change her clothes, slip into Bristol, board an America-bound ship as Mary Willcocks, and let the Worralls go on with their lives with only memories of their royal visitor. Both times, however, the Worralls mobilized a frantic search for the missing princess, and both times she was spotted by someone who knew her as Caraboo before she was able to embark. So she was obliged to remain behind the Caraboo mask and beg Elizabeth Worrall's pardon by explaining in pantomime that she had wandered off because she was homesick for her native Javasu.

"Caraboo" happened because a desperate woman with a linguistic talent collided with an ideology that put language at the center of identity and an empire that brought human otherness into view. Language isn't the only thing that mattered in Mary Willcocks's life: her boundary-crossing and in some ways queer sexuality, her poverty, or her chronic illness might have occupied more of her attention. Those were among the circumstances that made her vulnerable and relatively powerless. She had a linguistic opportunity to seize a little more power over her identity and her body; she seized it and went where it took her.[21]

The Caraboo Archive

From the perspective of two centuries later, Mary Willcocks's season as Caraboo is a vivid and creative episode in an ambitious life filled with strangeness and traumas. She grew up very poor in a small village in southwestern England, where her father was a shoemaker. An athletic child with "a wild disposition" and a competitive streak, Willcocks learned to read (but not write) in school and began work early as an agricultural laborer. From age fifteen, she suffered from recurring episodes of what we would call a mental illness, though in nineteenth-century medical terms it was deemed "a rheumatic fever, which affected her head," "a brain fever," or "a frenzy fever." Still, she was healthy enough at sixteen to reenter the workforce as a live-in servant at a farmhouse a few miles from her home, where for more than a year she took care of the children and helped out around the farm. A dispute about her compensation led to her quitting the job, much to the frustration of her parents, who "used her ill on account of leaving her place" of employment. Years later, when Mary Willcocks's father was asked why his daughter no longer lived at home, Thomas Willcocks responded that he "could not tell the reason of her leaving him," but "it was not on account of his beating her with a strap, though he had once done so, for going with another girl to a fair at Exeter." In fact, he acknowledged, that was not the only time he had "flogged her well." Whether for reasons of physical abuse or for other reasons, Mary Willcocks ran away from home. She was seventeen. She spent much of the next eight years either homeless or institutionalized.[22]

Sketchy as these details of Mary Willcocks's early years are, this is far more information than has survived about the vast majority of nineteenth-century working-class women. For this, the credit is due to Elizabeth Worrall. As the Caraboo story unraveled, Worrall wanted to know who had been living in her house for the past two months. She sent friends to London and to Willcocks's hometown to see what they could find out. They conducted more than a dozen interviews, including with her parents, her pastor, three former employers, and five former landladies—collecting what amounts to a small archive of personal correspondence, institutional records, oral histories, press clippings, and pictures. Worrall then collaborated with John Mathew Gutch, a Bristol newspaper editor who interviewed Willcocks at length after the truth came out, to collate their research into a pamphlet published just two months after the "Caraboo hoax" became public. The pamphlet is subtitled *A Narrative of a Singular Imposition*, but it's much more an archive than a narrative, reflecting written and oral contributions from more than thirty different people. Gutch organized the materials for publication with considerable restraint and transparency, separately presenting information gleaned from each source and allowing points of contradiction among the different accounts to remain unresolved. He also claims to report Willcocks's own account of herself largely as she gave it and in her own words—even the parts that he and Worrall determined to be untrue.[23]

Like all archives, the Gutch–Worrall pamphlet is very uncertain evidence. Its depiction of Mary Willcocks is mediated by what Willcocks was willing to say, what her relatives and former employers were willing to share, what Elizabeth Worrall was willing to hand over to Gutch, and what Gutch was willing to print. "Princess Caraboo" is a robust figure in the historical record, mentioned as princess, fraud, or both in hundreds of articles, poems, letters, novels, and advertisements—but Mary Willcocks is not. Except for what Gutch and Worrall printed in their pamphlet, very little of Mary Willcocks's life beyond Caraboo was preserved. Only one known document survives in her hand (shown in the preceding section), and it is a very difficult one. Still, the Gutch–Worrall pamphlet amounts to one of the richer caches of information that exists about any nineteenth-century working-class woman.[24]

In spite of the illness that "affected her head" during her adolescence, Mary Willcocks lived within the expected parameters of working-class life in rural England until she was seventeen—living with her parents or nearby and contributing her meager wages to support her family. After she quit her job and left her parents, however, her life became significantly more abject. With nowhere in particular to go, she spent a few months wandering up and down a sixty-mile corridor between Exeter and Bristol on foot, stopping at houses and cottages to beg. She slept in barns, did not get enough to eat, and came very close to hanging herself.[25] Turning her steps toward London, she covered more than a hundred miles on foot, then hitched the last thirty miles into the city. Suffering from "illness and fatigue," she collapsed at the door of one of London's ninety workhouses—institutions of last resort for the poor and starving—and was carried to its infirmary, where she was gravely ill for months.[26]

Going Viral: The [Caraboo script]tion of the Caraboo Language

Years later, when Willcocks arrived in Philadelphia, she was immediately invited into the homes of elite Philadelphians, where she delighted them with "private exhibitions" at which she "wr[ote] the Carraboo language with great facility," producing scraps of Carabooish text like the one shown earlier.[27] Visitors wanted to see her do her Caraboo act—evidently appreciating the Caraboo character as artifice rather than as reality. When private exhibitions did not satisfy demand, the theatrical performance was arranged. But most of Caraboo's appearances in the United States were in the newspapers, not on the stage. The American Caraboo newspaper event was enormous and truly national. The story about Caraboo broke in the British press in early June; Willcocks sailed from Bristol in late June; and by the end of August—before Willcocks herself even arrived—dozens of articles about her had already appeared in the American press. By the end of October, more than ninety newspapers had run articles about her, including in dozens of nonmetropolitan locations far beyond the mid-Atlantic centers of print culture (New Bern, North Carolina; Petersburg, Virginia; Hallowell, Maine) and on the distant frontier (Lexington, Kentucky; Natchez, Mississippi; St. Louis, Missouri).[28]

Since "Caraboo" arrived in North America not as an ostensibly real Indian princess but as a confessedly faux-Indian princess, she provided an occasion for Americans to have a hearty laugh at British gullibility and to celebrate American shrewdness.[29] Gleefully summarizing the culmination of Willcocks's life as Caraboo in Britain, one New York newspaper correspondent wrote that "Miss Caraboo was beginning to be considered as a native of another planet—when lo! the bubble burst, and John Bull for the thousandth time looked like an ass."[30] It was an exercise in self-definition that took place, as it often does, by disidentifying with somebody else, in this case "John Bull," the personification of the English people; *we* would never be so foolish. "The citizens of Philadelphia did not go see this out-cast as the London folks did, supposing her to be a Japanese Princess," explained the editor of a small newspaper in Vermont, "but merely to see what awkward imitations of Royalty can impose upon the Credulity of Englishmen."[31] And they found something appealing, and even appealingly American—"highly to the honor of the American character," one journalist wrote—about Willcocks's multiethnic, multilingual performance of identity, the nuances of which had confounded the Old World.[32]

But "Caraboo" was not only an opportunity for affirming the American difference from England. She also touched off an opportunity for Americans to play linguistically with more exotic identities. Americans wanted to act à la Caraboo. Newspapers from that fall contain dozens of efforts to write, speak, and print Carabooishly. In Georgetown, D.C., a wag jokingly announced the formation of the "Carraboo Eerf dna yzae xaoh CLUB"—the Caraboo Free and Easy Hoax Club, with letters scrambled—in a notice that had purportedly been "Translated from the original Carraboo by command of the great Chow Chow."[33] The Orientalized linguistic playfulness extends beyond the ching-chong linguistic stereotype: it also breaks English into parts and then rearranges them to form something linguistic that isn't quite language, an *eerf dna yzae xaoh*. This is exactly what Caraboo did with her invented language and script.[34]

In dozens of newspapers, Caraboo provided an occasion to put familiar linguistic materials into unfamiliar configurations. In upstate New York, the *Albany Gazette* printed a facsimile of Caraboo's handwriting —copying the illustration from the *New-York Daily Advertiser*, which had copied it from the *Boston Intelligencer*, which had copied it from Philadelphia's *Freeman's Journal*, which had copied it from the *Bath Gazette*, which had copied it from Gutch's *Bristol Gazette*, which had copied it from Mary Willcocks.[35] This viral reengraving was extremely unusual and probably made Willcocks's Caraboo writing the year's most widely

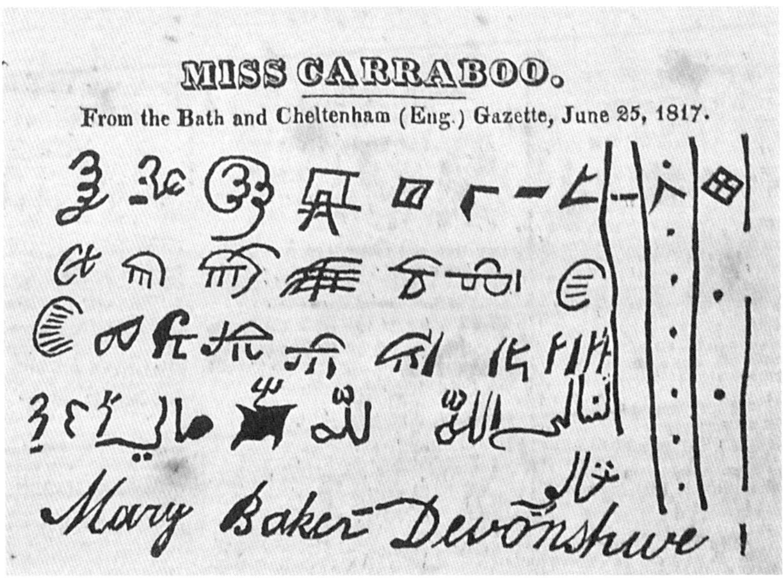

Caraboo's written language in the *Freeman's Journal* (Philadelphia), Sept. 6, 1817, engraved from a similar illustration in the *Bath Gazette*. "Mary Baker" is a name that Willcocks used on and off after 1812. The Arabic words اللّه (Allah), and تعالي (May He be exalted), appear to be attempted several times in the bottom row of characters.

reprinted illustration in American newspapers. Although newspaper *text* circulated widely, jumping easily from newspaper to newspaper by the convenience of movable type, very few graphic representations of anything (aside from stock images) came off multiple presses, ever, because each printer had to undertake or commission the laborious and imprecise process of engraving the design into a block of wood.[36] The newspaper editors who invested in the Caraboo illustration apparently expected significant readerly interest—or maybe they were also indulging their own enjoyment in tracing the pseudolinguistic shapes.

Even newspapers that did not have the resources to produce an engraved illustration for the Caraboo story got in on the grapho-linguistic fun. A newspaper in northern New Jersey jokingly published its own typographic simulation of Caraboo's writing, constructing what it winkingly describes as a signature "in the Caraboo language" out of about a dozen pieces of movable type: punctuation of various sizes, rarely used symbols, broken letters, and other typographic odds and ends, turned sideways and upside down and packed together to form an intricate patch of lines and curves that feel recognizably like printed language but don't add up to anything.[37] Unlike the facsimile, which required manufacturing a new printing block, this pseudo-signature was made out of movable type, so it could be reprinted without much trouble—and it was, in at least ten states. Some of the fifteen newspapers that reprinted the joke made an effort to retain the graphic form of the signature as they had received it, using roughly the same fourteen pieces of type as each other, in the same orientation, and producing graphically similar results (e.g., the four signatures in the left-hand column on the next page), while other compositors created their own more elaborate variations on the same theme, with twice as much type (e.g., those in the top-right and bottom-right). All of them, however, play with the conjunction of straight lines with curved ones; they all turn characters upside-down and sideways; they all mix different sizes of type together and subvert the eye's customary effort to sort printed characters into horizontal lines of type.

What was being "reprinted," therefore, was not a particular sequence of characters but a joke or game or fantasy about written communication. It was, perhaps, the same joke, game, or fantasy that Mary

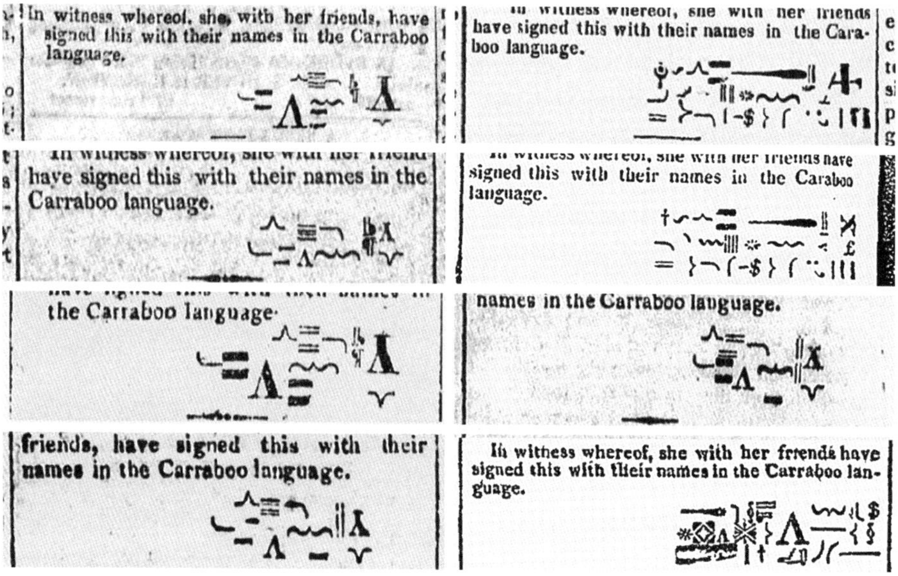

In witness whereof, she, with her friends, have signed this with their names in the Carraboo language.

In witness whereof, she with her friends have signed this with their names in the Cara-boo language.

In witness whereof, she with her friends have signed this with their names in the Carraboo language.

In witness whereof, she with her friends have signed this with their names in the Caraboo language.

the Carraboo language.

names in the Carraboo language.

friends, have signed this with their names in the Carraboo language.

In witness whereof, she with her friends have signed this with their names in the Carraboo language.

Eight newspaper printings of Caraboo's typographic "signature." From left to right and top to bottom: *New-York Daily Advertiser*, Sept. 26, 1817; *Northern Whig* (Hudson, N.Y.), Sept. 30, 1817; *Alexandria* (Va.) *Herald*, Oct. 1, 1817; *Albany Gazette*, Oct. 2, 1817; *Newburyport* (Mass.) *Herald*, Oct. 3, 1817; *Dedham* (Mass.) *Gazette*, Oct. 10, 1817; *Western Monitor* (Lexington, Ky.), Oct. 18, 1817; *American Yeoman* (Brattleboro, Vt.), Oct. 28, 1817. Courtesy of Readex.

Willcocks had played in England. Liberated from typography's ordinary semantic function—conveying meaning in words—the compositors were reaching into the rarely used corners of the type cabinet and playing with the common characters as shapes rather than as letters. How often does a compositor get a chance to use the ⟨ in his type drawer? Here was an occasion to use (or misuse) the compositor's expertise, intentionally making mistakes. The particles of language remain abstract nonsemantic shapes rather than cohering, as they usually do, into meaningful words. It is yet another exercise in breaking language apart and rearranging it into something that looks like language but isn't—the opposite, in a way, of what Benjamin Franklin did when he experimented with rearranging the letters into something that doesn't look like language but is (see chapter 2). Like Dufief, Mackintosh, Webster, Gilchrist, Fry, and Willcocks, the handful of American compositors who played this game went beyond manipulating language for the purposes of communication, the way poets do; they manipulated the medium, not the message. And like all the characters in this book, the American compositors undertook their metalinguistic manipulations in the context of imperial distance: Willcocks's transatlantic distance from Bristol, which they shared, and Caraboo's far greater distance from Javasu, which their typographic game gave them an opportunity to re-create.

Things Apart: London, 1810–1813

The brain fever at St. Giles's Workhouse hospital was Mary Willcocks's second encounter with serious illness and the second time that her illness had a mental component. Two years earlier, she had suffered "a rheumatic fever, which affected her head," and it was since then, according to her father, that "she was not right in her mind." In the London workhouse hospital, she was "insensible in a brain fever." Neither "brain fever" nor "rheumatic fever" was a particularly well-defined condition, nor did either diagnosis require the elevated temperature that the word "fever" now denotes; in nineteenth-century medicine, the word often simply means a state of agitation. A "rheumatic fever" entailed systemic pain, fatigue, nervous complaints, and other diffuse and typically shifting symptoms; the typical patient was an adolescent or young adult, and although most patients recovered, relapses were extremely common. The symptoms of "brain fever" were also vague, but more serious than rheumatic fever and more specifically cerebral, involving delirium, confusion, moaning, convulsions, catatonia, "noisy vociferation or screaming," sensitivity to light, and incoherent speech. The brain fever that Willcocks suffered at St. Giles's Workhouse hospital was a severe case. Doctors shaved her head and applied acids or suction to her scalp to raise blisters—the standard of care for insanity. Months passed. She scalded herself with a teakettle and nearly fell down a flight of stairs. She got better, then worse, then better.[38]

People liked her. Those who got to know Mary Willcocks during her pre-Caraboo young adulthood described her as "odd," "strange," "eccentric," and even "out of her mind"—but to the extent that she was insane, she was blessed with an extremely charming insanity, as some people are. She was a person you wanted to take care of, and she accumulated parental figures, up to and including Elizabeth Worrall. During her recovery at St. Giles's, she made an impression on a Presbyterian minister named William Pattenden, so that when the eighteen-year-old was discharged from the hospital, Pattenden made it his business to find her a permanent place to stay, as a maidservant to a well-to-do family just across the Thames in the London suburb of Kennington.[39]

The three years that Willcocks would spend as a servant in Kennington proved the most stable period of her young adulthood. Her mistress, Elizabeth Mathews, was "very partial to her" and later told Elizabeth Worrall's friend that "every one, who came to her house and saw her, took an interest in her"—even though "her behavior was always strange and eccentric, and her ways so mysterious." Pattenden and his wife, meanwhile, remained in Willcocks's life, even introducing her to their acquaintances as their "adopted child." Years later, the Pattendens said that "they did not think there was any harm in her; but she was always so odd and eccentric, that Mr. P. said it would fill a volume, if he were to transcribe all that he knew of her."[40]

Eccentricities and all, she was an excellent servant to the Mathewses, colorful and well liked, "correct in every respect, except that she told terrible stories," according to Elizabeth Mathews. Sometimes she announced that "she would not eat for several days together, to shew how long she could live without food" or said that "she should like to go and live in the woods." A woman who employed Willcocks a few years later recalled similarly first-rate performance of her servantly duties and a similar flood of implausible narratives pouring out of her: Willcocks was "the best servant she ever had in her house," Elizabeth Starling told Elizabeth Worrall's friend, and good with the children, though she told them "such strange stories about gypsies and herself, that she frightened them out of their wits." For example, "she told them she had been in the East-Indies and America; that she was in Philadelphia; was brought to bed by the side of a river; that a lady and gentleman going by in a carriage took her up, and had her taken care of." On one memorable occasion, Willcocks "came into the parlour, and had dressed herself up so like a gypsey, that the children did not know her." Although both mistresses thought "she must be out of her mind" and officially frowned on her wild storytelling ("correct in every respect, *except* that she told terrible stories"; "very fond of her children, *but* told them such strange stories"), they both liked her a great deal, and it's easy to imagine that the children adored her.[41] She had the storyteller's gift of capturing your imagination and whisking you away to fantasyland. This skill undoubtedly contributed to the success of her Caraboo story later on.

It was also during her three years in the Mathews household that Mary Willcocks learned to write, tutored by the Mathewses' teenage daughter Betsy.[42] As soon as she could operate her literacy well enough to do so, she wrote to her mother and father, with whom she had parted on bad terms two years earlier (but "not on account of his beating her with a strap," her father insisted). Her letter slips in and out of mundane epistolary formulations, and it's hard to know how much this letter constitutes impression management—saying what she thinks her parents or her employers want to hear. Years later, the Willcockses handed this letter over to Worrall and Gutch, who printed it with orthographic imperfections intact:

> Im in most delightful place and my mistress Treats me with all Imaginable kindness and my youn miss is Larnd me to write and ihope ishall nax Letter isen belebl to write befor I hve ver good friends . . . i do my work wil paleasure. . . . my dear mother I whe you wer so happy as im I hop my dear brothers will never let you want for ant thin I wich it was in my por to mker you comfortable but my dear mother I have send you wan pond not and I hop it wall be acceptable presents.*

These halting, formulaic reiterations of epistolary pieties stand in vivid contrast to the quenchless creative flood of original language that would pour out of her mouth and pen five years later as Caraboo. But these familiar formulations are also interwoven with less generic language—glimmers, perhaps, of the creativity and audacity with which she would wield a pen as Caraboo: "I wnt to now the situation that you Live in with it is beter now and it nas when i Live ther?" she asked, then cut

*I am in a most delightful place, and my mistress treats me with all imaginable kindness, and my young miss has learned me to write, and I hope I shall next letter [even be able?] to write [better?]. I have very good friends . . . I do my work with pleasure. . . . My dear mother, I [wish?] you were so happy as I am. I hope my dear brothers will never let you want for any thing. I wish it was in my power to make you comfortable, but, my dear mother, I have sent you a one-pound note and I hope it will be an acceptable present.

directly to the point: "it was bad Enough then with I hop it is beter now."* She closes the letter with an expression of uncertainty about one of the basic facts of her own identity. "I have got wan vever to beg of you," she wrote, "that is to send my aged for i wich to now how hold im": *one favor—send my age, for I wish to know how old I am.* It wasn't the last time that her legal identity would be a kind of stranger to her.

*I want to know the situation that you live in. Is it better now than it was when I lived there? It was bad enough then; I hope it is better now.

Her position in the Mathews household guaranteed Willcocks the basic necessities of food, shelter, and medical care, necessities of which at other times she was not at all assured. But the position also came with severe restrictions on her personal liberty. She was not permitted to leave the Mathewses' house except for church and for four times a year when she was allowed to visit the Pattendens at their house in Clerkenwell on the other side of London. She struck up a friendship with the cook who worked for the Jewish family next door, talking over the garden wall when their mistresses weren't around. In January 1813, when the cook invited her to a wedding down the street, she asked the Mathewses for permission to go.[43] They said no, but she went anyway and forged a note to cover her tracks. Elizabeth Mathews was angry and asked William Pattenden, the clergyman father figure, to come by to talk to Willcocks about the transgression. "Fearing to see Mr. P," however, Willcocks hid in the alley behind the house all through the January night until Pattenden left in the morning. Then she collected her belongings and moved out.

Perhaps the events that led up to her leaving the Mathewses were another episode in what we would call her series of mental health problems.[44] Perhaps it was an irrationally intense anxiety, or paranoia, that led her to flee the confrontation with Pattenden—the prospect of an angry father figure colliding, perhaps, with memories of abuse received from her actual father—or perhaps she envisioned a different life and swept away her existing arrangement with the extreme optimism that can accompany mania. Perhaps Elizabeth Mathews was not only angry at Willcocks but aware that something was off with her and concerned. On the other hand, there are entirely sane reasons for wanting out of a living arrangement in which you are not allowed to leave the house.

Still, freedom of movement may not be what Willcocks was after: she moved out of the Mathewses' and into a setting that was significantly more carceral, not less. She mailed her belongings to her parents with a note saying that she had quit the Mathewses and gone overseas, then walked up the road to a complex of several buildings anchored by a neat Georgian mansion and otherwise concealed from the street by high brick walls. It was the Magdalen Home for Penitent Prostitutes, an institution that she had passed on her way to or from visiting the Pattendens. She applied for admission under the name of Anne Burgess, using her mother's maiden surname.[45]

One way to look at this sequence of events is that Willcocks knew that she needed help and structure and astutely put herself in an institution where she would receive it. Or perhaps there really was a sexual past, professional or otherwise, about which she was penitent or willing to say she was. A third possibility is that she was out of touch with reality and inaccurately believed that she had been a prostitute. According to the Magdalen's intake notes, she told the staff that her parents were dead; that she had been "seduced by a gentleman . . . who brought her to London, lived with her a month"; and that after he deserted her, she "went on the town, and led a loose life."[46] The staff liked her, worried about her, and did not believe the part of her story about her parents being dead. One memorandum in her file, obtained by Worrall and

The Magdalen Hospital for the Reception of Penitent Prostitutes: Mary Willcocks's home from February to July 1813. Wellcome Library.

Gutch, noted that "*Anne Burgess* conducts herself with great propriety, and seems *repentant almost to despondence.*" She was "very eccentric," "unsettled from the time of her admission, till she left the house," and concerned above all else to avoid a reunion with her parents. When the staff pressed her to help them locate her family, "she became more restless than before" and threatened to kill herself "if it was discovered who she was." She then recanted her story about being a prostitute and petitioned for her release on the grounds that "she was not a fallen woman." The staff talked her out of leaving the institution, twice, but could not sway her a third time, and she left at the end of July 1813.[47]

Our [illegible], *Ourselves*

Four years later, at the Worralls', Willcocks would find herself again living in someone else's mansion, her every move carefully observed, the recipient of care and attention because of a not-entirely-true backstory involving sexual degradation: Caraboo indicated that she endured five months of captivity aboard her kidnappers' ship before she jumped overboard "in consequence of the ill usage she experienced"—implicitly, rape—and swam to shore. Her exotic Pacific sexuality intersected with her sentimental captivity-narrative sexuality to produce a character that audiences eroticized quite overtly in print as well as in person.[48] The well-connected intellectual Hester Lynch Piozzi, who watched the Caraboo incident unfold from her home in Bath, penned some light verse about "the bright Maid of Bristol, by all Men admired," and a raunchy ballad printed in a popular women's magazine a few months later elaborated the erotics of her escape:

> Did she leave her fine garments behind her,
> When she plung'd in the sea in a huff?
> Or did those who first happen'd to find her,
> Meet the beautiful creature *in buff?*
> She breasted thy waves, Bristol channel,
> *Sans* petticoat, stocking, or shoe,
> 'Till landed, *a Fay* [fairy] brought her flannel,
> 'stead of fig leaves, for poor Caraboo.[49]

At once poking fun at the rubes who were so aroused by the erotic narrative that they lost their critical perspective, and simultaneously enjoying that same arousal, the balladeer presents Caraboo gliding nakedly to shore like Botticelli's Venus. Going beyond the general description of "in buff," the poet offers a textual striptease, beginning with the pun on "breasted" and proceeding down the body from there: petticoat, stocking, shoe. She arrives on shore not in a state of Edenic innocence but, like postlapsarian Eve, in need of "fig leaves" because aware of her own sexuality. Newspapers universally described her as physically attractive. "She is very fond of bathing; and swims and dives with considerable activity," reported Charles Wilkinson, M.D., a physician and science buff in his midfifties who did more than anyone else to publicize Caraboo's presence.[50] More than one reader wondered about the circumstances under which Wilkinson became aware of just how considerably active Caraboo's swimming was; one newspaper poet fantasized that she was sleeping with Wilkinson or another of the men whose letters speculating about her origins were crisscrossing British print culture: "Wert thou with ALL the men so shy? / . . . Was there no *tender téte-a-téte*, / Thy *admirers* thus to fascinate, / Who puff'd thy beauty through the nation?"[51]

This hypersexualized Pacific fantasy—approximately the same fantasy that Herman Melville would invoke twenty-five years later in *Typee*—was complemented by an Orientalist chastity fantasy: the Caraboo fetish also rested on her intriguing aversion to men. She literally recoiled at their touch. Her scrupulous chastity played to Orientalist fantasies of female sexual purity and submission, fantasies of gender-oppressive Oriental societies that policed women's sexual agency even more strictly than Anglo-American culture did. The very first newspaper report about Caraboo characterized her as "very cautious in her conduct with respect to gentlemen; never allows them to take hold of her hand; and even if their clothes should casually come into contact with hers, she retires from them." She disappeared one evening and was discovered after a frantic search perched high in a tree, where she had fled, she indicated, "because all the females in the house had gone into the village, and she feared contamination from the men."[52]

Who feared contamination from the men—Caraboo, Mary Will-

Left: The uniform at the Magdalen (not Mary Willcocks), where Willcocks lived for five months in 1813. This rigorously deeroticized costume highlights the sexuality of the 1817 oil portrait, in which Caraboo's dress exposes considerable cleavage, underscored by her appearing to be fondling her left breast. The Magdalen shoes, stockings, dress, and petticoat obscure the skin as well as the shape of her legs, while Caraboo's sandals and considerably shorter dress reveal her bare legs, and her unpetticoated figure is visible through the fabric of her dress. Frontispiece to *An account of the Rise, Progress, and Present State of the Magdalen Hospital*, 5th ed. (London, 1776). Courtesy of the New York Academy of Medicine Library.

Right: Mary Willcocks as Caraboo, wearing clothes that she made herself with cloth supplied by Elizabeth Worrall, in an oil portrait painted in 1817 while she was still thought to be a princess. Portrait by Edward Bird, oil on panel, 1817. Bristol Museum and Art Gallery, U.K. (civic painting, transferred 1972). Bridgeman Images.

cocks, or both? Her interviews with Gutch provide plenty of reasons for why Willcocks might have shared Caraboo's "cautious"-ness, starting with the fact that she had been homeless and had lived in workhouses, two contexts in which sexual abuse was endemic. According to what she told Gutch, after she left the Magdalen she wanted to return to her childhood home, 175 miles away, but was concerned about the safety of traveling on foot as a single woman, especially through the notoriously crime-ridden Hounslow Heath, a shrubland that is now Heathrow Airport. So she pawned the clothes she had with her and bought men's clothes instead, removed her earrings, combed her short hair, and headed out on the road—as she had done when she left her parents' house four years earlier, except now dressed as a man. About three days from London, still in men's clothes, she encountered six bandits who invited her to join their gang. Things quickly got weird:

> They asked, whether she could fire a pistol? She told them no, that she had never learnt to fire. They gave her a pistol, bidding her to fire it off, showing her how to do it; at which she was frightened. They called her a chicken-heart; and said, that she would not be fit for their service, unless she plucked up a bold heart and courage. She fired off the pistol more dead than alive, and screamed out that she was murdered.—They threatened to destroy her, having ascertained thereby her sex, if she did not tell, whether she did not come there as a spy: then she fell on her knees, told them every thing, and begged pardon; hoping that they would let her go free. On which the captain drew a sword and said, if she would swear by the sword, and all the powers above never to betray them, they would let her go free. Which she did. They gave her a guinea and five shillings, and she went off.

Stranger things have happened, and this incident may have unfolded exactly as Willcocks reported it to Gutch four years later—though it could easily be invented or embellished, as encounters between outlaws and cross-dressing women are a standard device in adventure narratives. Willcocks's account bears a particular resemblance to a ballad called "The Female Robber," which includes the female-to-male transgender disguise, the gang of bandits, the sex-ascertainment, and the woman

The titular "Female Robber" from a broadside ballad printed around the same time as the Caraboo incident.

walking away with money—though in the case of the ballad, they rape her first and give her the money to render the sex act transactional and label her a prostitute. Willcocks's story invokes at least the threat of rape—first in her general anxiety about traveling as a single woman, and second in the specific scene where she is in the woods, "frightened," with six armed outlaws who have "ascertained . . . her sex," "scream[ing] out that she was murdered." But whether or not Willcocks had a sexual abuse history, Caraboo certainly did. As Caraboo, Willcocks spoke as an abuse victim who had the profound compassion of wealthy and powerful people. For reasons of class and gender, it would have been difficult for Mary Willcocks, as herself, to have persuaded authorities to care about her sexual abuse, if it existed; they would more likely have blamed her for it.[53]

Her male disguise may well have been a defense against sexual violence; but perhaps she also took some satisfaction in the subterfuge; perhaps she liked playing a character. Perhaps she also liked being male; this was not the only occasion on which she arranged to be so. Although she changed back into women's clothes to see her parents and did some domestic work (as a woman) in a nearby town, she soon quit that job, obtained another set of men's clothes, and hired herself as a male laborer on a farm nearby. This second transgender period went better than the first one, although it too culminated in a dangerous and traumatic disclosure of her sexual anatomy. Sent on an errand during a severe snowstorm, she collapsed en route and was unable to get up. She was rescued the next morning and resuscitated, but the resuscitation entailed taking off her clothes. So she quit that job too.[54]

These transgender episodes are intriguing, whether they actually happened or she invented them for Gutch. If these episodes, real or fantasized, represent a longstanding interest in inhabiting a male-gendered social role, then perhaps Mary Willcocks had been engaged in a kind of gendered "passing" long before she undertook the transracial passing of the Caraboo character. Hints of such an interest appear elsewhere in her story, such as in the facts that her mother was "uneasy at her way of life" and that "from a very early age . . . Mary evinced a strong inclination to follow the occupations and amusements of a boy." Willcocks's parents also told Elizabeth Worrall's investigator about two incidents in which their daughter had a relationship with another woman that they registered as improper in some way: first that her father whipped her "for going with another girl, to a fair," and second that they learned of her running away to London in 1810 "from a girl who ran away with her, and grew tired of her journey and returned."[55]

This isn't much to go on, but queer history often requires making use of mere scraps and possibilities; queerness, in the sense of forms of intimacy that do not fall into one of the normative or institutionally sanctioned categories, is poorly represented in archives, for the same reason that other socially illegible things are poorly represented in archives: most of what gets written down, printed, preserved, archived, and cataloged makes sense according to the prevailing norms of what counts as meaningful. Part of what makes Willcocks's illegible [illegible]es so intriguing is that they are a rare case in which "meaningless" expression has been carefully archived. Her destabilizing, counternormative use of language makes her counternormative engagement with gender expectations all the more interesting: perhaps it is not a coincidence that her Caraboo character destabilized both language and gender. Perhaps her Oriental passing alleviated her gender passing: with her audience's attention focused on Caraboo's language, Willcocks created a queer space where she was allowed to shun the presence of men, where women could take an extremely intimate interest in her, and where she herself was allowed to act beyond the role of nineteenth-century woman that was expected of her.[56]

After she almost froze to death in the snowstorm, about a year went by during which the people interviewed by Gutch and Worrall's agents—her family at home, and her parental figures and employers in London—lost track of Willcocks. When she resurfaced in London in 1815, she was pregnant. She called herself Mary Baker now, saying that she had married a man named John Baker who then deserted her. Privately, her friends and family were doubtful as to whether there really had been such a marriage. Worrall and Gutch were never able to find anyone who had actually met the man that Willcocks described as her husband, and two years earlier she had told some of the Magdalen inmates that she sometimes used Baker as a fake name. Whether or not the husband existed, the baby certainly did. John Baker Jr. was born in February and cared for at London's Foundling Hospital, as Willcocks had to go back to full-time domestic work, where she once again impressed her employers as a bright if eccentric young woman and an excellent servant. She won the hearts of Robert and Elizabeth Starling, the latest in the series of economically comfortable couples to whom she became like family: the Pattendens, the Mathewses, the Worralls. She saw her son during the foundling hospital's weekly visiting hours until he died in October, about six months before she would appear at the Worralls' house as Caraboo. Things went downhill after that. She set a bed on fire in the Starlings' house, and then, a few days later, another one. The Starlings thought she might have been trying to frame a coworker whom she disliked, though the death of her child also seems relevant. Fearing for their safety, the Starlings dismissed her—"yet they liked her," they told Elizabeth Worrall's friend, "and had it not been for the affair of the fire, would have kept her."[57]

Willcocks turned up at her parents' house later that winter, for only the second time since leaving home at seventeen (not because of flogging) eight years earlier. When Worrall's friend later asked the Willcockses if they had noticed anything unusual about their daughter's behavior during that visit, her father said that "she was very *learned*," and more than once talked in a foreign language that he did not understand, speaking "very fast: she used to talk for two or three hours in a morning to her sister in bed"—probably the glossolalic pseudolanguage that Caraboo would speak a few weeks later. After staying ten days, Willcocks told her parents that she was going "to the Indies," not specifying whether it was the East or West Indies, and left.[58] A few weeks later and eighty miles away, she was picked up for vagrancy, taken to the local magistrate, and cornered into the defensive linguistic maneuver for which she became famous. She had been experimenting with wearing her handkerchief on her head like a turban and begging in the persona of a nonspecific foreigner, since she found that she drew more lucrative donations this way, and she wanted money badly. In Bristol, she had inquired about passenger fares to North America and found a ship on which she could sail in two weeks' time—if she could raise £5 for the ticket. She didn't set out to pose as Princess Caraboo; she set out to beg for charity. When threatened with institutionalization, she deployed the Caraboo persona in an effort to dodge the apparatus of the state.

The Linguistic Investigation

Long before Caraboo made her appearance, a different young woman was wrested from her native land under the threat of violence and carried across the ocean to Bristol. It was Elizabeth Worrall, then nine years old and named Elizabeth Lechmere. Her exile was forced on her not by human traffickers or pirates but by the American Revolution: her parents were noted Loyalists in Cambridge, Massachusetts, and when the British army abandoned Boston in March 1776, the Lechmeres went with them. Along with several of their neighbors from Cambridge's "Tory Row" (Brattle Street), the Lechmeres moved across the ocean to Bristol and re-created in the Old World their old neighborhood from the New World.[59] Like Nicholas Gouin Dufief, Elizabeth Lechmere became one of the Age of Revolutions' permanent transoceanic refugees. Eighteen years later, she married Bristol's town clerk, Samuel Worrall, and they made their home at an estate on a hilltop seven miles outside of Bristol, with a view all the way to the ocean.

Perhaps part of what made her take such an interest in the young foreigner whom she found detained in her house when she returned from church on Good Friday 1817 was that she knew what it felt like to be young and vulnerable and very far away from home. Seeing how things stood, she took the young woman aside and spoke to her in "soothing and compassionate language." According to what she told Gutch later, she said to her something to this effect: "My good young woman, I very much fear that you are imposing upon me, and that you understand and can answer me in my own language; if so, and distress has driven you to this expedient, make a friend of me; I am a female as yourself, and can feel for you." Caraboo's first test was linguistic, and she passed it: her face remained perfectly blank, "making it apparent that she did not comprehend what Mrs. W. had said to her; and she immediately addressed Mrs. W. in her unknown tongue." The young woman's evident proficiency in a foreign language and her evident non-proficiency in English largely convinced Worrall of her authenticity, as it did the others who first evaluated Caraboo. A city magistrate agreed the next day that "her language and manners were such as he had never before heard or seen."[60]

Willcocks was not wearing any sort of a disguise, except for "a black cotton shawl on her head, and a red and black shawl round her shoulders; both loosely and tastefully put on, in imitation of the Asiatic costume." But accenting one's dress "in imitation of the Asiatic costume" was normal behavior for middle-class Englishwomen at this time and not an indication of being from Asia. Nor did Mary Willcocks's body bear any particular indications of racial Asianness. The portrait taken by Nathan Branwhite just after her unmasking depicts "Mary Wilcox . . . alias Caraboo" in approximately the dress in which she first appeared to the Worralls.[61] Neither this portrait nor the full-length portrait taken *before* Caraboo was shown to be not Asian resorts to any of the usual

Mary Willcocks wearing the outfit in which she first appeared as Caraboo. This portrait was taken after she was identified as Mary Willcocks. Engraving by Nathan Cooper Branwhite; frontispiece to Gutch–Worrall pamphlet.

visual tropes for marking racial Asianness: thick eyebrows, squinty eyes, bulbous noses, darkened skin, etc. Contemporary prints of Caraboo represent her skin by leaving the paper blank, per European monochrome representational conventions for white people.[62] The believability of Caraboo's Oriental identity was not based on her racial-visual appearance. It was fundamentally linguistic.

The Worralls and some of their friends now began reaching out to Orientalists with specimens of her language. "In what hand does she write?—In what tongue does she speak? / Is it Arabic, Persic, Egyptian, or Greek?" a young Bath poet wondered lightheartedly. The goal of their linguistic research was partly to communicate with her, partly to identify her, and partly to authenticate her. After Caraboo recovered from a life-threatening illness—diagnosed at the time as typhus fever, but it could also have been another brain fever episode—she wrote the thank-you letter to the doctor who treated her, and this is the document that was hand-copied and sent to relevant institutions (see the first illustration in the introduction; that document is also the basis for the Carabooish typography appearing in this chapter).[63] "Her letter was shewn to every person in Bristol and Bath, versed in Oriental literature, *but without success*," one of the Worralls' friends explained in a newspaper article: "a copy was sent to the India House, and submitted by the chairman of that company to the examination of Mr. Raffles, one of the best Oriental scholars, yet he could not decypher it."[64] A tutor at Oxford examined a copy of the letter and decided that it was a mixture of Portuguese and "the Humbug-language."[65] After it was all over, a satirist summed up this part of the story in a London entertainment magazine:

> Then she wrote such a delicate hand,
> In style not unlike *European*—
> But the characters none understand,
> Nor the wisest of linguists agree on.[66]

Since Caraboo did not use any recognized alphabet, it was impossible to circulate her writing in movable type, and the general public had access to it only through a much older broadcast technology: posting a copy of it in the town square—or in this case, in a consumer society, in the pump-room of one of the city's bathhouses. "A fac-simile of her letter is placed in the Kingston Pump-Room for examination," that establishment's proprietor announced, teasing the attraction in the *Bath Chronicle*: "All the assistance to be derived from a Polyglott Bible, Fry's Pantographia, or Dr. Hager's Elementary characters of the Chinese, do not enable us to ascertain either the nature of her language, or the country to which she belongs," although "one or two characters bear some resemblance to the Chinese" and others resemble Greek letters.[67] (There was no charge to look at the facsimile, but you might decide to spring for a bath or a glass of mineral water while you were there.[68]) The writing was sufficiently interesting that in the weeks after the story broke, four different newspaper editors in Bristol and Bath took the extremely unusual step of engraving copies of Willcocks's Caraboo writing into blocks of wood so that they could be printed in their newspapers.[69] "Your Ladyship will be amused by Caraboo's Invention of Characters," Hester Lynch Piozzi wrote to her daughter-in-law, referring to the newspaper illustrations: "Handwriting I mean; to perplex the University Students. She must be a very clever Girl."[70]

Nor did movable type allow the circulation of Caraboo's oral language in more than its very general outlines. "Nothing *perplexed the cognoscenti* . . . so much as her *pronunciation* of the language of Javasu," wrote one newspaperman. "Her *articulation* was unlike any thing ever heard before."[71] But that chief perplexity—that epitome of her linguistic distinctiveness—was incommunicable, except face-to-face. Still, the initial newspaper reports contained just enough sketchy phonetic information to render the linguistic identification of Caraboo a national project for a brief time. Around the British Isles, readers of those initial reports pondered the following specimens of her supposed tongue:

Caraboo	personal name (herself)
Javasu	place-name (her native island)
Justee	doctor
Alla-Tallah	the Supreme Being
Macratoo	rogue
Jesse-Mandue	personal name (her father)

In subsequent newspaper articles and in the Gutch–Worrall pamphlet, a total of seventy-six words from Caraboo's language were transliterated into Latin letters and printed in English-language publications (see table 3), and a few of them even spilled out of their quotation marks and into English sentences for a brief time. A London women's magazine, for example, published a suggestive poem envisioning a naked Caraboo being spied on while bathing by some "*Peeping Tom*—or *wanton Makratoo*."[72] The poet Horace Smith, known to Romanticists for losing a friendly competition with Percy Bysshe Shelley over who could write the best "Ozymandias" poem, used some of Caraboo's other words in a lighthearted satire:

> Caraboo had a mind on the pigeon to sup
> . . . She dress'd it, she ate it, she call'd it Rampoo—
> "This proves," swore the Doctor, "she's Queen Caraboo."[73]

In this way, the Caraboo media event that had begun as an effort to solve a puzzle of language and identity became an occasion for audiences to slip into the language (and identity) of the Caraboo character.

From around Britain, the Worralls began receiving letters attempting to decipher these few specimens of her language, which had been quickly reprinted in newspapers around the country. In Edinburgh, an exiled royal from an Ottoman-backed dynasty in Crimea suspected that Caraboo might hail from his native region: "Sultan Katagerry," as he was known in Britain, wrote to Elizabeth Worrall that he recognized parts of *Javasu*, *Jesse-Mandue*, and *Caraboo*, as meaningful lexemes "either in Tartar or in Circassian," two mutually unrelated languages spoken between the Black and Caspian Seas in modern-day Georgia and southwestern Russia.[74] "The part Java, of the name Javasu, in Circassian, may either signify a surface of any thing, or the second person imperative mode of the verb to drink," he explained, while "the latter part, su, signifies water in Tartar . . . The first part Jesse, in the name Jesse-Mandue, in Tartar signifies an owner."[75] Hoping to confirm his hypothesis, Kattı Geray (a modern rendering of his name) composed eight questions for Caraboo, translated all eight of them into both Circassian and Tartar, and then transliterated his translations into Latin

TABLE 3. A Vocabulary of the Caraboo Language

(Spellings and glosses are given as reported in the Gutch–Worrall pamphlet and the *Bath Chronicle*.)

CARABOO	ENGLISH	CARABOO	ENGLISH
Ake	*Come*	Pakey	*Child*
Alkader	*Lot*	Passa	*Flour*
Allah Tallah	*God*	Paza	*Peacock's Feathers*
Ana	*Water*	Prabha	*Head*
Anna	*Night*	Rampue, rambu	*a Pidgeon*
Apa	*Fire*	Sacco	*Supper*
Archee	*Potatoe*	Samen	*Heaven*
Arra	*an Eclipse*	Sanatoo	*the Sun*
Bardoo	*Dead, die*	Savee	*Rain*
Beek	*Good*	Savoo	*a Knife*
Bosve	*a Boat*	Sirrea	*Mother of Pearl*
Botee	*an Arrow*	Smache	*Cayenne*
Botin	*the Head*	Somens, sammens	*Servant Women*
Bras	*Rice*	Suso	*Sugar*
Brasidoo	*Breakfast*	Tamah	*Fowl*
Buis, Boogoos	*any Wild People*	Tarsa	*Earth*
Congee	*China*	Tenzenee	*a Sail*
Dosi	*Dinner*	Toose	*to Swim*
Doteau	*Gold Dust*	Toree	*a Stone*
Foso	*a Fork*	Tuzar	*a Ship*
Justo, justu, justee	*Doctor*	Vatan	*Gown*
Kala	*Time*	Vellee	*Bed*
Lazor	*Ladies*	Zee	*Tea*
Makey	*Pepper*	Eze	*One*
Makrittoo	*Servant Men*	Duce	*Two*
Manjintoo	*Gentlemen*	Trua	*Three*
Meller	*Yes*	Tan	*Four*
Mo	*Milk*	Zennee	*Five*
Mono	*Morning*	Sendee	*Six*
Mordains, Maudins	*the Malay*	Tamah	*Seven*
Mozum	*Fish*	Nunta	*Eight*
Nater	*the Arm*	Berteen	*Nine*
Nease	*the Foot*	Tashman	*Ten*
Nee	*Egg*	Limmenee	*Eleven*
No bo	*No good*	Judgbennee	*Twelve*
Nontee	*an Orange*	Artinne	*Thirteen*
Oree	*Onions*	Ferney	*Fourteen*
Oser	*Salt*	Fissmen	*Fifteen*

characters, hoping that Worrall would read them aloud to Caraboo and record her responses:

CIRCASSIAN	TARTAR	ENGLISH
Adigivzar uptshera?	*Nogoi tillĕn bēllasĕnma?*	Do you understand the [Circassian/Tartar] language?
Uadiga?	*Nogi sĕnma?*	Are you a [Circassian/Tartar]?
Set etsh ukyka?	*Nĕ jerden shukhansen?*	What land do you come from?
Ui yader adigit?	*Atang nogoi ĕdĕma?*	Was your father a [Circassian/Tartar]?
Etsar Setit?	*Ata nĕ ĕdĕ?*	What was his name?
Ui yaner adigit?	*Anang nogoi pĕshy ĕdĕma?*	Was your mother a [Circassian/Tartar]?
Ui tshema etsar set?	*Sĕnung jĕrungnung ata nēdēr?*	What is the name of your country?
Adigivzer uptshama, ege unjessa pesselthahema juap kuzat?	*Egĕr nogoi tillda bēllzung, sorrahan? humha juab bĕr?*	If you understand the [Circassian/Tartar] language, give an answer to the words now spoken.

Much like John Gilchrist, Kattı Geray confronts the problem of transmitting the sounds of an unfamiliar language on paper. "Sound all the letters as in English," he instructs Worrall; but, recognizing that many of the Latin characters mean more than one thing in English, he struggles to be more specific. For example, Worrall should pronounce "u, as in full" in all words, he says, except the Circassian word *kuzat* (where it should be pronounced "as in urn") and in the Tartar word *shukhansen* (where it should be pronounced "as in luck"). These convoluted instructions are not even theoretically possible to follow, however, because the writer's points of reference are themselves ambiguous: when he says to pronounce "u, as in full," does he mean *full* as pronounced in Edinburgh or as in upper-class Bristol? Those pronunciations differed from each other, and, moreover, since Kattı Geray learned English in Circassia and Elizabeth Worrall learned it in Massachusetts, there is no certainty that either of them would have had either standard in mind.[76]

This brief transnational effort by the imperially dislocated "Sultan Katagerry" to make a linguistic identification of the imperially dislocated "Princess Caraboo" via the imperially dislocated Elizabeth

Lechmere Worrall collided with the same technological limitations that troubled John Gilchrist, Duncan Mackintosh, and all the Americans who worried about the emergence of an American accent. Written language is silent over any distance, including imperial ones—and linguistic approaches to identity made that phonetic silence especially uncomfortable because phonetics, like other aspects of language, seemed to be one of the core components of the self. Empire exceeded its own phonetic technology: it was easier to move a princess from the South Pacific or the Caucasus to Britain than it was to move linguistic sounds between those locations—or even between England's immediate neighbors, such as Scotland or France. Thomas Willcocks initially told Worrall's agent that he had heard his daughter speaking French for hours at a time on her most recent visit. When pressed, he explained that he did not speak French and only thought it was French "because the folks in the village said it was so."[77] The folks in the village had no particular reason to learn French or even to hear French—so Willcocks's glossolalia was French to them. And although the wealthier and more globalized "folks" in Bristol and Philadelphia knew what French sounded like, they had no particular reason to learn or hear Chinese—so it was Chinese (or Chinese-ish) to them. The Scottish-Circassian-Crimean aristocrat in Edinburgh desperately needed the phonetic alphabet that John Gilchrist was then working on, in which he could have specified whether he meant *fəl* or *fʉl*, or Duncan Mackintosh's notation, in which he could have specified f$\overset{1}{u}$ll′ or f$\overset{2}{u}$ll′, or the much later International Phonetic Alphabet, in which he could have distinguished [ful] from [fʊl]. Or he needed an abecedareloge. Or a telephone.

The Unmasking of Mary Willcocks

By early June, descriptions of Caraboo's language, behavior, and general appearance had appeared in newspapers as far away as Edinburgh and Belfast. At least thirty British newspapers would report on the story over the next few weeks. In London, the Starlings—whose beds Willcocks had set on fire the previous fall—read about Princess Caraboo in the newspaper, "recognised the servant that had lived with them, and thought of writing to Mrs. Worrall about her, but feared, if she discovered that they had interfered, she would have returned to London, and waylaid Mr. Starling in his walks home, through the fields to Islington." Elizabeth Mathews also guessed that Caraboo was Mary Willcocks and "had frequently thought of writing to Mrs. W[orrall] since she had heard of CARABOO in the newspapers," but didn't do so.[78] In the end, the identification was made by two people who had known Willcocks not as a London servant but as a Bristol beggar: a boardinghouse keeper from whom Willcocks had tried to rent a room earlier that spring, and a concerned citizen who had seen Willcocks begging in the Bristol suburbs in a non-Caraboo persona the day before her encounter with the Worralls. Two Bristol newspapers ran stories about the purported princess on Saturday, June 7. On Monday, both witnesses got in touch with Elizabeth Worrall.[79]

Given the circumstances, Worrall dealt with these revelations in an exceptionally generous manner. Perhaps, as one critic surmises, Caraboo "was neither fully believed nor fully disbelieved," and the revelation was not as surprising as it might have been.[80] Worrall maintained a poker face for the rest of the day while quietly arranging a confrontation with minimal humiliation. The next morning, she indicated to Caraboo that they needed to go into Bristol so that she could finish posing for a full-length oil portrait being painted by Bristol's leading painter. She told the coachman, however, to drive not to Edward Bird's studio but to the house of William Mortimer, the physician recipient of Caraboo's earlier thank-you note. By prearrangement, the woman at whose boardinghouse Willcocks had sought a room months earlier was already waiting at the Mortimers'. But Worrall wanted to avoid that scene. The boardinghouse keeper and the Mortimers waited in another room while Worrall took Caraboo upstairs and spoke to her alone, laying out what she knew and offering to help her—on the condition that she "instantly give a faithful detail of her former course of life, disclose her real name, her parentage and history."[81]

Willcocks gave up right away. Having spent the past two months narrating Caraboo's biography in pantomime and Carabooish glossolalia, she now began to narrate Mary Willcocks's biography in English, using her native language for the first time in months. Understandably wary, Worrall asked Dr. Mortimer and his wife, Sophia Landeg, to let

Willcocks stay at their house while she looked into Willcocks's story to see if she had kept up her end of the bargain. It was for this reason that Worrall sent an emissary to Willcocks's parents' house, where the story Willcocks had given was more or less confirmed. So Worrall kept her promise to Willcocks. The whole affair had begun with Willcocks trying to earn £5 to pay for a ticket to America. When her story checked out, Worrall bought her the ticket, furnished her with Western clothing, and gave her the money she would need to start a new life in Philadelphia.[82]

The confrontation was on a Tuesday; on Saturday, the story broke wide as both Gutch's *Bristol Journal* and the rival *Bristol Mirror* ran breathless columns about the unmasking. "Her native language was soon discovered to be old mother English! . . . Oh *Allah Tallah!!*" wrote Gutch in the *Journal*. It would be two more weeks before she sailed for Philadelphia, and during this time "the public curiosity to gain a sight of her was rather increased than diminished," Gutch noted. "Some pitied her, some condemned her, & others upheld her." The same person who had received a stream of visitors at the Worralls' as Caraboo now received a stream of visitors at the Mortimers' as Mary Willcocks: "natives and foreigners, linguists, painters, physiognomists, craniologists, and gypsies." The Earl of Cork drove up from Bath "for the sole purpose of conversing with her." Once again there was something charming about Mary Willcocks and her stories, even though she broke the rules in telling them. Although in general "she shewed no signs of contrition for the part she had been acting," it was Gutch's perception that Willcocks felt genuinely moved by the generosity of Elizabeth Worrall. In a farewell letter that she wrote to her patroness just before embarking, Willcocks quoted a few lines from a hymn by Isaac Watts that calls friendship the "charmer of the mind": friendship entails making oneself vulnerable, and for that reason it yields both "the brightest moments mortals find / and sharpest pains we feel." Gutch took Willcocks's letter as an acknowledgment that she had hurt Worrall by deceiving her. Perhaps she wanted to tell Worrall that she could be proud of having fallen for the Caraboo deception; it was her openhearted spirit of friendship that led her astray, not some baser motive or weakness or gullibility.[83]

Yet Willcocks's "singular epistle," as Gutch called it, was in fact anything but singular: the Watts hymn, as well as Willcocks's comments on it, is taken verbatim from a model letter "on friendship" in a popular letter-writing manual.[84] It is in fact the first of thirty-six epistolary samples "on friendship, &c.," in that manual. Willcocks may well have found a copy of *The Universal Letter-Writer* in the Mortimers' house, turned to the "friendship" section, and copied out the first sample letter contained therein. But what this means about the authenticity of the sentiment it expresses is unclear. The premise of letter-writing manuals is that conveying your feelings in writing isn't easy. Mary Willcocks may have been, in a way, more articulate in her pseudolinguistic literacy than she was in her English literacy. Perhaps she conveyed a more powerful gratitude when she wrote to her doctor to thank him for   than when she wrote to Elizabeth Worrall to thank her for her friendship.

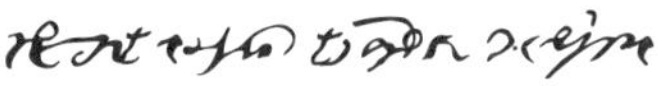

Princess Caraboo got to North America two weeks before Mary Willcocks did. Toward the end of August, American newspapers began receiving their usual copies of British newspapers from June. The mystery, the investigation, and the exposé hit American newspapers all at once, rather than unfolding over a period of weeks as they had in Britain, and the story went instantly viral. By the time Willcocks arrived a few weeks later, her story had already been widely reported in dozens of newspaper articles, as far north as Portland, Maine, and as far south as Norfolk, Virginia. News reports had included the name of Willcocks's ship, so as it proceeded up the Delaware River—bearing Mary Willcocks, three Moravian missionaries tasked with getting her started on the right foot in the New World, eighteen other passengers, sixteen casks of pickled fish, eleven baskets of cheese, and a great deal else—the vessel was hailed from shore with shouts of "How is the Princess?" and "Is the Princess on board?" A large crowd gathered at the Philadelphia docks when the passengers disembarked, "all crying out [asking] which was the Princess Carraboo." Willcocks's handlers escorted her off the ship, her face covered with a veil, fending off the crowd: *nothing to see here, this is not the Princess.*[85]

The plan was for Willcocks to find a servant position, and her chaperones had no trouble getting her an offer of employment in a respectable household. But perhaps Willcocks had taken enough domestic jobs found for her by well-intentioned elites. This time she had other options. By the end of her first week in Philadelphia, she had "made several private exhibitions of her capability" for "writ[ing] the Carraboo language," had taken meetings with a show promoter, and was busy arranging a public appearance. Her chaperones' perception was that Willcocks was being exploited by greedy showmen, but it's not hard to imagine that Willcocks knew exactly what she was doing. To her chaperones' dismay, she turned down the job offer that they had arranged for her and asked them in no uncertain terms to leave her alone: "she had met with kinder friends in America than she had in England, and . . . tho' she was obliged to us for the interest we took in her welfare, she thought she was quite old enough to think and act for herself." Five days after her arrival in North America, the *Freeman's Journal* announced that "Miss Carraboo . . . intends shortly to gratify the ladies and gentlemen of Philadelphia, with an exhibition of herself, at a proper time and place." After a few days of planning, newspaper advertisements announced that a Grand Concert of Vocal and Instrumental Music, "for the benefit of Miss Carraboo," would be held next Tuesday and Thursday. A more detailed program was announced the day before: eight vocal performances and eight instrumental ones; doors at seven, curtain at seven-thirty. The very last words of the advertisement, almost as if they were an afterthought, were these: "Miss Carraboo will make her appearance at 8 o'clock." A New York newspaper noted drily: "whether she is to sing a song, or tell a story, we are not informed."[86]

What must it have been like to perform her own character, openly, and to have that character celebrated not as a reality but as a performance? If we take her at her word, it was a triumph: "if you had seen me handed on and off the Stage by two gentlemen," she wrote to Sophia Landeg a few weeks later, "you had thought I really was a Princess, as I really did at the time." Back in England, her elite audience had demanded that she be either Caraboo or Mary Willcocks. In Philadelphia, her American audience delighted in her being both at the same time. It is easy to imagine how it might have been profoundly cathartic to have permission to unleash her Caraboo creativity openly, with no deception, and no danger of criminal penalties. She had actually daydreamed about a similar scenario to Gutch before she left Bristol: "After the discovery," he wrote, "she more than once expressed a wish, that the tale might be dramatized; and nothing, she said, would have given her greater pleasure, than to have acted the part of CARABOO!!" In fact, within months, "A new harlequinade . . . founded on the adventures of Caraboo" was playing at the Bristol Theatre—but with a professional actress, not Mary Willcocks, in the lead role.[87]

Although the Tuesday night concert was declared a success in Philadelphia's *True American* newspaper, Willcocks—or her backers—canceled the Thursday night performance, and she prepared to decamp for New York.[88] She was finding her life as a full-time celebrity boring. "I am obliged to dress immediately after breakfast to see the company who are constantly calling to look at me," she wrote in a letter to Elizabeth Worrall, "but I do not come down to everyone where curiosity brings them to the house, or I should not have a moment to myself."[89] She spent her alone time "improving my reading and writing" and going for walks in the evenings.

Much like Nicholas Dufief, Mary Willcocks's linguistic self-reinvention coincided with a dramatic change in her social position, a relocation to the New World, a handful of new names, and the subjective experience of becoming a foreigner. Willcocks had not, in fact, been a displaced young woman in a foreign land when she met Elizabeth Worrall in April; but now, in October in Philadelphia, that is exactly what she was. She hated it. "You have no idea how prejudiced the people are against old England," she told Worrall: it was "hardly possible to sit in their company without being obliged to listen to the greatest illiberality" about England. She quarreled with Americans about their nationalities and found herself "frequently under the necessity of expressing my opinion pretty freely." In England, her foreignness was a conceit that she controlled, largely through her language; in America, she found herself foreign in a national dimension that she could not control. "Here they call English foreigners," she told Worrall, "which is not done by the English when speaking of America."

Although she got "any books I want from the ladies and Gentlemen," and had "the best of everything," and "live[d] as I aught like a Princess"—even so, she confessed that she wasn't happy. "After the flattering descriptions I heard in England of America, I am much disappointed," she told Sophia Landeg: everything was expensive, the countryside was ugly, and as for the people, they were for "the most part Quakers, and very distant in their manner, they seem to think of little else but business." She told Landeg that she "hope[d] one day or other to see old England again and those kind friends I left in it," and while this was a strategically appropriate thing to say, there's no particular reason to doubt her when she says she was feeling lonely. "I should very much like to hear from you," she wrote to Landeg, "if you would do me the favor of writing to me."[90] A month later, she wrote to Elizabeth Worrall from New York that she had "been much disappointed in America, as the Country is by no means to be Compared to England, and the people especially." Although her intended New York concert never came together, New York's celebrity culture was if anything even more intense than Philadelphia's. "The House I lived in here has ever since my being in it was known filled with visitors, their curiosity and impertinence was so great that I have been scarcely able to walk out, and could never eat my dinner without people staring in at the windows," she told Worrall. A Philadelphia print of her portrait was all over New York too, and she claimed that "several Ladies have been taken for me at the Theatre and in the Streets and some followed by crouds to their great discomposure." Plus, she still had nothing to do. She spent the last two weeks of October 1817 "very ill," perhaps depressed. She wrote to Worrall that she was going back to Philadelphia.[91]

And with that, Mary Willcocks dropped out of public view. A decade later, she had returned to England—not to the Devonshire of her childhood, nor to the London of her young adulthood, but to the Bristol of her Caraboohood.[92] Perhaps Bristol became her true home when she became Caraboo there, speaking and writing a new identity into existence. She lived there for the rest of her life—not as a domestic servant, either, but as the proprietor of a small medical supply business: she imported leeches from the Continent and earned a decent living selling them to Bristol pharmacies and hospitals.[93] She married, and raised a daughter, Mary Ann, and quietly and non-Carabooishly lived to the age of seventy-three. Someone who knew her when she was in her fifties remembered later that "nothing annoyed her more than when a neighbour's child ventured to call after her 'Caraboo!'"[94] She's buried in Bristol. But the name on her tombstone isn't Princess Caraboo, or Mary Willcocks, or Mary Baker, or Mary Burgess, or Anne Burgess, or Hannah Baker, or any of the other names she used during her lifetime. There is no tombstone at her grave. It's unmarked.

Haranai Patch and Oach Patch at Parker Dam, Arizona, 1939.
Courtesy of the Metropolitan Water District of Southern California.

Coda

Language Makes the  between Now and Then

IN 1939, THE Metropolitan Water District of California arranged for a 103-year-old Mojave Indian named Haranai Patch to look at the new Parker Dam and say "Javasu." Actually, what the U.S. Interior Department's casually racist press release says is that he "grunted admiringly, 'Javasu'"—which means *blue* in Mojave—because he was impressed by "the white man's magic" that had transformed the muddy red waters of the Colorado River to a blue lake covering some twenty thousand acres of what had traditionally been Mojave land.[1] A non-Mojave decision-maker evidently felt that "Lake Javasu" had a nice ring to it, because months later the U.S. Board on Geographic Names announced that the lake had been given an "Indian name" meaning "Lake of the Blue Waters" in Mojave. Princess Caraboo's homeland, therefore, was not the last "Javasu" to become a pseudo-Indian place-name eagerly embraced by English-speaking white people.

This is mostly a coincidence, but not entirely so. Haranai Patch doubtless said other words while he was there. But Lake "Havasu" (the spelling has been anglicized) has the same appealing phonetics as "Caraboo": three consonants separated by three vowels that make it easy for English speakers to say. That balance of the exotic and the familiar is probably among the reasons that Mary Willcocks went with *Javasu* as the name of Caraboo's birthplace. In fact, Willcocks used that

CVCVCV pattern of vowels and consonants, or something close to it, in numerous of Caraboo's other words, such as *sanatoo* (sun), *limmenee* (eleven), *brasidoo* (breakfast), *makrittoo* (men). Today, Lake Havasu supplies half of southern California's drinking water. Mary Willcocks left other, less metaphorical material legacies: a beaded bracelet, an ivory spoon. But I think Lake Havasu best captures the projections and fantasies and otherness and unequal power and hearing-but-not-listening that were concentrated into linguistic form when Willcocks taught her caretaker- captors to say "Caraboo" and "Javasu."

I also like thinking of Lake Havasu as Willcocks's legacy because it is big—far out of proportion to her little-remembered story. Other characters in this book left similarly disproportionate material legacies. John Gilchrist's estate funded a prominent adult education program from the 1860s until World War II, offering "Gilchrist Lectures" that were attended by at least a hundred thousand people. Edmund Fry coined the word "phonology." "Webster's dictionaries" are in middle-class households everywhere—though Americans often conflate the lexicographer with his younger cousin, the most significant nineteenth-century American politician who was never elected president. I once eavesdropped as a tour guide stood in front of an enormous bronze statue of Daniel Webster in Central Park explaining to a group of schoolchildren that nineteenth-century lexicographers had been regarded as celebrities in their day because reading dictionaries was a popular form of entertainment at that time—hence the statue. And while this isn't literally true, I love the idea of it: someone's willingness to confront a perplexing set of apparent facts (*why is there a huge statue of a lexicographer in Central Park?*) and to infer a history from them, a history in which some things about the past are different (entertainment content) while other things are similar (celebrity culture). Also, the tour guide's contextualization of that monument captures at least a little of the thesis of this book: it says that language was of intense public interest in the nineteenth century.

There are real statues of Noah Webster in West Hartford, Connecticut, and Amherst, Massachusetts, but I prefer the "Webster" statue in Manhattan: it's a kind of failure, the way Noah Webster was a kind of failure. It's not really a representation of Noah Webster, the way the "Noah Webster" we know isn't really a representation of Noah Webster, the linguistic separatist and media troll. All of the characters in this book failed: neither Duncan Mackintosh's phonetic notation nor John Gilchrist's *yoneversul* alphabet was ever used in any texts other than their own promotional materials (until now!); Edmund Fry's *Pantographia* was forgotten by nineteenth-century linguistics in favor of a similar work produced slightly later by a professional academic; Nicholas Gouin Dufief was mocked; Mary Willcocks was unmasked. On the other hand, they all managed the exceptional achievement of registering some part of themselves in archives, to be listened to later. Perhaps they only seem more like failures now because the logic that governed their ideas and choices has lost its purchase.

For a brief moment in 1818, the hybrid success-failures of Willcocks and Dufief occupied overlapping spaces in transatlantic media culture: they were both famous for linguistic innovations that were not considered entirely legitimate. Dufief seemed Carabooish: about six months after the Princess Caraboo media event, a Philadelphia editorialist panned *Nature Displayed* as a scam and "a serious Carraboo imposition which daily gains ground."[2] Another satirist represented Dufief offering "to instruct a small class in the CARABOO LANGUAGE."[3] But while their voices and personas intersected in newspaper columns, the material Dufief and the material Willcocks passed each other like ships in the night—possibly on actual ships in the actual night, in July 1817, when Willcocks was crossing the Atlantic on her post-Caraboo westbound voyage to Philadelphia, while Dufief was on an eastbound ship from Philadelphia to London to find a British publisher for *Nature Displayed*.

There is no record of Dufief, Webster, Gilchrist, Fry, Willcocks, or Mackintosh ever meeting in material reality. But they did cross remarkably close to each other's paths. Before Mary Willcocks left Bristol in 1817, she was treated with particular kindness by Joseph Storrs Fry—local bigwig, founder of the world's first industrial-scale chocolate manufactory, and older brother of the typefounder whose *Pantographia* had not identified Princess Caraboo earlier that spring. Years later, in 1824, Willcocks was reportedly receiving visitors in London in her Caraboo persona (admission: one shilling) a few hundred yards from where John Gilchrist was living on a fashionable street in Mayfair. The next year, Gilchrist was carting his newly cast universal type among several shops in London's printing district while Noah Webster was making the rounds in the same neighborhood seeking a British publisher for his *American Dictionary*. Two decades earlier, Webster had received a smarmy letter from Dufief, who was seeking Webster's endorsement for *Nature Displayed* and trying to position himself as the older and more famous man's intellectual heir, "for you have shewn me the laudable example of attacking, on this side of the Atlantic the powerful prejudices, which render the task of Education so difficult to Young minds."[4] (Webster did not give Dufief the blurb he was looking for.) Dufief spent most of the 1820s in London teaching French classes at a schoolroom three blocks away from the lecture hall where John Gilchrist was doing a brisk business teaching Hindustani to India-bound EIC doctors. They were two non-Englishmen in London teaching non-English languages to English students. Later, Dufief and Fry would retire to the same London suburb, Pentonville, where they would die down the street from each other in 1834–35.

These are remarkably close encounters for five people born in four different nations into widely divergent socioeconomic circumstances: their fathers were an absent deadbeat (Gilchrist), a peasant (Willcocks), a farmer (Webster), an artisan (Fry), and a nobleman (Dufief). They all turned up in London selling their respective linguistic products—all but Duncan Mackintosh, though he sounded a lot like he was fishing for an opportunity to do so when he closed his *Essay* by saying that he would not "hes′itat*e* go′ing, with′ my Fa′mily, to E′ng-land; in o′rder to rece*i*′ve pro′per advic′*e*" as to the most correct English pronunciation.[5] But he never did go there, with his Fa′mily or without it, and although he came within about a hundred miles of John Gilchrist (when a young Gilchrist was serving in the British Navy in Grenada) and Edmund Fry (when Fry was a young apprentice in Bristol), Mackintosh's intersections with the other figures in this book were only distant and intellectual, unless any of the sugar he grew in Dominica ended up in someone's tea.

Every year or two in our contemporary world, a media panic kicks up about some sort of linguistic phenomenon—a word, an intonation, an abbreviation, a grammatical construct—that is taken as evidence of some social ill. A recent iteration of this panic concerned the so-called vocal fry, which is one of six types of phonation that humans can produce. (The others include whispering and falsetto.) Vocal fry, or "creaky voice," was noncontroversial until 2011, when a poorly designed study purported to show that employers were less likely to hire college-aged women who spoke this way than college-aged women who spoke in a "normal voice."[6] What the study actually shows is that when college-aged women recorded themselves reading a statement two ways—once in their natural voice and once with an *affected* vocal fry—listeners preferred the unaffected version. But the factoid about vocal fry and young women's employability circulated widely as evidence that young women "today" are not doing their part to seize the social and economic opportunities painstakingly won for them by previous generations of female professionals. "Young women, give up the vocal fry and reclaim your strong female voice," urged Naomi Wolf in 2015, one of many distinguished critics and journalists who heard in the vocal fry the sound of women being complicit in their own submission.

I think also of *omg*, *idk*, *brb*, *ur welcome*: the shorthands and abbreviations that have evolved over successive generations of text-based electronic media—from the Usenet message boards of the early internet, to instant messaging platforms in the 1990s, to SMS text messaging—and have been taken as evidence of the ignorance, insincerity, or carelessness of corresponding generations of young people. In a recent essay called "Texting Makes U Stupid," Niall Ferguson issued this unhappy prediction:

> Seconds before the earth is hit by a gigantic asteroid or engulfed by a super tsunami, millions of lithe young fingers will be typing the human race's last inane words to itself: C u later NOT :(

What would be the problem with that, exactly? I take it that Ferguson would prefer that end-of-the-world text messages use standard spelling and punctuation, rather than the phonetic shorthand *c u* and the ideograph at the end: *See you later . . . not! This is sad.* There is a long history of worrying about attenuated forms of informal language; Duncan Mackintosh, for example, was particularly upset about contractions:

"Mi′sers clip′ ôûr côin′, with a viêw′ to enrich′ themse′lves," he wrote, "But *why* should′ *E′nglishmen* clip′ their word′s?" I take it, however, that Ferguson finds these hypothetical last words "inane" and "stupid" not only because of the shorthand but also because of the . . . *not!* construction, the affect of which (I agree with him here) seems all wrong for the end of the world. As Ferguson is evidently aware, . . . *not!* runs on irony, in that the speaker says the opposite of what he or she means, and then cues the listener to invert it. *See you later . . . not!* might be restated as something like *Wouldn't it be funny if I said "See you later" right now? Since I won't?* Ferguson might well understand the end of the world as an inappropriate occasion for kidding around. Possibly he would prefer that the statement be given without the irony: *I will not see you later. This is sad.*[7]

Fair enough. I can see where Ferguson is coming from, in the sense that I can imagine wishing that humanity would take the end of the world seriously rather than experiencing it from a position of ironic detachment. However, I would note that the SMS medium is equally capable of transmitting sincere messages as ironic ones. "Texting Makes U Stupid"? If teenagers spend the end of the world sending each other ironic messages, I fail to understand the argument that Texting Made Them do that. In fact, I will go so far as to say that if teenagers retreat into sarcasm instead of talking about painful or scary feelings, that has more to do with the nature of teenagers than the nature of any communications technology or shorthand. Ferguson's fantasy that young people will write *C u later NOT :(* expresses his perception that "young people today" are "stupid" and insincere. But he perceives that stupid insincerity in their linguistic shorthand and in a communications medium over which they exchange it, rather than in the actual communicative content of the messages they exchange. What is remarkable about Ferguson's thesis is not that it's a particularly ludicrous instance of an incoherent cliché, but that it *is* a cliché: you don't need research to know that tens of millions of adults agree that text-message language is damaging young people's minds. (But that research does exist.[8])

When I was growing up, the word "like" was the focus of a similar moral panic. No one is, like, entirely sure why this particular discourse particle became controversial when others such as *um*, *er*, *uh*, *well*, *you know*, *I mean*, and *look* remained unproblematic. "Teenagers sprinkle their sentences with the word 'like' because they don't wish to commit themselves to anything," runs one account of this linguistic plague, positing a hypothetical teenager who tells a driver to "make, like, a right" turn. "Increasingly in society, people are unwilling or unable to commit to *anything*. (No wonder some kids view married people as self-deluded buffoons.) Our teens see a lack of commitment all around them, and this image rubs off in their language use."[9] For the author of that account, *make, like, a right* evidently represents the same teenage insincerity that *C u later NOT :(* represents for Ferguson—while also registering some broader fecklessness "in society," and the long-term decline in Western marriage rates. Somehow, all of this is perceptible in *Make, like, a right turn* (but not in *Make, uh, a right turn*). Round and round we go. This kind of linguistic evidence *always* appears to confirm an existing narrative, and usually quite an ancient one: civilization's going to pieces, women aren't behaving properly, a new communications technology is rotting our brains. We project these well-worn anxieties onto bits and pieces of language, and then "discover" the linguistic evidence that our worst fears are coming true. In Niall Ferguson's end-of-the-world fantasy, humanity's last words go to the "lithe young fingers" of the texting generations. The non-"young," nontexting generations are absent from his fantasized apocalypse: one generation passeth away, and another generation texteth, unmindful of the long arc of "the human race," the precious traditions that have been left in their hands. I think on some level this is Ferguson's anxious fantasy about being forgotten. That is an eminently valid anxiety and has been one of the chief concerns of Western literature, from *The Iliad* forward, but it has very little to do with text messages.

Do I really want a world, though, in which a person like Ferguson is obligated to rage head-on against the dying of the light, instead of raging against the saying of the "like"? Maybe not. Denial is important. Many things are too painful to think about directly; we need to be able to project them onto other things. Language seems to be one of the most available receptors for this projection—a good punching bag. If believing that the world is getting worse helps a person cope with the knowledge that he will someday leave that world, then I would rather that he perceive that worsening in terms of young people saying *like* than in terms of, say, immigrants or gay marriage. Similarly, if ironic detachment helps you handle the knowledge that an asteroid is speeding apocalyptically toward the earth, it's fine with me if you want to detach. If thinking about the wrongness of "10 items or less" or "could care less" or "nucular" helps you blow off existential steam, maybe that's okay.

But I confess that I find it much easier to pardon the linguistic alarmism of the eighteenth- and nineteenth-century writers quoted in this book than to pardon present-day linguistic alarmists such as Niall Ferguson, my mother, and the many other smart people who indulge and even cultivate their capacity for outrage about formal elements of language that don't interfere with communication. When their outrage is directed at a person or group less privileged than themselves (young women and the vocal fry), I'm offended; when it's directed at someone more powerful (President George W. Bush and "nucular"), I'm simply impatient. By contrast, I could listen all day to Noah Webster's enemies railing against the replacement of *wharfs* with *wharves*: I'm fascinated by it even though I don't myself have a preference between *wharfs* and *wharves*. Neither do I myself want to see the "notorious cacography" of the world's many alphabets replaced by an "omnilingual" replacement, but I could spend untold hours tracing Gilchrist's designs for his universal alphabet—and I did. In historical retrospect, I'm interested in linguistic passions of all kinds, whether or not they seem valid to me. In the present, I resent linguistic passions that I see as misplaced. If I encountered Webster, Gilchrist, Mackintosh, or Dufief in my present world, I would tell them to calm down. But when I look at them across archival time and space, I want to tell them to act up. I want to hear them predict linguistic catastrophes and dream impossibly large linguistic dreams. They are the tonic of wildness to my self-imposed linguistic sobriety, the fantasized tempest to my even linguistic keel, the vicarious outlet for my hidden dreams of remaking the self through language. The less interested I become in policing the linguistic boundaries of my own world, the more I like to lose myself in the strangeness, the wonder, and the sheer  of the past's linguistic imagination.

NOTES

INTRODUCTION

1. *Bath Chronicle*, June 5, 1817, [4]; *Bristol Mirror*, June 21, 1817, [3].

2. *Bath Chronicle*, June 5, 1817, [4].

3. Gutch and Worrall, *Caraboo*, 19.

4. [Kattı Geray] to Elizabeth Worrall, June 14, 1817, in ibid., 21–23.

5. Hester Lynch Piozzi to Sir James Fellowes, July 1, 1817, in Bloom and Bloom, *Piozzi Letters*, 6:97.

6. Gutch and Worrall, *Caraboo*, 15, 12.

7. Ibid., 54.

8. *Bath Chronicle*, June 12, 1817, [4].

9. Dufief, "Language Makes the Difference"; Cardell, *Essay on Language*, 3; John Gilchrist, quoted in *Asiatic Journal* (March 1827): 417.

10. *Encyclopaedia Britannica*, 3rd ed. (1797), 9:534, s.v. "language."

11. Darnton, *The Great Cat Massacre*, 4–5.

12. Mackintosh, *A Plain, Rational Essay on English Grammar* (1797), xviii; hereafter cited as Mackintosh, *Essay* (1797).

13. Ibid., 98.

14. Extrapolated from data in Boberg, *The English Language in Canada*, 55–79; Conklin and Lourie, *A Host of Tongues*, 65–69; De Fréine, "The Dominance of the English Language in the 19th Century"; Haines and Steckel, *A Population History of North America*; Holm, "English in the Caribbean"; Ross, "The 'White' Population of South Africa in the Eighteenth Century"; Schofield and Wrigley, *The Population History of England 1541–1871*; R. Wells, *The Population of the British Colonies in America before 1776*; Withers, *Gaelic in Scotland 1698–1981*.

15. Mackintosh, *Essay* (1797), 228.

16. J. G. Chambers, *Elements of Orthography* (1812), dedication (unpaginated).

17. *Hampshire Gazette* (Northampton, Mass.), Aug. 28, 1799, 1; *Encyclopaedia Britannica*, 3rd ed. (1797), 9:548, s.v. "language." For earlier concerns about the unruliness of English, see Nevalainen and Tieken-Boon van Ostade, "Standardisation," esp. 277–79; Crowley, *Language in History*, 54–98.

18. Annotation in Mackintosh's hand in his untitled 1799 pamphlet (Portland Collection, Pl C 23/1).

19. J. Wilson, *A Volume for All Libraries*, 83.

20. For identity categories available in the eighteenth century, see Wahrman, *The Making of the Modern Self*, 7–82, 127–53, 166–97, 265–311. During most of the eighteenth century, "race" and "nation" could be used interchangeably, but the later decades of the century saw "race" develop a specialized sense "as a term for the biological subdivision of humanity" into four or five large groups with recognizable physiological differences, while "nation" acquired a specifically political and social meaning (Hudson, "From 'Nation' to 'Race,'" 248). For the rising significance of nationality as an identity category in the late eighteenth and early nineteenth centuries, see B. Anderson, *Imagined Communities*, 44–46; Hobsbawm, *Nations and Nationalism since 1780*; Kidd, *British Identities before Nationalism*. For "conceptions of Christianity, civility, and rank" as "*more explicitly* important . . . than physical attributes such as skin color," see R. Wheeler, *The Complexion of Race*, 1–48, 7. On the other eighteenth-century identity categories mentioned, see Colley, *Britons*, 11–54; Nechtman, *Nabobs*, 37–69; Nussbaum, *The Limits of the Human*, 23–132.

21. For more on how imperial distance and contact with otherness deepened English speakers' attention to languages, see chapters 2 and 3, as well as Paxman, *Voyage into Language*, 69–129.

22. Judges 12:1–6. The meaning of *shibboleth* is uncertain; it might also mean "stream of water" (Hendel, "Sibilants and *šibbōlet*," 69–70). The twelfth-century dating is also uncertain (Mandel, *Who's Who in the Jewish Bible*, 193). Of course, the historical phonetic incident may not have occurred as the Deuteronomists present it in the text (or at all).

23. See Damrosch, "Scriptworlds." Cuneiform, like the Latin alphabet, can be used to write many different languages.

24. Axtell, "Babel of Tongues," 31–34; Taylor, "Indian Lingua Francas." Conversely, for Europeans' use of Native American languages, see, e.g., Kupperman, *Indians and English*, 77–109. On New World language encounters in early British America more broadly, see Dillard, *A History of American English*, 1–31; Fiering and Gray, *The Language Encounter in the Americas 1492–1800*; Grandjean, *American Passage*, 76–109; Paxman, *Voyage into Language*, 67–129; Spengemann, *A New World of Words*.

25. Roger Williams, *A Key into the Language of America*, [ii]; Axtell, "Babel of Tongues," 33–34, 42–43; Grandjean, *American Passage*, 94–95; Gray, *New World Babel*, 48–49, 80–83. As I discuss in chapter 2, virtually all of the spellers, grammars, dictionaries, and pronunciation guides used by English speakers in Britain and colonial America alike were intended to match the prestige dialect of southeastern England, even though few American colonists actually came from southeastern England.

26. Locke, *An Essay Concerning Humane Understanding*, 185 (bk. 3, chap. 1). For a detailed account of ancient, medieval, and early modern thinking about languages as political hazards, see Gustafson, *Representative Words*, 66–194. On the Act of Union (1707) and the ensuing debates about the meaning of "Britain" and of England and Scotland within it, see Colley, *Britons*; Crawford, *Devolving English Literature*, 45–110; Davis, *Acts of Union*, 74–143; Gottlieb, *Sympathy and National Identity*. For eighteenth-century discomfort with British multilingualism in general and with Gaelic in particular, see Crowley, *Language in History*, 67–73; Sorensen, *Grammar of Empire in Eighteenth-Century British Writing*, 28–62; Stroh, *Gaelic Scotland in the Colonial Imagination*, 65–72.

27. Kenrick, *A New Dictionary of the English Language* (1773), dedication (unpaginated). For Scottish migration to London, see Nenadic, *Scots in London in the Eighteenth Century*. Touchstones of eighteenth-century linguistic de-Scotticization include David Hume's *Scotticisms* (1752); John Walker's "rules to be observed by the natives of Scotland . . . for avoiding their respective Peculiarities," prefaced to his *Critical Pronouncing Dictionary* (1791); and James Beattie's *List of Two Hundred Scoticisms* (1779). See Basker, "Scotticisms and the Problem of Cultural Identity in Eighteenth-Century Britain"; Sorensen, *Grammar of Empire*, chap. 4.

George I, who took the throne at the age of fifty-four, had only "the most rudimentary knowledge of English," while George II "spoke English volubly, though with a thick German accent" (*Dictionary of National Biography*, s.v. "George I"; "George II"; Hatton, *George I*, 130–32, 267, 296).

28. Johnson, preface to *A Dictionary of the English Language*, 1:[x]. Matthew Lauzon shows that the English and French languages were persistently defined against each other in the eighteenth century (*Signs of Light*, chaps. 5–6), extending arguments made by Linda Colley (*Britons*) and Gerald Newman (*The Rise of English Nationalism*) that "Britishness" and "English National Identity" arose in the eighteenth century as counterformations against (stereotypes of) the French. For eighteenth- and nineteenth-century thinking about the differences between Saxons and Celts, see Kidd, *British Identities before Nationalism*; Young, *The Idea of English Ethnicity*, 11–70.

29. Aarsleff, "Locke's Influence," 271 ("later commentator"); Ong, *Orality and Literacy*, 172–73. Locke's empiricist argument, which is a response to the "innatism" of Descartes, is in books 1 and 2 of the *Essay Concerning Humane Understanding*. His "disturbing picture of the insufficiency of language as a vehicle of thought" is in book 3 (Harris and Taylor, *Landmarks in Linguistic Thought*, 114). For the "two-faced" nature of Locke's philosophy of language, see Aarsleff, "Philosophy of Language," 453–54.

30. Aarsleff, "Philosophy of Language," 453, 452. On Locke, see also Aarsleff,

From Locke, 146–209; Harris and Taylor, *Landmarks in Linguistic Thought*, 120–35; Paxman, *Voyage into Language*, 203–12. On Condillac, see Aarsleff, "Philosophy of Language," 458–66; Ricken, *Linguistics, Anthropology and Philosophy in the French Enlightenment*, chap. 8; Robins, *A Short History of Linguistics*, 154–55. The *Encyclopédie*'s philosophies of language are covered by Aarsleff, "Philosophy of Language," 469–72; Simone, "The Early Modern Period," 210–11. For the Prussian Academy's contest and Johann David Michaelis's winning essay, see Lifschitz, *Language and Enlightenment*, 119–42.

31. Humboldt, quoted in Koerner, *Toward a History of American Linguistics*, 49; Christy, "Steinthal and the Development of Linguistic Science," 491. For specific lineages from Humboldt to Sapir and Whorf, see Koerner, *Toward a History of American Linguistics*, 39–62. Other accounts identifying the Herder-Humboldt cluster as the main source of the idea that "any specific language constituted a specific 'cosmovision' (*Weltansicht*)" which "determin[ed] human thought" include Barth et al., *One Discipline*, 61–156, 69; Darnell, *Invisible Genealogies*, 179; Harris and Taylor, *Landmarks in Linguistic Thought*, 151–64; Jankowsky, "Comparative, Historical, and Typological Linguistics," 640–42; Paxman, *Voyage into Language*, 221–34; Robins, *A Short History of Linguistics*, 155–68.

32. The mutual influence of these German and Scottish intellectual traditions at the turn of the nineteenth century was surprisingly slight. Less has been written about this Scottish eighteenth-century tradition of linguistic deterministic thinking than about their German contemporaries, but see Murray Cohen, *Sensible Words*, 102–3, 115, 120–27; Rysiew, "Thomas Reid on Language."

33. G. Campbell, *The Philosophy of Rhetoric*, 2:102; *Encyclopaedia Britannica*, 3rd ed. (1797), 9:534, s.v. "language"; D. Stewart, *Elements of the Philosophy of the Human Mind*, 221–22. On the anthropomorphosis of the English language with "bold," "nervous" (muscular), and other gendered qualities, see Michele Cohen, *Fashioning Masculinity*; Sklar, "So Male a Speech."

34. Because nineteenth-century linguists turned away from researching the relationship between language and thought, this Scottish intellectual tradition has often been treated as ancillary, "unfortunate," "pitiful and even laughable" relative to the history of linguistics proper (Robins, *A Short History of Linguistics*, 159–60; Aarsleff, "Philosophy of Language," 484). Even if the Scottish Enlightenment writers did not meaningfully contribute to the disciplines that emerged later in the nineteenth century, they gave the "language makes the difference between man and man" idea a meaningful academic imprimatur in the English-speaking world at the turn of the nineteenth century.

35. Dwight, "Observations on Language," [365–66], [365], [368] (misnumbered 126–27, 126, 129).

36. Kames, *Elements of Criticism*, 2:150n.

37. Beattie, *Dissertations Moral and Critical*, 477.

38. M., "On the Origin, Nature, and Necessity of Different Languages," 620.

39. Blair, *Lectures on Rhetoric and Belles Lettres*, 1:118.

40. Roebuck, *Annals of the College of Fort William*, 25; *Essays by the Students of the College of Fort William in Bengal*, 73, 81. The students are William Martin and Charles Metcalfe, respectively.

41. *Essays by the Students*, 81. On British anxieties about losing one's Britishness in the alterity of Indian others, see Nechtman, *Nabobs*, 60–91.

42. On the common Orientalist fantasy that Asian languages are unusually complex and therefore instruments of "Oriental despotism," see Irvine, "Ideologies of Honorific Language," 64.

43. Dwight, "Observations on Language," [368–69]. On the virtue of "copiousness" in eighteenth- and nineteenth-century linguistic thought, see Lauzon, *Signs of Light*, 150–55, 183–86. For the information that was available to Dwight about Arabic and its speakers, see Einboden, *The Islamic Lineage of American Literary Culture*, 33–64.

44. For Dwight's scholarship, see C. Wells, *The Devil and Doctor Dwight*.

45. For a recent theoretical conceptualization of projective tasks in general and the Rorschach in particular, see Tuber, *Understanding Personality through Projective Testing*.

46. Robins, *A Short History of Linguistics*, 164. For the nineteenth-century rise of historical linguistics and the declining prestige of research into the relationship between language and thought, see ibid., 160–70, 189–221; Aarsleff, *From Locke to Saussure*; Aarsleff, *The Study of Language in England, 1780–1860*, 3–11; Andresen, *Linguistics in America, 1769–1924*, 1–39; Foucault, *Order of Things*; Harris and Taylor, *Landmarks in Linguistic Thought*; Hudson, "Theories of Language."

In addition to the works of intellectual history cited elsewhere, I have drawn on the following works of cultural and literary history touching on the history of linguistic thinking beyond the formal history of ideas circa 1800: Baron, *English-Only Question*, 28; Cmiel, "Broad Fluid Language of Democracy," 923–24; Murray Cohen, *Sensible Words*, 102–4; Davidson, *Breeding*, 124–48; Gray, *New World Babel*, 5–7; Gustafson, *Representative Words*.

47. Sapir, "The Status of Linguistics as Science," 162. For the rise and fall of the Sapir-Whorf hypothesis in the twentieth century, see Darnell, *Edward Sapir*; Koerner, *Toward a History of American Linguistics*, 39–62.

48. Whorf, "An American Indian Model of the Universe," 58. For space-time, see Chase, *Power of Words*, 146; Livingstone, "Perception and Commitment." Armin Geertz provides a detailed history of the "Hopi time controversy" in *The Invention of Prophecy*.

49. Wittgenstein, *Tractatus Logico-Philosophicus*, 68; Harpham, *Language Alone*. Twentieth-century theory is rich with similarly evocative declarations of the linguistic bonds encompassing consciousness and communication, such as Jacques Derrida's "There is no 'outside-the-text'" (*Of Grammatology*, 158) and Raymond Williams's *Keywords*. On the relationship between Sapir-Whorf linguistic relativity and twentieth-century literary theory, see Hawkes, *Structuralism and Semiotics*.

50. For Hopi time, see Malotki, *Hopi Time*. For linguistic universals, see Bickel, "Linguistic Diversity and Universals."

51. See Cook and Newsom, *Chomsky's Universal Grammar*, for a clear survey of this line of thinking.

52. For the recent rise of neuroimaging and cognitive neuroscience and their relevance to linguistic relativity research, see Pederson, "Linguistic Relativity and Mainstream Linguistics." The cross-linguistic cognitive differences that have been identified so far are fascinating but relatively subtle; they do not approach anything like a different worldview. For different grammars corresponding to different neural pathways, see Janzen, Haun, and Levinson, "Tracking Down Abstract Linguistic Meaning." For other recent "neo-Whorfian" findings, see, e.g., Blomberg and Zlatev, "Language May Indeed Influence Thought"; Thierry, "Neurolinguistic Relativity."

53. Quoted in Boroditsky, "Lost in Translation"; Mackintosh, *Essay* (1797), iv. Boroditsky's view of linguistic relativity is not accepted by most linguists; John McWhorter calls it "utterly incoherent, and even dangerous" (*The Language Hoax*, xviii).

54. *Times* (London), Oct. 25, 1822, 1.

55. McKitterick, "Old Faces and New Acquisitions."

56. Gitelman, "The Phonograph's New Media Publics"; Hochman, *Savage Preservation*.

57. *Jamaica Lady*, 35–36; Hudson, "From 'Nation' to 'Race,'" 256, 248; Wahrman, *The Making of the Modern Self*; R. Wheeler, *The Complexion of Race*. In *Breeding: A Partial History of the Eighteenth Century*, Davidson offers a thoughtful investigation of how the eighteenth-century concept of "breeding"—which might refer to a person's biological background or to her education—also straddled the nature-nurture line for eighteenth-century thinkers.

58. Elliott, *The Culture Concept*, 13, 14.

59. See Kuper's *Culture: The Anthropologists' Account*, as well as classic statements about the history of cultural anthropology by anthropologists, such as Kluckhohn and Kroeber, *Culture*; Stocking, *Race, Culture, and Evolution*, chap. 9.

60. Skeptics of the benevolence of "cultural" analysis include Kuper, *Culture*, chap. 7; Michaels, *Our America*; Young, *Colonial Desire*.

CHAPTER ONE

1. Dufief, *Nature Displayed* (1804), 1:130–31. Hereafter cited as *ND* (followed by year of publication).

2. Dufief did not speak Spanish; for the Spanish editions, he collaborated with Louis Hargous, Manuel Torres, and Mariano Velázquez de la Cadena (García Aranda, "La enseñanza del léxico en el método Dufief").

3. *ND* (1810), 1:xxii.

4. The marginal quotations are from *ND* (1806).

5. For the conversion of English colonists into "Americans," see, e.g., R. Ferguson, *The American Enlightenment, 1750–1820*, who places the tipping point in 1764 (90); Yokota, *Unbecoming British*, 159. For the political history of Martinique, see Geggus, "The Slaves and Free Coloreds of Martinique." For France, see Furet, *Revolutionary France, 1770–1880*.

6. On how cartographers handled the shifting political boundaries in the Age of Revolutions, see Branch, *The Cartographic State*, 36–67.

7. Irving, *The Sketch Book of Geoffrey Crayon, Gent.*, 83, 86, 87. *Oxford English Dictionary*, s.v. "identity," n., sense 2b. This kind of "identity" has not always existed and is neither an inevitable nor a universal way of experiencing the self. Since the eighteenth century each person in a Western society has been obliged to develop an account of himself or herself in terms of certain historically specific categories. Today, for example, I must know how to place myself in terms of my race, nationality, sex, gender, age, sexual orientation, class, profession, religion, education, and so forth, and I am strongly encouraged to develop an understanding of myself in which at least some of those attributes are significant. That compulsory self-understanding within a bounded set of categories is what I mean by identity. My thinking on this is shaped by Louis Althusser, Lauren Berlant, Michel Foucault, Eve Kosofsky Sedgwick, Michael Warner, and Slavoj Žižek.

8. The "August Decrees" of Aug. 4–5, 1789. Furet, *Revolutionary France*, 70–73; Klooster, *Revolutions in the Atlantic World*, 55–57.

9. For his citizenship, see M. Stern, *Nicholas Gouin Dufief of Philadelphia*, 75. Dufief's bookselling business is the only aspect of his life that has received focused historiographical attention (Hayes and Wolf, *The Library of Benjamin Franklin*, 40–48; M. Stern, *Nicholas Gouin Dufief of Philadelphia*).

10. Dufief, "Language Makes the Difference." At the same time that this phrase announces a vision of human diversity in which languages create and reflect the crucial differences among people and peoples, it is also probably operating as an advertisement for Dufief's French classes—an invitation to gain a competitive advantage over other "men" by developing superior language. In

1806, "language makes the difference between man and man" would have been understood as applying to both men and women. However, its gendering is also noteworthy, especially at a time when some languages were considered more "masculine" than others (Michele Cohen, *Fashioning Masculinity*, 38–41, 83–84).

11. Dufief, "Language Makes the Difference."

12. *ND* (1804), 1:xxi.

13. Dufief, "Language Makes the Difference."

14. *Morning Chronicle* (London), July 29, 1823, [1].

15. For the adolescent metaphor of the American Revolution, see Fliegelman, *Prodigals and Pilgrims*. For France, see Desan, *The Family on Trial in Revolutionary France*.

16. Gourdon de Genouillac, *Dictionnaire des fiefs*, 183. For the history of the Bretons and Brittany, see Galliou and Jones, *The Bretons*, esp. 128–48, 230–52.

17. Planhol, *An Historical Geography of France*, 82–87; Wmffre, *Breton Orthographies and Dialects*, 616.

18. Hettier, *Relations de la Normandie et de la Bretagne avec les îles de la Manche pendant l'émigration*, 317 (on Désiré Gouin); L'Estourbeillon, *Les familles françaises à Jersey pendant la Révolution*, 535, 267 (on the parents).

19. *Philadelphia Gazette*, Sept. 10, 1800, [1]; M. Stern, *Nicholas Gouin Dufief of Philadelphia*, 75; entries dated March 17 and April 21, 1796, in Membership Book 1, Montgomery Lodge No. 19, Masonic Library and Museum of Philadelphia, 179 (quoted in correspondence with Glenys Waldman, librarian, Nov. 2014); Gilreath, *Federal Copyright Records, 1790–1800*, 38; *Philadelphia Gazette*, Oct. 9, 1795, [2].

20. Dufief appears to have believed that he was born a year later, in September 1776; he indicates in *Nature Displayed* that he was fifteen in summer 1792 and sixteen in July 1793 (*ND* [1818], 1:ii–iii), when in fact he was sixteen and seventeen. Dufief's error has led to his birth being given as "1776?" in bibliographies. The Nantes parish register, however, clearly shows that Nicolas was born Sept. 21, 1775, while his brother Henri-Constant was born in fall 1776. "Nantes—Gil à Guz," s.v. "Gouin," 126, no. 59, Fonds Freslon, Archives départementales de Loire-Atlantique, archives.loire-atlantique.fr/jcms/chercher/archives-numerisees/genealogie/fonds-freslon/fonds-freslon-fr-t1_6156.

21. Cullen, *The Brandy Trade under the Ancien Régime*; C. Miller, *The French Atlantic Triangle*, xi, 40–61; Pruitt, "Nantes Noir."

22. Pruitt, "Nantes Noir," 43. For the significance of Saint-Domingue for France and for Nantes, see Chaussinand-Nogaret, *French Nobility in the Eighteenth Century*, 84–116; Cheney, *Cul de Sac*, 7–8, 20–24; Klooster, *Revolutions in the Atlantic World*, 84–86.

23. *ND* (1806), 1:91–92. Dufief's paternal uncle César managed several

plantations north of Port-au-Prince. On the other side of the island, Dufief's mother's brother, Pierre Julien Libault, owned a plantation near Cap Français.

24. The "August Decrees" of Aug. 4–5, 1789.

25. Carlyle, *The French Revolution*, 2:35. My account of the Marine Royale's participation in this invasion draws on *ND* (1818), 1:i–iii; Bélizal, "Journal et lettres d'un émigré," esp. 94–96; Bittard des Portes. *Histoire de l'armée de Condé*, 7–53; Merland, "Le comte d'Hector," 284; d'Agay, "A European Destiny"; Schneid, *European Armies of the French Revolution, 1789–1802*.

26. Sept. 21, 1792 (*Archives parlementaires*, 52:73–74; Furet, *Revolutionary France*, 115–18).

27. Goethe, *Campaign in France, in the Year 1792*, 87, 143–45; Bélizal, "Journal et lettres d'un émigré," 94–95.

28. The Marine Royale was disbanded in October 1792, and Dufief says he arrived in Philadelphia "in July, 1793" (*ND* [1818], 1:iii). Winter transatlantic crossings were avoided (Furstenberg, *When the United States Spoke French*, 76–77), so Dufief likely left Europe between March and May 1793. Draft riots began on March 3 in Cholet, and Paris ordered an army of fifteen thousand troops to subdue the region on March 23 (Hussenet, *"Détruisez la Vendée!"*, 31–32).

29. L'Estourbeillon, *Les familles françaises à Jersey*, 535, 267; "W.," *L'intermédiaire*, Aug. 25, 1885, 495–96. Most exiles from the French Revolution tried to find refuge in Britain or Jersey, not the Caribbean or the United States. See Harsanyi, *Lessons from America*, 50–53; B. Oliver, *Surviving the French Revolution*, 19–50.

30. For the Haitian Revolution up to summer 1793, see Dubois, *Avengers of the New World*, 91–159; Klooster, *Revolutions in the Atlantic World*, 84–105.

31. Popkin, *You Are All Free*, 2 (quotation); *ND* (1806), 1:114; Dubois, *Avengers of the New World*, 30, 157–59; Klooster, *Revolutions in the Atlantic World*, 102; White, *Encountering Revolution*, 22–23, 58.

32. Dufief evidently left Saint-Domingue in June or early July for the three-week passage to Philadelphia, "where I arrived in July, 1793" (*ND* [1818], 1:iii). César Gouin du Fief, Dufief's paternal uncle in Port-au-Prince, on whose hospitality Dufief likely would have relied in Saint-Domingue, died in Kingston, Jamaica, Jan. 24, 1800.

33. *ND* (1806), 1:v–vii. Charitable organizations and the city government of Philadelphia provided immediate financial assistance to the two or three thousand refugees who arrived from Saint-Domingue in the summer of 1793 (White, *Encountering Revolution*, 51–73).

34. B. G. Smith, *Ship of Death*, 187–241.

35. Dufief, *Logic of Facts*, 6; *ND* (1806), iv–vii; Furstenberg, *When the United States Spoke French*, 65; B. G. Smith, *Ship of Death*, 210; *ND* (1804), xi ("it was deemed"); *ND* (1806), iv ("more sensibly").

36. Thomas Berry, *Vraie méthode pour apprendre facilement*, 101, 48. On the popularity of Berry's *Vraie méthode*, see Gallet-Blanchard, "L'enseignement de la langue anglaise en France au dix-huitième siècle," 41; for other "treatises on English written for speakers of French," see Alston, *A Bibliography of the English Language*, 2:37–72.

37. *ND* (1806), 1:v–viii.

38. Although inductive language pedagogy had been explored in "experimental methods scattered here and there," mainstream teaching in Dufief's day was still focused on "deductive learning and memorization of grammar rules" (G. Wheeler, *Language Teaching through the Ages*, 110). A more inductive method that involved working at the level of the sentence, now known as the grammar-translation method, was coming into use at the same time; but Dufief's method goes much further, anticipating the "series," "direct," and "natural" methods of Maximilian Berlitz, François Gouin (no relation to Dufief), and Lambert Sauveur. Like those later practitioners, Dufief emphasized orality and whole phrases, alleged that his system replicated the process by which children learn first languages, and erroneously believed that his insight was completely new (McLelland, *Teaching and Learning Foreign Languages*; Tomalin, "The Torment of Every Seminary"; G. Wheeler, *Language Teaching*, 112–43).

39. *ND* (1806), 1:vii.

40. B. G. Smith, *Ship of Death*, 234–35.

41. *ND* (1818), 1:iii; *ND* (1806), 1:vii; John Adams to Edmund-Charles Genêt, May 17, 1780 (Sparks, *The Diplomatic Correspondence of the American Revolution*, 5:102). For British and American interest in learning French, see Görlach, *Aspects of the History of English*, 179–99; Furstenberg, *When the United States Spoke French*. On the teaching of French classes by refugees from the French and Haitian revolutions, see Moutray, *Refugee Nuns, the French Revolution, and British Literature and Culture*, 146–51; White, *Encountering Revolution*, 36. For other ways émigrés supported themselves, see Merland, "Le comte d'Hector," 285; B. Oliver, *Surviving the French Revolution*, 35–50; White, *Encountering Revolution*, 26–37.

42. *ND* (1806), 1:vii–viii; *Philadelphia Gazette*, Oct. 9, 1795, [2]; Furstenberg, *When the United States Spoke French*, 110–15.

43. Dufief, *Logic of Facts*, 22; *ND* (1806), 1:viii–x; *ND* (1818), 1:ii–iii; M. Stern, *Nicholas Gouin Dufief of Philadelphia*, 36–50. On French exiles at the American Philosophical Society, see Harsanyi, *Lessons from America*, 66–67.

44. These are the opening statements in Perrin, *A Grammar of the French Tongue* (1768), Wanostrocht, *A Grammar of the French Language* (1789), Chambaud, *A Grammar of the French Tongue* (1775), Labute, *A French Grammar* (1790), and Boyer, *The Complete French Master for Ladies and Gentlemen* (1779),

respectively. According to one study, between 1740 and 1800, two-thirds of the English grammars that define "grammar" define it as "the art of speaking and writing correctly" (Michael, *English Grammatical Categories and the Tradition to 1800*, 189).

45. *ND* (1804), 2:12–14.

46. Specifically, 1.31 pounds (B. G. Smith, *Lower Sort*, 95–103).

47. Franklin, *Autobiography*, 75–77. Dufief was almost certainly familiar with Franklin's autobiography, having purchased the remnants of Benjamin Franklin's library in 1801.

48. *ND* (1804), 1:xxxiii.

49. *ND* (1818), 1:xxxv. For a brief analysis of this "oral drill," see W. Miller, "Nature Displayed."

50. *ND* (1806), 1:71.

51. *ND* (1823), 1:14n.

52. *Atlas* (London), July 31, 1831, 523.

53. Thomas Jefferson to Samuel R. Demaree (enclosure), Oct. 4, 1789, *Founders Online*, founders.archives.gov/documents/Jefferson/ 03-01-02-0453-0002. For Jefferson's view of *Nature Displayed*, see Carrière, "Mr. Jefferson Sponsors a New French Method"; for Poe, see Quinn, *Edgar Allan Poe*, 103; for Irving, see S. Williams, *Journal of Washington Irving (1823–1824)*, 65, 83; for Lidian Jackson Emerson (Ralph Waldo Emerson's wife), see Emerson, *Life of Lidian Jackson Emerson*, 28, 216n58. Astor owned one of the Spanish-language editions of *ND* (K. Porter, *John Jacob Astor*, 1:500). For forty years later: *Dufief's French Self-Interpreter* (1874).

54. "Proposals for Printing by Subscription *The French Grammatical Companion*," *Sun* (Dover, N.H.), Dec. 2, 1795, 4; *Times* (London), July 3, 1823, 2.

55. Dufief, "Proposals for Publishing [. . .] Nature Displayed," [2]; *ND* (1823), 1:14n; *Times* (London), Dec. 5, 1829, 2.

56. *Kaleidoscope* (Liverpool), Oct. 6, 1818, 43.

57. *Monthly Anthology* (Boston), Nov. 1805, 591.

58. *Times* (London), Oct. 25, 1822, 1.

59. *ND* (1806), 1:xxvii–xxviii.

60. *Times* (London), Oct. 25, 1822, 1.

61. Dufief, "To the Subscribers," 10.

62. *ND* (1806), 1:iii.

63. *ND* (1823), 1:t.p.

64. "Dr. Tromp's *Nature Perfected*," *Edinburgh Magazine*, Dec. 1818, 534–38.

65. *Edinburgh Magazine*, Oct. 1818, 358–62.

66. *National Gazette* (Philadelphia), Nov. 25, 1823, [3].

67. *ND* (1806), 1:xxvii–xxviii.

68. Dufief could mean *anxious* in the sense of "earnestly desirous" (*Oxford English Dictionary*, s.v. "anxious," sense 3). In the context, however, and given the contrast with the mother, "troubled or uneasy" (sense 1a) seems like a better fit.

69. *ND* (1818), 1:iii.

70. *ND* (1806), 1:xxx.

71. I am drawing on Friedrich Kittler's essay, "The Mother's Mouth" (*Discourse Networks*, 25–69), which argues that the affective scene of maternal language acquisition is an imaginative creation of Dufief's historical moment. Dufief could be understood as participating in the invention of that scene. For Freud's oral stage (the first 18–24 months of life, during which the child's paradigmatic experience of pleasure is the total fulfillment of needs that he or she enjoys during breastfeeding), see his *Three Essays on the Theory of Sexuality* (1905).

72. N. G. Dufief to Thomas Jefferson, April 4, 1817, *Founders Online*, founders.archives.gov/documents/Jefferson/03-11-02-0203; N. G. Dufief, *Monthly Magazine* (London), Aug. 1, 1819, 18. He returned to the United States in 1823, taught classes in Boston and New York, and then returned permanently to Europe in 1825. *National Advocate* (New York), Sept. 27, 1823, [3]; *Evening Post* (New York), Sept. 28, 1824, [3]; *Independent Chronicle* (Boston), May 25, 1825, [3]; *Commercial Advertiser* (New York), Oct. 20, 1825, 3.

73. *Quarterly Literary Advertiser* (London), Oct. 1828, 23.

74. Opponents of working-class education were deeply concerned about the consequences of cultivating working-class critical thinkers (Hopkins, *Childhood Transformed*, 128–29). The Parochial Schools Bill of 1807 passed the House of Commons but died in the House of Lords (Paz, *The Politics of Working-Class Education in Britain, 1830–50*, 5–6). In preindustrial Britain, masters had typically provided some kind of education to young people apprenticed to them; this system became conspicuously inadequate as work shifted to factories (Hopkins, *Childhood Transformed*, 1–8, 128–58; Paz, *The Politics of Working-Class Education*, 3–5).

75. *Royal Lady's Magazine*, Aug. 1831, 108–9.

76. For the economic challenges, see Sanderson, *Education, Economic Change and Society in England 1780–1870*, 13–19. The Lancaster and Madras systems are often seen as equivalent and grouped together under the rubric of "monitorial" pedagogy (Silver and Silver, *The Education of the Poor*, 9–16, 35–73; Tomlinson, *Head Masters: Phrenology, Secular Education, and Nineteenth-Century Social Thought*, 115–214), although Frances Ferguson has recently identified some key theoretical differences between the two systems; see F. Ferguson, "The Social Organization of Schools (around 1800)."

77. *London Courier and Evening Gazette*, Nov. 24, 1827, 4; *Morning Post* (London), Feb. 1, 1819, 4.

78. *Daily National Intelligencer* (Washington, D.C.), Oct. 17, 1843, [3].

79. *Literary Chronicle* (London), Sept. 11, 1819, 264.

80. *Times* (London), Jan. 20, 1821, 4.

81. [Charles Knight?], *London Magazine* (London), Feb. 1829, 185–86. On the *London Magazine*'s conspicuously independent politics, see Parker, *Literary Magazines and British Romanticism*, 59–105.

82. *Atlas* (London), Jan. 14, 1827, 4. On the LMI, see Flexner, "The London Mechanics' Institution."

83. *Mechanics' Magazine*, Aug. 4, 1827, 48.

84. Number of students: *Morning Advertiser* (London), Oct. 16, 1827, 4; *London Courier and Evening Gazette*, Nov. 24, 1827, 4; *Quarterly Literary Advertiser* (London), Oct. 1828, 23. Required texts: *Morning Advertiser* (London), June 9, 1827, 1.

85. *London Literary Gazette*, Aug. 3, 1822, 494.

86. *Poulson's American Daily Advertiser* (Philadelphia), Dec. 6, 1820, [3]; *New-York Evening Post*, Dec. 26, 1820, [4]; *City Gazette* (Charleston, S.C.), Dec. 27, 1820, [2]; *Daily National Intelligencer* (Washington, D.C.), Jan. 1, 1821, [4].

87. *ND* (1818), 1:vi–vii.

88. *ND* (1831), 1:vii.

89. His inscription to Charles X is in a copy of *ND* (1828) that is now at the Huntington Library (call no. 109597).

90. *Morning Chronicle* (London), July 30, 1823, [1].

91. *ND* (1810), 1:xxiin.

92. *Times* (London), Dec. 11, 1818, 1. On this teacher, Charles-Pascal Buquet, see Levée, *Biographie*, 59; Anthiaume, *Le Collège du Havre*, 2:386–87.

93. *Bristol Mercury*, Nov. 1, 1819, 2. On this teacher, Claude Guiot, see Faber, *Bibliothèque de la Providence*, 89. Other highborn French exiles who associated themselves with Dufief include Dominique Auguste Fichet des Jardins (ca. 1796–1864) (*Leeds Intelligencer*, Aug. 13, 1836, [1]); and Mariette Yvonnet (1802–69) and her father, Alexis Yvonnet (1773–1859) (*Columbian Centinel* [Boston], May 22, 1819, [1]; July 8, 1820, [1]; Sept. 8, 1824, [3]).

94. *Ipswich Journal*, Nov. 19, 1825, 3.

95. Suliot, "The Teaching of Foreign Languages," 339. Dufief is also quoted as telling "a *leetle* story" in *Mirror* (London), Dec. 19, 1835, 419.

96. See, e.g., Fogleman, *Two Troubled Souls*; Waldstreicher, *Runaway America*; Jasanoff, *Liberty's Exiles*.

97. "W.," *L'intermédiare*, Aug. 25, 1885, 495–96; *ND* (1804), 1:vi–vii.

98. This was the Battle of Torfou-Tiffauges, Sept. 19, 1793. See Cretineau-Joly, *Histoire de la Vendée militaire*, 1:232.

99. Ibid., 2:226. On women's participation in the Vendée insurgency and

the broader French Revolution, see Smart, *Citoyennes*, 180–85; Dupuy, "Les femmes et la Contre-Révolution dans l'ouest."

100. Beauchamp, *Histoire de la guerre de la Vendée*, 2:257; Muret, *Histoire des guerres de l'ouest*, 2:161; "Mémoires de Bodereau," 2:203–4.

101. *ND* (1806), dedication (unpaginated).

102. An intense public controversy about the applicability of this term followed the publication of Sécher's *Le génocide franco-français* (1986).

103. Estimates of deaths range from about 15 percent to more than 50 percent of the regional population (Hussenet, *"Détruisez la Vendée!"*, 415–32; Martin, *La Vendée et la France*, 312–17; Sédillot, *Le coût de la Révolution française*, 28).

CHAPTER TWO

1. J. G. Chambers, *Elements of Orthography* (1817), 6, 5. For the little that is known about Joseph Gaston Chambers (1756?–1829), see D. Chambers, "Sketch of the Life of David Chambers," 33–37; Looney and Woodward, *Princetonians, 1791–1794*, 481–88. Chambers's alphabetic proposal was printed four times (1791, 1811, 1812, 1817), with Chambers's material access to nonstandard type improving over time. I have used Chambers's 1817 spellings where possible.

American public opinion was bitterly divided about the prospect of war in 1812 (Eustace, *1812*, 1–35). Chambers's respectful dedications to President Madison and the Prince Regent suggest that the English language was (at least for Chambers) able to transcend a maximally polarizing debate.

2. J. G. Chambers, *Elements of Orthography* (1812), dedication (unpaginated).

3. "Advertisement, by an English Friend," in Ramsay, *The History of the American Revolution*, 1:iii–viii, at 1:vi.

4. For establishment and policing of distinctions between Britain and the United States, see Eustace, *1812*, 1–33; Perl-Rosenthal, *Citizen Sailors*, esp. 140–207.

5. Webster, *Dissertations on the English Language*, 406.

6. Gordon Wood, *Empire of Liberty*, 49. For Webster's place in the historiography of American nationalism, see note 85 in this chapter.

7. [William Cobbett], *Rush-Light*, Feb. 28, 1800, 50n–51n.

8. Abigail Adams to John Quincy Adams, Aug. 20, 1790, *Founders Online*, founders.archives.gov/documents/Adams/04-09-02-0049.

9. Webster's partisan activities are covered in Daniel, *Scandal and Civility*, 177–80; Kendall, *The Forgotten Founding Father*, 221–26; Rollins, *Long Journey of Noah Webster*, 89–105. Yet Lepore, Cmiel, and Simpson have all argued that Webster was "a conservative with liberal ideas" who had "the very bad biparti-

san luck of offending nearly everybody" (Lepore, "Noah's Mark," 80, 81; Lepore, *A Is for American*, 15–41; Cmiel, "Broad Fluid Language of Democracy," 915, 921–25; Simpson, *Politics of American English*, 63–90). On the norms of print politeness that Webster violated, see Warner, *Letters of the Republic*, chaps. 2–3.

A recent biographer suggests that Webster might today be diagnosed with obsessive-compulsive personality disorder (Kendall, *The Forgotten Founding Father*, 7–8). See also Lepore's reflections on Webster's likeability as a research subject in "Historians Who Love Too Much."

10. Webster, *Dissertations on the English Language*, 179.

11. For the English-speaking populations inside and outside of England, see introduction, note 14. For many other structural similarities between the French Caribbean and the United States, see White, *Encountering Revolution*, 13–22.

12. Quoted by Benjamin Vaughan in Franklin, *Political, Miscellaneous, and Philosophical Pieces*, 475n. On Franklin's phonetic alphabet, see Lepore, *A Is for American*, 31–39; Lepore, *Book of Ages*, 211–13; Looby, "Phonetics and Politics." More generally on Franklin's prerevolutionary years in London, see Morgan, *The Devious Dr. Franklin*.

13. On uncertainties about correct English in North America, Scotland, and other imperial frontiers, see Bann and Corbett, *Spelling Scots*, 78–83; Krapp, *The English Language in America*, 1:57–60; Looby, "Phonetics and Politics," 6; Sorensen, *Strange Vernaculars*, 133–48. Franklin's access to Anglophone print culture is detailed in Hayes and Wolf, *Library of Benjamin Franklin*, 3–56. On British phonetic texts and Americans' importation of them, see R. Bailey, *Speaking American*, 12, 67–69; Beal, "The Place of Pronunciation in Eighteenth-Century Grammars of English"; Boggs, "William Kenrick's Pronunciations"; Monaghan, *A Common Heritage*, 31–49.

14. The owner was probably Zaccheus Collins (1764–1831), who donated this copy of Walker's *Critical Pronouncing Dictionary* (1797) to the American Philosophical Society in 1815 (call no. 423 W15). Collins may have made some use of a published *Vocabulary of Such Words as Are of Dubious or Unsettled Accentuation; in Which the Pronunciation of Sheridan, Walker, and Other Orthoepists Is Compared* (London, 1797). For a recent comparison of eight eighteenth-century dictionaries' recommended pronunciations, see Beal and Condorelli, "Cut from the Same Cloth?," 31–36.

15. Pickering, *A Vocabulary*, v.

16. Franklin, *Political, Miscellaneous, and Philosophical Pieces*, 469; Benjamin Franklin to [Mary Stevenson], July 20, 1768, American Philosophical Society, Bradford Collection, MSS.B.F85.bra; Stevenson to Franklin, Sept. 26, 1768, in Franklin, ibid., 472; Franklin to Stevenson, Sept. 28, 1768, in Franklin,

ibid., 473–78. Franklin and Stevenson met in 1757, when she was eighteen, and carried on a flirtatious correspondence for decades; see Morgan, *Devious Dr. Franklin*, 19, 69.

17. Mackintosh, *A Plain, Rational, and Patriotic Essay on English Grammar* (1808), unpaginated front matter. Mackintosh and his printers applied his system to his texts to varying degrees of rigor, sometimes leaving off the numbers.

On the English language in the eighteenth-century Caribbean, see Holm, "English in the Caribbean," 346–50; Schneider, "Contact Englishes and Creoles in the Caribbean," 479–82.

18. Mackintosh, *A Plain, Rational, and Patriotic Essay* (1808), xviii.

19. *Critical Review* (Dec. 1808): 446.

20. Bhabha, *The Location of Culture*; Crawford, *Devolving English Literature*, 38. On the Scottish "invention" of English linguistic correctness, see Beach, "The Creation of a Classical Language in the Eighteenth Century"; Crawford, *Scottish Invention of English Literature*. For American analogies, see Baron, *Grammar and Good Taste*, 22–24; Longmore, "Good English without Idiom or Tone."

21. Weed, *The American Orthographer*, vi.

22. Cardell, *Essay on Language*, 43. See chapter 3 for more on the intersection of (musical) instruments and phonetic technology.

23. "On Alphabetic Reformations," *Literary Magazine* (Philadelphia), April 1805, 267. On the centuries-long fantasy of "a one-to-one correspondence between grapheme and phoneme," see Venezky, "In Search of the Perfect Orthography," 139; see also Hudson, *Writing and European Thought, 1600–1830*, 92–118.

24. For exclusively British accounts of eighteenth-century spelling and alphabet reform, see Beal, "Out in Left Field"; C. Jones, *English Pronunciation in the Eighteenth and Nineteenth Centuries*, 137–65. For exclusively American accounts, see Lepore, *A Is for American*, 30–60; Baron, *Grammar and Good Taste*, 69–83; Brückner, *The Geographic Revolution in Early America*, 101–2; Venezky, *The American Way of Spelling*, 217–24.

One exception to this tendency to bound the genre within national borders is Simpson's *Politics of American English*, which places Webster and Thornton in dialogue with Spence and Elphinston (59–63).

25. For the weight and value of Thomas's equipment, see Shipton, *Isaiah Thomas*, 86–90. On the expense and logistics of type manufacturing, see chapter 4. The problem of creating new type for alphabetic reformations and the various typographic workarounds that have been tried by alphabetic innovators over the years—turning letters, borrowing characters from Greek founts, etc.—is discussed in Drucker, *The Alphabetic Labyrinth*, 247–61.

26. Ewing, *The Columbian Alphabet*, 4. On Ewing, see Baron, *Grammar and Good Taste*, 77–79; Lepore, *A Is for American*, 76, 204n46.

27. See for example *Specimen of Isaiah Thomas's Printing Types* (1785), 28; *Specimen of Printing Types, by Fry and Steele* (1794), [55]; *Specimen of Printing Types, by Wm Caslon* (1796), [53].

28. Jane Mecom to Benjamin Franklin, March 3, 1781, *Founders Online*, founders.archives.gov/documents/Franklin/01-34-02-0321. On Mecom, her spelling, and her relationship with her brother, see Lepore, *Book of Ages*, esp. 103–10, 211–13.

29. Benjamin Franklin to Jane Mecom, July 4, 1786, quoted in Ford, *Notes on the Life of Noah Webster*, 1:119n–120n; Franklin to Stevenson, Sept. 28, 1768, 474.

30. "His study of linguistics (no doubt influenced by his egalitarianism) was responsible for his opinion, 'I think the worst Spelling is the best'," writes a recent biographer (Lemay, *The Life of Benjamin Franklin*, 74). See also Scragg, *A History of English Spelling*, 103–4.

31. Bourdieu, "The Economy of Linguistic Exchanges," 57.

32. Sorensen, *Grammar of Empire*, 138. Other accounts that place Scottish and American linguistic self-"improvement" efforts in primary relation to the socioeconomic power of the London prestige district include Colley, *Britons*, 120–32; Flavell, *When London Was Capital of America*, 63–83, esp. 71; C. Jones, *English Pronunciation*, 117–21; Longmore, "They . . . Speak," 293–94; Mugglestone, "*Talking Proper*"; O. Smith, *The Politics of Language, 1791–1819*.

33. Elphinston, *Propriety Ascertained in Her Picture*, 1:312; Southey, *Letters from England*, 3:302.

34. To the best of my knowledge, Mackintosh's *Plain, Rational Essay on English Grammar* has never been discussed beyond very brief bibliographical references such as Alston, *A Bibliography of the English Language*, 6:511; C. Jones, *English Pronunciation*, 149; Read, "Projected English Dictionaries," 349–50.

35. See Goudie, "The Caribbean Turn," on this scholarship.

36. For the history of printing in Martinique, see Banks, *Chasing Empire across the Sea*, 180–81, 205–6; Dibbell, "History of the Book in the Caribbean and Bermuda," 711.

37. The sketch of Duncan Mackintosh that follows relies on the prefatory materials to *Essay* (1797) and *A Plain, Rational, and Patriotic Essay* (1808), and the following manuscript documents: Registre paroissial, 1779, Le Fort, Sainte-Pierre, Martinique (*Archives nationales d'outre-mer*, anom.archivesnationales.culture.gouv.fr); an untitled pamphlet by Mackintosh, dated April 12, 1799 ([St. Pierre?], 1799), with marginalia in Mackintosh's hand throughout; letters by Mackintosh to the faculty of the University of Oxford, to a hypothetical

printer, and to the Duke of Portland, all dated July 20, 1779 (Portland Collection, Pl C 23/1–7); and Mackintosh to James Grant, Feb. 10, 1779 (*James Grant of Ballindalloch Papers*, reel 39, folder 8).

38. Mackintosh to Grant, Feb. 10, 1779.

39. Mackintosh, *Essay* (1808), unpaginated front matter.

40. Byres, *References to the Plan of the Island of Dominica*, [1], 9, 16; Mackintosh to Grant, Feb. 10, 1779. On Dominica in the eighteenth century, before and after the British invasion in 1761, see Baker, *Centring the Periphery*, 34–97; Honychurch, *The Dominica Story*, 49–115; Paugh, *Playing with Languages*, 30–33. The British government changed the official language to English, but it was adopted only very gradually (Paugh, *Playing with Languages*, 9–11).

41. Mackintosh to Grant, Feb. 10, 1779.

42. Marie-Louise-Guillemette Bègue, marquise de Bouillé; François de Cours de Thomazeau; and Etienne-Marie-George Cacqueray de Valmenier, respectively. Baptism of Marie George Mackintosh, Oct. 4, 1779. Registre paroissial, 1779, Le Fort, Sainte-Pierre, Martinique, 37, no. 205 (*Archives nationales d'outre-mer*, anom.archivesnationales.culture.gouv.fr).

43. Abjuration of Eliza Barnes Mackintosh, May 2, 1779. Registre paroissial, 1779, Le Fort, Sainte-Pierre, Martinique, 21, no. 111 (*Archives nationales d'outre-mer*, anom.archivesnationales.culture.gouv.fr).

44. Mackintosh to Grant, Feb. 10, 1779. On the legal status of British aliens in French territory during the ancien régime, see Sahlins, *Unnaturally French*.

45. Schloss, *Sweet Liberty*, 1–71.

46. In contrast to enslaved persons in mainland North America, most slaves in the West Indies spoke African languages or Afro-Caribbean creoles (Mullin, *Africa in America*, 192). On the African, European, and creole languages spoken by slaves in Caribbean colonies, see also Paugh, *Playing with Languages*, 7–8; John Thornton, *Africa and Africans in the Making of the Atlantic World, 1400–1680*, 192–205.

47. Mackintosh, *Essay* (1797), vii–viii. Military conflicts between European imperial powers in the eighteenth-century Caribbean were almost constant, and Britain would cede Martinique back to France in 1802; see O'Shaughnessy, *An Empire Divided*.

48. Mackintosh, *Essay* (1797), 170, [ii], 228; Mackintosh, *Essay* (1808), t.p.

49. Mackintosh, *Essay* (1797), xi, 30, x.

50. Ibid., viii, ix.

51. Mackintosh, *Essay* (1808), xxiv, xxvii, xxviii. On climatic accounts of human diversity, see Nechtman, *Nabobs*, 37–69; Wahrman, *The Making of the Modern Self*, 127–53; R. Wheeler, *The Complexion of Race*, 1–48.

52. Mackintosh, *Essay* (1808), xxviii–xxix.

53. B. Anderson, *Imagined Communities*, 83–86, 132–34.

54. The early modern great powers and their languages: Britain (English), France (French), Spain (Spanish), Portugal (Portuguese), the Dutch Republic (Dutch), Prussia (German), Poland (Polish), Sweden (Swedish), Russia (Russian), the Ottoman Empire (Turkish). In reality, these states were not actually monolingual, but each had its own dominant vernacular, distinct from the others'. The English-speaking United States (est. 1776) and German-speaking Austrian Empire (est. 1804) were the first geopolitically significant nation-states that were understood as sharing their dominant vernacular with another such nation-state.

55. Though I am suggesting that Anderson overstates the nationalizing function of the English language, my thinking about how languages affect the work of "imagining" of national communities has been deeply influenced by Anderson and the many studies that have built on his work, especially Cmiel, *Democratic Eloquence*; Crain, *Story of A*; Looby, *Voicing America*; St. Clair, *The Reading Nation in the Romantic Period*; Tennenhouse, *The Importance of Feeling English*; Warner, *Letters of the Republic*; Young, *Idea of English Ethnicity*.

For the actual history of linguistic differences between American and British Englishes up to 1825—as distinct from my concern with the cultural history of *perceived* differences—see R. Bailey, *Speaking American*, 3–120; Dillard, *A History of American English*, 1–92.

56. J. G. Chambers, *Elements of Orthography* (1812), dedication; Croft, *A Letter, from Germany*, 2 (emphasis added), 3.

57. Chastellux, *Travels in North-America*, 2:202. The Hebrew anecdote first appears in English in excerpts of Chastellux's memoir in the *Gentleman's Magazine*, Dec. 1786, 1119, and then in Chastellux, *Travels*, 2:265–66. By 1807, the story was circulating in the United States as fact (*Port-Folio*, Nov. 21, 1807, 323). Other than the two sentences in Chastellux, no one has ever turned up any evidence that Hebrew was proposed as an American language, seriously or otherwise (Mencken, *The American Language*, 137–39; Withington, "The Marquis de Chastellux on Language and Peace"). On the German myth, see Baron, "Legendary English-Only Vote of 1795," pbs.org/speak/seatosea/officialamerican/englishonly/; Mencken, *The American Language*, 139–40.

58. Archibald McCalester to Thomas Jefferson, Nov. 1, 1791, *Founders Online*, founders.archives.gov/documents/Jefferson/01-22-02-0241.

59. Chastellux, *Travels*, 2:202.

60. John Adams to C. W. F. Dumas and William Short, Sept. 11, 1785, *Founders Online*, founders.archives.gov/documents/Adams/06-17-02-0234. On Adams's linguistic activism, see Baron, *Grammar and Good Taste*, 17–18; Simpson, *Politics of American English*, 29–32.

61. William Thornton received the APS medal for his *Cadmus* on January 27, 1793, and won the Capitol design contest on April 2, 1793. See Baron, *Grammar and Good Taste*, 75–77; Lepore, *A Is for American*, 44–60.

62. Sprague, *Oration*, 18–19. On expressions of American identity at Fourth of July and other civic occasions, see S. Newman, *Parades and the Politics of the Street*; Waldstreicher, *In the Midst of Perpetual Fetes*.

Notable studies of early national language ideologies that keep the nationalist paradigm at arm's length include Cmiel, "Broad Fluid Language of Democracy"; Looby, "Phonetics and Politics"; M. Nash, "Contested Identities"; Simpson, *Politics of American English*. Taking note of the early republic's relative friendliness toward non-English-speaking communities within its borders, Shirley Brice Heath has suggested that "language was not yet a national ideological symbol" at that time but functioned merely as "a pragmatic instrument" and medium of communication, unburdened by the political baggage that language would eventually bear in American identity ("Why No Official Tongue?," 30). I would revise this somewhat: Americans saw great national and ideological significance in the status of language in the United States, but not in a way that prioritized having that English language be nationally differentiated from British English.

63. Embree, *Orthography Corrected*, 142, iv, 26. My thinking on this is influenced by numerous studies of the ongoing investment in Britishness in the early United States and the ambivalences and contradictions within American nationalism, especially Loughran, *The Republic in Print*; McGill, *American Literature and the Culture of Reprinting, 1834–1853*; Rezek, *London and the Making of Provincial Literature*; Tamarkin, *Anglophilia*; Tennenhouse, *The Importance of Feeling English*; Yokota, *Unbecoming British*.

64. "Account of the College and Academy of Philadelphia," *American Magazine* (Philadelphia), Oct. 1758, 631. See also R. Bailey, *Speaking American*, 65–68; Davidson, *Breeding*, 128, 140–48; Kamensky, *Governing the Tongue*, 50–54; Longmore, "Good English"; Simpson, *Politics of American English*, 22–24. On British Americans' similar attunement to other norms of English civility, see Shields, *Civil Tongues and Polite Letters in British America*.

65. Flavell, *When London Was Capital*, 71, 128–29; Longmore, "Good English"; Read, "British Recognition of American Speech in the Eighteenth Century," 313–34. For the patchwork of English dialects in eighteenth- and nineteenth-century England, see Beal, *English Pronunciation in the Eighteenth Century*; Görlach, *English in Nineteenth-Century England*, 28–36. For the linguistic diversity of Wales, Scotland, and Ireland at the time, see Hickey, *Irish English*, 41–48; C. Jones, *A Language Suppressed*; Löffer, "English in Wales," 351.

66. Those thirty-six were Perry (13 printings, 1788–1813); Walker (9 printings,

1808–18); Entick (7 printings, 1800–12); Sheridan (4 printings, 1789–96); Johnson (1805, 1813). The two failures were Caleb Alexander's *Columbian Dictionary* (1800; see Latimer, "American Classical Scholarship and Caleb Alexander," esp. 419–20; Simpson, *Politics of American English*, 49–50), and Webster's *Compendious Dictionary* (1806).

Although Americans evidently preferred not to buy dictionaries touting their Americanness, they were quite willing to buy conspicuously "American" spellers and grammars. On spellers, see Monaghan, *Common Heritage*; on grammars, see Schweiger, "A Social History of English Grammar in the Early United States."

67. Isaiah Thomas, dedication, in Perry, *Royal Standard English Dictionary* [. . .] *First American Edition* (1788). For Thomas's "Royal Standard" advertisements, see, e.g., *Massachusetts Spy* (Worcester), March 30, 1786, [3]. On Thomas's politics, see Shipton, *Isaiah Thomas*, 17–73, 53 (for 54,000 copies).

68. [Francis Horner], *Edinburgh Review*, Oct. 1804, 185; Pickering, *Vocabulary*, 11, 17. See Read, "British Recognition." On early national Americans' stigma against Americanisms, see Andresen, *Linguistics in America*, 27–29; Cmiel, "Broad Fluid Language of Democracy," 914–27; Simpson, *Politics of American English*, 42, 48–50. For the actual history of Americanisms as now understood by historical linguists, see R. Bailey, *Speaking American*.

69. Webster, *Letter to Pickering*, 26–27, [52] (misnumbered 60).

70. Rollins, introduction to *Long Journey of Noah Webster*, 5.

71. *Freeman's Journal* (Philadelphia), Nov. 14, 1787, [1].

72. "Aristarchus," *New-England Palladium* (Boston), Nov. 6, 1801, [1].

73. Noah Webster to Benjamin Franklin, May 24, 1786, *Papers of Benjamin Franklin*, franklinpapers.org/franklin/yale?vol=44&page=132; Webster, *Dissertations on the English Language*, 23; Webster, *Letter to Pickering*, [48] (misnumbered 56); Webster, *Dissertations*, 20–21.

74. Webster, *Dissertations*, 179, 406, 171; Looby, *Voicing America*, 1, 32–33; Webster, *Dissertations*, 24.

75. Webster, *Dissertations*, 394, 397.

76. Haines and Steckel, *A Population History of North America*, 306; Monaghan, *Common Heritage*, 216. Webster's spelling book was first published in 1783 under the title *Grammatical Institute of the English Language* [. . .] *Part I*. It bore the more famous title of *American Spelling Book* from 1787 onward (Skeel, *Bibliography*, 5–12).

77. Monaghan claims that even an "ultra-conservative estimate" suggests fifty-five million copies sold by 1883, and perhaps fifteen million after that; see her exhaustive study of the speller's commercial and cultural impact (*Common Heritage*, 219). On the logistical and ideological challenges of interregional

communication in the early national period, see Gross and Kelley, *A History of the Book in America*, chaps. 2, 9, 11; Loughran, *Republic in Print*; Warner, *Letters*, chap. 5.

78. [William Cobbett], *Rush-Light*, Feb. 28, 1800, 50n.

79. *Aurora General Advertiser* (Philadelphia), June 9, 1800, [2].

80. *Monthly Anthology* (Boston), Oct. 1809, 259.

81. *United States' Gazette* (Philadelphia), April 4, 1807, [2].

82. *General Advertiser* (New York), June 23, 1800, [2].

83. *Argus* (New York), May 30, 1796, [1].

84. Warfel, *Noah Webster: Schoolmaster to America*; Kendall, *The Forgotten Founding Father*; Daniel Walker Howe, quoted on the dust jacket to Kendall. On the recuperation of Webster after 1828, see Kendall, *The Forgotten Founding Father*, 307–18, 329–34; Micklethwait, *Noah Webster and the American Dictionary*, 222–308. Horace Scudder's 1888 biography set off a series of adulatory magazine articles celebrating Webster as a lexicographical patriot.

85. Smith-Rosenberg, *This Violent Empire*, 5, 54, 57; Lepore, *A Is for American*, 5; Gordon Wood, *Empire of Liberty*, 49. Using Webster as an avatar, exemplum, or representative case study in the rise of American nationalism is commonplace: see Brewer, "Johnson, Webster, and the *OED*," 116; Burstein, *Sentimental Democracy*, 151–52; Gustafson, *Representative Words*, 308–23; Lepore, *A Is for American*, 15–60; Lerer, *Inventing English*, 182; Schneider, *Postcolonial English*, 276–78; Weinstein, "Noah Webster and the Diffusion of Linguistic Innovations for Political Purposes."

86. In fact, my primary concern is not with Webster or his ideas but with the ideas of the people who rejected him. Interpretations of Webster that deal in depth with his public rejection include Jonathon Green, *Chasing the Sun*, 304–26; Park, "The Bonds of Union"; Simpson, *Politics of American English*, 52–90; Rollins, *Long Journey of Noah Webster*.

87. "C." [Charles Brockden Brown], "On the Scheme of an American Language," *Monthly Magazine* (Philadelphia), July 1800, 1.

88. "Aristarchus," *New-England Palladium* (Boston), Nov. 6, 1801, [1]. For Babel in early American thought, see Axtell, "Babel of Tongues"; Erben, *A Harmony of the Spirits*, 17–61; Gray, *New World Babel*. On Webster's relationships with college presidents Samuel S. Smith (Princeton), Ezra Stiles (Yale), and Timothy Dwight (Yale), see Monaghan, *Common Heritage*, 91. For local and regional periodicals in early U.S. print culture, see Daniel, *Scandal and Civility*, 148–86; Haveman, *Magazines and the Making of America*.

89. For example, Webster declared in a New York newspaper in 1806 that "the lexicographer . . . has no right to prescribe words; he is to present them as they are" (*New-York Commercial Advertiser*, Aug. 19, 1806, [3]). But the next

year he took exactly the opposite position in a Boston magazine: "The lexicographer's business is to search for truth, to proscribe error, and repress anomaly" (*Panoplist*, Aug. 1807, 125).

90. Brown, "On the Scheme," 1; "Aristarchus," *New-England Palladium*, Nov. 6, 1801, [1]; Pickering, *Vocabulary*, vi. For the positive American reception of Pickering, see, e.g., *North American Review*, Sept. 1816, 355–62; *Portico* (Baltimore), July–Aug. 1817, 1–11; *Western Review* (Lexington, Ky.), Sept. 1820, 67.

91. *Aurora General Advertiser* (Philadelphia), June 9, 1800, [2]; *Monthly Anthology* (Boston), Oct. 1809, 259. For all of the eighteenth century and much of the nineteenth, Americans read far more British literature than (what we now call) American literature; see James N. Green, "English Books and Printing in the Age of Franklin"; St. Clair, *The Reading Nation in the Romantic Period*, chap. 19; Tennenhouse, *The Importance of Feeling English*.

92. Ellis, *After the Revolution*, 184. On the similarity of Webster's text to Thomas Dilworth's 1744 speller, see Kramer, *Imagining Language in America*, 38–44; Monaghan, *Common Heritage*, 31–56. On the inconsistent orthographic agendas in editions of Webster's speller, see Weinstein, "Noah Webster and the Diffusion," 96.

93. Webster, *Compendious Dictionary*, t.p., 194, 220, 201, 168; Webster, *New-York Commercial Advertiser*, Aug. 19, 1806, [3].

94. N[oah] Webster to Hudson and Goodwin, Sept. 4, 1788, in Warfel, *Letters*, 80. On Webster's early dreams of "federal language," see Lepore, *A Is for American*, 15–17; Brückner, *The Geographic Revolution in Early America*, 102–7.

95. Webster, *New-York Commercial Advertiser*, Aug. 19, 1806, [3]. On postrevolutionary American regionalisms and their perceived dangers, see R. Bailey, *Speaking American*, 90–97; Loughran, *Republic in Print*, 303–443; M. Nash, "Contested Identities," 421–33; Waldstreicher, *In the Midst of Perpetual Fetes*, 246–94.

96. *Connecticut Herald* (New Haven), Aug. 12, 1806, [1] (originally printed in *Albany Centinel*, July 29, 1806, per Skeel, *Bibliography of the Writings of Noah Webster*, 227). On the Americas' supposed linguistic hyperdiversity, see Gray, *New World Babel*, chap. 1; Harvey, *Native Tongues*, 59–62.

97. Coleman, *New-York Evening Post*, July 23, 1806, [2].

98. [James Savage?], *Monthly Anthology*, Oct. 1809, 263. Earlier in his career, Webster had himself expressed concern about interregional linguistic ridicule; see Gustafson, *Representative Words*, 313–14; Kramer, *Imagining Language*, 60–61; Park, "Bonds of Union," 405.

99. "A Citizen of Ohio," *Washington Gazette* (D.C.), May 18, 1821, [2].

100. Ngai, *Ugly Feelings*.

101. This is the founding insight of "variationist" sociolinguistics, which

holds "that the variation witnessed at all levels of language is not random" but "structured" in a way that corresponds to social phenomena (Bayley, "Variationist Sociolinguistics," 11).

102. *Monthly Anthology* (Boston), Sept. 1804, 510; *New-York Gazette*, June 16, 1800, [3]. Webster himself was troubled by the difficulty of reconciling the democratic promise of liberal individualism with his desire for socioeconomic stability (Gustafson, *Representative Words*, 301–23). On socioeconomic conflict in the early United States, and American elites' reluctance to actually distribute power in a "democratic" fashion, see Beeman, *The Varieties of Political Experience in Eighteenth-Century America*, 276–92; G. Nash, *The Unknown American Revolution.*

103. David Shields's reassessment of colonial American aesthetic preferences is informative. Shields maintains that British Americans pursued aesthetic values not just as instruments of social and political power but as "modes of communicating desires and pleasures" (*Civil Tongues*, xxiv). Anti-Webster writers share these motives, which cannot always be mapped onto nationalism or class conflict.

104. *Port-Folio*, Nov. 21, 1807, 323; *New-Hampshire Gazette* (Portsmouth), Jan. 15, 1791, [3].

105. *Gazette of the United States* [Philadelphia], June 16, 1800, [3]. Cf. a later satirical phoneticization of a German-speaking night watchman: "Basht dree o'-glock" (*Boston Recorder*, Feb. 10, 1826, 24).

106. *Aurora General Advertiser* (Philadelphia), June 9, 1800, [2].

107. Webster worked on the *American Dictionary* in three successive residences in New Haven and Amherst. The study with sand-insulated walls was in the house in New Haven where he moved in 1822. See Kendall, *The Forgotten Founding Father*, 296–98; Rollins, *Autobiographies of Noah Webster*, 11.

108. *New-York Evening Post*, May 16, 1826, [2]; Pickering, "Americanism," 1:10–11. On shifting attitudes about Americanisms in the antebellum period, see Andresen, *Linguistics in America*, 68–119; Cmiel, "Broad Fluid Language of Democracy," 918–20; Simpson, *Politics of American English*, 140–41, 170–201.

109. Rollins, *Long Journey of Noah Webster*, 127. On the bombastic American nationalisms of the 1810s and 1820s, see Waldstreicher, *In the Midst of Perpetual Fetes*, 294–348.

110. E.g., "the father of American lexicography" (Venezky, *American Way of Spelling*, 220); Kendall, *The Forgotten Founding Father*; Schulman, *Websterisms.*

111. Webster, *Dissertations on the English Language*, 22. The standard work on the present-day pronunciation differences between British and American English is John C. Wells, *Accents of English.* For the aural distinguishability of British and American dialects, see Bent et al., "Classification of Regional Dialects." For spelling differences, see Venezky, *American Way of Spelling.*

112. J. W. Clark, "American Spelling," 184–85; Lynch, "Four Centuries of Lexicographical Belligerence," 119; D. Wilson, *United Irishmen, United States*, 96. Other recent articulations of this myth include Hitchings, *The Language Wars*; Lerer, *Inventing English*, 185; Venezky, *American Way of Spelling*, 218–21, 220.

113. Those who have questioned the Webster truism include Algeo, "English around the World," 424–25; Jonathon Green, "Language," 150–51; Simpson, "American English to 1865."

114. The trends discussed are based on a quantitative analysis of Readex's *Early American Newspapers* database and the British Library's *British Newspaper Archive*, taking newspaper spellings as a reasonable proxy for spellings considered correct by a general reading public at a given time. I compared the number of hits for each spelling of each word in five-year increments from 1750–54 to 1880–84.

115. Hitchings, *Language Wars*, 112. See also N. Bailey, *An Universal Etymological English Dictionary* (1783); Entick, *The New Spelling Dictionary* (1782); Fisher, *An Accurate New Spelling Dictionary* (1773).

116. Hitchings, *Language Wars*, 112; Webster, *Grammatical Institute of the English Language*, 11.

117. Malone, "A Linguistic Patriot," 29.

118. Shea, "A Sure Uncertainty."

CHAPTER THREE

1. More properly, Gilchrist was teaching "Hindustani," the language construct of which Hindi and Urdu can be thought of as dialects. "Hindustani" is a problematic term, as will be discussed later.

2. Gilchrist, *A Grammar of the Hindoostanee Language* (1796), 1:10; Gilchrist, *Dialogues* (1804), iii–iv. For Gilchrist as teacher of Hindustani at Calcutta's College of Fort William, see Kidwai, *Gilchrist and the "Language of Hindoostan,"* 67–81; Steadman-Jones, *Colonialism and Grammatical Representation*, 78–80.

3. Gilchrist, *Dialogues* (1804), viii–ix.

4. Gilchrist, *British Indian Monitor* (1806), 1:13. Gilchrist is describing a voiceless uvular stop, which is transcribed in the International Phonetic Alphabet the same way: [q]. His *kh* and *gh* are the velar fricative consonants represented in IPA as [x] and [ɣ].

5. Gilchrist, *Dialogues* (1804), v–vi, xix–xx.

6. Ibid., 139–41; Gilchrist, *Grammar of the Hindoostanee Language* (1796), 1:19–20.

7. Gilchrist, *A Dictionary, English and Hindoostanee* (1787), xxxiv; Gilchrist, *Parliamentary Reform on Constitutional Principles* (1815), 181. To the best of my

knowledge, Gilchrist's abecedarian clock has never been discussed in modern scholarship.

8. [Gilchrist], *Asiatic Journal*, June 1816, 535, and Aug. 1816, 118.

9. Franklin, *Political, Miscellaneous, and Philosophical Pieces*, 475n; Gilchrist, *Dictionary* (1787), xxxiv–xxxv; Gilchrist, *Asiatic Journal*, Nov. 1816, 437–42; Gilchrist, *Dialogues, English and Hindoostanee* (1826), app., xvi, xv, xx.

As far as I know, the only modern study that has discussed Gilchrist's universal alphabet is Raley's "Teleology of Letters." Raley is most interested in the earlier phase of Gilchrist's career in which he is optimistic about the representability of all languages within the Latin alphabet. She reads Gilchrist as a champion of vernacular as opposed to classical education (¶13).

10. Gilchrist, *Morning Chronicle* (London), Dec. 14, 1821, [4].

11. Gitelman, "The Phonograph's New Media Publics"; Rubery, *The Untold Story of the Talking Book*.

12. The *Oxford English Dictionary* dates this sense of "loudspeaker" to 1879; s.v. "loud-speaking," adj.

13. Most histories of sound recording deal primarily with music (e.g., Horning, *Chasing Sound*; Katz, *Capturing Sound*). Lisa Gitelman emphasizes the initial (1878–ca. 1890) reception of the phonograph as a speaking machine in *Always Already New* (25–44), *Scripts, Grooves, and Writing Machines* (62–96), and "Souvenir Foils" (157–73); Matthew Rubery has also elaborated early visions of the phonograph as a literary medium (*The Untold Story of the Talking Book*, 29–55). On the cultural and ideological processes whereby communications media become associated with particular types of content, see Kittler, *Gramophone, Film, Typewriter*; Sterne, *The Audible Past*, 31–85.

14. Gitelman, *Scripts*, 24–51; Wheatstone, "On the Vowel Sounds, and on Reed Organ Pipes," 41.

15. Kövecses, *American English*, 222–23; J. C. Wells, *Accents of English*, 1:117.

16. Gilchrist, *Dictionary* (1787), vii–viii; Gilchrist, *Parliamentary Reform* (1815), 172 (quotation); Hakala, *Negotiating Languages*, 34–41; Steadman-Jones, *Colonialism and Grammatical Representation*, 74–77. On British thinking about Indian languages in the early 1780s, see Kopf, *British Orientalism and the Bengal Renaissance*, 18, 50, 57–58; Momma, "A Man on the Cusp," 163–69; Steadman-Jones, *Colonialism and Grammatical Representation*, 21–131.

17. *Asiatic Journal*, March 1827, 421 ("changed his European appearance"); Gilchrist, *Succinct Narrative of Dr. Gilchrist's Services* (1821), 4 ("unrestricted intercourse"); Gilchrist, *Dictionary* (1787), vii–viii ("surrounded"); Gilchrist, *Parliamentary Reform* (1815), 174 ("a lexicographical slavery").

18. Gilchrist, *Dictionary* (1787), iv, xxxii. Hindi and Urdu were never the popular speech of "all Hindoostan"; even today, after considerable linguistic

consolidation, less than half of South Asians speak Hindi or Urdu as a first language (Bashir and Hock, *The Languages and Linguistics of South Asia*, 9–240). Many linguists now refer to Hindi and Urdu as two dialects of "Hindustani," but the term remains problematic because it effaces colonial, national, and religious conflicts (Cohn, "The Command of Language and the Language of Command"; Hasnain and Rajyashree, "Hindustani as an Anxiety between Hindi-Urdu Commitment"; R. King, "The Poisonous Potency of Script"). On languages as ideological constructions, see Hakala, *Negotiating Languages*, 76–114; C. King, *One Language, Two Scripts*, 53–87; Young, "That Which Is Casually Called a Language." On Gilchrist's significant role in the history of the Hindustani language, see Cohn, *Colonialism and Its Forms of Knowledge*; Kidwai, *Gilchrist and the "Language of Hindoostan,"* 89–96; Steadman-Jones, *Colonialism and Grammatical Representation*, 28–41.

Although the switch to English officially took place in 1837, Viswanathan and others have shown that movement in this direction began much earlier, arguably in 1813 (Viswanathan, *Masks of Conquest*, 23, 30–44). On the shifting ideologies of language that drove British language policy in India in the first half of the nineteenth century, see also Momma, *From Philology to English Studies*, 96–99; Roy, "'Englishing' India."

19. Gilchrist, *The Hindee-Roman Orthoepigraphical Ultimatum* (1804). On Gilchrist's romanization system and its adoption in the nineteenth century, see Kidwai, *Gilchrist and the "Language of Hindoostan,"* 117–23; Kopf, *British Orientalism*, 82–83, 110–11; Raley, "A Teleology of Letters," ¶¶4–5, 11–15; Steadman-Jones, *Colonialism and Grammatical Representation*, 77–78; Tarantelli, "Voice into Text," 110–18.

Gilchrist's literary and pedagogical activities in India (1782–1804) are also well covered by Steadman-Jones and Kidwai; Steadman-Jones covers Gilchrist's later repackaging and promotion of his Hindustani pedagogical materials in the British print market, 1804–26. Gilchrist's other activities between 1804 and 1841 remain underexplored: his radical antimonarchist politics; his teaching career in London; and his founding roles in three of the nineteenth century's most significant working-class educational institutions: the London Mechanics' Institution (now Birkbeck College, University of London), the University of London (now University College London), and the Gilchrist Educational Trust.

20. Wellesley hired Gilchrist to teach "Hindoostanee and Persian" in February 1799; his classes became part of the new college in 1800 (Roebuck, *Annals of the College of Fort William*, 5; Wellesley, *Letters of the Marquis Wellesley*, 63). On the College of Fort William and the conflicts it provoked between the EIC and the British government, see Kopf, *British Orientalism*, 51–84. British

rule in India was an enterprise not of the British state but of a state-chartered (but not state-owned) corporation. The British governor-general had formal authority only over the Fort William complex until 1833, when Crown authority was greatly expanded. The EIC was nationalized in 1858 (see P. Stern, *The Company-State*).

21. On Gilchrist's paranoid style, see Raley, "A Teleology of Letters," e.g., ¶¶2–3; Steadman-Jones, *Colonialism and Grammatical Representation*, 125–31. The quotation is from the title page to *The Moral Preceptor, or Ukhlaq i-Hindee* (Calcutta, 1803). On Fort William College's publication of Indian poetry and prose, see Ahmad, *Oriental Presses in the World*, 108–13; Ghosh, *Power in Print*, 48–49, 73–75; Siddiqi, *Origins of Modern Hindustani Literature*, 156–60. On Gilchrist's own publishing frenzy during this period, see Ahmad, *Oriental Presses*, 156–72; Gilchrist, *Introductory Address* (1806), 17–18; Kopf, *British Orientalism*, 81–84; Steadman-Jones, *Colonialism and Grammatical Representation*, 264–65; Wellesley, *Letters*, 2–8, 80, 84.

22. Ahmad, *Oriental Presses*, 168–69; Gilchrist, *Introductory Address* (1806), 17; Gilchrist, *Succinct Narrative* (1821), 5; Steadman-Jones, *Colonialism and Grammatical Representation*, 87; *Dictionary of National Biography*, s.v. "Gilchrist, John Borthwick."

23. Gilchrist, in Brelvi, *Poems of Dr. John Gilchrist*, 61.

24. Gilchrist recorded his abhorrence in a letter that later became evidence in a lawsuit over his estate: see *Whicker v. Hume* (1851), 371–72.

25. Gilchrist, *The Oriental Green Bag!!!* (1820), 105.

26. *Whicker v. Hume* (1858), 51–52.

27. Ibid.

28. Gilchrist, *General East India Guide* (1825), 654–55.

29. *Asiatic Journal*, Nov. 1816, 437–42, at 437. Gilchrist's *w* represents the diphthong in *foul*.

30. *Morning Chronicle* (London), Dec. 14, 1821, [1]; *Asiatic Journal*, Nov. 1816, 437.

31. Benjamin Franklin to Erasmus Darwin, Aug. 1, 1772 (King-Hele, *The Letters of Erasmus Darwin*, 65); *Asiatic Journal*, Nov. 1816, 437. This Irish automaton is probably apocryphal.

For the early history of cuckoo clocks, see Chapuis, *History of the Musical Box and of Mechanical Music*. The mechanical intersection between clocks and automata is broad (Riskin, *The Restless Clock*; Voskuhl, *Androids in the Enlightenment*, 128–69; Gaby Wood, *Edison's Eve*, 3–59).

32. On other real and imagined speaking automata, see Connor, *Dumbstruck*, 338–61; Sterne, *Audible Past*, 71–76. On a typewriter's isolation of graphemes

from semantic meaning, see Kittler, *Gramophone, Film, Typewriter*, 16. On longitude and the chronometer, see Sudan, *The Alchemy of Empire*, 153–54.

33. *Asiatic Journal*, Aug. 1816, 118; "a panglossal prospectus," *Asiatic Journal*, June 1825, unpaginated fold-out; *Asiatic Journal*, June 1816, 535; *Asiatic Journal*, Aug. 1816, 118; *Morning Chronicle* (London), Dec. 14, 1821, [1]; *Asiatic Journal*, June 1816, 534; *Classical Journal*, Dec. 1823, 376.

34. Gilchrist, *Dictionary* (1787), xviii–xix, where he also affirms the "intimate connection . . . between *speech* & *reason*" and cites Scottish Enlightenment writers Lord Monboddo (*Of the Origin and Progress of Language*) and D. Stewart (*Elements of the Philosophy of the Human Mind*) on the subject.

35. *Asiatic Journal*, March 1827, 417; *Classical Journal*, Dec. 1823, 376; Gilchrist, *Dialogues* (1826), app., xv.

36. *Journal des Savans* (Paris), May 1822, 316. For a detailed account of the Volney prize, see Kemp, "Transcription, Transliteration and the Idea of a Universal Alphabet."

37. *Oriental Herald*, Aug. 1825, 302.

38. Gilchrist, *Dialogues* (1826), app., x; *Asiatic Journal*, June 1825, 796; *Dialogues* (1826), app., xv.

39. Between 1818 and 1825, more than 1,500 India-bound EIC employees attended his classes (*Oriental Herald*, March 1826, 571–73; Dec. 1826, 517–29). Notices that Gilchrist is ready to publish "as soon as a fount of appropriate symbols can be cast" appear in the *Classical Journal*, Dec. 1823, 376, and *Asiatic Journal*, March 1824, 276. The first appearance of the type in print is in *Asiatic Journal*, June 1825.

40. Mirambell appears to have modified existing pieces of type or carved individual pieces of type out of wood or type metal one at a time rather than casting them. The anonymous 1741 volume titled *The Methodist* contains full pages of real cast type (Underhill, "John Byrom and the Contexts of Charles Wesley's Shorthand," 52–53; Yale, *The Languages of Disenchantment*, 93–94).

Raley, possibly the only critic who has written about Gilchrist's universal alphabet in the past century, describes it as "curiously among the most serious and extensive attempts to devise a universal alphabet" ("A Teleology of Letters," ¶14), though she downplays its originality: "In its appearance on the page, it basically resembles all of the other phonetic projects and plans for a universal alphabet; that is to say that his translated textual object (the Lord's Prayer) is more or less legible, but only at the level of general meaning" (ibid.). This is true, although I also think that its typographic form makes it highly discontinuous with most of the other projects.

41. *Examiner* (London), Sept. 17, 1826, 608. In 1825, the *Asiatic Journal* was

printed in Great Queen Street, while the *Oriental Herald* was printed in Bolt Court, per title pages.

42. Gilchrist, *Dialogues* (1826), app., i, xvi.

43. Gilchrist, *Parliamentary Reform* (1815), 181.

44. Gilchrist, *General East India Guide* (1825), 660–61. See Raley, "A Teleology of Letters," ¶¶11–12.

45. Gilchrist, *Dialogues* (1826), app., v (Quixote), 103 ("the british," "every national"), 106 ("the appropriate precursor"), iv ("grand beneficial"). (Gilchrist's text renders the Spanish/German pronunciation of *Quixote* as **kekot**, which appears to be a typographical error.)

46. "A. C. C.," "Stray Thoughts on Language," *Gentleman's Magazine*, June 1829, 495; [John Herschel], *Edinburgh Review*, Jan. 1848, 226n; [Isaac Pitman and Alexander John Ellis], "The Completion of the Phonotypic Alphabet," *Phonotypic Journal*, June 1845, 105; [Isaac Pitman?], "The Phonetic Principle in Relation to Education," *Phonetic Journal*, April 30, 1853, 139. For the increasing interest in phonetic typography in the 1830s, see Gitelman, *Scripts*, 24–37; Kemp, "The Development of Phonetics"; Tarantelli, "Voice into Text," 108–53.

To the best of my knowledge, no histories of the IPA reference Gilchrist's universal character. A typical history of pre-IPA phonetic notation, such as MacMahon, "Phonetic Notation" (831–36), covers Walker (1791), Jones (1788), Pickering (1818), Lepsius (1853), and Pitman (1869). Other Gilchristless histories of the IPA include Kemp, "Development of Phonetics"; Robins, *A Short History of Linguistics*, 227–28; Tarantelli, "Voice into Text," 108–53.

47. Monier-Williams, "The Duty of English-Speaking Orientalists," 620.

48. For the significance of Jones and the Indo-European hypothesis to the founding of the discipline that would later be called linguistics, see Momma, *From Philology to English Studies*, 28–59, 147–82; Robins, *A Short History of Linguistics*, 168–70, 189–221.

49. Gilchrist, *General East India Guide* (1825), 666; Raley, "A Teleology of Letters," ¶4; Gilchrist, *Dictionary* (1787), xviii–xix.

50. Gitelman, "Souvenir Foils," 157; Weber, *The Talking Machine*.

51. Dudley and Tarnoczy, "The Speaking Machine of Wolfgang von Kempelen"; *Cabinet of Curiosities*, 2:58–60. Erasmus Darwin contemplated a similar device in 1803 (*The Temple of Nature*, 119–20). On von Kempelen's chess-playing "Mechanical Turk," see Gaby Wood, *Edison's Eve*, 60–110.

52. Bell, *Visible Speech*. I am conflating the conceptual history of the telephone with that of the phonograph. The shared and reciprocal significance of these technologies, as received by their initial audiences in the 1870s, is explored by Sterne in *The Audible Past*. On the Bells, Visible Speech, and the telephone, see Connor, *Dumbstruck*, 348–49, 356–57; Robins, *A Short History of Linguistics*, 227.

53. G. Anderson, *Landmarks of Rensselaer County, New York*, 2:363.

54. Gilchrist, *Oriental Green Bag!!!* (1820), 69; *Dialogues* (1826), app., ii. It's not clear why he thought that repeating words uttered by a machine would be less stultifying than repeating words uttered by a Frenchman.

55. Gilchrist, *A Practical Appeal to the Public* (1833), 29–30, 26–27.

56. Ibid., 75, 71, 54.

57. Gilchrist, *Hindee-Roman Orthoepigraphical Ultimatum* (1820), li.

58. *Whicker v. Hume* (1858), 52. The legal dispute is detailed in Reynolds, *William Balmain and John Gilchrist*, 35–52.

59. *Whicker v. Hume* (1858), 52, 51.

60. On the history of the Gilchrist Educational Trust and its activities, see Cranage and Kay-Shuttleworth, *Gilchrist Educational Trust*; Reynolds, *William Balmain and John Gilchrist*, 83–84, 100.

61. *Whicker v. Hume* (1858), 56n.

CHAPTER FOUR

1. Gilchrist, *Dialogues* (1826), app., x, 103.

2. *Philosophical Magazine*, Oct. 1807, 366–67.

3. There appear to be more than 4,000 distinct custom characters in *Pantographia*; the usual rate of four hours per punch would have required 16,000 hours. For four hours per punch, see *Public Ledger and Daily Advertiser* (London), May 8, 1819, [3]; H. Caslon, "Developments in Typefounding since 1720," 496–97.

4. Fry, *Pantographia*, xxiii; Webster, *Collection of Essays and Fugitiv Writings*, xi. Fry quoted a price of two guineas (£2.2s.) per matrix in 1809; an urban parish church typically cost £2,000 to £3,000 in the 1790s. Edmund Fry to J. W. Morris, Feb. 21, 1809, Grolier Club, Autograph Collection, box 2, folder 9; Norris, *The Financing of John Wesley's Methodism*, 68.

5. Gilchrist, *General East India Guide* (1825), 660–61.

6. *London Review*, Nov. 1799, 409.

7. Fry, *Pantographia*, xxii.

8. E.g., Joseph Banks, president of the Royal Society; John Nichols, editor of the *Gentleman's Magazine*; Benjamin West, president of the Royal Academy; and John Henniker Major, Charles Shaw Lefevre, Richard Sullivan, and Andrew Strahan, MPs (ibid., xxx–xxxvi).

Pantographia was advertised in 1799 at "2l. 2s.," i.e., forty-two shillings. In 1800, shoes were five and a half shillings per pair; beef was about 8d. (two-thirds shilling) per pound. *Times* (London), Aug. 26, 1799, [1]; G. Clark, "Average Earnings and Retail Prices, UK, 1209–2010," 2011, 49, 37, www.measuringworth.com/datasets/ukearncpi/earnstudynew.pdf.

9. *British Critic*, Oct. 1799, 425; *Gentleman's Magazine*, Oct. 1799, 880. *Pantographia* was also noticed appreciatively in *Edinburgh Magazine*, Oct. 1799, 287–91; *Monthly Magazine*, Jan. 1800, 1058; *Monthly Review*, May 1800, 14–17; *New London Review*, Nov. 1799, 409–17; *Universal Magazine*, Sept. 1799, 189–93.

10. *Encyclopaedia Britannica*, 3rd ed. (1797), 9:534, s.v. "language."

11. *London Review*, Nov. 1799, 413.

12. The literature about eighteenth-century concepts of media and mediation is large, but see especially Guillory, "Genesis of the Media Concept"; Lupton, *Knowing Books*; McDowell, "Mediating Antiquarians"; McLuhan, *The Gutenberg Galaxy*; Siskin and Warner, *This Is Enlightenment*. For eighteenth-century thinking about language(s) as a type of mediation, see Guillory, "Enlightening Mediation"; Sorensen, *Grammar of Empire*, 104–37.

13. Fry, *Pantographia*, xiii, xi; *Encyclopaedia Britannica*, 9:533–34, s.v. "language."

14. Dufief, "Language Makes the Difference."

15. Sorensen, *Grammar of Empire*; Young, *Idea of English Ethnicity*, chaps. 1–2. On eighteenth-century encyclopedism, see Yeo, *Encyclopaedic Visions*.

16. In reality, Macpherson composed most of the Ossian poems himself; see McDowell, "Mediating Antiquarians." For Fry's discussions of Celtic languages, see *Pantographia*, 26–27, 164–67, 268–69, 304–7.

17. Fry, *Pantographia*, 61.

18. Crompton, "How to Look at a Reading Font," 82. For eighteenth-century thinking about the mediating effects of typography, see also Dane, *Out of Sorts*, 72–90, 164–90.

19. For example, on Massachusetts printer Isaiah Thomas's difficulties stocking clean type during the American Revolution, see Shipton, *Isaiah Thomas*, 35, 40, 41. On eighteenth- and nineteenth-century readers' and printers' careful attention to type, see Bidwell, "Printers' Supplies and Capitalization," 171; Darnton, *The Great Cat Massacre*, 222–24; Gross, "Introduction," 45; Piper, *Dreaming in Books*, 58; O. Smith, *Politics of Language*, 205.

20. Franklin, *Autobiography*, 169–70; *Aberdeen Journal*, April 7, 1800, [1].

21. *Oxford Journal*, Dec. 27, 1788, [4].

22. *Monthly Mirror* (London), Jan. 1800, unpaginated preface. For the price, see *Derby Mercury*, Jan. 30, 1800, [4].

23. The chief sources for the history of the Fry foundry are Reed, *A History of the Old English Letter Foundries*, 298–310; prefaces to the Frys' many specimen books (especially those of 1785, 1786, and 1794); and a circular issued by Fry when he put the foundry up for sale, Feb. 14, 1828.

24. Quoted in Mores, *A Dissertation upon English Typographical Founders and Founderies*, 93n.

25. Benjamin Franklin to John Baskerville, 1764, quoted in J. Chambers, *A Dissertation upon English Typographical Founders and Founderies*, 373–74.

26. Fry, *Pantographia*, 167.

27. This strategic realignment is discussed in Fry's 1828 circular (qtd. in Reed, *History of the Old English Letter Foundries*, 310–13).

28. D. Chambers, introduction to *Specimen of Modern Printing Types*, 8. On the process of manufacturing type, see Lawson, *Anatomy of a Typeface*, 381–403; Mores, *Dissertation*; Reed, *History of the Old English Letter Foundries*, 1–26, 97–114. The type-manufacturing process is also lucidly demonstrated on video by historian Stanley Nelson in *From Punch to Printing Type*.

29. Since Fry did not intend to mass manufacture the *Pantographia* type, he could have skipped several steps, such as by carving the letters into blocks of type metal instead of steel. Johnston suggests that Fry took even more drastic shortcuts, simulating cast type by engraving many of the specimens as woodcuts, with only "a minority of the types [being] real" (Johnston, *Alphabets to Order*, 19). Contemporary audiences, however, accepted the book's implication that the specimens are printed from metal type (e.g., *British Critic*, Oct. 1799, 425). Writing in the 1880s, Reed also appears to have believed that *Pantographia* was printed from cast metal type (*History of the Old English Letter Foundries*, 305–6).

30. *Specimen of Printing Types, by Edmund Fry and Co.* (1787). For the father's retirement in 1787, see Reed, *History of the Old English Letter Foundries*, 303. English printers did not quote sizes in "points" until the 1820s. I have converted the eighteenth-century sizes into points per Richardson, "Correlated Type Sizes and Names for the Fifteenth through Twentieth Century."

31. *Specimen of Printing Types, by William Caslon, Letter-Founder to His Majesty* (1785); *A Specimen of Printing Types, by Joseph Fry and Sons, Letter-Founders to the Prince of Wales* (1786).

32. Fry, *Pantographia*, 315.

33. See, e.g., "To the Public," *Specimen of Printing Types, by William Caslon* (1785); "To the Public," *Specimen of Printing Types, by Joseph Fry and Sons* (1786); Reed, *History of the Old English Letter Foundries*, 313–14. The Caslon foundry was at 22/23 Chiswell Street, at the corner of Type Street (since renamed Moor Lane). Fry's foundry was a few doors down at 6 Type Street.

34. *Kentish Gazette*, Feb. 8, 1788, [1]; *Derby Mercury*, Jan. 28, 1790, [3].

35. Edmund Fry to Isaiah Thomas, Aug. 16, 1786, American Antiquarian Society, Isaiah Thomas Papers, box 2, folder 7.

36. Crompton, "How to Look at a Reading Font," 89, 79. Recent scholarship on other kinds of nonnormative reading includes Drucker, "Reading Interface"; Fleming, "How to Look at a Printed Flower"; Hall and Reilly, "Modalities of Reading"; G. Stewart, *Look of Reading*; Knott, *Sensibility and the American*

Revolution, chap. 1; Piper, *Dreaming in Books*; Warner, "Uncritical Reading." On the broader history of reading, see Cavallo and Chartier, *A History of Reading in the West*; Febvre and Martin, *The Coming of the Book*.

37. This convention originated with Caslon in 1734. See Dibdin, *The Bibliographical Decameron*, 2:381–82; Johnston, *Alphabets to Order*, 13–16.

38. Garrett Stewart also helpfully calls such medium-foregrounding texts "demediating" ("Bookwork as Demediation," 413n, 457).

Most of the scholarly attention to specimen books has come from historians of typography. See, e.g., Berry and Johnson, *Catalogue of Specimens of Printing Types*; Annenberg, *Type Foundries of America and Their Catalogues*; Mosley, *British Type Specimens before 1831*. Among the few works to approach type specimens in terms of literary and cultural history are Gitelman's *Paper Knowledge* (38–52); Johnston, *Alphabets to Order*; and Raven, *Publishing Business in Eighteenth-Century England*, chap. 3.

39. *Critical Review*, Jan. 1800, 82; Reed, *History of the Old English Letter Foundries*, 308; Gilchrist, *Dialogues* (1826), app., 103. Fry received his MD from Marischal College, University of Aberdeen, in 1795 (P. J. Anderson, *Fasti Academiae Mariscallanae Aberdonensis*, 2:137; contra Reed, 302).

40. Wiles, *Serial Publication in England before 1750*, 181–84, 210. The face-to-face scene of eighteenth-century book purchasing is notoriously difficult to document, but see Belanger, "From Bookseller to Publisher"; Fergus and Porter, "Provincial Bookselling in Eighteenth-Century England."

41. *Salisbury and Winchester Journal*, Nov. 5, 1787, [4]; *Kentish Gazette*, Feb. 3, 1779, [1].

42. *Hampshire Chronicle*, June 25, 1792, [2].

43. *The Following Is a Specimen of the Lexicography of Webster's Dictionary*; see Skeel, 231–32.

44. St. Clair, *Reading Nation*, 43–65.

45. *British Critic*, Oct. 1799, 425.

46. *Times* (London), April 22, 1797, [2]; *Times*, April 28, 1798, [1]; *List of the Governors and Officers of the Asylum*, 74; Fry, *Pantographia*, ix.

47. Reed erroneously says that Fry was educated as a doctor but went into typefounding because "the infirmity of deafness prevented him from" practicing medicine (302), a claim that has been repeated in other type histories. Fry earned his medical degree in 1795, long *after* he went into typefounding in 1782. Other than Reed's assertion in the 1880s, there is no known evidence that Fry was deaf and considerable evidence that he was not in the form of various records of people interacting face-to-face with Fry without mentioning any hearing impairment. For example, he testified and was cross-examined in court in 1813 (*Times* [London], July 15, 1813, [3]) and had a wide-ranging conversation with

John Coakley Lettson on Lettson's deathbed in 1815 (*Monthly Magazine*, Dec. 1815, 438). Nor do any of the obituaries published on his death in 1835 make any reference to deafness.

Given Fry's involvement with the London Asylum for the Deaf and Dumb Children of the Poor, it's possible that Reed either got confused or jumped to a conclusion in trying to reconcile Fry's vocation with the curious fact of his medical degree. On the other hand, Reed inherited the corporate remnants of Fry's foundry business from his father, who bought them from the person who bought them from the person who bought them from Fry. It is conceivable, therefore, that Reed had access to revealing business documents or industry lore.

48. On the sometimes acrimonious interplay of these evolving standards, see Oliphant, "Touching the Light."

49. *Blackwood's Edinburgh Magazine*, July 1820, 446.

50. *Report by a Committee of the Society of Arts in Scotland*, 13, 13n.

51. *Oxford English Dictionary*, s.v. "sanserif," n. The first sans serif typeface was created by William Caslon III in 1816, but it is not known to have been used until the 1830s (Loxley, *Type*, 37–39).

CHAPTER FIVE

1. "Miss Carraboo," *Freeman's Journal*, Sept. 22, 1817; "Miss Caraboo," *True American*, Sept. 22, 1817, [3], and Sept. 23, 1817, [3]; "Communication," *True American*, Sept. 25, 1817, [2]; Mary Willcocks to Sophia Landeg, Sept. 30, 1817. The theater was Washington Hall; see Keels, *Forgotten Philadelphia*, 54–55, 93.

2. Willcocks to Landeg, Sept. 30, 1817. Willcocks might have been stretching the truth about the finery.

3. *Repertory* (Boston), Sept. 23, 1817, [1]; *True American*, Sept. 25, 1817, [2]; *Columbian Register* (New Haven), Sept. 20, 1817, [3]; Willcocks to Worrall, Nov. 3, 1817.

4. In this paragraph I have accepted the general outlines of the account of her life that she gave to Gutch (Gutch and Worrall, *Caraboo*, 28–53), though that biography is problematic for reasons discussed later in this chapter. Willcocks was born in Witheridge, Devonshire, Nov. 11, 1791 (not 1792 as sometimes reported).

5. Actually, her name is a complicated issue, and I am making a somewhat unconventional choice by using the name she was born with, Mary Willcocks. At various times, she also went by Hannah Baker, Mary Baker, Anne Burgess, Mary Burgess, and (Caraboo). Most accounts of the 1817 Caraboo story give her name as Mary Baker because two years earlier, Mary Willcocks had become pregnant and told some sympathetic middle-class Londoners that she had married a man named John Baker who had subsequently deserted her.

No one else ever met the husband, and privately her friends and acquaintances doubted that any marriage had taken place; nevertheless, and perhaps mostly for the sake of appearances, she was known (inconsistently) from then on as Mary Baker (Gutch and Worrall, *Caraboo*, 36, 49). The morality requirements of the charitable institutions on which Willcocks depended gave her a strong motive to introduce this story. There is also good evidence that she had already been using the pseudonym Baker for at least two years by the time she supposedly married "John Baker" (52–53).

It seems to me that the jilted spouse "Mary Baker" was, like Princess Caraboo, a character that she played for the sake of expediency. Calling her Mary Baker seems like participating in a Victorian effort to sanitize her sexual life. A decade later, she was going by Mary Burgess. In an absolutely García-Márquezian twist, however, Mary Willcocks later married a man named Richard Baker, in 1828, and thus really did become Mary Baker.

6. [Mary Willcocks] to the *True American*, Sept. 13, 1817. Although "Caraboo" has gone down in history as the standard spelling, "Carraboo" was equally common in the American media event of fall 1817.

7. *American Yeoman* (Brattleboro, Vt.), Nov. 4, 1817, [3].

8. Mary Willcocks has been the subject of two chapter-length scholarly treatments: Lee, *Romantic Liars*, 139–99; and Russett, "The 'Caraboo' Hoax," adapted as part of Russett's *Fictions and Fakes*, 113–36. John Wells's *Princess Caraboo: Her True Story* (1994), a nonfiction account published as a mass-market paperback, is the most extensively researched work on Willcocks; it lacks footnotes but is generally transparent about its sources. The most widely circulated retelling of Mary Willcocks's season as "Princess Caraboo" is the film *Princess Caraboo* (1994), written by the abovementioned John Wells, with Phoebe Cates in the title role.

9. On the American bootstrap narrative that figures prominently in iconic texts by Horatio Alger, Frederick Douglass, and Benjamin Franklin, see Bjorklund, *Interpreting the Self*, 66–88. On trickster-huckster figures in American literature and culture, see L. Cohen, *The Fabrication of American Literature*; Landay, *Madcaps, Screwballs, and Con Women*, 32–46.

10. Gutch and Worrall, *Caraboo*, 54. The long eighteenth century "abounded in frauds" and in curiosity about frauds (Lynch, *Deception*, viii). Those who understood Mary Willcocks's Caraboo performance as a hoax or imposture recognized an antecedent in George Psalmanazar—a native of France who, in London from 1703 to 1706, claimed to have been born and raised in Taiwan (Keevak, *The Pretended Asian*, 56–59).

11. Davenport, *Sketches of Imposture*, 159.

12. *Weekly Entertainer* (Sherborne), July 7, 1817, 521; Gutch and Worrall, *Caraboo*, 4n–5n.

13. On antibegging policies in early-nineteenth-century England, see Snell, *Parish and Belonging*, 81–161. As Lynch points out, there is a long tradition of critics taking the side of accused impostors and reframing their untruths more sympathetically (*Deception and Detection in Eighteenth-Century Britain*, 2–3). One common pitfall is for the critic to overcorrect and become the subject's advocate. Like Lynch, I hope to have steered a middle course.

Glossolalia was associated with Methodism in Mary Willcocks's day (Hargrave, "Glossolalia"; Taves, *Fits, Trances, and Visions*, esp. 328–40). Secular glossolalia like Willcocks's, however, awaits detailed scholarly attention.

14. The *-oo* of "Caraboo" probably reflects the prevailing hypothesis at the time that the languages of less civilized peoples were highly vocalic, i.e., that they had many vowels (see table 1). More than 80 percent of Princess Caraboo's recorded words end in a vowel sound, compared to only 20 percent of the English glosses of those words: *Javasu, Mandu, bardoo, makritoo, brasidoo*, etc. For the complete Princess Caraboo lexicon, see table 3.

15. Gutch and Worrall, *Caraboo*, 6–7; Bonner, *Carraboo, Carraboo*, 7. It is likely that the name of her fictional island was at least partly influenced by the real island of Java; see Lee, *Romantic Liars*, 139–200.

Gutch gives the Portuguese sailor's name as Manuel Eynesso, and nothing else is known of him. It is unclear whether he thought he understood Willcocks, conspired with her to concoct a story, or invented the kidnapped princess narrative himself, perhaps to avoid admitting that he didn't understand her after all. He seems to have provided only the superstructure of the narrative that Willcocks would fill in through pantomime (Gutch and Worrall, 7). Lee's claim that additional details were contributed by a "Capt. Palmer" (*Romantic Liars*, 185–86) appears to rest on a misreading of Charles Wilkinson's June 9, 1817, letter to the *Bath Chronicle* (Gutch and Worrall, 25).

16. Gutch and Worrall, 7.

17. For Willcocks's access to *Pantographia*, see ibid., 15, 55; Wilkinson, *Bath Chronicle*, June 5, 1817, [4], and June 19, 1817, [3]. Wells suggests that Willcocks made particular use of the "Lampoon" and "Rejang" specimens that appear in the last five pages of *Pantographia* (230–31).

Many accounts of the Caraboo story have assumed that Mary Willcocks had some kind of help in developing her "Oriental" language and character—perhaps from a band of gypsies, a Jewish neighbor, a mysterious foreigner she claimed to have married, or the Portuguese sailor who claimed to understand her a little. Willcocks never hints at any kind of collaboration, however, and the simplest explanation is that she had a good ear for languages, a good tongue for glossolalia, an inventive mind, and a copy of *Pantographia*. The hunt for Mary Willcocks's unknown collaborator has sometimes verged on an assumption that the Caraboo character is too complex and impressive to have been the work of a poor, provincial, uneducated, and/or female mind. See Gutch and Worrall, *Caraboo*, 36n, 56; Lee, *Romantic Liars*, 158, 185–87.

18. *Kentish Weekly Post*, Nov. 18, 1817, [2]; *Liverpool Mercury*, June 20, 1817, 406; Gutch and Worrall, *Caraboo*, 25; *American Star* (Petersburg, Va.), Sept. 9, 1817, [3]; *Belfast Commercial Chronicle*, July 7, 1817, [1]; "Sporting Intelligence Extra," *Bristol Mirror*, reprinted in Gutch and Worrall, *Caraboo*, 65–66.

19. Gutch and Worrall, *Caraboo*, 9, 13–15.

20. Ibid., 8–9.

21. Neither of the two existing scholarly treatments of Willcocks deals with her language more than passingly. Russett is interested in Willcocks's sources for the Caraboo performance ("The 'Caraboo' Hoax"); Lee's interest is in Willcocks's (conjectured) use of Stamford Raffles's *History of Java* (1817) and in the social and economic possibilities available to "obscure women who became impostors" (*Romantic Liars*). I share Russett's and Lee's interest in understanding the Caraboo story as much from Mary Willcocks's perspective as possible. Russett does not, however, try to use the biographical material in the Gutch and Worrall pamphlet to place the Caraboo events in the context of Willcocks's life; she focuses on the choices Willcocks made during her ten weeks as Caraboo. Lee uses the Gutch and Worrall pamphlet and other sources to construct a detailed but ultimately unreliable account of Willcocks's subjective experiences that treats primary sources uncritically and embellishes those sources with conjectural details presented as historical facts. My account also differs from Lee's and Russett's in that I do not frame the story as a "hoax" or "imposture"; I trace the American phase of Willcocks's story; and I give more attention to Willcocks's mental problems.

22. Gutch and Worrall, *Caraboo*, 28, 31, 41–43. For literacy among England's female, poor, and rural populations in the long eighteenth century, see Fergus, *Provincial Readers in Eighteenth-Century England*, 59–60, 75–81; Stephens, "Literacy in Devon during the Industrial Revolution."

23. The pamphlet, *Caraboo: A Narrative of a Singular Imposition*, was published in London in August 1817. I will refer to this document as "the Gutch–Worrall pamphlet." Previous discussions of the Caraboo story have always recognized Gutch as the "author" of the pamphlet, but it is probably better understood as an archive jointly compiled by Gutch and Elizabeth Worrall than as a single text "authored" by Gutch or anyone else. Gutch states in a prefatory note that the pamphlet's text "has in many instances been printed

verbatim, as it was spoken or dictated" by the sources he interviewed. Worrall was one of his chief sources, and she also evidently directed and compiled the research comprising the pamphlet's third quarter.

24. Most of the women from this period whose lives can be extensively documented belonged to the middle or upper classes (cf. Abigail Adams, Elizabeth Drinker, Hester Lynch Piozzi, Mary Wollstonecraft); see Cook and Culley, *Women's Life Writing, 1700–1850*. For other working-class women whose lives can be documented to an unusual extent, see Gagnier, "The Literary Standard, Working-Class Lifewriting and Gender."

Other than what appears in the Gutch–Worrall pamphlet, the extant known documents from Mary Willcocks's mouth and pen consist of a scrap of paper with Carabooish characters on it (Houghton Library, Harvard University, *EC8.B1752.817C); a newspaper halftone of a brief note in her handwriting (*Western Daily Press* [Bristol], Aug. 27, 1926, 7–8); three woodcuts of her Carabooish and English writing, originally printed in the *Bristol Mirror*, June 21, 1817, [3], and the *Bristol Journal*, June 21, 1817, [3]; one letter from Willcocks to Sophia Landeg, Sept. 30, 1817, probably dictated as it is not in her hand (Cambridge University Library, G.32.54, no. 7); and handwritten transcripts of two letters by Mary Willcocks (to Elizabeth Worrall, Sept. 17, 1817, and Nov. 3, 1817) and one letter about her (Ann H. Lamb to Elizabeth Worrall, Sept. 10, 1817), probably made years later by Elizabeth Worrall or her son Henry Lechmere Worrall (Bristol Museum, K6152).

25. Gutch–Worrall pamphlet, 43, 29–30. For the socioeconomic expectations facing rural working-class nineteenth-century women, see Verdon, *Rural Women Workers in Nineteenth-Century England.*

26. It was the infirmary of St. Giles's Workhouse (Gutch–Worrall pamphlet, 30–31, 51).

27. *Repertory* (Boston), Sept. 23, 1817, [1]. The American chapter in Mary Willcocks's Caraboo story has not been explored in previous scholarship.

28. *Western Monitor* (Lexington, Ky.), Sept. 20, 1817, [2]; *Mississippi Free Trader* (Natchez), Sept. 27, 1817, [3]; *Missouri Gazette and Public Advertiser* (St. Louis), Oct. 4, 1817, [3]; *Carolina Federal Republican* (New Bern, N.C.), Sept. 6, 1817, [2]; *American Star* (Petersburg, Va.), Sept. 18, 1817; *Kennebec Advertiser* (Hallowell, Me.), Sept. 13, 1817.

29. "The joke was published as evidence of John Bull's credulity," reports *Poulson's American Daily Advertiser* (Philadelphia), Sept. 30, 1817, [3].

30. *Republican Chronicle* (New York), Aug. 23, 1817, repr. in *Poulson's American Daily Advertiser* (Philadelphia), Aug. 25, 1817, [3].

31. *American Yeoman* (Brattleboro, Vt.), Oct. 28, 1817, [3].

32. *Poulson's American Daily Advertiser* (Philadelphia), Sept. 30, 1817, [3].

33. *National Messenger* (Georgetown, D.C.), Nov. 3, 1817, [3].

34. Edgar Allan Poe's newspaper hoaxes of the 1830s and 1840s provide another point of reference for the spirited, playful performance of untruths before American publics; see L. Cohen, *The Fabrication of American Literature*, 23–64.

35. *Freeman's Journal* (Philadelphia), Sept. 6, 1817, [2]; *Boston Intelligencer*, Sept. 27, 1817, [4]; *New-York Daily Advertiser*, Sept. 29, 1817, [2]; *Albany Gazette*, Oct. 4, 1817, [2].

36. On the vigorous "culture of reprinting" that defined newspaper content in the antebellum United States, see McGill, *American Literature and the Culture of Reprinting*; for recent efforts to map the networks through which "viral" newspaper content circulated, see Cordell, "Reprinting, Circulation, and the Network Author in Antebellum Newspapers." Before the advent of the "illustrated newspaper" later in the nineteenth century, newspaper illustrations were extremely rare in both British and American newspapers (P. Anderson, *The Printed Image and the Transformation of Popular Culture, 1790–1860*, 16–49).

37. This apparently originated in the *Bergen Express and Paterson Advertiser*, Sept. 24, 1817. In addition to the printings reproduced in the accompanying illustration, it was also printed in the *Evening Post* (New York), Sept. 25, 1817; *New-York Herald*, Sept. 27, 1817; *Patriot* (Utica, N.Y.), Oct. 7, 1817; *Connecticut Herald* (New Haven), Oct. 7, 1817; and *Huntsville* (Ala.) *Republican*, Nov. 4, 1817.

38. Gutch–Worrall pamphlet, 43, 31; *Oxford English Dictionary*, s.v. "fever," n1, senses 1 and 3. In modern medicine, "rheumatic fever" is the name of a different disease, a rare condition caused by a specific bacterial infection (English, *Rheumatic Fever in America and Britain*). Nineteenth-century brain fever could be caused by "fear, anxiety, disappointments, long continued watching on a sick bed, intense study, [or] want of sleep" (Peterson, "Brain Fever in Nineteenth-Century Literature," 447–48). For its standard treatments, see Laffey, "Psychiatric Therapy in Georgian Britain."

39. Gutch–Worrall pamphlet, 48, 50–52.

40. Ibid., 50, 32, 48.

41. Ibid., 50, 51–52. On other eighteenth- and nineteenth-century women who claimed to be able to live without food, see Lee, *Romantic Liars*, 21–78.

42. Gutch–Worrall pamphlet, 31, 51. Willcocks was at the Mathewses' from about 1810 to January 1813. Elizabeth (Betsy) Mathews evidently worked with her in 1811.

43. Ibid., 32.

44. For evolving concepts of the phenomena that we now understand as "mental illness," see Miller and Torrey, *The Invisible Plague*; R. Porter, *Mind Forg'd Manacles*.

45. On the Magdalen Hospital, see Pearce, *Changing Sentiments and the Magdalen Hospital.*

46. Gutch–Worrall pamphlet, 53. This could indeed have happened in 1810 between her running away from home and her being hospitalized at St. Giles's Workhouse. On the other hand, if it was not true, then Willcocks was expertly deploying elements of the seduction fiction genre.

47. Ibid., 53n, 53.

48. Gutch–Worrall pamphlet, 8. "Caraboo's" history draws on several related genres of eighteenth- and nineteenth-century prose narrative, including the captivity narrative, seduction fiction, and transcultural travel writing. Like much long-eighteenth-century fiction, Caraboo's story centers on a threat to a young woman's chastity while she is being held against her will by a man intending sexual violence (see Beach, "Aubin's *The Noble Slaves*, Montagu's Spanish Lady, and English Feminist Writing"). This man is often religiously or racially othered, e.g., as a Catholic or a Turk (see Colley, *Captives*). Princess Caraboo is kidnapped for sexual enslavement by Orientalized and vaguely Islamized pirates; their leader "wore a turban" (Gutch–Worrall pamphlet, 10). The heroine in this genre is frequently of noble birth; Caraboo is a princess. And while the prototypical protagonist of these stories is a white woman, a significant subgenre features light-skinned nonwhite women in this role (the so-called tragic mulatta trope; see Manganelli, *Transatlantic Spectacles of Race*); Princess Caraboo is a light-skinned biracial.

Narratives that present the Orient as a place of rape or enslavement also commonly figure the Orient—and especially the Pacific—as a place of exciting sexual pleasure (see Lewis, *Gendering Orientalism*; Said, *Orientalism*). The sexualization of Caraboo (by Willcocks and by her observers) follows this pattern.

49. Hester Lynch Piozzi to Sir James Fellowes, July 1, 1817, in Bloom and Bloom, *Piozzi Letters*, 6:97; "Caraboo—A New Ballad," *La Belle Assemblée*, August 1817, 82–83.

50. Wilkinson, *Bath Chronicle*, June 5, 1817, [4]. On Wilkinson, see J. L. Thornton, "Charles Hunnings Wilkinson."

51. H. Smith, "YOUNG CARABOO!," in Gutch–Worrall pamphlet, 64–65.

52. Wilkinson, *Bath Chronicle*, June 5, 1817, [4]; Gutch–Worrall pamphlet, 14.

53. Gutch–Worrall pamphlet, 34–35. For other cross-dressing female bandits in English balladry, see S. Clark, *Women and Crime in the Street Literature of Early Modern England.* On the class-mediated treatment of nineteenth-century women who reported sexual violence, see Siena, *Venereal Disease, Hospitals and the Urban Poor*, 181–218; Toulalan, "Is He a Licentious Lewd Sort of a Person?"

54. The Gutch–Worrall pamphlet reports this episode without the transgender element (35–36). Willcocks told a different journalist, Harry Bonner, that she took this job "under the disguises of a Footman" and that "in [male] disguise she actually lived in her native place, close to her father's house" (Bonner, *Carraboo, Carraboo*, t.p.; Bonner, *Full Particulars of the Life, Character, and Adventures of Carraboo*). For other transgender episodes in the long eighteenth century, see Klein, "Eighteenth-Century Female Cross-Dressers and Their Beards."

55. *La Belle Assemblée*, Nov. 1817, 237–38; Bonner, *Full Particulars*; Gutch–Worrall pamphlet, 41, 42. Willcocks's white-to-nonwhite transracial "passing" is atypical but by no means singular (Chang, *Britain's Chinese Eye*, 56–70; Yang, *Performing China*, 75–113).

56. On queer historiography's archival challenges, see, e.g., Cvetkovich, *An Archive of Feelings*; Halperin, "How to Do the History of Male Homosexuality."

57. Gutch–Worrall pamphlet, 50–53; John Wells, *Princess Caraboo*, 206.

58. Gutch–Worrall pamphlet, 43.

59. V. Oliver, *Caribbeana*, 2:139. For the broader history of Loyalist refugees from the American Revolution who settled in Britain, see Jasanoff, *Liberty's Exiles*, 113–47.

60. Gutch–Worrall pamphlet, 3–4, 4n.

61. Ibid., 1; Russett, "'Caraboo' Hoax," 31–32; John Wells, *Princess Caraboo*, 114.

62. See Henry Meyer's engraving of Edward Bird's portrait of Willcocks as Caraboo, and Nathan Branwhite's engraving of his own portrait of Mary Willcocks, both of which are included in the Gutch–Worrall pamphlet. Russett reads the Bird portrait as "'orientalized': the mouth made smaller, the nose narrower, the eyes more almond-shaped," details that I strain to perceive ("Caraboo Hoax," 33–34). On the convention of using the blank page to represent racial whiteness, see Senchyne, "Bottles of Ink and Reams of Paper."

63. Gutch–Worrall pamphlet, 20–21; *Bristol Mirror*, June 21, 1817, [3]. Charles Wilkinson also presented the thank-you letter at the May 19, 1817, meeting of the Bath Literary and Philosophical Society (*Bath Gazette*, June 4, 1817, [4]).

64. *Royal Cornwall Gazette*, June 21, 1817, [4]. On Stamford Raffles and his examination of the Caraboo manuscript, see Lee, *Romantic Liars*, 139–99.

65. [Richard] Whately, "Notice of the Pretended Princess Caraboo," *The Rose, the Shamrock, and the Thistle*, April 1863, 517.

66. "Caraboo—A New Ballad," *La Belle Assemblée*, August 1817, 82–83.

67. Gutch–Worrall pamphlet, 22, 20–21.

68. *Historical and Local New Bath Guide*, 33.

69. *Bristol Mirror*, *Bristol Gazette*, *Bristol Journal*, and *Bath Gazette*. American reengravings of the same illustration have been noted earlier.

70. Hester Lynch Piozzi to Harriet Maria Salusbury, June 25[–26], 1817, in Bloom and Bloom, *Piozzi Letters*, 6:93.

71. *Bristol Mirror*, June 21, 1817, [3]; Bonner, *Carraboo, Carraboo*, 8.

72. Gutch–Worrall pamphlet, 64.

73. H. Smith, "YOUNG CARABOO!," in Gutch–Worrall pamphlet, 64–65.

74. The languages called "Tartar" and "Circassian" in this letter are now more commonly known as Nogai and Adyghe. See Gordon, *Ethnologue*, 518, 552, 556.

75. "A. B." to Elizabeth Worrall, June 14, 1817, in Gutch–Worrall pamphlet, 21n–23n. The sender of this letter has not been previously identified, but it was almost certainly Kattı Geray (1789?–1847), nephew of the last dynastic khan to rule Crimea before its annexation by the Russian Empire in 1783. Kattı Geray grew up in exile in Circassia, where he became the star student at the Edinburgh Missionary Society's mission in Karas. He spent 1816–17 in Scotland (Kirimli, "Crimean Tatars, Nogays, and Scottish Missionaries").

76. See C. Jones, *English Pronunciation*, 199–201, 320, 336–38.

77. Gutch–Worrall pamphlet, 43.

78. Ibid., 52, 50.

79. Ibid., 27. The story ran in Gutch's *Bristol Journal*, June 7, 1817, [4], and in the *Bristol Mirror*, June 7, 1817, [3], both reprinting Wilkinson's letter in the *Bath Chronicle*, June 5, 1817, [3].

80. Swiderski, *Lives between Cultures*, 79.

81. Gutch–Worrall pamphlet, 27–28.

82. Ibid., 46–47. Sophia Mansell Landeg and William Mortimer's acquaintances regarded their relationship as legitimate even though they were not legally married until after the death of Landeg's estranged husband in 1833.

83. *Bristol Journal*, June 14, 1817, [3]; Gutch–Worrall pamphlet, 47.

84. Cooke, *The Universal Letter-Writer*, 92–93.

85. John Wells, *Princess Caraboo*, 124–26; *True American* (Philadelphia), Sept. 4, 1817, [2]; *Weekly Entertainer* (Sherborne), Nov. 24, 1817, 929; Willcocks to Landeg, Sept. 30, 1817.

86. Lamb to Worrall, Sept. 10, 1817; *Lang's Gazette*, reprinted in *Repertory* (Boston), Sept. 23, 1817, [1]; *Freeman's Journal* (Philadelphia), Sept. 8, 1817, [2]; *Freeman's Journal* (Philadelphia), Sept. 17, 1817; *National Advocate* (New York), Sept. 25, 1817, [2]. For Philadelphia's place in a very active transatlantic theater culture, see Gibbs, *Performing the Temple of Liberty*.

87. Willcocks to Landeg, Sept. 30, 1817; Gutch–Worrall pamphlet, 67n; *Caledonian Mercury*, Dec. 13, 1817, [2].

88. "Communication," *True American* (Philadelphia), Sept. 25, 1817, [2]; "Miss Carraboo," *Freeman's Journal* (Philadelphia), Sept. 25, 1817.

89. Willcocks to Worrall, Sept. 30, 1817. On transatlantic celebrity culture in the early nineteenth century, see Eastman, "The Transatlantic Celebrity of Mr. O."

90. Willcocks to Worrall, Sept. 30, 1817.

91. Willcocks to Worrall, Nov. 4, 1817.

92. She was reported back in the British Isles in 1821 and 1824 (*Bristol Mercury*, Oct. 13, 1821, 3; *New Times* [London], Dec. 17, 1824, 4), and she married in Bristol in 1828.

93. George Pryce, *Notes and Queries*, 3rd ser., 7, April 15, 1865, 310; "Bristoliensis," *Notes and Queries*, 3rd ser., 7, May 20, 1865, 409; John Wells, *Princess Caraboo*, 292–98.

94. "Bristoliensis," 409.

CODA

1. *Colorado River Aqueduct News*, Jan. 25, 1939, 9; *Arizona Republic*, June 7, 1939, 1.

2. "Anti-Carraboo," *Ladies Literary Museum; or, Weekly Repository* (London), Feb. 3, 1818, 24.

3. *Rutland Vermont Herald*, Jan. 7, 1818, [4].

4. Dufief to Webster, Oct. 2, 1804, New York Public Library, Noah Webster Papers, Series 1B.

5. Mackintosh, *Essay* (1797), 229.

6. R. Anderson, "Vocal Fry May Undermine the Success of Young Women in the Labor Market."

7. N. Ferguson, "Texting Makes U Stupid"; Mackintosh, *Essay* (1797), xix.

8. Thurlow and Mroczek, *Digital Discourse*.

9. Gevirtzman, *An Intimate Understanding of America's Teenagers*, 14.

BIBLIOGRAPHY

Aarsleff, Hans. *From Locke to Saussure: Essays on the Study of Language and Intellectual History*. Minneapolis: University of Minneapolis Press, 1982.

———. "Locke's Influence." In *The Cambridge Companion to Locke*, edited by Vere Chappell, 252–89. Cambridge: Cambridge University Press, 1994.

———. "Philosophy of Language." In *The Cambridge History of Eighteenth-Century Philosophy*, edited by Knud Haakonssen, 1:451–95. Cambridge: Cambridge University Press, 2006.

———. *The Study of Language in England, 1780–1860*. Minneapolis: University of Minnesota Press, 1983.

Ahmad, Nazir. *Oriental Presses in the World*. Lahore: Qadiria, 1985.

Alexander, Caleb. *Columbian Dictionary of the English Language*. Boston, 1800.

Algeo, John. "English around the World." *American Speech* 68 (1993): 420–25.

Alston, R. C. *A Bibliography of the English Language*. 20 vols. Leeds: Arnold and Son, 1965–.

Amory, Hugh, and David D. Hall, eds. *A History of the Book in America: Volume 1, The Colonial Book in the Atlantic World*. Chapel Hill: University of North Carolina Press, 2007.

Anderson, Benedict. *Imagined Communities: Reflections on the Origin and Spread of Nationalism*. 2nd ed. New York: Verso, 1991.

Anderson, George. *Landmarks of Rensselaer County, New York*. Syracuse: Mason, 1897.

Anderson, Patricia. *The Printed Image and the Transformation of Popular Culture, 1790–1860*. Oxford: Clarendon Press, 1991.

Anderson, Peter John, ed. *Fasti Academiae Mariscallanae Aberdonensis: Selections from the Records of the Marischal College and University*. 3 vols. Aberdeen, 1898.

Anderson, Rindy, Casey A. Klofstad, William J. Mayew, and Mohan Venkatachalam. "Vocal Fry May Undermine the Success of Young Women in the Labor Market." *PLoS ONE* 9 (2014).

Andresen, Julie Tetel. *Linguistics in America, 1769–1924: A Critical History*. New York: Routledge, 1990.

Annenberg, Maurice. *Type Foundries of America and Their Catalogues.* 1975; New Castle, Del.: Oak Knoll, 1994.

Anthiaume, Albert. *Le Collège du Havre: Contribution à l'histoire de l'enseignement.* 2 vols. Le Havre: Havre-Éclair, 1905.

Archives parlementaires de 1787 à 1860. 101 vols. Paris, 1868–1913.

Axtell, James. "Babel of Tongues: Communicating with Indians in Eastern North America." In *The Language Encounter in the Americas 1492–1800*, edited by Norman Fiering and Edward Gray, 15–60. New York: Berghahn, 2000.

Bailey, Nathan. *An Universal Etymological English Dictionary.* 25th ed. London, 1783.

Bailey, Richard. *Speaking American: A History of English in the United States.* Oxford: Oxford University Press, 2012.

Baker, Patrick. *Centring the Periphery: Chaos, Order, and the Ethnohistory of Dominica.* Buffalo: McGill-Queen's University Press, 1994.

Banks, Kenneth. *Chasing Empire across the Sea: Communications and the State in the French Atlantic, 1713–1763.* Montreal: McGill-Queen's University Press, 2002.

Bann, Jennifer, and John Corbett. *Spelling Scots: The Orthography of Literary Scots, 1700–2000.* Edinburgh: Edinburgh University Press, 2015.

Baron, Dennis. *The English-Only Question: An Official Language for Americans?* New Haven: Yale University Press, 1990.

———. *Grammar and Good Taste.* New Haven: Yale University Press, 1982.

Barth, Fredrick, Andre Gingrich, Robert Parkin, and Sydel Silverman. *One Discipline, Four Ways: British, German, French, and American Anthropology.* Chicago: University of Chicago Press, 2005.

Bashir, Elena, and Hans Heinrich Hock, eds. *The Languages and Linguistics of South Asia: A Comprehensive Guide.* Boston: De Gruyter, 2016.

Basker, J. G. "Scotticisms and the Problem of Cultural Identity in Eighteenth-Century Britain." *Eighteenth-Century Life* 15 (1991): 81–95.

Bayley, Robert. "Variationist Sociolinguistics." In *The Oxford Handbook of Sociolinguistics*, edited by Robert Bayley, Richard Cameron, and Ceil Lucas, 11–30. Oxford: Oxford University Press, 2013.

Beach, Adam. "Aubin's *The Noble Slaves*, Montagu's Spanish Lady, and English Feminist Writing about Sexual Slavery in the Ottoman World." *Eighteenth-Century Fiction* 29 (2017): 583–606.

———. "The Creation of a Classical Language in the Eighteenth Century: Standardizing English, Cultural Imperialism, and the Future of the Literary Canon." *Texas Studies in Literature and Language* 43 (2001): 117–41.

Beal, Joan C. *English Pronunciation in the Eighteenth Century: Thomas Spence's*

"Grand Repository of the English Language." Oxford: Clarendon Press, 1999.

———. "'Out in Left Field': Spelling Reformers of the Eighteenth Century." *Transactions of the Philological Society* 100 (2002): 5–23.

———. "The Place of Pronunciation in Eighteenth-Century Grammars of English." *Transactions of the Philological Society* 111 (2013): 165–78.

Beal, Joan C., and Marco Condorelli. "Cut from the Same Cloth? Variation and Change in the Cloth Lexical Set." *Token* 3 (2014): 15–36.

Beattie, James. *Dissertations Moral and Critical.* London, 1783.

———. *List of Two Hundred Scoticisms.* Aberdeen, 1779.

Beauchamp, Alphonse. *Histoire de la guerre de la Vendée.* 3 vols. Paris, 1806.

Beeman, Richard. *The Varieties of Political Experience in Eighteenth-Century America.* Philadelphia: University of Pennsylvania Press, 2004.

Belanger, Terry. "From Bookseller to Publisher: Changes in the London Book Trade, 1750–1850." In *Book Selling and Book Buying: Aspects of the Nineteenth-Century British and American Book Trade*, edited by Richard Landon, 7–16. Chicago: American Library Association, 1978.

Bélizal, vicomte de [André-Marie de Gouzillon]. "Journal et lettres d'un émigré." *Revue de Bretagne*, 2nd ser. 27 (1902): 92–113.

Bell, Alexander Melville. *Visible Speech: The Science of Universal Alphabetics* [. . .]. New York, 1867.

Bent, Tessa, Eriko Atagi, Amal Akbik, and Emma Bonifield. "Classification of Regional Dialects, International Dialects, and Nonnative Accents." *Journal of Phonetics* 58 (2016): 104–17.

Berry, Thomas. *Vraie méthode pour apprendre facilement à parler, à lire, et à l'écrire l'anglois.* Paris, 1762.

Berry, W. Turner, and A. F. Johnson. *Catalogue of Specimens of Printing Types by English and Scottish Printers and Founders 1665–1830.* 1935. New York: Garland, 1983.

Bhabha, Homi. *The Location of Culture.* London: Routledge, 1994.

Bickel, Balthasar. "Linguistic Diversity and Universals." In *The Cambridge Handbook of Linguistic Anthropology*, edited by N. J. Enfield, Paul Kockelman, and Jack Sidnell, 101–24. Cambridge: Cambridge University Press, 2014.

Bidwell, John. "Printers' Supplies and Capitalization." In Amory and Hall, *A History of the Book in America*, 1:163–83.

Bittard des Portes, Réné. *Histoire de l'armée de Condé pendant la Révolution française.* Paris, 1896.

Bjorklund, Diane. *Interpreting the Self: Two Hundred Years of American Autobiography.* Chicago: University of Chicago Press, 1998.

Blair, Hugh. *Lectures on Rhetoric and Belles Lettres*. 2 vols. London, 1783.

Blomberg, Johan, and Jordan Zlatev. "Language May Indeed Influence Thought." *Frontiers in Psychology* 6, no. 1631 (2015): n.p.

Bloom, Edward Alan, and Lillian Doris Bloom, eds. *The Piozzi Letters: Correspondence of Hester Lynch Piozzi, 1784–1821*. 6 vols. Newark: University of Delaware Press, 1989–2002.

Boberg, Charles. *The English Language in Canada: Status, History and Comparative Analysis*. Cambridge: Cambridge University Press, 2010.

Boggs, W. Arthur. "William Kenrick's Pronunciations." *American Speech* 39 (1977): 131–34.

[Bonner, Harry]. *Carraboo, Carraboo: The Singular Adventures of Mary Baker* [. . .]. London, 1817.

———. *Full Particulars of the Life, Character, and Adventures of Carraboo, Alias Mary Baker* [. . .]. Bristol, [1817].

Boroditsky, Lera. "Lost in Translation." *Wall Street Journal*. July 23, 2010.

Bourdieu, Pierre. "The Economy of Linguistic Exchanges." In *Language and Symbolic Power*, edited by John Thompson, trans. Gino Raymond and Matthew Adamson, 37–102. Cambridge, Mass.: Harvard University Press, 1991.

Boyer, Abel. *The Complete French Master for Ladies and Gentlemen*. 24th ed. London, 1779.

Branch, Jordan. *The Cartographic State: Maps, Territory, and the Origins of Sovereignty*. Cambridge: Cambridge University Press, 2014.

Brelvi, Ebadat, ed. *Poems of Dr. John Gilchrist*. Lahore: University Oriental College, 1977.

Brewer, Charlotte. "Johnson, Webster, and the *OED*." In Matto and Momma, *A Companion to the History of the English Language*, 113–21.

Brosses, Charles de. *Traité de la formation méchanique des langues*. Paris, 1765.

Brückner, Martin. *The Geographic Revolution in Early America: Maps, Literacy, and National Identity*. Chapel Hill: University of North Carolina Press, 2006.

Burstein, Andrew. *Sentimental Democracy: The Evolution of America's Romantic Self-Image*. New York: Hill and Wang, 1999.

Byres, John. *References to the Plan of the Island of Dominica, as Surveyed from the Year 1765 to 1773*. London, 1777.

Cabinet of Curiosities, Natural, Artificial, and Historical. 2 vols. Hartford, 1822.

Campbell, George. *The Philosophy of Rhetoric*. 2 vols. London, 1776.

Cardell, William. *Essay on Language, as Connected with the Faculties of the Mind* [. . .]. New York, 1825.

Carlyle, Thomas. *The French Revolution: A History*. 2 vols. New York, 1851.

Carrière, J.-M. "Mr. Jefferson Sponsors a New French Method." *French Review* 19 (1946): 394–405.

Caslon, H. Daniel. "Developments in Typefounding since 1720." *Journal of the Royal Society of Arts* 82 (1934): 489–505.

Cavallo, Guglielmo, and Roger Chartier, eds. *A History of Reading in the West.* Amherst: University of Massachusetts Press, 1999.

Chambaud, Louis. *A Grammar of the French Tongue.* 6th ed. London, 1775.

Chambers, David. Introduction to *Specimen of Modern Printing Types by Edmund Fry, 1828: A Facsimile.* London: Printing Historical Society, 1986.

———. "Sketch of the Life of David Chambers." In *Chambers History: Trails of the Centuries*, ed. William Chambers, 33–37. Muncie, Ind.: Scott, 1925.

Chambers, John. *Biographical Illustrations of Worcestershire.* Worcester, Mass., 1820.

[Chambers, Joseph Gaston.] "Elements of Orthography; or an Attempt to Form a Complete System of Letters." *Universal Asylum and Columbian Magazine* (Philadelphia), July–October 1791, 33–37, 113–17, 175–78, 225–28.

[———.] *Elements of Orthography* [. . .]. Washington, Penn., 1811.

[———.] *Elements of Orthography* [. . .]. Zanesville, Ohio, 1812.

[———.] *Elements of Orthography* [. . .]. Philadelphia, 1817.

Chang, Elizabeth. *Britain's Chinese Eye: Literature, Empire, and Aesthetics in Nineteenth-Century Britain.* Stanford, Calif.: Stanford University Press, 2010.

Chapuis, Alfred. *History of the Musical Box and of Mechanical Music.* Trans. Joseph Roesch. Summit, N.J.: Music Box Society, 1992.

Chase, Stuart. *Power of Words.* New York: Harcourt, Brace, 1955.

Chastellux, Marquis de. *Travels in North-America, in the Years 1780, 1781, and 1782.* Trans. "by an English gentleman." 2 vols. London, 1787.

Chaussinand-Nogaret, Guy. *French Nobility in the Eighteenth Century: From Feudalism to Enlightenment.* Cambridge: Cambridge University Press, 1985.

Cheney, Paul. *Cul de Sac: Patrimony, Capitalism, and Slavery in French Saint-Domingue.* Chicago: University of Chicago Press, 2017.

Christy, T. Craig. "Steinthal and the Development of Linguistic Science: The Convergence of Psychology and Linguistics." In *Papers in the History of Linguistics: Proceedings of the Third International Conference on the History of the Language Sciences*, edited by Hans Aarsleff, L. G. Kelley, and Hans-Josef Niederehe, 491–99. Philadelphia: John Benjamins, 1987.

Clark, John W. "American Spelling." In *Spelling*, rev. ed., edited by George Henry Vallins, 184–202. London: Deutsch, 1965.

Clark, Sandra. *Women and Crime in the Street Literature of Early Modern England.* New York: Palgrave, 2003.

Cmiel, Kenneth. "'A Broad Fluid Language of Democracy': Discovering the American Idiom." *Journal of American History* 79 (1992): 913–36.

———. *Democratic Eloquence: The Fight over Popular Speech in Nineteenth-Century America.* Berkeley: University of California Press, 1990.

Cohen, Lara Langer. *The Fabrication of American Literature: Fraudulence and Antebellum Print Culture.* Philadelphia: University of Pennsylvania Press, 2012.

Cohen, Michele. *Fashioning Masculinity: National Identity and Language in the Eighteenth Century.* London: Routledge, 1996.

Cohen, Murray. *Sensible Words: Linguistic Practice in England, 1640–1785.* Baltimore: Johns Hopkins University Press, 1977.

Cohn, Bernard. *Colonialism and Its Forms of Knowledge: The British in India.* Princeton, N.J.: Princeton University Press, 1996.

———. "The Command of Language and the Language of Command." In *Subaltern Studies IV: Writings on South Asian History and Society*, edited by Ranajit Guha, 276–329. Delhi: Oxford University Press, 1996.

Colley, Linda. *Britons: Forging the Nation 1707–1837.* New Haven: Yale University Press, 1992.

———. *Captives: Britain, Empire, and the World, 1600–1850.* New York: Random House, 2002.

Conklin, Nancy Faires, and Margaret Lourie. *A Host of Tongues: Language Communities in the United States.* New York: Free Press, 1983.

Connor, Steven. *Dumbstruck: A Cultural History of Ventriloquism.* Oxford: Oxford University Press, 2000.

Cook, Daniel, and Amy Culley, eds. *Women's Life Writing, 1700–1850: Gender, Genre and Authorship.* New York: Palgrave Macmillan, 2012.

Cook, Vivian, and Mark Newson. *Chomsky's Universal Grammar: An Introduction.* 3rd ed. Malden, Mass.: Wiley-Blackwell, 2007.

Cooke, Thomas. *The Universal Letter-Writer.* London, 1812.

Cordell, Ryan. "Reprinting, Circulation, and the Network Author in Antebellum Newspapers." *American Literary History* 27 (2015): 417–45.

Crain, Patricia. *The Story of A: The Alphabetization of America from the New England Primer to the Scarlet Letter.* Stanford, Calif.: Stanford University Press, 2000.

Cranage, David Herbert, and J. Kay-Shuttleworth. *Gilchrist Educational Trust: Pioneering Work in Education.* Cambridge: Cambridge University Press, 1930.

Crawford, Robert. *Devolving English Literature*. 2nd ed. Edinburgh: Edinburgh University Press, 2000.

———, ed. *The Scottish Invention of English Literature*. Cambridge: Cambridge University Press, 1998.

Cretineau-Joly, J. *Histoire de la Vendée militaire*. 4 vols. 2nd ed. Paris, 1843.

Croft, Herbert. *A Letter, from Germany* [. . .] *on the English and German Languages*. Hamburg, 1797.

Crompton, Andrew. "How to Look at a Reading Font." *Word & Image* 30 (2014): 79–89.

Crowley, Tony. *Language in History: Theories and Texts*. New York: Routledge, 1996.

Cullen, L. M. *The Brandy Trade under the Ancien Régime*. Cambridge: Cambridge University Press, 2002.

Cvetkovich, Ann. *An Archive of Feelings: Trauma, Sexuality, and Lesbian Public Cultures*. Durham, N.C.: Duke University Press, 2003.

D'Agay, Frédéric. "A European Destiny: The Armée de Condé, 1792–1801." In *The French Émigrés in Europe and the Struggle against Revolution, 1789–1814*, edited by Kirsty Carpenter and Philip Mansel, 28–42. New York: St. Martin's, 1999.

Damrosch, David. "Scriptworlds: Writing Systems and the Formation of World Literature." *Modern Language Quarterly* 68 (2007): 195–219.

Dane, Joseph. *Out of Sorts: On Typography and Print Culture*. Philadelphia: University of Pennsylvania Press, 2011.

Daniel, Marcus. *Scandal and Civility: Journalism and the Birth of American Democracy*. Oxford: Oxford University Press, 2009.

Darnell, Regna. *Edward Sapir: Linguist, Anthropologist, Humanist*. Berkeley: University of California Press, 1990.

———. *Invisible Genealogies: A History of Americanist Anthropology*. Lincoln: University of Nebraska Press, 2001.

Darnton, Robert. *The Great Cat Massacre and Other Episodes in French Cultural History*. Rev. ed. New York: Basic Books, 2009.

Darwin, Erasmus. *The Temple of Nature*. London, 1803.

Davenport, Richard Alfred. *Sketches of Imposture, Deception, and Credulity*. London, 1837.

Davidson, Jenny. *Breeding: A Partial History of the Eighteenth Century*. New York: Columbia University Press, 2009.

Davis, Leith. *Acts of Union: Scotland and the Negotiation of the British Nation*. Stanford, Calif.: Stanford University Press, 1998.

De Fréine, Seán. "The Dominance of the English Language in the 19th

Century." In *The English Language in Ireland*, edited by D. Ó Muirithe, 71–87. Dublin: Mercier Press, 1977.

Derrida, Jacques. *Of Grammatology*. Trans. Gayatri Chakravorty Spivak. Baltimore: Johns Hopkins University Press, 1976.

Desan, Suzanne. *The Family on Trial in Revolutionary France*. Berkeley: University of California Press, 2004.

Dibbell, Jeremy. "History of the Book in the Caribbean and Bermuda." In *The Book: A Global History*, edited by Michael Suarez and H. R. Woudhuysen, 710–16. Oxford: Oxford University Press, 2013.

Dibdin, Thomas. *The Bibliographical Decameron*. 2 vols. London, 1817.

Dillard, J. L. *A History of American English*. New York: Longman, 1992.

Drucker, Johanna. *The Alphabetic Labyrinth: The Letters in History and Imagination*. London: Thames and Hudson, 1995.

———. "Reading Interface." *PMLA* 128 (2013): 213–20.

Dubois, Laurent. *Avengers of the New World: The Story of the Haitian Revolution*. Cambridge, Mass.: Harvard University Press, 2004.

Dudley, Homer, and T. H. Tarnoczy. "The Speaking Machine of Wolfgang von Kempelen." *Journal of the Acoustical Society of America* 22 (1950): 151–66.

Dufief, Nicholas Gouin. "[Language Makes the Difference between Man and Man]." *United States' Gazette* (Philadelphia), daily, July 10–18, 1806; *Aurora General Advertiser* (Philadelphia), daily, July 11–17, 1806; *Independent Chronicle* (Boston), July 17, 1806.

[———.] *The Logic of Facts*. Philadelphia, 1806.

———. *Nature Displayed, in Her Mode of Teaching Language to Man* [. . .] *Adapted to the French*. 2 vols. Philadelphia, 1804, 1806, 1810, 1823, 1827; Paris, 1817 (as *New French-English Grammar*); London, 1818, 1819, 1831, 1833; New York, 1825; London and Philadelphia, 1834.

[———.] "Proposals for Publishing [. . .] Nature Displayed." Philadelphia, 1806.

———. "To the Subscribers and Purchasers of the First Edition of 'Nature Displayed.'" Appendix to Dufief, *Logic of Facts*. Separately paginated. Philadelphia, 1806.

Dufief, Nicholas Gouin, Manuel Torres, and Louis Hargous. *Nature Displayed* [. . .] *Adapted to the Spanish*. Philadelphia, 1811; London, 1817.

Dufief, Nicholas Gouin, Manuel Torres, Louis Hargous, and Mariano Velázquez de la Cadena. *Nature Displayed* [. . .] *Adapted to the Spanish*. New York, 1825; London, 1826.

Dufief's French Self-Interpreter. Birmingham: W. M. Robinson, 1874.

Dupuy, Roger. "Les femmes et la Contre-Révolution dans l'Ouest." *Bulletin d'histoire économique et sociale de la Révolution française* (1979): 61–70.
Dwight, Timothy. "Observations on Language." *Memoirs of the Connecticut Academy* 1 (1816): [365]–386.
Eastman, Carolyn. "The Transatlantic Celebrity of Mr. O: Oratory and the Networks of Reputation in Early Nineteenth-Century Britain and America." *Comparative American Studies* 14 (2016): 7–20.
Einboden, Jeffrey. *The Islamic Lineage of American Literary Culture: Muslim Sources from the Revolution to Reconstruction*. Oxford: Oxford University Press, 2016.
Elliott, Michael. *The Culture Concept: Writing and Difference in the Age of Realism*. Minneapolis: University of Minnesota Press, 2002.
Ellis, Joseph. *After the Revolution: Profiles of Early American Culture*. New York: Norton, 1979.
Elphinston, James. *Propriety Ascertained in Her Picture*. 2 vols. London, 1786–87.
Embree, Thomas. *Orthography Corrected*. Philadelphia, 1813.
Emerson, Ellen Tucker. *Life of Lidian Jackson Emerson*. Lansing: Michigan State University Press, 1992.
English, Peter. *Rheumatic Fever in America and Britain: A Biological, Epidemiological, and Medical History*. New Brunswick, N.J.: Rutgers University Press, 1999.
Entick, John. *The New Spelling Dictionary*. London, 1782.
Erben, Patrick. *A Harmony of the Spirits: Translation and the Language of Community in Early Pennsylvania*. Chapel Hill: University of North Carolina Press, 2012.
Essays by the Students of the College of Fort William in Bengal. Calcutta, 1802.
Eustace, Nicole. *1812: War and the Passions of Patriotism*. Philadelphia: University of Pennsylvania Press, 2012.
Ewing, James. *The Columbian Alphabet*. Trenton, N.J., 1798.
Faber, Reginald Stanley. *Bibliothèque de la Providence: Catalogue of the French Hospital*. London, 1890.
Febvre, Lucien, and Henri-Jean Martin. *The Coming of the Book: The Impact of Printing, 1450–1800*. Trans. David Gerard. London: New Left Books, 1976.
The Female Robber. [London?], [1780?].
Fergus, Jan. *Provincial Readers in Eighteenth-Century England*. Oxford: Oxford University Press, 2006.
Fergus, Jan, and Ruth Porter. "Provincial Bookselling in Eighteenth-

Century England: The Case of John Clay Reconsidered." *Studies in Bibliography* 40 (1987): 147–65.

Ferguson, Frances. "The Social Organization of Schools (around 1800)." *SEL* 56 (2016): 823–43.

Ferguson, Niall. "Texting Makes U Stupid." *Newsweek* (Sept. 19, 2011): 11.

Ferguson, Robert. *The American Enlightenment, 1750–1820*. Cambridge, Mass.: Harvard University Press, 1994.

Fiering, Norman, and Edward Gray, eds. *The Language Encounter in the Americas 1492–1800*. New York: Berghahn, 2000.

Fisher, Anne. *An Accurate New Spelling Dictionary, and Expositor of the English Language*. 2nd ed. London, 1773.

Flavell, Julie. *When London Was Capital of America*. New Haven: Yale University Press, 2010.

Fleming, Juliet. "How to Look at a Printed Flower." *Word & Image* 22 (2006): 165–87.

Flexner, Helen Hudson. "The London Mechanics' Institution: Social and Cultural Foundations, 1823–1830." PhD dissertation. University College London, 2014.

Fliegelman, Jay. *Prodigals and Pilgrims: The American Revolution against Patriarchal Authority, 1750–1800*. Cambridge: Cambridge University Press, 1982.

Fogleman, Aaron. *Two Troubled Souls: An Eighteenth-Century Couple's Spiritual Journey in the Atlantic World*. Chapel Hill: University of North Carolina Press, 2015.

The Following Is a Specimen of the Lexicography of Webster's Dictionary [. . .]. [New Haven?], [1826?].

Ford, Emily Ellsworth Fowler, comp. *Notes on the Life of Noah Webster*. 2 vols. New York, 1912.

Foucault, Michel. *The Order of Things: An Archaeology of the Human Sciences*. Trans. Alan Sheridan. New York: Pantheon, 1971.

Franklin, Benjamin. *The Autobiography of Benjamin Franklin*. Edited by Leonard Larabee, Ralph L. Ketcham, Helen C. Boatfield, and Helene H. Fineman. 2nd ed. New Haven: Yale University Press, 2003.

———. *Political, Miscellaneous, and Philosophical Pieces*, edited by Benjamin Vaughan. London, 1779.

Freud, Sigmund. *Three Essays on the Theory of Sexuality*. 1905.

Fry, Edmund. *Pantographia: Containing Accurate Copies of All the Known Alphabets in the World* [. . .]. London, 1799.

Furet, François. *Revolutionary France, 1770–1880*. Trans. Antonia Nevill. Oxford: Blackwell, 1992.

Furstenberg, François. *When the United States Spoke French: Five Refugees Who Shaped a Nation*. New York: Penguin, 2014.

Gagnier, Regenia. "The Literary Standard, Working-Class Lifewriting and Gender." *Textual Practice* 3 (1996): 36–55.

Gallet-Blanchard, Liliane. "L'Enseignement de la langue anglaise en France au dix-huitième siècle." *Franco-British Studies* 12 (1991): 39–54.

Galliou, Patrick, and Michael Jones. *The Bretons*. Oxford: Blackwell, 1996.

García Aranda, María Ángeles. "La enseñanza del léxico en el método Dufief: *La naturaleza descubierta en su modo de enseñar las lenguas a los hombres* (Filadelfia, 1811)." *Verba* 43 (2016): 329–59.

Geertz, Armin. *The Invention of Prophecy: Continuity and Meaning in Hopi Indian Religion*. Berkeley: University of California Press, 1994.

Geggus, David. "The Slaves and Free Coloreds of Martinique during the Age of the French and Haitian Revolutions: Three Moments of Resistance." In *The Lesser Antilles in the Age of European Expansion*, edited by Robert L. Paquette and Stanley L. Engerman, 280–301. Gainesville, Fla.: University Press of Florida, 1996.

Gevirtzman, Bruce. *An Intimate Understanding of America's Teenagers: Shaking Hands with Aliens*. Westport: Praeger, 2008.

Ghosh, Anindita. *Power in Print: Popular Publishing and the Politics of Language and Culture in a Colonial Society, 1778–1905*. Oxford: Oxford University Press, 2006.

Gibbs, Jenna. *Performing the Temple of Liberty: Slavery, Theater, and Popular Culture in London and Philadelphia, 1760–1850*. Baltimore: Johns Hopkins University Press, 2014.

Gilchrist, John. *The British Indian Monitor*. 2 vols. Edinburgh, 1806.

———. *Dialogues, English and Hindoostanee*. Calcutta, 1804. 2nd ed., Edinburgh, 1809. 3rd ed., London, 1820. 4th ed., London, 1826.

———. *A Dictionary, English and Hindoostanee*. Calcutta, 1787.

———. *General East India Guide and Vade Mecum*. 3rd ed. London, 1825.

———. *A Grammar of the Hindoostanee Language*. 2 vols. Calcutta, 1796.

———. *The Hindee-Roman Orthoepigraphical Ultimatum*. Calcutta, 1804; London, 1820.

———. *Introductory Address to the Honorable Court of Proprietors of the East India Company*. London, 1806.

———. *The Oriental Green Bag!!!* London, 1820.

———. *Parliamentary Reform on Constitutional Principles*. Glasgow, 1815.

———. *A Practical Appeal to the Public, through a Series of Letters* [. . .]. London, 1833.

[———.] *A Succinct Narrative of Dr. Gilchrist's Services from 1782 to 1821.* [London], [1821].

Gilreath, James, ed., and Elizabeth Carter Wills, comp. *Federal Copyright Records, 1790–1800.* Washington, D.C.: Library of Congress, 1987.

Gitelman, Lisa. *Always Already New: Media, History, and the Data of Culture.* Cambridge, Mass.: MIT Press, 2006.

———. *Paper Knowledge: Toward a Media History of Documents.* Durham, N.C.: Duke University Press, 2014.

———. "The Phonograph's New Media Publics." In *The Sound Studies Reader*, edited by Jonathan Sterne, 283–303. New York: Routledge, 2012.

———. *Scripts, Grooves, and Writing Machines: Representing Technology in the Edison Era.* Stanford, Calif.: Stanford University Press, 1999.

———. "Souvenir Foils: On the Status of Print at the Origin of Recorded Sound." In *New Media, 1740–1915*, edited by Lisa Gitelman and Geoffrey Pingree, 157–73. Cambridge, Mass.: MIT Press, 2003.

Goethe, Johann Wolfgang von. *Campaign in France, in the Year 1792.* Trans. Robert Farie. London, 1849.

Gordon, Raymond, Jr., ed. *Ethnologue: Languages of the World.* 15th ed. Dallas: SIL International, 2005.

Görlach, Manfred. *Aspects of the History of English.* Heidelberg: Universitätsverlag C. Winter, 1998.

———. *English in Nineteenth-Century England: An Introduction.* Cambridge: Cambridge University Press, 1999.

Gottlieb, Evan. *Sympathy and National Identity in Scottish and English Writing, 1707–1832.* Lewisburg, Penn.: Bucknell University Press, 2007.

Goudie, Sean X. "The Caribbean Turn in C19 American Literary Studies." In *Turns of Event: Nineteenth-Century American Literary Studies in Motion*, edited by Hester Blum, 127–50. Philadelphia: University of Pennsylvania Press, 2016.

Gourdon de Genouillac, H. *Dictionnaire des fiefs* [. . .] *de l'ancienne France.* Paris, 1862.

Grandjean, Katherine. *American Passage: The Communications Frontier in Early New England.* Cambridge, Mass.: Harvard University Press, 2015.

Gray, Edward. *New World Babel: Languages and Nations in Early America.* Princeton, N.J.: Princeton University Press, 1999.

Green, James N. "English Books and Printing in the Age of Franklin." In Amory and Hall, *A History of the Book in America*, 1:248–98.

Green, Jonathon. *Chasing the Sun: Dictionary Makers and the Dictionaries They Made.* New York: Henry Holt, 1996.

———. "Language: Spelling Chuckers." *Critical Quarterly* 43 (2001): 147–51.

Gross, Robert. "Introduction: An Extensive Republic." In Gross and Kelley, *A History of the Book in America*, 2:1–52.

Gross, Robert, and Mary Kelley, eds. *A History of the Book in America, Volume 2: An Extensive Republic: Print, Culture, and Society in the New Nation*. Chapel Hill: University of North Carolina Press, 2010.

Guillory, John. "Enlightening Mediation." In Siskin and Warner, *This Is Enlightenment*, 37–63.

———. "Genesis of the Media Concept." *Critical Inquiry* 36 (2010): 321–62.

Gustafson, Thomas. *Representative Words: Politics, Literature, and the American Language*. Cambridge: Cambridge University Press, 1992.

[Gutch, John Mathew, and Elizabeth Worrall, comps.] *Caraboo: A Narrative of a Singular Imposition, Practised upon the Benevolence of a Lady Residing in the Vicinity of the City of Bristol*. London, 1817.

Haines, Michael R., and Richard Steckel, eds. *A Population History of North America*. Cambridge: Cambridge University Press, 2000.

Hakala, Walker. *Negotiating Languages: Urdu, Hindi, and the Definition of Modern South Asia*. New York: Columbia University Press, 2016.

Hall, David D., and Elizabeth Carroll Reilly. "Modalities of Reading." In Amory and Hall, *A History of the Book in America*, 1:404–10.

Halperin, David. "How to Do the History of Male Homosexuality." *GLQ* 6 (2000): 87–123.

Hargrave, Vessie. "Glossolalia: Reformation to the Twentieth Century." In *The Glossolalia Phenomenon*, edited by Charles Conn, 97–139. Cleveland: Pathway, 1966.

Harpham, Geoffrey Galt. *Language Alone: The Critical Fetish of Modernity*. New York: Routledge, 2002.

Harris, Roy, and Talbot Taylor. *Landmarks in Linguistic Thought: The Western Tradition from Socrates to Saussure*. New York: Routledge, 1989.

Harsanyi, Doina Pasca. *Lessons from America: Liberal French Nobles in Exile, 1793–1798*. University Park: Pennsylvania State University Press, 2010.

Harvey, Sean. *Native Tongues: Colonialism and Race from Encounter to the Reservation*. Cambridge, Mass.: Harvard University Press, 2015.

Hasnain, S. Imtiaz, and K. S. Rajyashree. "Hindustani as an Anxiety between Hindi-Urdu Commitment." In *The Yearbook of South Asian Languages and Linguistics*, edited by Rajendra Singh, 247–66. Berlin: Mouton de Gruyter, 2004.

Hatton, Ragnhild. *George I: Elector and King*. New ed. 1978; New Haven: Yale University Press, 2001.

Haveman, Heather. *Magazines and the Making of America: Modernization, Community, and Print Culture, 1741–1860*. Princeton, N.J.: Princeton University Press, 2015.

Hawkes, Terence. *Structuralism and Semiotics*. 1977; New York: Routledge, 2003.

Hayes, Kevin J., and Edwin Wolf 2nd. *The Library of Benjamin Franklin*. Philadelphia: American Philosophical Society and Library Company of Philadelphia, 2006.

Heath, Shirley Brice. "Why No Official Tongue?" In *Language Loyalties: A Source Book on the Official English Controversy*, edited by James Crawford, 20–31. Chicago: University of Chicago Press, 1992.

Hendel, Ronald. "Sibilants and *šibbōlet* (Judges 12:6)." *Bulletin of the American Schools of Oriental Research* 301 (1996): 69–75.

Hettier, Charles. *Relations de la Normandie et de la Bretagne avec les îles de la Manche pendant l'émigration*. Caen, France, 1885.

Hickey, Raymond. *Irish English: History and Present-Day Forms*. Cambridge: Cambridge University Press, 2007.

The Historical and Local New Bath Guide. Bath, England, [1823].

Hitchings, Henry. *The Language Wars: A History of Proper English*. New York: Farrar, Straus and Giroux, 2011.

Hobsbawm, Eric. *Nations and Nationalism since 1780: Programme, Myth, Reality*. Cambridge: Cambridge University Press, 1990.

Hochman, Brian. *Savage Preservation: The Ethnographic Origins of Modern Media Technology*. Minneapolis: University of Minneapolis Press, 2012.

Holm, John. "English in the Caribbean." In *Cambridge History of the English Language*, vol. 5, edited by Robert Burchfield, 328–81. Cambridge: Cambridge University Press, 1994.

Honychurch, Lennox. *The Dominica Story: A History of the Island*. 3rd ed. London: Macmillan, 1995.

Hopkins, Eric. *Childhood Transformed: Working-Class Children in Nineteenth-Century England*. New York: Manchester University Press, 1994.

Horning, Susan Schmidt. *Chasing Sound: Technology, Culture, and the Art of Studio Recording from Edison to the LP*. Baltimore: Johns Hopkins University Press, 2015.

Hudson, Nicholas. "From 'Nation' to 'Race': The Origin of Racial Classification in Eighteenth-Century Thought." *Eighteenth-Century Studies* 29 (1996): 247–64.

———. "Theories of Language." In *Cambridge History of Literary Criticism*, edited by H. B. Nisbet and Claude Rawson, 4:335–48. Cambridge: Cambridge University Press, 1997.

———. *Writing and European Thought, 1600–1830*. Cambridge: Cambridge University Press, 1994.

Hume, David. *Scotticisms*. [Edinburgh, 1752?].

Hussenet, Jacques, ed. *"Détruisez la Vendée!": Regards croisés sur les victimes et destructions de la guerre de Vendée*. Roche-sur-Yon, France: Centre Vendéen de Recherches Historiques, 2007.

Irvine, Judith. "Ideologies of Honorific Language." In *Language Ideologies: Practice and Theory*, edited by Bambi Schieffelin, Kathryn A. Woolard, and Paul V. Kroskrity, 51–67. Oxford: Oxford University Press, 1998.

Irving, Washington. *The Sketch Book of Geoffrey Crayon, Gent.* New York, 1819.

The Jamaica Lady. London, 1720.

James Grant of Ballindalloch Papers 1740–1819. Microfilm. Edinburgh: National Archives of Scotland, 2003.

Jankowsky, Kurt. "Comparative, Historical, and Typological Linguistics Since the Eighteenth Century." In *The Oxford Handbook of the History of Linguistics*, edited by Keith Allan, 635–54. Oxford: Oxford University Press, 2013.

Janzen, Gabriele, Daniel B. M. Haun, and Stephen C. Levinson. "Tracking Down Abstract Linguistic Meaning: Neural Correlates of Spatial Frame of Reference Ambiguities in Language." *PLoS ONE* 7 (2012).

Jasanoff, Maya. *Liberty's Exiles: American Loyalists in the Revolutionary World*. New York: Knopf, 2011.

Johnson, Samuel. *A Dictionary of the English Language*. 2 vols. London, 1755.

Johnston, Alastair. *Alphabets to Order: The Literature of Nineteenth-Century Typefounders' Specimens*. New Castle, Del.: Oak Knoll, 2000.

Jones, Charles. *English Pronunciation in the Eighteenth and Nineteenth Centuries*. New York: Palgrave Macmillan, 2006.

———. *A Language Suppressed: The Pronunciation of the Scots Language in the 18th Century*. Edinburgh: John Donald, 1995.

Jones, William. "Dissertation on the Orthography of Asiatick Words in Roman Letters." *Asiatick Researches* 1 (1788): 1–56.

Kamensky, Jane. *Governing the Tongue: The Politics of Speech in Early New England*. Oxford: Oxford University Press, 1999.

Kames, Lord (Henry Home). *Elements of Criticism*. 2 vols. 6th ed. Edinburgh, 1785.

Katz, Mark. *Capturing Sound: How Technology Has Changed Music*. Rev. ed. Berkeley: University of California Press, 2010.

Keels, Thomas. *Forgotten Philadelphia: Lost Architecture of the Quaker City*. Philadelphia: Temple University Press, 2007.

Keevak, Michael. *The Pretended Asian: George Psalmanazar's Eighteenth-Century Formosan Hoax*. Detroit: Wayne State University Press, 2004.

Kemp, Alan. "The Development of Phonetics from the Late 18th to the Late 19th Century." In *History of the Language Sciences: An International Handbook on the Evolution of the Study of Language from the Beginnings to the Present*, edited by Sylvain Auroux, E. F. K. Koerner, Hans-Josef Niederehe, and Kees Versteegh, 1468–80. Berlin: De Gruyter, 2001.

———. "Transcription, Transliteration and the Idea of a Universal Alphabet." In *The Prix Volney: Its History and Significance for the Development of Linguistic Research*, vol. 1b, edited by J. Leopold, 476–569. London: Kluwer Academic, 1999.

Kempelen, Wolfgang von. *Le mécanisme de la parole, suivi de la description d'une machine parlante*. Vienna, 1791.

———. *Mechanismus der menschlichen Sprache nebst der Beschreibung seiner sprechenden Maschine*. Vienna, 1791.

Kendall, Joshua. *The Forgotten Founding Father: Noah Webster's Obsession and the Creation of an American Culture*. New York: Putnam, 2010.

Kenrick, William. *A New Dictionary of the English Language*. London, 1773.

Kidd, Colin. *British Identities before Nationalism: Ethnicity and Nationhood in the Atlantic World, 1600–1800*. Cambridge: Cambridge University Press, 1999.

Kidwai, Sadiq-ur-Rahman. *Gilchrist and the "Language of Hindoostan."* New Delhi: Rachna Prakashan, 1972.

King, Christopher. *One Language, Two Scripts: The Hindi Movement in Nineteenth Century North India*. Oxford: Oxford University Press, 1994.

King, Robert. "The Poisonous Potency of Script: Hindi and Urdu." *International Journal of the Sociology of Language* 150 (2001): 43–59.

King-Hele, Desmond, ed. *The Letters of Erasmus Darwin*. Cambridge: Cambridge University Press, 1981.

Kirimli, Hakan. "Crimean Tatars, Nogays, and Scottish Missionaries: The Story of Kattı Geray and Other Baptised Descendants of the Crimean Khans." *Cahiers du Monde Russe* 45 (2004): 61–108.

Kittler, Friedrich. *Discourse Networks 1800/1900*. Trans. Michael Metteer. Stanford, Calif.: Stanford University Press, 1990.

———. *Gramophone, Film, Typewriter*. Trans. Geoffrey Winthrop-Young and Michael Wutz. Stanford, Calif.: Stanford University Press, 1999.

Klein, Ula Lukszo. "Eighteenth-Century Female Cross-Dressers and Their Beards." *Journal for Early Modern Cultural Studies* 16 (2016): 119–43.

Klooster, Wim. *Revolutions in the Atlantic World: A Comparative History*. New York: New York University Press, 2009.

Kluckhohn, Clyde, and Alfred Kroeber. *Culture: A Critical Review of Concepts and Definitions*. Cambridge: Peabody Museum, 1952.

Knott, Sarah. *Sensibility and the American Revolution*. Chapel Hill: University of North Carolina Press, 2009.

Koerner, E. F. K. *Toward a History of American Linguistics*. New York: Routledge, 2002.

Kopf, David. *British Orientalism and the Bengal Renaissance: The Dynamics of Indian Modernization, 1773–1835*. Berkeley: University of California Press, 1969.

Kövecses, Zoltán. *American English: An Introduction*. Orchard Park, N.Y.: Broadview, 2000.

Kramer, Michael P. *Imagining Language in America*. Princeton, N.J.: Princeton University Press, 1992.

Krapp, George Philip. *The English Language in America*. 2 vols. New York: Century, 1925.

Kuper, Adam. *Culture: The Anthropologists' Account*. Cambridge, Mass.: Harvard University Press, 1999.

Kupperman, Karen Ordahl. *Indians and English: Facing Off in Early America*. Ithaca: Cornell University Press, 2000.

Labute, R. *A French Grammar*. Cambridge, [England], 1790.

Laffey, Paul. "Psychiatric Therapy in Georgian Britain." *Psychological Medicine* 33 (2003): 1285–97.

Landay, Lori. *Madcaps, Screwballs, and Con Women: The Female Trickster in American Culture*. Philadelphia: University of Pennsylvania Press, 1998.

Latimer, John. "American Classical Scholarship and Caleb Alexander." *Transactions and Proceedings of the American Philological Association* 80 (1949): 403–22.

Lauzon, Matthew. *Signs of Light: French and British Theories of Linguistic Communication, 1648–1789*. Ithaca, N.Y.: Cornell University Press, 2010.

Lawson, Alexander. *Anatomy of a Typeface*. Boston: Godine, 1990.

Lee, Debbie. *Romantic Liars: Obscure Women Who Became Impostors and Challenged an Empire*. New York: Palgrave Macmillan, 2006.

Lemay, J. A. Leo. *The Life of Benjamin Franklin, Volume 1: Journalist, 1706–1730*. Philadelphia: University of Pennsylvania Press, 2006.

Lepore, Jill. *A Is for American: Letters and Other Characters in the Newly United States*. New York: Vintage, 2002.

———. *Book of Ages: The Life and Opinions of Jane Franklin*. New York: Vintage, 2013.

———. "Historians Who Love Too Much: Reflections on Microhistory and Biography." *Journal of American History* 88 (2011): 129–44.

———. "Noah's Mark: Webster and the Original Dictionary Wars." *New Yorker*, Nov. 6, 2006, 78–87.

Lerer, Seth. *Inventing English: A Portable History of the Language*. New York: Columbia University Press, 2007.

L'Estourbeillon, Régis de. *Les Familles françaises à Jersey pendant la Révolution*. Nantes, 1886.

Levée, Jerome Balthazar. *Biographie, ou, Galerie historique des hommes célèbres du Havre*. Paris, 1828.

Lewis, Reina. *Gendering Orientalism: Race, Femininity, and Representation*. New York: Routledge, 1996.

Lifschitz, Avi. *Language and Enlightenment: The Berlin Debates of the Eighteenth Century*. Oxford: Oxford University Press, 2012.

List of the Governors and Officers of the Asylum for [. . .] *Deaf and Dumb Children* [. . .]. Bermonsey [London], 1817.

Livingstone, Robert. "Perception and Commitment." *Bulletin of the Atomic Scientists* 19 (1963): 16.

Locke, John. *An Essay Concerning Humane Understanding*. London, 1689.

Lodwick, Francis. *An Essay towards an Universal Alphabet*. London, 1686.

Löffer, Marion. "English in Wales." In Matto and Momma, *A Companion to the History of the English Language*, 350–57.

Longmore, Paul K. "'Good English without Idiom or Tone': The Colonial Origins of American Speech." *Journal of Interdisciplinary History* 37 (2007): 513–42.

———. "'They [. . .] Speak Better English Than the English Do': Colonialism and the Origins of National Linguistic Standardization in America." *Early American Literature* 40 (2005): 279–314.

Looby, Christopher. "Phonetics and Politics: Franklin's Alphabet as a Political Design." *Eighteenth-Century Studies* 18 (1984): 1–34.

———. *Voicing America: Language, Literary Form, and the Origins of the United States*. Chicago: University of Chicago Press, 1996.

Looney, J. Jefferson, and Ruth Woodward, eds. *Princetonians, 1791–1794: A Biographical Directory*. Princeton, N.J.: Princeton University Press, 1991.

Loughran, Trish. *The Republic in Print: Print Culture in the Age of U.S. Nation Building, 1770–1870*. New York: Columbia University Press, 2007.

Loxley, Simon. *Type: The Secret History of Letters*. London: Tauris, 2006.

Lupton, Christina. *Knowing Books: The Consciousness of Mediation in Eighteenth-Century Britain*. Philadelphia: University of Pennsylvania Press, 2011.

Lynch, Jack. *Deception and Detection in Eighteenth-Century Britain*. Burlington, Vt.: Ashgate, 2008.

———. “Four Centuries of Lexicographical Belligerence: The Edward J. Bloustein Dictionary Collection.” *Library Quarterly* 78 (2008): 115–21.
“M.” “On the Origin, Nature, and Necessity of Different Languages.” *Westminster Magazine* (Dec. 1777): 628–30.
Mackintosh, Duncan. *A Plain, Rational, and Patriotic Essay on English Grammar*. London, 1808.
———. *A Plain, Rational Essay on English Grammar* [. . .]. Boston, 1797.
MacMahon, Michael. “Phonetic Notation.” In *The World's Writing Systems*, edited by Peter Daniels and William Bright, 821–46. Oxford: Oxford University Press, 1996.
Malone, Kemp. “A Linguistic Patriot.” *American Speech* 1 (1925): 26–31.
Malotki, Ekkehart. *Hopi Time: A Linguistic Analysis of the Temporal Concepts in the Hopi Language*. Amsterdam: Mouton, 1983.
Mandel, David. *Who's Who in the Jewish Bible*. Philadelphia: Jewish Publication Society, 2007.
Manganelli, Kimberly Snyder. *Transatlantic Spectacles of Race: The Tragic Mulatta and the Tragic Muse*. New Brunswick, N.J.: Rutgers University Press, 2012.
Martin, Jean-Clément. *La Vendée et la France*. Paris: Seuil, 1987.
Matto, Michael, and Hal Momma, eds. *A Companion to the History of the English Language*. Malden, Mass.: Wiley-Blackwell, 2011.
McDowell, Paula. “Mediating Antiquarians in Britain, 1760–1830: The Invention of Oral Tradition, or, Close Reading before Coleridge.” In Siskin and Warner, *This Is Enlightenment*, 229–46.
McGill, Meredith. *American Literature and the Culture of Reprinting, 1834–1853*. Philadelphia: University of Pennsylvania Press, 2003.
McKitterick, David. “Old Faces and New Acquisitions: Typography and the Association of Ideas.” *Papers of the Bibliographical Society of America* 87 (1993): 163–86.
McLelland, Nicola. *Teaching and Learning Foreign Languages: A History of Language Education, Assessment and Policy in Britain*. New York: Routledge, 2017.
McLuhan, Marshall. *The Gutenberg Galaxy: The Making of Typographic Man*. Toronto: University of Toronto Press, 1964.
McWhorter, John. *The Language Hoax: Why the World Looks the Same in Any Language*. Oxford: Oxford University Press, 2014.
“Mémoires de Bodereau.” In *Documents pour server a l'histoire de la Révolution française*, edited by Gustave Bord and Charles d'Héricault, 2:203–16. Paris, 1885.

Mencken, H. L. *The American Language: Supplement One*. 1945; New York: Knopf, 1962.
Merland, C. "Le comte d'Hector, lieutenant général de la marine." *Revue de Bretagne et de Vendée* 45 (1879): 276–93.
The Methodist [. . .] *a New and Universal Alphabet*. London, 1741.
Michael, Ian. *English Grammatical Categories and the Tradition to 1800*. Cambridge: Cambridge University Press, 1970.
Michaels, Walter Benn. *Our America: Nativism, Modernism, and Pluralism*. Durham, N.C.: Duke University Press, 1995.
Micklethwait, David. *Noah Webster and the American Dictionary*. Jefferson: McFarland, 2000.
Miller, Christopher. *The French Atlantic Triangle: Literature and Culture of the Slave Trade*. Durham, N.C.: Duke University Press, 2008.
Miller, Judy, and Edwin Fuller Torrey. *The Invisible Plague: The Rise of Mental Illness from 1750 to the Present*. New Brunswick, N.J.: Rutgers University Press, 2002.
Miller, William. "Nature Displayed." *Modern Language Journal* 26 (1942): 251–55.
Mirambell y Giol, Francisco. *Anocújeni, ó alphabéto* [. . .] *universal, para todas las lenguas*. Manresa, Spain, 1813.
Momma, Haruko. *From Philology to English Studies: Language and Culture in the Nineteenth Century*. Cambridge: Cambridge University Press, 2012.
———. "A Man on the Cusp: Sir William Jones's 'Philology' and 'Oriental Studies.'" *Texas Studies in Literature and Language* 41 (1999): 160–79.
Monaghan, E. Jennifer. *A Common Heritage: Noah Webster's Blue-Back Speller*. Hamden: Archon, 1983.
Monboddo, Lord (James Burnett). *Of the Origin and Progress of Language*. 6 vols. Edinburgh and London, [1773–]1792.
Monier-Williams, Sir Monier. "The Duty of English-speaking Orientalists in regard to [. . .] Jones's Principles of Transliteration." *Journal of the Royal Asiatic Society* 22 (1890): 607–29.
Mores, Edward Rowe. *A Dissertation upon English Typographical Founders and Founderies*. 1778; London: Oxford University Press, 1961.
Morgan, David. *The Devious Dr. Franklin, Colonial Agent: Benjamin Franklin's Years in London*. Macon, Ga.: Mercer University Press, 1996.
Mosley, James. *British Type Specimens before 1831: A Hand-List*. Oxford: Oxford Bibliographical Society, 1984.
Moutray, Tonya. *Refugee Nuns, the French Revolution, and British Literature and Culture*. New York: Routledge, 2016.

Mugglestone, Lynda. *"Talking Proper": The Rise of Accent as Social Symbol.* Oxford: Clarendon, 1995.

Mullin, Michael. *Africa in America: Slave Acculturation and Resistance in the American South and the British Caribbean, 1736–1831.* Champaign: University of Illinois Press, 1992.

Muret, Théodore César. *Histoire des guerres de l'ouest.* 5 vols. Paris, 1848.

Nash, Gary. *The Unknown American Revolution: The Unruly Birth of Democracy and the Struggle to Create America.* New York: Penguin, 2005.

Nash, Margaret. "Contested Identities: Nationalism, Regionalism, and Patriotism in Early American Textbooks." *History of Education Quarterly* 49 (2009): 417–41.

Nechtman, Tillman. *Nabobs: Empire and Identity in Eighteenth-Century Britain.* Cambridge: Cambridge University Press, 2010.

Nelson, Stanley. *From Punch to Printing Type: The Art and Craft of Hand Punchcutting and Typecasting.* Dir. Peter Herdrich. Charlottesville: Book Arts Press, 1985.

Nenadic, Stana. *Scots in London in the Eighteenth Century.* Lewisburg, Penn.: Bucknell University Press, 2010.

Nevalainen, Terttu, and Ingrid Tieken-Boon van Ostade. "Standardisation." In *A History of the English Language*, edited by R. Hogg and D. Denison, 271–311. Cambridge: Cambridge University Press, 2006.

Newman, Gerald. *The Rise of English Nationalism: A Cultural History 1740–1830.* New York: St. Martin's, 1987.

Newman, Simon P. *Parades and the Politics of the Street: Festive Culture in the Early American Republic.* Philadelphia: University of Pennsylvania Press, 1999.

Ngai, Sianne. *Ugly Feelings.* Cambridge, Mass.: Harvard University Press, 2005.

Norris, Clive. *The Financing of John Wesley's Methodism c. 1740–1800.* Oxford: Oxford University Press, 2017.

Nussbaum, Felicity. *The Limits of the Human: Fictions of Anomaly, Race, and Gender in the Long Eighteenth Century.* Cambridge: Cambridge University Press, 2003.

Oliphant, John. "'Touching the Light': The Invention of Literacy for the Blind." *Paedagogica Historica* 44 (2008): 67–82.

Oliver, Bette. *Surviving the French Revolution: A Bridge Across Time.* Lanham, Md.: Lexington Books, 2013.

Oliver, Samuel. *A General Critical Grammar of the Inglish Language.* London, 1825.

Oliver, Vere Langford, ed. *Caribbeana.* 6 vols. London, 1910–19.

Ong, Walter. *Orality and Literacy: The Technologizing of the Word*. 1982. New York: Routledge, 2002.

O'Shaughnessy, Andrew. *An Empire Divided: The American Revolution and the British Caribbean*. Philadelphia: University of Pennsylvania Press, 2000.

Park, Benjamin. "The Bonds of Union: Benjamin Rush, Noah Webster, and Defining the Nation in the Early Republic." *Early American Studies* 15 (2017): 382–408.

Parker, Mark. *Literary Magazines and British Romanticism*. Cambridge: Cambridge University Press, 2001.

Paugh, Amy. *Playing with Languages: Children and Change in a Caribbean Village*. New York: Berghahn, 2012.

Paxman, David. *Voyage into Language: Space and the Linguistic Encounter, 1500–1800*. Burlington, Vt.: Ashgate, 2003.

Paz, Denis. *The Politics of Working-Class Education in Britain, 1830–50*. New York: Manchester University Press, 1980.

Pearce, Mary. *Changing Sentiments and the Magdalen Hospital: Luxury, Virtue and the Senses in Eighteenth-Century Culture*. New York: Routledge, 2017.

Pederson, Eric. "Linguistic Relativity and Mainstream Linguistics." In *Oxford Handbook of Linguistic Analysis*, 2nd ed., edited by Bernd Heine and Heiko Narrog, 693–706. Oxford: Oxford University Press, 2015.

Perl-Rosenthal, Nathan. *Citizen Sailors: Becoming American in the Age of Revolution*. Cambridge, Mass.: Harvard University Press, 2015.

Perrin, John. *A Grammar of the French Tongue*. 8th ed. London, 1793.

Perry, William. *The Royal Standard English Dictionary* [. . .] *First American edition*. Worcester, Mass., 1788.

Peterson, Audrey. "Brain Fever in Nineteenth-Century Literature: Fact and Fiction." *Victorian Studies* 19 (1976): 445–64.

Pickering, John. "Americanism." In *Encyclopaedia Americana*, edited by Francis Lieber, 1:210–11. Philadelphia, 1830–47.

———. *An Essay on a Uniform Orthography for the Indian Languages of North America*. Cambridge, 1820.

———. *A Vocabulary, or Collection of Words and Phrases Which Have Been Supposed to Be Peculiar to the United States of America*. Boston, 1816.

Pignotti, Lorenzo. *The History of Tuscany*. 4 vols. Translated by John Browning. London, 1823.

Pinkerton, John. *Dissertation and Progress of the Scythians or Goths*. London, 1787.

Piper, Andrew. *Dreaming in Books: The Making of the Bibliographic Imagination in the Romantic Age*. Chicago: University of Chicago Press, 2009.

Planhol, Xavier de. *An Historical Geography of France*. Trans. Janet Lloyd. Cambridge: Cambridge University Press, 1994.

Popkin, Jeremy. *You Are All Free: The Haitian Revolution and the Abolition of Slavery*. Cambridge: Cambridge University Press, 2010.

Porter, Kenneth. *John Jacob Astor: Business Man*. 2 vols. Cambridge, Mass.: Harvard University Press, 1931.

Porter, Roy. *Mind Forg'd Manacles: A History of Madness in England from the Restoration to the Regency*. Cambridge, Mass.: Harvard University Press, 1987.

Portland Collection. Papers of W. H. C. Cavendish-Bentick, 3rd Duke of Portland. University of Nottingham Library.

Princess Caraboo. Directed by Michael Austin. Written by John Wells. Columbia Tristar, 1994.

Pruitt, Dwain. "Nantes Noir: Living Race in the City of Slaves." PhD dissertation. Emory University, 2005.

Quinn, Arthur Hobson. *Edgar Allan Poe: A Critical Biography*. 1941; Baltimore: Johns Hopkins University Press, 1998.

Raffles, Stamford. *History of Java*. London, 1817.

Raley, Rita. "A Teleology of Letters; or, From a 'Common Source' to a Common Language." In *The Containment and Re-Deployment of English India*, edited by Daniel O'Quinn, Romantic Circles Praxis Series, 2000, www.rc.umd.edu/praxis/containment/raley/raley.html.

Ramsay, David. *The History of the American Revolution*. 2 vols. London, 1791.

Raven, James. *Publishing Business in Eighteenth-Century England*. Woodbridge: Boydell Press, 2014.

Read, Allen Walker. "British Recognition of American Speech in the Eighteenth Century." *Dialect Notes* 6 (1933): 313–34.

———. "Projected English Dictionaries, 1755–1828 (Continued)." *Journal of English and Germanic Philology* 36 (1937): 347–66.

Reed, Talbot Baines. *A History of the Old English Letter Foundries*. London: E. Stock, 1887.

Report by a Committee of the Society of Arts in Scotland on the Best Alphabet and Method of Printing for the Use of the Blind. Edinburgh, 1837.

Reynolds, Peter. *William Balmain and John Gilchrist: Family and Property*. Balmain: Leichhardt Historical Journal, 2003.

Rezek, Joseph. *London and the Making of Provincial Literature: Aesthetics and the Transatlantic Book Trade, 1800–1850*. Philadelphia: University of Pennsylvania Press, 2015.

Richardson, John, Jr. "Correlated Type Sizes and Names for the Fifteenth through Twentieth Century." *Studies in Bibliography* 43 (1990): 251–72.

Ricken, Ulrich. *Linguistics, Anthropology and Philosophy in the French Enlightenment*. Trans. Robert Norton. London: Routledge, 1994.

Riskin, Jessica. *The Restless Clock: A History of the Centuries-Long Argument over What Makes Living Things Tick*. Chicago: University of Chicago Press, 2015.

Robins, Robert Henry. *A Short History of Linguistics*. 4th ed. New York: Routledge, 2013.

Roebuck, Thomas, ed. *Annals of the College of Fort William*. Calcutta, 1819.

Rollins, Richard M. "Introduction." *The Autobiographies of Noah Webster: From the Letters and Essays, Memoir, and Diary*, 5–12. Columbia: University of South Carolina Press, 1989.

———. *The Long Journey of Noah Webster*. Philadelphia: University of Pennsylvania Press, 1980.

Ross, Robert. "The 'White' Population of South Africa in the Eighteenth Century." *Population Studies* 29 (1975): 217–30.

Roy, Modhumita. "'Englishing' India: Reinstituting Class and Social Privilege." *Social Text* 39 (1994): 83–109.

Rubery, Matthew. *The Untold Story of the Talking Book*. Cambridge, Mass.: Harvard University Press, 2016.

Russett, Margaret. "The 'Caraboo' Hoax: Romantic Woman as Mirror and Mirage." *Discourse* 17 (1994–95): 26–47.

———. *Fictions and Fakes: Forging Romantic Authenticity, 1760–1845*. Cambridge: Cambridge University Press, 2006.

Rysiew, Patrick. "Thomas Reid on Language." In *Linguistic Content: New Essays on the History of the Philosophy of Language*, edited by Margaret Cameron and Robert Stainton, 223–44. Oxford: Oxford University Press, 2015.

Sahlins, Peter. *Unnaturally French: Foreign Citizens in the Old Regime and After*. Ithaca: Cornell University Press, 2004.

Said, Edward. *Orientalism*. New York: Pantheon, 1978.

Sanderson, Michael. *Education, Economic Change and Society in England 1780–1870*. 2nd ed. Cambridge: Cambridge University Press, 1995.

Sapir, Edward. "The Status of Linguistics as Science." *Language* 5 (1929): 207–14. Reprinted in *The Selected Writings of Edward Sapir in Language, Culture, and Personality*, edited by David Mandelbaum. Berkeley: University of California Press, 1949, 160–66.

Schloss, Rebecca Hartkopf. *Sweet Liberty: The Final Days of Slavery in Martinique*. Philadelphia: University of Pennsylvania Press, 2009.

Schneid, Frederick, ed. *European Armies of the French Revolution, 1789–1802*. Norman: University of Oklahoma Press, 2015.

Schneider, Edgar. "Contact Englishes and Creoles in the Caribbean." In *Handbook of Language Contact*, edited by Raymond Hickey, 478–97. Malden: Wiley-Blackwell, 2010.

———. *Postcolonial English: Varieties Around the World*. Cambridge: Cambridge University Press, 2007.

Schofield, R. S., and E. A. Wrigley. *The Population History of England 1541–1871*. Cambridge: Cambridge University Press, 1989.

Schulman, Arthur, comp. *Websterisms: A Collection of Words and Definitions Set Forth by the Founding Father of American English*. New York: Free Press, 2008.

Schweiger, Beth Barton. "A Social History of English Grammar in the Early United States." *Journal of the Early Republic* 30 (2010): 533–55.

Scragg, D. G. *A History of English Spelling*. New York: Harper & Row, 1974.

Scudder, Horace. *Noah Webster*. Boston, 1882.

Sécher, Reynald. *Le génocide franco-français: La Vendée-Vengé*. Paris: PUF, 1986.

Sédillot, René. *Le coût de la Révolution française*. Paris: Perrin, 1987.

Senchyne, Jonathan. "Bottles of Ink and Reams of Paper." In *Early African American Print Culture*, edited by Lara Langer Cohen and Jordan Stein, 140–58. Philadelphia: University of Pennsylvania Press, 2012.

Shea, Ammon. "A Sure Uncertainty: On Some Difficulties Using *OED* Online Data to Establish Shakespeare Coinages." *Dictionaries* 35 (2014): 121–45.

Shields, David. *Civil Tongues and Polite Letters in British America*. Chapel Hill: University of North Carolina Press, 1997.

Shipton, Clifford. *Isaiah Thomas: Printer, Patriot, and Philanthropist, 1749–1831*. Rochester: Leo Hart, 1948.

Siddiqi, M. Atique. *Origins of Modern Hindustani Literature, Source Material: Gilchrist Letters*. Aligarh: Naya Kitab Ghar, 1963.

Siena, Kevin. *Venereal Disease, Hospitals and the Urban Poor: London's 'Foul Wards', 1600–1800*. Rochester: University of Rochester Press, 2004.

Silver, Pamela, and Harold Silver. *The Education of the Poor: The History of the National School, 1824–1974*. London: Routledge, 1974.

Simone, Rafaelle. "The Early Modern Period." In *History of Linguistics, Volume III: Renaissance and Early Modern Linguistics*, edited by Giulio Lepschy, 149–214. New York: Routledge, 2013.

Simpson, David. "American English to 1865." In Matto and Momma, *A Companion to the History of the English Language*, 254–62.

———. *The Politics of American English, 1776–1850*. New York: Oxford University Press, 1986.

Siskin, Clifford, and William Warner, eds. *This Is Enlightenment*. Chicago: University of Chicago Press, 2010.

Skeel, Emily Ellsworth Ford. *A Bibliography of the Writings of Noah Webster*. New York: New York Public Library, 1958.

Sklar, Elizabeth. "So Male a Speech: Linguistic Adequacy in Eighteenth-Century England." *American Speech* 64 (1989): 372–79.

Smart, Annie. *Citoyennes: Women and the Ideal of Citizenship in Eighteenth-Century France*. Newark: University of Delaware Press, 2011.

Smith, Billy G. *The "Lower Sort": Philadelphia's Laboring People, 1750–1800*. Ithaca: Cornell University Press, 1990.

———. *Ship of Death: A Voyage That Changed the Atlantic World*. New Haven: Yale University Press, 2013.

Smith, H. "YOUNG CARABOO!" In Gutch and Worrall, *Caraboo*, 64–65.

Smith, Olivia. *The Politics of Language, 1791–1819*. Oxford: Clarendon Press, 1984.

Smith, Samuel Stanhope. *Essay on the Causes of the Variety of Complexion and Figure in the Human Species*. New ed. [Edinburgh], 1788.

Smith-Rosenberg, Carroll. *This Violent Empire: The Birth of an American National Identity*. Chapel Hill: University of North Carolina Press, 2010.

Snell, K. D. M. *Parish and Belonging: Community, Identity and Welfare in England and Wales*. Cambridge: Cambridge University Press, 2006.

Sorensen, Janet. *The Grammar of Empire in Eighteenth-Century British Writing*. Cambridge: Cambridge University Press, 2000.

———. *Strange Vernaculars: How Eighteenth-Century Slang, Cant, Provincial Languages, and National Jargon Became English*. Princeton, N.J.: Princeton University Press, 2017.

[Southey, Robert.] ("Don Manuel Alvarez Espriella"). *Letters from England*. 2nd ed. 3 vols. London, 1808.

Sparks, Jared. *The Diplomatic Correspondence of the American Revolution*. 12 vols. Boston, 1829–30.

A Specimen of Isaiah Thomas's Printing Types. Worcester, 1785.

A Specimen of Printing Types, by Edmund Fry and Co. Letter-Founders to the Prince of Wales. London, 1787, 1788.

A Specimen of Printing Types, by Fry and Steele, Letter-Founders to the Prince of Wales. London, 1794, 1798, 1800.

A Specimen of Printing Types, by Joseph Fry and Sons, Letter-Founders to the Prince of Wales. London, 1786.

A Specimen of Printing Types, by William Caslon, Letter-Founder to His Majesty. London, 1785, 1786.

A Specimen of Printing Types, by Wm Caslon, Letter-Founder to the King. London, 1795, 1796, 1798.

A Specimen of Printing Types, Made by Joseph Fry and Sons, Letter-Founders. London, 1785.

Spengemann, William. *A New World of Words: Redefining Early American Literature.* New Haven: Yale University Press, 1994.

Sprague, Charles. *An Oration, Delivered on Monday, Fourth of July, 1825, in Commemoration of American Independence.* Boston, 1825.

St. Clair, William. *The Reading Nation in the Romantic Period.* Cambridge: Cambridge University Press, 2004.

Steadman-Jones, Richard. *Colonialism and Grammatical Representation: John Gilchrist and the Analysis of the 'Hindustani' Language in the Late Eighteenth and Early Nineteenth Centuries.* Oxford: Blackwell, 2007.

Stephens, W. B. "Literacy in Devon during the Industrial Revolution." *Journal of Education Administration and History* 8 (1976): 1–5.

Stern, Madeleine. *Nicholas Gouin Dufief of Philadelphia: Franco-American Bookseller, 1776–1834.* Philadelphia: Philobiblion Club, 1988.

Stern, Philip. *The Company-State: Corporate Sovereignty and the Early Modern Foundations of the British Empire in India.* Oxford: Oxford University Press, 2011.

Sterne, Jonathan. *The Audible Past: Cultural Origins of Sound Reproduction.* Durham, N.C.: Duke University Press, 2003.

Stewart, Dugald. *Elements of the Philosophy of the Human Mind.* 3rd ed. London, 1792.

Stewart, Garrett. "Bookwork as Demediation." *Critical Inquiry* 36 (2010): 410–457.

———. *The Look of Reading: Book, Painting, Text.* Chicago: University of Chicago Press, 2006.

Stocking, George W., Jr. *Race, Culture, and Evolution: Essays in the History of Anthropology.* New York: The Free Press, 1968.

Stroh, Silke. *Gaelic Scotland in the Colonial Imagination: Anglophone Writing from 1600 to 1900.* Evanston: Northwestern University Press, 2017.

Sudan, Rajani. *The Alchemy of Empire: Abject Materials and the Technologies of Colonialism.* New York: Fordham University Press, 2016.

Suliot, Theodore. "The Teaching of Foreign Languages." *Ohio Educational Monthly* (Nov. 1861): 337–41.

Swiderski, Richard. *Lives between Cultures: A Study of Human Nature, Identity, and Culture.* Juneau: Denali Press, 1991.

A System of Geography. 4 vols. Glasgow, 1805–7.

Tamarkin, Elisa. *Anglophilia: Deference, Devotion, and Antebellum America.*

Chicago: University of Chicago Press, 2007.
Tarantelli, Valentina. "Voice into Text: Case Studies in the History of Linguistic Transcription." PhD dissertation. University of Sheffield, 2015.
Taves, Ann. *Fits, Trances, and Visions: Experiencing Religion and Explaining Experience from Wesley to James*. Princeton, N.J.: Princeton University Press, 1999.
Taylor, Allan. "Indian Lingua Francas." In *Language in the USA*, edited by Shirley Brice Heath and Charles Ferguson, 175–95. Cambridge: Cambridge University Press, 1981.
Tennenhouse, Leonard. *The Importance of Feeling English: American Literature and the British Diaspora, 1750–1850*. Princeton, N.J.: Princeton University Press, 2007.
Thierry, Guillaume. "Neurolinguistic Relativity: How Language Flexes Human Perception and Cognition." *Language Learning* 66 (2016): 690–713.
Thornton, J. L. "Charles Hunnings Wilkinson." *Annals of Science* 23 (1967): 277–86.
Thornton, John. *Africa and Africans in the Making of the Atlantic World, 1400–1680*. Cambridge: Cambridge University Press, 1992.
Thornton, William. *Cadmus*. Philadelphia, 1793.
Thurlow, Crispin, and Kristine Mroczek, eds. *Digital Discourse: Language in the New Media*. Oxford: Oxford University Press, 2011.
Tomalin, Marcus. "'The Torment of Every Seminary': The Teaching of French in British Schools, 1780–1830." *Journal of the History of Education* 40 (2011): 446–64.
Tomlinson, Stephen. *Head Masters: Phrenology, Secular Education, and Nineteenth-Century Social Thought*. Tuscaloosa: University of Alabama Press, 2005.
Toulalan, Sarah. "'Is He a Licentious Lewd Sort of a Person?': Constructing the Child Rapist in Early Modern England." *Journal of the History of Sexuality* 23 (2014): 21–52.
Tuber, Steven. *Understanding Personality through Projective Testing*. Lanham: Jason Aronson, 2012.
Underhill, Timothy. "John Byrom and the Contexts of Charles Wesley's Shorthand." *Wesley and Methodist Studies* 7 (2015): 27–53.
Vallancey, Charles. *A Grammar of the Iberno-Celtic, or Irish Language*. 2nd ed. Dublin, 1782.
Venezky, Richard. *The American Way of Spelling: The Structure and Origins of American English Orthography*. New York: Guilford, 1999.

———. "In Search of the Perfect Orthography." *Written Language & Literacy* 7 (2004): 139–63.

Verdon, Nicola. *Rural Women Workers in Nineteenth-Century England: Gender, Work and Wages.* Woodbridge: Boydell, 2002.

Viswanathan, Gauri. *Masks of Conquest: Literary Study and British Rule in India.* New York: Columbia University Press, 1989.

Vocabulary of Such Words as Are of Dubious or Unsettled Accentuation [. . .]. London, 1797.

Voskuhl, Adelheid. *Androids in the Enlightenment: Mechanics, Artisans, and Cultures of the Self.* Chicago: University of Chicago Press, 2013.

Wahrman, Dror. *The Making of the Modern Self: Identity and Culture in Eighteenth-Century England.* New Haven: Yale University Press, 2004.

Waldstreicher, David. *In the Midst of Perpetual Fetes: The Making of American Nationalism, 1776–1820.* Chapel Hill: University of North Carolina Press, 1997.

———. *Runaway America: Benjamin Franklin, Slavery, and the American Revolution.* New York: Hill and Wang, 2004.

Walker, John. *Critical Pronouncing Dictionary and Expositor of the English Language.* London, 1791, 1797.

Wanostrocht, Nicolas. *A Grammar of the French Language, with Practical Exercises.* 3rd ed. London, 1789.

Warburton, William. *The Divine Legation of Moses.* 2nd ed. 2 vols. London, 1742.

Warfel, Harry, ed. *Letters of Noah Webster.* New York: Library Publishers, 1953.

———. *Noah Webster: Schoolmaster to America.* New York: Macmillan, 1936.

Warner, Michael. *The Letters of the Republic: Publication and the Public Sphere in Eighteenth-Century America.* Cambridge, Mass.: Harvard University Press, 1990.

———. "Uncritical Reading." In *Polemic: Critical or Uncritical*, edited by Jane Gallop, 13–38. New York: Routledge, 2004.

Weber, James. *The Talking Machine: The Advertising History of the Berliner Gramophone and Victor Talking Machine.* Midland: Adio, 1997.

Webster, Noah. *American Spelling Book.* Philadelphia, 1787.

———. *An American Dictionary of the English Language.* 2 vols. New York, 1828.

———. *Collection of Essays and Fugitiv Writings.* Boston, 1790.

———. *Compendious Dictionary.* New Haven, 1806.

———. *Dissertations on the English Language.* Boston, 1789.

———. *Grammatical Institute of the English Language* [. . .] *Part 1*. Boston, 1783.
———. *A Letter to the Honorable John Pickering, on the Subject of his Vocabulary*. Boston, 1817.
Weed, Enos. *The American Orthographer*, vol. 1. [New York], [1805?].
Weinstein, Brian. "Noah Webster and the Diffusion of Linguistic Innovations for Political Purposes." *International Journal of the Sociology of Language* 38 (1982): 85–108.
[Wellesley, Richard.] *Letters of the Marquis Wellesley, respecting the College of Fort William*. London, 1812.
Wells, Colin. *The Devil and Doctor Dwight: Satire and Theology in the Early American Republic*. Chapel Hill: University of North Carolina Press, 2002.
Wells, John. *Princess Caraboo: Her True Story*. London: Pan Books, 1994.
Wells, John C. *Accents of English*. 3 vols. Cambridge: Cambridge University Press, 1982.
Wells, Robert. *The Population of the British Colonies in America before 1776*. Princeton, N.J.: Princeton University Press, 1975.
[Wheatstone, Charles.] "On the Vowel Sounds, and on Reed Organ Pipes." *London and Westminster Review* (Oct. 1837): 27–41.
Wheeler, Garon. *Language Teaching through the Ages*. New York: Routledge, 2013.
Wheeler, Roxann. *The Complexion of Race: Categories of Difference in Eighteenth-Century British Culture*. Philadelphia: University of Pennsylvania Press, 2000.
Whicker v. Hume (1851). In *Reports of Cases in Chancery* [. . .] 13:389–402. London, 1853.
Whicker v. Hume (1858). In *The English Reports*, vol. 11: *House of Lords*, 50–67. Edinburgh, 1901.
White, Ashli. *Encountering Revolution: Haiti and the Making of the Early Republic*. Baltimore: Johns Hopkins University Press, 2010.
Whorf, Benjamin. "An American Indian Model of the Universe." Written ca. 1936. *International Journal of American Linguistics* 16 (1950): 67–72. Reprinted in *Language, Thought, and Reality: Selected Writings of Benjamin Whorf*, edited by John Carroll, 57–64. Cambridge: MIT Press, 1956.
Wiles, R. M. *Serial Publication in England before 1750*. Cambridge: Cambridge University Press, 1957.
Wilkins, John. *Essay towards a Real Character and a Philosophical Language*. London, 1668.

Williams, Raymond. *Keywords: A Vocabulary of Culture and Society*. Rev. ed. Oxford: Oxford University Press, 1985.
Williams, Roger. *A Key into the Language of America*. London, 1643.
Williams, Stanley, ed. *Journal of Washington Irving (1823–1824)*. Cambridge, Mass.: Harvard University Press, 1931.
Wilson, David. *United Irishmen, United States: Immigrant Radicals in the Early Republic*. Cornell University Press, 1998.
Wilson, John. *A Volume for All Libraries*. Washington City, [D.C.], 1814.
Withers, C. W. J. *Gaelic in Scotland 1698–1981*. Edinburgh: John Donald, 1984.
Withington, Robert. "The Marquis de Chastellux on Language and Peace." *New England Quarterly* 16 (1943): 316–19.
Wittgenstein, Ludwig. *Tractatus Logico-Philosophicus*. 1921. Trans. David Pears and Brian McGuinness. New York: Routledge, 1974.
Wmffre, Iwan. *Breton Orthographies and Dialects, Volume 2: The Twentieth-Century Orthography War in Brittany*. Bern: Peter Lang, 2007.
Wood, Gaby. *Edison's Eve: A Magical History of the Quest for Mechanical Life*. New York: Knopf, 2002.
Wood, Gordon. *Empire of Liberty: A History of the Early Republic, 1789–1815*. Oxford: Oxford University Press, 2009.
Yale, Robert. *The Languages of Disenchantment: Protestant Literalism and Colonial Discourse in British India*. Oxford: Oxford University Press, 2013.
Yang, Chi-ming. *Performing China: Virtue, Commerce, and Orientalism in Eighteenth-Century England, 1660–1760*. Baltimore: Johns Hopkins University Press, 2011.
Yeo, Richard. *Encyclopaedic Visions: Scientific Dictionaries and Enlightenment Culture*. Cambridge: Cambridge University Press, 2001.
Yokota, Kariann. *Unbecoming British: How Revolutionary America Became a Postcolonial Nation*. Oxford: Oxford University Press, 2011.
Young, Robert. *Colonial Desire: Hybridity in Theory, Culture and Race*. New York: Routledge, 1995.
———. *The Idea of English Ethnicity*. Malden: Blackwell, 2008.
———. "That Which Is Casually Called a Language." *PMLA* 131 (2016): 1207–21.

INDEX

IMPRESSIONS

Studies in the Art, Culture, and Future of Books

Playful Letters
A Study in Early Modern Alphabetics
ERIKA MARY BOECKELER

Figures of Speech
Six Histories of Language and Identity in the Age of Revolutions
TIM CASSEDY

Mass Authorship and the Rise of Self-Publishing
TIMOTHY LAQUINTANO

Metamedia
American Book Fictions and Literary Print Culture after Digitization
ALEXANDER STARRE

The Portrait and the Book
Illustration and Literary Culture in Early America
MEGAN WALSH

COLOPHON

Figures of Speech was designed and typeset using Adobe InDesign CC page layout software. The primary typeface is Adobe Caslon Pro, designed by Carol Twombly, with Big Caslon, by Matthew Carter, used for display. Both of these fonts are digital revivals based on the metal types of the English typefounder William Caslon (1692–1766).

The text includes more than twenty additional typefaces—a number of them created by the author, from primary sources, using Adobe Illustrator and the font editing software Birdfont. Cassedy based the Caraboo script on a wood engraving of Mary Willcocks's writing that was printed in the *Bristol Mirror* in 1817. He drew the Gilchrist typeface from John Gilchrist's "Panglossal Prospectus" of 1825. The so-called Ethiopic, Irish, Nagari, and Samaritan characters were developed from tracings of glyphs in *Pantographia*. Types in chapter two, including Duncan Mackintosh's tightly registered superscript and subscript numerals and diacritics, are modifications of Junicode, an open-source typeface by Peter Baker.

The Caraboo and Gilchrist types used in this book are available as open-source typefaces at timcassedy.com.

Printed at McNaughton & Gunn in Saline, Michigan, on 60# Glatfelter Natures Smooth Antique paper using a KBA Press.